THE
PHANTOM KILLER

THE
PHANTOM KILLER

UNLOCKING THE MYSTERY OF
THE TEXARKANA SERIAL MURDERS:
THE STORY OF A TOWN IN TERROR

JAMES PRESLEY

PEGASUS CRIME

NEW YORK LONDON

THE PHANTOM KILLER

Pegasus Books LLC
80 Broad Street, 5th Floor
New York, NY 10004

Copyright © 2014 by James Presley

First Pegasus Books cloth edition November 2014

Interior design by Maria Fernandez

Library of Congress Cataloging-in-Publication Data is available.

ISBN: 978-1-60598-642-5

10 9 8 7 6 5 4 3 2 1

Printed in the United States of America
Distributed by W. W. Norton & Company

To the memory of
the Phantom's victims
and to their families and friends.
May they always be remembered.

I have arrived in Texarkana, the home of the Phantom Killer. I have met a newspaperman named Graves. I have checked into the Grim Hotel, and the hair is rising on my neck.

—Kenneth Dixon,
International News Service dispatch

The people were panicky. They were really panicky. I had never in my life run into anything like it.

—Texas Ranger Captain M. T.
"Lone Wolf" Gonzaullas

CONTENTS

AUTHOR'S NOTE

My personal interest in the Phantom murders, officially unsolved since 1946, traces from boyhood. My uncle, Bill Presley, served as sheriff of Bowie County, Texas, where most of the attacks took place. Later as a teenaged police reporter for the *Texarkana Gazette* I came to know the investigators, as well as reporters and editors who'd covered the story. Eventually doctoral studies in history enabled me to add perspective to the ravages of a willful domestic terrorist.

The case cried out for a reliable record to preserve the known facts, dig up new ones, and separate the substantive evidence from the spurious and imaginary. This book applies the tools of history to explain how and why the crimes and the panic happened—and seek a solution.

The Texas Department of Public Safety labeled it "the Number One unsolved murder case in Texas history." That's a lot of crimes over many decades in a state hardly celebrated for its peacefulness. "As a puzzle," wrote Dallas columnist Kent Biffle, "the case remains more popular than sudoku, but seemingly uncrackable." National and regional media continue to revisit the tantalizing case. The Internet, with Wikipedia in the lead, ripples with references. The Learning Channel's "Ultimate

Ten," on which I appeared, classified it as one of "the most notorious and intriguing unsolved crimes in history," in a dead heat with Jack the Ripper's 1888 London rampage. The Ripper killed five women. The Phantom killed five victims, badly injured three others, as he hunted couples at a disadvantage in the dark.

This account offers an antidote for the rumors and distortions caused by time, journalistic excesses, and, on occasion, clumsy police work. With the principal participants dead (most of whom I interviewed at some point in their final years) and documentary evidence fragile and scattered and possibly on the way to being lost forever, this was the last chance to set the record straight and close a popular but vexing old mystery.

THE TOWN

Tucked away in the far northeastern corner of Texas—or southwestern edge of Arkansas, if you prefer—Texarkana mostly goes unnoticed, the abandoned stepchild of both states. Occasionally its geographical anomaly rescues it from oblivion, by attesting to Texas's size. Such as the hoary anecdote of the salesman whose home office in Chicago orders: "Check on our new customer in Texarkana." The salesman, based in El Paso, fires back: "Go yourself. You're closer than I am!" It's true. Texarkana, spilling over into Arkansas and near the boundaries of Louisiana and Oklahoma, is nearer to Lake Michigan than to its sister city on the Mexican border.

Commonly spoken of as one city, Texarkana actually is a shorthand term for two separate political entities sprawled carelessly astride the state line: Texarkana, Texas, and Texarkana, Arkansas, each with its own mayor, municipal government, police, and firemen. The United States and the Republic of Texas set the boundary in 1841, before there was a Texarkana. East is Arkansas and West is Texas: Numbered streets are preceded by either a W or an E to designate which side of town they're on. East 16th is in Arkansas, but cross the state line in search of the nearest counterpart and you'll find West 23rd in Texas. Fitted together like asymmetrical line dancers glued to each other, the cities were, and are, joined physically at the hip, sharing utilities and a chamber of commerce, while periodically behaving like dysfunctional Siamese twins.

In a solidly Southern town, with nearly a third of the population black, the obligatory Confederate memorial features a stone soldier forlornly staring southward. Yet a cosmopolitan mix of ethnic groups—Irish, Italian, German, Jewish, Greek, and French—not found in most Southern towns its size, by the 1920s supplemented the predominant English and Scotch-Irish Caucasian stock. Baptists and Methodists led in numbers, with Catholics a significant minority, and with one Jewish temple.

Duality has characterized—or plagued—Texarkana from its founding in 1873, in the waning days of Reconstruction. Each side of town had its own separate post office until 1892, when the first joint one was built on its present site on the state line. That one was razed in 1930. Three years later the present one was built, combining Texas pink granite and Arkansas limestone in its materials. The state line defined even religious jurisdictions. The city's two Catholic parishes—Sacred Heart in Texas, St. Edward in Arkansas—were in different dioceses, Dallas and Little Rock. Protestant denominations experienced similar realities. Crosstown rivalries flourished. The annual football game between Texas High's Tigers and Arkansas High's Razorbacks often included fistfights in the stands. One photo promoting the city portrayed a pair of young twins with boxing gloves confronting each other. The most popular symbol of duality, though, was a postcard that depicted a man on the Texas side clutching a rope tied to a donkey on the other side of the state line. In the background the massive United States Courthouse and Post Office, billed as the only one in America situated in two states, imposingly straddles State Line Avenue. The postcard's caption signified, perhaps humorously, perhaps not, a potential for friction.

A MAN IN TEXAS AND HIS ASS IN ARKANSAS

To balance things out, a competing card placed a Biblical ass in Texas.

In the nineteenth century the timber industry flourished in both states with an abundant supply of pine and hardwood, creating jobs, albeit often dangerous ones, and a number of local fortunes. Texarkana's location made it a natural railroad center as lines crossed from almost every direction en route to either coast. The town became known as "that lively railroad village" festooned with saloons and bawdy houses and rampant with crime. "Texarkana is the gateway between the East and Texas, and the half-way house, where burglars, thieves and robbers stop momentarily to recuperate," commented one early observer.

The most horrifying tragedy of those days occurred on a July night in 1882. A violent storm drove dozens inside the Paragon Saloon and gambling house for refuge. Lightning struck the building next door, under construction, and strong winds blew a wall onto the saloon, shattering timbers, knocking over kerosene lamps. A fierce fire broke out, compounding the plight of those trapped beneath the rubble. At least forty men perished. One, pinned painfully and hopelessly, ended his agony with a gunshot to his own head.

With its location "a veritable magnet for the criminally inclined," an early editor charged, "the great majority of Texarkana's early settlers were gamblers, gunmen and other lawless individuals who flocked into towns where law enforcement was weak." By 1888, by one accounting, the fledgling city boasted twenty-three saloons, eighteen of them on Broad Street, with flashy names like Cosmopolitan, Hole-in-the-Wall, Gateway, Triangle, Golden Star, and Red River. Over the years the city—or cities—grew out of its frontier roughness but never shook off the image entirely. Open saloons and gambling dens vanished in time; brothels continued to flourish. Organized prostitution persisted well beyond World War II.

Texarkana has since remained a crossroads. Four major highways intersect in the town today. In the 1940s, four rail lines provided passenger service, which was on par for a city several times Texarkana's size. American and Mid-Continent Airlines each offered two flights daily. American's DC-3s landed and departed from either coast; Mid-Continent flew north and south. Buses and automobiles brought in people of all descriptions and statuses. A large sign above U.S. Highway 67, a major artery connecting Dallas and Little Rock, proclaimed the city to be the "Gateway to the Southwest." Texarkana, as the unofficial capital of this Four States Area, became a stopover for national travelers, as well as a regional hub for commerce—and for crime. Law enforcement grew knottier, as criminals crossed state lines to avoid arrest.

Intensifying Texarkana's crossroads status, World War II jerked the region out of the Great Depression. Red River Ordnance Depot, later elevated to Arsenal status, and Lone Star Army Ammunition Plant nearly doubled the population. Workers and their families swarmed in from all points, as far off as Illinois and Michigan. The economy boomed. So did the work of the police.

A duality of both dark and light emerged. Old-timers remembered an idyllic small town where everyone knew everybody else and enjoyed a sense of community and a pleasant life—unless, perhaps, you were black or poor. They'd cite a long roster of men and women who came from their town to achieve fame or fortune: Byron Nelson the legendary golfer; politicians Wright Patman, longtime chairman of the House Banking and Currency Committee, and Morris Sheppard (Senate tenure, 1913-1941), to name a few.

Undismayed by negative distractions, the business sector's ingrained booster spirit burst forth most forcibly in the 1940s with an Old West do-or-die slogan emblazoned on city buses: *Pull for Texarkana or Pull Out.*

It didn't work. True to the town's dual nature, denizens of a darker side continued, in counterpoint, to scar its sunny face, neither pulling for nor pulling out.

The nether side was almost never completely out of view. One observer reported the most frequent datelines in the *Police Gazette* to be Peoria, Illinois, and Texarkana. Some occasionally referred to their hometown as Little Chicago. As a lawman of the time, Max Tackett, put it, Texarkana was "calloused to murder."

Selected headlines from the 1940s seem to bear out Tackett's contention. The gruesome Arkansas-side murder of Gertrude Hutchinson O'Dwyer on July 24, 1940, was one of the most shocking: her head smashed by a car axle, her throat slit from ear to ear, her bed soaked with blood. The case remains unsolved.

The next year a sixteen-year-old boy, on parole for a shotgun killing in Alabama four years earlier, fatally slugged a younger boy with a pop bottle in Fouke, Arkansas, about ten miles from Texarkana.

A rigidly segregated Southern city, Texarkana's last recorded lynching had occurred on July 13, 1942, about seven months into World War II. The chain of events began near the little town of Hooks, a dozen miles west of Texarkana and next door to the defense plants. An intruder dragged a twenty-two-year-old white woman, asleep with her baby at her side while her husband worked a night shift, from her trailer home. She broke free and escaped. He fled. She identified him only as a black man. A group of white men—none a police officer—started looking for suspects. At a café they tried to arrest Willie Vinson, thirty-one years old, who was visiting from Louisiana. He refused to go with them. One of the men shot him in the abdomen. Vinson was taken to the hospital. The woman never positively identified Vinson or any other man. Vinson languished near death. Around midnight Sunday several white men wrenched a groaning Vinson, begging for his life, from his unguarded hospital bed. They dragged him by car through the streets and hanged his corpse at a cotton compress a mile away. Relegating the global war to lesser headlines, the *Texarkana Gazette* thundered forth with a bold, all-capitals 8-column banner:

NEGRO LYNCHED BY MOB HERE

The case made national news. Racial tensions rose exponentially; rumors flew. The FBI entered the case. No arrests were made, no culprits named, no charges filed.

Months later, on the Arkansas side, a war-plant worker, H. H. Hasselberg, was shot and left for dead. Before he died he named Curtis Lee Jones, nineteen, as the man who had shot him. Jones, on probation for car theft, fled. Arrested in Houston and returned to Texarkana, he jumped bail and escaped to Mexico. Extradited, he pleaded guilty to avoid a death sentence and received life in the penitentiary. It was not the end of his criminal career; he ended up with a long rap sheet. After his early release, he continued to add to his record.

On December 9, 1944, Walker L. Curtner, age thirty, a used-car salesman, was found shot in the head and dying in a Texas-side street. He'd been robbed of $1300 in cash. The year ended with no break in the mystery. With the case his top priority, the new Bowie County sheriff, Bill Presley, and Texarkana police chief Jack Runnels posted a hefty reward and received a tip leading to the arrest and conviction of Guy Brantley, an escaped convict. Assessed a life sentence, he later died in prison.

The Japanese surrender brought no end to violence in Texarkana. On October 20, 1945, Ernest F. Bryers, an overseas Army veteran discharged two days earlier in Oklahoma, was found dead, almost decapitated, in a pool of blood near downtown on the Texas side. He'd had a brief lay-over en route home to Louisiana. Subsequently Jarvis Andrew Elliott, twenty-three, and Vera Jackson, seventeen, confessed to the grisly murder, claiming Bryers had resisted their robbery, leading to the killing. Elliott, a black man, was sentenced to the electric chair; his teen-aged confederate, life in prison.

Holdups, cuttings, burglaries also vied for headlines. At the edges of four states, Texarkana lay in the direct path of traffickers in illicit goods. Scofflaws ran whiskey from wet Louisiana to dry Oklahoma through the area. Specially rigged automobiles carried from fifty to seventy cases of liquor; a stake-bed truck, a hundred. High-speed chases, at times in town and accompanied by gunfire, might register as high as ninety miles per hour. It was a lively atmosphere, during a lively time.

The old year 1945 went out—literally—with a bang. In a shootout at nearby Fulton, Arkansas, the day before New Year's Eve, Arkansas State Policemen Charley Boyd and Max Tackett, both war veterans back at their old jobs, returned fire from James W. Moore, a thirty-five-year-old ex-convict from Missouri, fatally wounding him.

An ominous foreshadowing, with sequel over the next several weeks of the new year 1946: a $485 holdup of a liquor store in Arkansas (the only side with legal liquor sales), shootings, the sentencing of three men for robbery with firearms, a war veteran's fatal blow with a hammer to an adversary's head in an alcohol-fueled fracas, a gunshot suicide, a fatal knife fight, a string of burglaries and thefts netting from five dollars to as much as seven hundred. One Texas-side pistol-backed holdup yielded only thirty-eight dollars. Clothing, radios, jewelry, vehicles, saddles and horses—nothing was off limits to thieves. Highway crashes snuffed out two lives and injured others.

The unexpected kept cropping up. Weeks after New Year's, three inches of snow covered Texarkana, which was extremely rare. Even more unusual, a rabid dog meandered about Pleasant Grove, a rural community north of town. Hydrophobic dogs came and went, but mostly in the heat of summer, hardly ever in the midst of winter.

The two anomalies soon faded from memory. The snow melted. The weather grew cooperative. Fears of a roving mad dog evaporated. The war was over.

What could happen next?

THE
PHANTOM KILLER

CHAPTER 1

STRANGER IN THE DARK

When they met in February, 1946, tall, bespectacled Jimmy Hollis and petite, brunette Mary Jeanne Larey were married, but not to each other. He was twenty-five; she, nineteen. Each was in the process of dissolving a wartime marriage that hadn't worked out. While awaiting their final divorce decrees, they felt free to date, and did. Their lives, like the rest of the town and the world, were in flux.

Jimmy and Mary Jeanne may have been scarcely aware of how unsettled and unruly the times were. The evidence, however, lay on every hand. In twin-city Texarkana (pop. 52,393) crime tormented both sides of the Texas-Arkansas line. The unexpected had become so common as to lose its ability to surprise.

Hollis, captivated by Mary Jeanne's striking good looks, asked her out for the evening of Friday, February 22. He arranged a double date for them with his younger brother Bob and a girl to whom he'd introduced Bob, Virginia Lorraine Fairchild. Bob, on the shy side, benefitted from Jimmy's gift of gab.

With the war a fresh memory, people avidly flocked to a broad range of entertainment. Wrestling at the Arkansas Armory featured headliners like the Purple Phantom, whose mask would come off only at his defeat. But movies were the main draw.

Jimmy Hollis chose Warner's freshly minted *Three Strangers* at the classy Paramount theater. A trip to the Paramount was almost a formal event, the men wearing coats and ties, the women in high heels and their best dresses, sometimes even gloves. The best place in town, for a fifty-cent admission fee. Unlike the other "white" theaters, the Paramount featured a "Colored" entrance at the side, next to an alley, that led up to a segregated portion of the balcony.

Three Strangers, a black-and-white film billed as "a masterpiece of suspense," was one of Geraldine Fitzgerald's earlier movies, with heavies Sidney Greenstreet and Peter Lorre. It had its moments, but not many. Set in London in the spring of 1938, the film climaxes when a desperate Greenstreet viciously slams Miss Fitzgerald over the head with a brass Chinese idol, killing her. Not exactly a happy ending.

About a quarter after ten the couples left the theater. Jimmy Hollis, driving an old-model gray Chevrolet, took them to a drive-in café where they sipped soft drinks and chatted. Then he drove Bob and his date home. It was a long drive from there to the little town of Hooks, in Texas, where Mary Jeanne lived.

Texarkana was small. You could drive across town in a matter of minutes. By eleven, less than an hour after leaving the theater, Jimmy and Mary Jeanne drove onto New Boston Road on the Texas side, which would take them to Highway 82 and west to Hooks. First he detoured to graveled Richmond Road, north of town. They were "young and frivolous," as Jimmy was to put it; they followed Richmond Road about a hundred yards past the last row of city houses and turned off onto a dirt lane and parked. They were near the rural Pleasant Grove community, scene of the mad dog scare the previous month. By that time of night, traffic was sparse. All was quiet and peaceful.

Earlier there had been a light drizzle with some fog. It was pleasantly cool, in the upper sixties, with a slight breeze. The moon was nearing the last quarter and wouldn't be rising for more than an hour.

They were in pitch-black darkness as they chatted and Hollis, always an easy conversationalist, told a few jokes. Fancying himself a bit of a crooner, he drew on his experience with a dance band in Fort Worth and began singing to Mary Jeanne. It was a romantic interlude for both. Utter privacy. Whatever might be said of Texarkana, its lovers' lanes were secluded, peaceful, quiet, and safe, a commonly accepted lure to the young set.

For some reason Hollis never could explain later, to himself or anyone else, he impulsively got out of the car and studied the dark sky, searching for stars.

As he stood in the unpaved lane in the dark, suddenly a powerful flashlight's beam switched on, seemingly out of nowhere, about twenty feet away, and focused in his eyes, blinding him. From around the halo of light he saw what appeared to be a pistol barrel aimed his way, backed up by a rough voice barking orders in a mean tone. Judging from the voice and level of the flashlight, Hollis assessed the man as tall and fairly young. Who was he? What did he want?

"Take off your fucking pants!" the gruff voice ordered.

Hollis, partially in shock, partially in denial, couldn't fathom what was going on. He knew the man was holding a gun on him. He could tell by the orders that the man was uncouth, to put it mildly, and intended to have his way. His mind groped for a reasonable explanation. This must be some kind of strange game, he told himself. A prankster had mistakenly zeroed in on him.

Hollis, startled, knew he had never heard the voice before. "Fellow, you've got me mixed up with someone else. You've got the wrong man."

Hollis's words drove the man, now moving closer, into a spasm of anger.

"I don't want to kill you, fellow," the man spat the words back. "So you better do what I tell you! Take off your goddamned pants. Now!"

The second command shook Hollis out of any residual denial or confusion. There was no joke behind the man's snarled words. Incongruously Hollis ran a question over and over in his mind: *What would Dick Tracy do now?* Even as he thought it, he realized the comic-strip detective would have found himself just as helpless in a situation like this.

From inside the car he heard Mary Jeanne, pleading. "Jimmy, please take them off," she said, thinking that might keep them from being harmed.

Hollis had no choice. He loosened his belt, lowered his trousers, and eased out of them, one leg almost snagging as he tried to keep from falling. Then the intruder moved closer and slammed Hollis viciously on the head with a heavy blunt object like an iron pipe or pistol's barrel, once—*whock!*—then a second time—*whock!* The force knocked his glasses off. He crumpled to the ground. The man kicked him, hard. Hollis could feel metal cleats in the man's shoes or boots stomping his chest. Then the stranger struck Hollis again on the head as he lay on the ground.

Mary Jeanne thought Hollis had been shot. She was mistaken. She'd heard his skull cracking.

With Hollis disabled on the ground, the assailant turned his attention to the petite teenager. She got out of the car. She leaned over to pick up Hollis's trousers and took out his billfold, showing it to the assailant.

"Look," she said, "he doesn't have any money."

"You're lying!" the man shouted.

"No, look. You can see."

He bent over to where Hollis lay and searched his trousers.

He turned to her. "Where's your purse?"

"I don't have one," she said weakly.

Angered, he hit her on the head. It felt like an iron pipe. She fell to the ground.

Somehow she managed to get up.

"Take off!" the man growled. "Run!"

She tried to obey. She headed for a nearby ditch.

"Not that way!" he shouted. "Go up the road."

She was wearing high-heeled shoes. She did the best she could. She could hear Hollis, still on the ground, groaning. The thug turned his attention back to Hollis, beating and stomping him. As she ran she could hear the thud of the blows and could hear Hollis's groans. Terrified, she blindly ran down the road. At times stumbling, she dashed off wildly. Would he let her escape, or was he going to shoot her? In the dark she ran and ran, despite her high heels, as if her life depended on every step.

She came upon an old model car parked by the side of the road. It faced toward Hollis's car. *Someone to help me!* She stopped momentarily and glanced inside. She saw no one. Her brief hope evaporated. In her panic, she didn't realize it may have been the stranger's car, parked unnoticed with the lights off before he stalked them.

Then, suddenly, as if the gunman had decided to turn the bizarre aggression into a sport, he took off and chased her down the isolated road. She could hear his footsteps thudding on the dirt road. Just after she'd passed the old car, he caught up with her.

"What the hell are you running for?" he demanded.

"You told me to run," she answered in a trembling voice.

"You're a goddamned liar!" he yelled back at her.

In that moment she knew he was going to kill her. Fear and anticipation paralyzed her. She stopped in her tracks. She was so frightened, she couldn't move. She could think of nothing she could do. It was the end.

He then slammed her—harder than before—with the blunt object, opening a wound on her scalp. She dropped to the ground again.

Then the game changed. Helpless on the ground, she felt a violent tug at her panties and then the sudden intrusion of a metallic object like a pistol muzzle. She cried out in excruciating pain. She feared it would never end. Yet he didn't try to rape her.

Somehow, and she never was able to remember afterward how she did it, she rose unsteadily to her feet.

The abuse was so painful, so humiliating that, once on her feet and knowing she didn't want him to ever touch her again, she begged him, "Go ahead and kill me!"

She remembered little of the scene after that. She believed he intended to force her into his car and later kill her. Then suddenly he turned and left her in the middle of the road. Days later she decided the headlights of a car had frightened him away.

As soon as the man was gone, Mary Jeanne ran pell-mell, despite her high heels, to sound the alarm. She kept thinking, *I've got to get help for Jimmy!*

She ran to the first house she saw on Richmond Road.

"Help me! Help me!" she screamed as she pounded on the front door.

Just then a car came along. She yelled for it to stop. It cruised on past.

Frantic, she ran to the back of the house, shouted and pounded on the door. A man came to the door.

"Call the police!" she said. She explained what had happened. The man immediately called the sheriff's office.

Meanwhile Hollis, taking advantage of the gunman's momentary absence, had regained consciousness and faced the most horrible moment of his life. He instantly remembered what had happened. Where is the guy? he thought. If he sees me move he'll finish killing me. Nearly blind and helpless, he tried to clear his foggy mind enough to decide what to do, what he *could* do. Blood oozed from his head wounds, down his face and into his eyes. His trousers were gone, back in the road somewhere. He was clad only in underwear from the waist down. His glasses were in the dirt somewhere. Through his hazy and impaired eyesight he saw car lights on Richmond Road. He concentrated on making his way to Richmond Road to find help from a passing motorist. He rubbed the congealed blood from his eyes. He groggily rose to his feet and stumbled toward the graveled road. He fell back to the ground but crawled on. He saw a car's lights. He flagged it down. The car eased to a halt and pulled up.

Reflexively Hollis experienced a new fear. *Is the guy behind the wheel the one who tried to kill me? Will he finish me off?* Then his more immediate needs took over. He had no choice but to seek help.

"I've got to see a doctor," said Hollis. "I'm hurt bad. Take me to the hospital."

A man and a woman were in the car, the man driving. Hollis, knowing he had to have medical care fast, tried to open the door of the sedan and crawl into the back seat.

"Don't do that," the driver shouted. "You'll get blood in my car!"

What is wrong with him? Hollis thought. What is he thinking? Here I am dying, and he refuses to help, afraid of getting a little blood on his back seat. The man's actions added to Hollis's confusion.

"I'll call an ambulance for you, soon as I can get to a telephone," the motorist promised. He didn't have to. Presently, with Hollis leaning on the car, a siren going full blast rent the air. An ambulance pulled up. Its driver rushed to Hollis. Immediately afterward a city policeman, with siren screaming, arrived. Hollis, barely conscious, stumbled toward the ambulance. The policeman stopped to talk to the motorist. It was the last Hollis saw of the man.

Minutes later the ambulance whisked Hollis to Texarkana Hospital, a few blocks from downtown. Mary Jeanne, seeing the ambulance coming, hurried from the house, in time to ride with the policeman to the hospital.

Groggy, semiconscious, Hollis's mind raced. Why had the motorist acted so strangely? Had he seen anything that might help identify the attacker? Or had the motorist been his assailant? His sense of time was deranged. He didn't even know if the man in the car could have even been the criminal.

Afterward Hollis would learn that the police tried to locate the man in the car but never could. Hollis's mind returned to the slight possibility that the motorist had been his assailant and had narrowly escaped from the police by spinning a fictitious identity. But how could he explain the woman in the car with him, who had said nothing at all? Didn't even gasp at the sight of such a brutally beaten person. One thing made as much sense as another.

In his confusion and pain, it was understandable that Hollis failed to accept a perfectly logical explanation: Who was likely to let a stumbling, bleeding stranger in his underwear into his car, particularly in a place with Texarkana's reputation? Even if the cautious driver had been willing, it's doubtful that his female companion would have wanted a stranger in the car.

Once in the ambulance, Hollis obsessively recited to the attendant his name, address, and where his brother Bob could be reached, over and over again. His trousers and wallet were gone. He had no identification. He was afraid no one would know who he was if he died.

Though it seemed like an eternity to the two victims, the entire action in the dark had taken not more than ten minutes. Likely, no more than five to eight minutes.

Long after both victims had arrived at the hospital, a fading moon—a day away from the last quarter—began almost tentatively to peek faintly beyond the tree line to the east. It would take a while for it to cast any light.

The mass movement of people during World War II is the simplest way to explain why Jimmy Hollis and Mary Jeanne Larey met in Texarkana in 1946.

James Mack Hollis was born in 1920, in little Dubach in northern Louisiana, a short drive from the Arkansas line. Months after his birth, his parents moved to El Dorado, Arkansas, to open a general store and restaurant and profit from the huge oil discovery. It was a typical rough-and-ready boomtown. The elder Hollis ran the store; his wife cooked for the restaurant. Jimmy, his two brothers, and two sisters grew up in El Dorado.

Later Hollis and his parents moved to California for a while, where he attended high school and obtained his Social Security card. When the war came, he hurried to join the Navy but failed the physical examination because of a congenital heart defect. He opted for the next best, a job in aircraft manufacturing at Fort Worth, Texas. On the side he sang in a dance band. It was during this time that he met and married his first wife, Dora Louise Nichols. Hollis took her to El Dorado where, in December 1942, they married. He was twenty-two; she, nineteen. As the war wound down, so did their marriage. In January 1946 they separated for good. Hollis left Fort Worth. He went first to Texarkana, where his two brothers lived, and then on to El Dorado where he filed for divorce.

El Dorado was several hours east of Texarkana on Highway 82. Hollis's older brother Edmond managed the Texarkana office of the Reliable Life Insurance Company. Reliable Life was a debit insurance company that collected premiums on a door-to-door basis. Edmond pointed out that their younger brother Robert Jr., recently returned from Europe, was already working for the company in Texarkana. Why didn't Jimmy, by then at loose ends, also join the Reliable Life team? It made sense. He moved in with Bob in an apartment on the Arkansas side. Texarkana was a good way-station.

Mary Jeanne Harris was born in Tishomingo, Oklahoma, in 1927. When the war boom came, her father took his family to Texarkana, finding a job at Red River Ordnance Depot. As government housing became available closer to work the family moved to East Hooks Courts, a short distance from the gate to the defense plant. Mary Jeanne enrolled at Hooks High School.

Mary Jeanne, a lovely dark-eyed brunette with a fraction of Indian blood, met Roland L. "Stretch" Larey, eighteen, in Texarkana and married him in the Miller County Courthouse, on the Arkansas side, in 1943. His father, local attorney Clyde Larey, signed as security on the marriage license bond, required by Arkansas law. Mary Jeanne listed her birthday as January 11, 1925, which made her, for the record, eighteen and old enough to marry without parental permission.

Actually, she was sixteen; she'd bumped her age up by two years.

The marriage was brief. Larey went into the Navy. By time he returned from the war, the marriage had deteriorated. Larey left for college in Arkadelphia, Arkansas, eighty miles from Texarkana. She remained in Hooks, living with her parents; by the end of 1945 their separation was permanent.

An uncontested divorce suited both parties. Larey filed; Mary Jeanne waived her appearance in court. They had no children and no community property. She signed the waiver in January 1946, two days before her true nineteenth birthday—in Harlingen, Texas, where she was visiting a friend in the service as the wartime airfield there was shutting down.

After she returned to Hooks, she met Jimmy Hollis, recovering from his own unhappy marriage.

CHAPTER 2

CONFLICTING PERCEPTIONS

The vicious beatings disrupted what had promised to be a routine, though hardly boring, Friday night for Bowie County Sheriff Bill Presley.

Since taking office slightly more than a year before, William Hardy Presley, a personable fifty-year-old widower who had served in France during World War I, had grown used to unexpected disturbances of sleep and schedule. He lived in the little town of Nash, a few miles west of Texarkana. His household consisted of his aged mother in her eighties and his teenaged daughter. Presley's wife and older daughter had died from injuries after a drunken driver had intentionally crashed into the Presley vehicle in 1936; only Presley and his younger daughter had survived.

Unlike the stereotypical tall Texas sheriff, ruddy-faced, usually mild-mannered Presley stood slightly under average height. Though he packed a pistol, he usually kept it on the car seat beside him, not on his hip. He dressed immaculately in a neat business suit and felt hat instead of the

ten-gallon version popularized by brawny sheriffs in the movies. Even
without a gun at his side, he wasn't an easy man to confront. Growing
up in rough-and-tumble rural Bowie County, he'd had his share of fistfights. As sheriff, however, he'd drawn his gun only once, to tame a husky,
crazed drunk.

He hadn't called it a day yet when the call came late that Friday
night. He had just a few deputies for the entire county, so he sped to the
scene himself. Although the attack had occurred in the county's jurisdiction, outside the Texarkana city limits, three city policemen had also
answered the call. With a small staff to cover a large county, Presley
granted special deputy commissions to city policemen. This enabled
them to respond beyond their usual range, particularly in emergencies
such as this one.

The sheriff and the policemen checked out what little was known of
the Friday night attack, then scoured the area in search of the assailant.
Tracking what they believed to be the route of the gunman's automobile,
they traced him to the house to which Mrs. Larey had fled. This suggested
that she had narrowly escaped him a second time. From there they followed the tracks eastward to Summerhill Road, another graveled branch
north of the city. They found Hollis's trousers about a hundred yards from
the scene of the attack.

The culprit had made a clean getaway. Presley and the policemen drove
downtown to interview the victims. Both were still at the hospital, where
Hollis would remain for weeks.

Hollis was barely conscious and in critical condition, hovering between
life and death, his skull fractured in three places. There was no hope of
talking with him. Mrs. Larey was being treated in the emergency room
when the officers arrived. She had deep cuts on her head. The doctor used
eight stitches to close the wounds. She was in a state of severe emotional
distress. She just wanted to go home.

Presley and his deputy Frank Riley gently questioned her at the hospital. What, exactly, had happened?

In a semi-hysterical condition, her mind jumped about. She worried
about Hollis. Was he going to survive? She did the best she could to
describe the experience.

The stranger had driven up and ordered them out of the car, she said. He told Hollis to remove his trousers, after which he bludgeoned Hollis in the head with a heavy blunt object. Then he turned to her.

Who was he? What did he look like? Did you know him? Did Hollis know him? Had she ever seen him before? What kind of gun did he have?

"I don't know," she said. "I never saw or heard him before. I'd never forget that voice, how mean it was. He had on a white mask. It had cut-out places for his eyes and mouth."

She felt certain he was a Negro, of light complexion. This was based partially on her interpretation of the way he talked.

Clearly she was not in the best frame of mind to be interrogated. The sheriff drove her home to East Hooks Courts, still in a mild state of shock. He'd question her again when she regained her equilibrium.

Hollis, in a coma, was in no position to corroborate, refute, or add to what she said. The impression from her statement left the focus on a black man with a sadistic streak who had tried to rob them—and wore a mask. The mask became a sensational part of the front-page story in the *Daily News*, the following afternoon with an eight-column headline.

MASKED MAN BEATS TEXARKANIAN AND GIRL

The report named Hollis as a victim, identifying him as an insurance man and noting his residence, while identifying Mrs. Larey only as his "19-year-old girl companion." The newspaper didn't use her name until later. On Sunday morning the *Gazette* ran a one-column page-one report that essentially rehashed the afternoon newspaper's story. The story didn't fade for days.

Upon reflection and further questioning, officers grew uncertain about the accuracy of her description, vague though it was. Considering the locale of the attack and the type of crime, it didn't fit the pattern of a black criminal, as attackers such as these tend to "hunt" within their own ethnic groups. They considered part of her statement open to question, or at least incomplete. And the mask: the more officers thought about it, the more they wondered. The main reason for wearing a mask would be to hide his features so he wouldn't be identified. In the dark that seemed unlikely. Darkness would have shielded a black man even more. So why had he worn a mask? And a white mask, no less? Did he believe they were someone else? Did mistaken identity explain the beatings? And how, in the dark, was she even able to see a mask? One deputy raised the possibility that she, and perhaps Hollis, actually knew the man and out of fear *claimed* he had worn a mask, an effort to prevent retaliation.

As the days wore on, this possibility gained strength. Both victims were married, the sheriff learned, but not to each other. She explained she was estranged from her husband and that, as far as she knew, he was in college in Arkansas. They were in process of obtaining a divorce by mutual agreement. Was the attacker a boyfriend? Absolutely not!

The next day, officers interviewed her again. She could only reiterate what she had told them previously. Her husband's alibi, readily checked, held firm. So the jilted-lover hunch was now off the table.

The nightmarish experience dominated her days and nights. In her dreams she saw the blurred image of a vicious man almost every time she fell asleep.

She insisted, though, that she could identify him by his snarling voice.

"I'll never forget that voice, as long as I live," she said. "It rings always in my ears."

Two days after the incident, her fears intensified when, unrelated to the beating, a house fire in a small frame building in Hooks, close enough to see and smell the smoke and flames, burned a woman to death. The sirens that responded, the general commotion, and the subsequent reports and rumors all became another hideous reminder that death, accidental or otherwise, lurked in unexpected places, even near at hand. A few days later a two-car crash on a curve on Highway 67 West, eight miles out in the rural community of Red Springs, injured seven motorists from New York and Tennessee; one died the next day. The traffic casualties were names in the newspaper, from other regions, on another highway, but the home fire in Hooks was one witnessed and lamented by the entire little town, adding to the painful emotions of the attack.

Meanwhile, the question remained whether Hollis would survive. Officers learned from his brothers, however, that he also was in the process of obtaining a divorce, which might come through almost any day. They assured officers that they knew of no one who would want to do harm to him, and that Hollis's divorce was mutually desired by both parties.

The viciousness of the attack suggested a vengeful nature, which guided officers into a theory that someone had sought to get even. But they could uncover no one bearing a grudge against Hollis or likely to beat up either of them. Still, officers refused to shake the feeling that an angry suitor had been involved.

Hollis, unconscious and in critical condition, spent days in the hospital before he slowly began to improve. Barely conscious when he arrived at the hospital, he later recalled, the last thing he had heard before slipping into a weeklong coma was the sound of surgical scissors snipping off his blood-clotted hair, preparing him for the operating room.

For many days, it seemed doubtful that he would live. His family gathered at his bedside. His encounter with the stranger replayed over and over in his mind. Although he'd been raised in a Baptist atmosphere where one took care with one's language, his parents and brothers heard him repeatedly vow, "You sonofabitch, I'll get you if it takes me twenty years!" His body reacted as if he was struggling with the gunman while lying in the hospital bed. Periodically a family member or friend would have to help hospital attendants restrain him. He flailed about, at times punching one of his brothers in the jaw, throwing the other one over the foot of the bed. He kept reliving his close brush with death.

Sheriff Presley arranged for a round-the-clock guard at Hollis's hospital room. Whoever the criminal was, Hollis was an eyewitness and the fear that the gunman might try to eliminate him was a reasonable one. The sheriff remembered, from 1942, when his predecessor had failed to mount a guard on Willie Vinson's hospital room, enabling lynchers to spirit the dying black man away with impunity. Protection from further harm was paramount. Hollis's physician wouldn't allow lawmen to interrogate him just yet, citing his fragile condition.

When he came out of the coma, Hollis's nightmare lived on. He would fall asleep and wake in a cold sweat. He would see, vaguely outlined, a monster standing over him as he lay on the ground. His helplessness terrified him.

Fifteen days after the beating, the hospital released him. He was taken home in an ambulance. Afterward, at his apartment, Hollis talked to investigators for the first time. Who was the man? Had you ever seen him before? What did he look like? Did Mrs. Larey recognize him? Do you know why he attacked you? Tell us what he did and said. Describe him.

Hollis did the best he could. No, he did not know him. He'd never seen him before, to his knowledge. Mary Jeanne hadn't known him either. It had just happened out of the blue—or, more accurately, out of the dark.

Hollis focused on the assailant's behavior. The man was tall and mean. His words were vile, bristling with anger and projecting violence that immediately followed. Then Hollis summarized his characterization of the gunman.

"I think he is a young white man, not over thirty years old, and he's desperate."

"What else did you see? Anything about his face?"

"No, I don't know what he looked like."

"Did he have anything on his face or head?"

"No, I didn't see anything."

"He wear a mask?"

"I didn't see any." He was willing to accept his date's version of a mask, though.

It wasn't much, really, to go on, except that two essential points of his statement conflicted with the teenaged woman's assessment, adding a serious complication. The gunman was a Negro, she had insisted, and he wore a white mask over his head with holes cut out for his eyes and mouth. Hollis hadn't seen a mask of any kind and was certain that he was a white man. Most of all, he was sure about the man's mindset.

"That man's dangerous," he said. "He's a potential murderer. The next one he gets ahold of will be killed. Evidently he thought he killed me that night. I know he was crazy. The crazy things he said. I know his mind was warped."

The discrepancies in the two eyewitness reports created a problem from the beginning. Instead of narrowing down a search for suspects, it opened it up to almost anyone: young and uncouth—and vicious. In Texarkana at the time, this description would apply to hundreds of men.

Some lawmen suspected one or both victims—especially the girl—of concealing the identity of the gunman. Officers didn't believe a black man had attacked them, thus siding with Hollis on that point. And if Hollis hadn't seen a mask, why would she claim the man wore one? They acknowledged that in a time of panic a strong-beamed flashlight in your eyes might create the illusion of a hood, or a halo, from the reflection. But the concept gained little support. Instead officers began to insist that she knew her attacker and was protecting him, perhaps out of fear, by claiming he was black and wore a mask.

On a Wednesday afternoon in March, while Hollis lay in bed at home four weeks after the episode, Texas Ranger Stewart Stanley visited him. He followed up on the earlier questioning by Presley and Riley. The line of questioning soon ruffled Hollis.

"Who would try to do this kind of thing to you?" he was asked. "Which of your enemies would do it?"

"I don't have any enemies!" Hollis shot back. "I don't know anybody who'd do this to me."

"Are you sure you don't know him? Not covering up for him?"

This provoked Hollis even more.

"Are you kidding? After what I've gone through, if it was my grand-mother I'd want to see her hang! I'm trying to tell you that this man is brutal. He's a potential killer. If you don't find him, the next thing you know he's going to kill someone!"

This interview, Hollis remembered, occurred on Wednesday, March 20, nearly a month after the incident.

What was the underlying motive? The intruder had brutalized Hollis before demanding money. He gained no more than twenty dollars from Hollis's wallet. He'd abused the girl but hadn't tried to rape her. Was it an act of jealousy or revenge? No one could say. Was it a case of mistaken identity? Hollis thought so. The case puzzled the lawmen and everyone else.

Both victims agreed their attacker was sadistic and that he was tall, close to six feet. In those hectic moments in the dark with a raging madman, it was understandable that their memories of the horror wouldn't mesh exactly, and there was no way to reconcile their differing impressions of the man's race and whether he wore a mask or not.

They agreed, emphatically, however, that he was capable of anything.

The experience unnerved the young woman so deeply that she fled Texarkana, moving to Frederick, Oklahoma, to live with an aunt and uncle. Mary Jeanne was afraid the man would pursue her and kill her. Even there, safe in a secure small town in another state, she feared being alone or going upstairs by herself.

Although no one mentioned it then or later, the gunman's abuse of his female victim followed the pattern of the fictional character Popeye, a small-time crook in William Faulkner's horrific 1931 novel, *Sanctuary*. In one scene Popeye violates the teenaged female character Temple Drake with a corncob. Popeye, as drawn by Faulkner, was a vicious thug, but impotent. Did this sexual abuse in Texarkana suggest the perpetrator was impotent? Or was there another reason he used the gun barrel in such a bizarre and sexually sadistic manner?

Little progress was made in the case. Suspects were cleared as soon as they were thoroughly checked out. The teenaged woman's husband was out of the Navy and in college eighty miles away, apparently nursing no resentment over their break-up. As perfect an alibi as one might imagine.

On March 12 Hollis, while still in the hospital, was granted a divorce from his wife Louise in Union County, Arkansas, where he had filed his complaint in early February.

Even after he was released from the hospital Hollis still had a long recuperation ahead of him. One of his scars was easily discerned, on the left side of his forehead going into the hairline; his hair, growing back, covered the rest of his scars. His physician ordered him not to go back to work for six months. Like his companion of that night, he continued to feel uncomfortable even away from the scene. He moved to Shreveport, Louisiana, seventy-five miles to the south.

"You can't forget a thing like that," he said. "Last night in Shreveport, I was riding in a car with a friend. We stopped to wait on a red traffic light. A friend came running up and jumped on the running board, and I began shaking."

He was still recuperating from his injuries. His voice was weak and low as he talked to a reporter. His physician told him it would be "some time" before he would be completely well.

On April 22—two months to the day after the beatings—Mary Jeanne's husband was granted an uncontested divorce in district court in Bowie County, Texas. Subsequently Hollis traveled to Frederick, Oklahoma, where Mary Jeanne was living. He spent a week there. They reviewed their night of terror and discussed the future. Hollis was interested in a more permanent relationship. It was obvious, however, that he was far from recovered. Even his behavior reflected as much. If he'd had marriage in mind when he made the trip, the week in Frederick ended the dream. There was simply too much residual trauma from that fateful night to ever hope to salvage a relationship.

In early May, Hollis took a job as a clerk at Arkansas Natural Gas in Shreveport. His Texarkana experience kept him, literally, gun-shy for a long time. The next year in Shreveport, where he met a young woman who was to become his second wife, Addie Nell "Snookie" Thompson, he took her out to a wooded area where they were going target practicing with a rifle. He wanted to teach her how to shoot, as commonly practiced in the region, and it helped him maintain his own skill, should he need it. As they were walking toward the woods, they heard gunshots in the distance. Without a word, Hollis reacted as if he were alone, turning immediately and sprinting back to his parked car. She ran after him. He was already inside and turning the key before she caught up with him and got into the car as it was rolling. He'd never told her about the Texarkana nightmare etched indelibly in his psyche.

Hollis's brother Bob was more fortunate. He had not only avoided the attack by turning in early that fateful Friday night, he got along so well with his date that they married later the same year, a union that lasted until his death.

"Persons of interest"—to use a later term—were in short supply in the months following the attack. The conflicting impressions compounded the case. Despite its not being unusual for witnesses to offer differing accounts of an attacker, lawmen still believed that one or both of these two knew their assailant.

Investigators gave little or no thought to another element that may have explained why a nineteen-year-old woman, in a desperate moment of high-tension fear, had mistakenly identified the assailant as black. Mary

Jeanne had been a young girl when Vinson, a black man, had been lynched in Texarkana several years earlier. The precipitating event had been the seizing of a white woman from her mobile home near Hooks. Though the woman was not injured and the lynched black man was apparently innocent, there was much talk of the event in Hooks. The emotional tide may have literally colored her perceptions of the February incident. If she had expected a black perpetrator, based on stories she'd heard, her mind would have been geared in that direction.

Too much else was going on for the public to brood over the beatings. Veterans, like AAF Sergeant George Reese and Seaman First Class Bob Mundella, a *Gazette* reporter, returned home to wide welcome. Professionals resumed interrupted careers. One man met his Australian wife's train and saw their months-old son for the first time. Some enrolled in two-year Texarkana College or a larger college elsewhere. The unemployed ranks reached 9,707, a huge number. Ex-GIs searched for jobs or joined the 52-20 Club to draw twenty dollars a week for a year or until they found suitable work.

Emblematic of the changing times, peace had ended War Savings Time. Darkness now came an hour earlier than during the war. Months later the USO Club on the Texas side shut down. (The Negro USO Club of that Jim Crow era operated a few blocks away.) In a seamless transition, the local Veterans of Foreign Wars chapter snapped up the lease on the USO building. The management changed; the dance continued.

Meanwhile, crime maintained its lively pace. A purse thief netted $312. Three men forced an out-of-town man into their car downtown, drove him out five miles, and robbed him of a wrist watch, pocket knife, and fifteen dollars. Safecrackers hit the New Boston, Texas, school for $500 and tried to do the same at Hooks. In other cases, men wanted elsewhere were arrested: an ex-convict in Hooks for two murders in Iowa, a Louisiana man possessing a cache of dynamite and two pistols.

The traffic and accident toll grew: six-year-old Charles Elvey Whitlock killed by a car; two veterans dead in a Highway 82 crash; just outside the city, a wagon's driver injured. A farmhouse fire near Redwater, in Texas, claimed the lives of a young couple and their year-old child.

Yet optimism peeked through. Bridal showers, like the one for Jacqueline Hickerson at the fashionable Hotel Grim, dominated the society pages. At the post office downtown, mail-order baby chicks, cheeping in their boxes while awaiting delivery, heralded the advent of spring.

Even as uncertainty fueled instability, life flowed on. It would take a heavy jolt, indeed, to shake the town and plunge every individual into panic. Until 1946, no event had quite achieved that questionable distinction. The savage Hollis-Larey beatings didn't come close.

CHAPTER 3

DOUBLE DEATH IN A CAR

I n a word, "rambunctious" aptly described Texarkana in 1946. It had a reputation as a rough little town. Yet if you were prudent in what you did and where you went, by all odds you would be safe. Stay out of dives. Avoid overindulging in alcohol and shun those who did. Beware of contentious situations. Choose your company carefully. In other words, mind your own business, much as you would anywhere else, and, chances were, you'd live a long and injury-free life.

The horrible O'Dwyer murder in 1940 in her bed and the vicious lynching of Willie Vinson were memorable exceptions. Most residents recognized and kept away from the relatively few danger zones. Children were free to roam downtown and in their neighborhoods. Boys as young as ten rode bicycles to Spring Lake Park, miles north of the city, or deep into the countryside without fear.

It was a small town of vibrant neighborhoods. Billie Hargis House remembered how, as a girl of twelve, she played outside with her friends, at times as late as ten o'clock at night, with no anxiety or incidents.

In many ways it was an idyllic, wholesome place to grow up. Among the most reliably safe places around Texarkana were its movie theaters and its sequestered off-road parking spots where young couples could cuddle, pet, or quietly chat in as private a setting as was likely to be found outside of a private home or motel room. The vicious assault upon Jimmy Hollis and Mary Jeanne Larey was dismissed by most as a rarity, probably sparked by jealousy or some weird desire for revenge, unlikely to recur.

With the world in flux, the movies continued to draw with films like the war drama *They Were Expendable* vying with more sinister titles like *The Last Ride* ("Lives Are Cheap by Their Standards").

They were both young with their lives before them, he a veteran, she a recent high school graduate now working at a defense plant.

Twenty-nine-year-old Richard Lanier Griffin, relieved that he had gotten through the war alive and unwounded, had served in the Navy's Construction Battalions, or SeaBees, in the South Pacific. Griffin, a handsome man with dark auburn hair and freckles, was the oldest boy of a Cass County, Texas, farm family of five children—two girls, three boys. His father had served as the county's tax collector before resigning to go back to farming. They all knew, first hand, hard work and how difficult times were during the Great Depression. They plowed, chopped cotton in the spring, picked it in the summer and fall. Richard and his brother Welborn never made more than 75 cents for a twelve-hour day for wages except when they picked cotton, which paid by weight and thus by how much you picked. Somehow the family managed. Everyone worked all week and on Sunday attended, virtually without fail, Methodist church services. Norman Rockwell could have used them as models to paint a *Saturday Evening Post* cover celebrating salt-of-the-earth rural America.

Richard's two brothers also served in World War II. David, the youngest, joined the peacetime Army in 1940, eventually participating in the European invasion soon after D-Day. Richard, as a carpenter and cabinet-maker, worked for a contractor before the war. After Pearl Harbor he went with the contractor to Hawaii, repairing damage sustained during the Japanese attack, as well as new construction for wartime needs. Some of his work was on one of the bombed ships at Pearl Harbor. He returned from Hawaii, still single and eminently eligible for the draft. He joined the Navy and, because of his experience, was welcomed into the SeaBees. His brother Welborn was conscripted. By early 1942 all three were in uniform.

The family suffered two tragedies before the war was over. In April 1941, months before the war, a sailor brother-in-law, who was married to Richard's older sister Hattie Merle, was fatally shot in an accident aboard ship at Pearl Harbor. Then in 1943, in the middle of the war, their father died. Welborn and David attended the funeral on emergency furloughs. Richard, by then in the Pacific theater building bases and landing strips for Marines and soldiers as they seized island after island from the entrenched Japanese, was unable to go home.

After the father's death, their mother, Bernice Griffin, moved in with her daughter Eleanor, who worked at Lone Star Army Ammunition Plant west of Texarkana. They lived in Robison Courts, wartime housing on the western edge of Texarkana, near the bus line for Eleanor. After the war, David lived with them while he looked for work.

Following his discharge Richard returned to his civilian work, carpentry. He joined his mother and two siblings at the Texarkana apartment but spent most of his time in Cass County, where he worked on a long-term project. Because of the distance, close to forty miles, he usually went to Texarkana only on weekends.

In February 1946, Richard began dating Polly Ann Moore, also from Cass County. He hadn't known her when he went off to war. She had been a little girl. When he returned, she had grown up and was an attractive young woman, brown-haired, blue-eyed. He was twenty-nine; she, only seventeen. In those days, the twelve-year difference in age didn't generate a great deal of conversation. She was an emotionally mature young woman.

Polly and her younger brother Mark were reared by their mother, Lizzie, after their father, George Moore, died of a stroke when Polly was eight. Polly attended Atlanta (Texas) High School for her last two years, graduating in 1945 at age sixteen. Before the war was over in the Pacific, she took a job at Red River Ordnance Depot as a checker of ammunition and other materiel being loaded onto trucks, helping maintain records of the inventory. With the war soon over, the ammunition was stored in igloos.

The family's situation created a transportation crisis for Polly. No one nearby, with whom she could ride, worked at the defense plant. A solution came through her mother's cousin. Ardella Campbell lived in Texarkana, just a few steps off State Line on the Texas side. She had an extra room that she rented to Polly. Ardella worked nights as a telephone operator. Polly could take the city bus downtown and catch another bus to the defense plant.

The arrangement worked well. Ardella and her mother soon grew fond of their new roomer. Polly was quiet and easy to like.

The little family kept in touch. About once a month Lizzie and her son would ride the bus from Douglassville, or Polly would take the bus there, where someone would meet her and take her the rest of the way home.

On Saturday, March 23, Texas-side police recovered a 1940 Hudson sedan found abandoned in Robison Courts, not far from where the Griffin family lived. It had been stolen ten days earlier at another location. For four years the public had to make do with prewar models. Waiting lists for new cars were long. Car thefts had become common. A columnist in the weekly *Two States Press* summed it up. "Suggested Slogan: There's an auto in your future—if you live long enough." Or if you were inclined to steal. If you owned a car, no matter how old, you were advised to keep a close eye on it.

Like millions of other veterans, Richard Griffin yearned for a normal life. He had located a four-door 1941 Oldsmobile sedan in Shreveport. It was the best he could do. The Olds had been used as a taxicab during the war, sustaining considerable wear and tear. Practically worn out, it nonetheless provided transportation at a time when a new car was out of the question.

Unlike Richard, Polly had known little of life outside her circumscribed area. She'd turned seventeen a few months earlier. Like others in her family, she was quiet, had been a good student with good manners, serious, wholesome—the kind of young woman who would impress a man like Richard, despite their difference in age. Polly's dating was confined to spending time with Richard. Several weeks into March, they had been "going together" for six weeks.

On Saturday evening, March 23, Richard drove to 1215 Magnolia and picked up Polly. They were going to dinner at the popular Canary Cottage, then to a movie. The Canary Cottage was an all-night restaurant specializing in steak and chicken, situated at the edge of the city limits on West Seventh. A very short distance further, the Texas & Pacific railroad track crossed the street. Past that, near Waggoner Creek, the city-limit sign marked the beginning of the rural environs "out in the country." West Seventh Street was the Texas-side route of U.S. Highway 67 as it wound through the city, conveying motorists to Dallas and beyond. A string of cafés, some merely beer joints, dotted the route.

Richard and Polly met Richard's unmarried sister Eleanor and her boyfriend Jesse A. Proctor at the restaurant and enjoyed a leisurely, pleasant supper. Afterward, the two couples went their separate ways. Richard drove Polly back to her Magnolia Street address. She had spilled something on her blouse, and she went to her room to change. Later they headed to the midnight movie at the Paramount Theater downtown. *SNAFU* was a 1945 Columbia comedy just making its way to Texarkana.

It had been a pleasantly cool day, the temperature never moving out of the sixties. After the movie, popcorn and all, they went to a West Seventh café for an after-movie snack, leaving around two A.M. Before taking Polly home, Richard drove out West Seventh, less than a half-mile past the city limits near the Stockman's Cafe, where he turned south onto a dirt road. About fifty yards off the highway he stopped at a parking area in a low marshy spot, the ditch nearby banked by willows. Behind the willows a dense stand of trees and bushes made the off-road stretch practically impenetrable. Across the road was a gravel pit, its gate locked. In the darkness, the road was as secluded as anyone could want. Perfect privacy. No one around for blocks. He killed the engine.

After a short while another car drove up and parked. More lovers, no doubt. Then a man stealthily walked up, unnoticed, his movements cloaked by darkness. Unaware of the intruder's presence, Richard and Polly continued their conversation. Suddenly the shadowy figure was upon them. Brandishing a handgun, he ordered Griffin to drop his trousers. Griffin did so. They fell to his ankles.

We cannot be certain exactly what happened next. Eventually the gunman shot both Richard and Polly, first restricting Richard's movement by forcing him to drop his trousers and then, inside the car, shooting him twice in the back of the head, spattering blood all over the inside of the car and, probably, onto himself. He shot Polly twice outside the car on a blanket. Her blood soaked the blanket and the ground beneath it. Outwardly there was no sign of a beating or of rape.

His night's atrocity completed, the killer moved Polly's body into the car with her body slumped in a sitting position while Richard's body leaned forward from the back seat and on his face, his trousers to his ankles. In the darkness there was no way the murders would be noticed from the highway. By the time the moon, waning into the last quarter, sluggishly appeared over the trees high enough to cast any light on the tragic scene, the murderer had long escaped.

There had been light rain during the day. In a few hours, more rain patted the dirt in the lane and dampened the trees and vegetation, obscuring any tracks the killer might have left.

Daylight, Sunday morning, broke hours later.

Texarkanians had to fish their Sunday *Gazettes* off wet lawns. There was plenty to read about. The Cold War hadn't yet been officially declared, but sparks were beginning to appear. Baseball, another interrupted pleasure, was poised to return. "Gabby" Lusk looked forward to playing for and managing the city's professional team, the Texarkana Bears.

The *Tarzan* strip in the *Gazette*'s comics was to become of more than casual interest as the day wore on. The day's particular episode, "Dance of the Dum-Dum," involved the Apeman's violent encounter with a panther. At the end of the strip, a preview teaser heralded, as if a foreshadowing: *Next Week: Trail of Blood.*

CHAPTER 4

A BAFFLING CASE

While residents sipped coffee and read their newspapers, there was nothing at the lovers' lane to alert the casual observer who might pass and glance at Richard Griffin's parked Oldsmobile in the early-morning light. The road saw little traffic, even less on a quiet Sunday morning. But at nine o'clock, a passing motorist glanced at the car and wondered why it was there at that time of day. There appeared to be two persons inside. There was something unnatural about it. His suspicions rose. On closer inspection, he grew alarmed and concluded that something worth reporting had happened. As soon as he reached a telephone he called the police.

City policemen immediately sped to the scene. The police dispatcher relayed the message to the Bowie County sheriff's office.

War veterans Byron Brower, Jr., and his brother-in-law Edward Brettel with his young son Eddie set out that morning to fetch a Sunday newspaper and some kerosene. They drove to a Texaco station on Highway 67 just west of the Texarkana city limits. They picked up a newspaper and purchased the kerosene. Then their eyes followed a string of automobiles down by the little dirt road that branched off the highway.

"Wonder what's going on there," Brower said. They turned off the highway and parked behind a long row of cars. They got out to take a closer look. Policemen and curious observers crowded around a car at the end of the row. Immediately they realized that it was a crime scene. There was no police line. They walked within eight feet of the car on which all eyes were focused. They saw two bodies in an Oldsmobile. A man's body lay between the seats, his face down. A woman was slumped over in the front seat on the passenger side. Brower had only a side view of her face, but could see she had turned dark.

It was Sunday morning in a small city. The dispatcher directed a squad car to the new crime scene before the sheriff or his deputies could be alerted. The sheriff's Texarkana office was upstairs at 214½ Main over a popular café, John's Place, in the heart of downtown; the city police headquarters and city jail lay a block away.

By time Sheriff Bill Presley arrived, a "very large" crowd had assembled. The milling throng and light showers throughout the morning obliterated any tracks in the dirt around the car. Very few clues were left. About twenty feet from the car, a section of the ground was saturated with dried blood, indicating that one of the victims—Polly Moore, it was later decided—had been murdered outside, and Griffin had been shot inside the car. Griffin was found on his knees behind the front seat, his trousers down to his ankles, his head resting on his hands. She was found sprawled in the front.

The Oldsmobile was spotted throughout with blood. Blood had seeped through the bottom of the car's door and onto the running board, where it had congealed. Griffin's trouser pockets were turned inside out, as if to suggest robbery. Judging from the amount of blood, both inside and outside the car, the killer could hardly have avoided getting blood all over himself as well.

The presence of police cars and other automobiles piqued the curiosity of others who turned off the highway to see what was going on. It became a major chore to keep people away.

Who were the victims? Griffin's identification was readily established. His wallet contained his driver's license. The young woman's purse contained no identification. But she wore an Atlanta High School Class of 1945 ring, which narrowed the search. Inside the ring were initials: PAM. Presley called Homer Carter, city marshal of Atlanta in the next county. Contacting Atlanta school officials, Carter learned the ring apparently belonged to Polly Ann Moore, who had graduated the year before. He passed on the finding to Bowie County. Presley and others began backtracking the couple's activities the night of their deaths, learning that they'd eaten supper at the Canary Cottage with Griffin's sister and her boyfriend.

The newspaper soon learned of the deaths. A reporter immediately asked, "Was this a murder and suicide?"

"No, definitely not," replied the sheriff. "Both were shot in the back of their heads. It's a double murder. We're still looking for clues and leads. We've found no weapon."

But there was so little to go on.

The sheriff immediately launched an area-wide investigation. He notified both Texas and Arkansas-side lawmen at city, county, and state levels, along with the Federal Bureau of Investigation, the Texas Department of Public Safety, and the Texas Rangers. The Rangers promised to dispatch a man.

By the end of the day, the only certainty was that two persons had been murdered. What the rain hadn't washed away, officers and gawkers had destroyed by plodding around the scene. After the bodies were taken away, the Oldsmobile remained at the site for hours until moved to the Arkansas-side police station, where a more thorough fingerprint examination could be undertaken.

Polly Moore's immediate family didn't learn the dismal news until her school ring had been identified. Lizzie Moore's telephone was on a large party line in the rural community. Her ring was one long and two shorts—she didn't have to wait long to know whether a call was for her or not.

The caller identified himself as the Cass County sheriff.

"Mrs. Moore, they've found two bodies over in Texarkana. A man and a young woman. We think she's your daughter Polly."

Lizzie Moore, shocked by the words, maintained her composure. She'd never been an emotional person.

"Why? What happened?"

"They were shot to death, in a car. The girl was wearing an Atlanta High School class ring with the initials PAM. The school thinks it belongs to your daughter. They would like for you to go to Texarkana and verify this."

It was the Moore family's introduction to the tragic news. Lizzie Moore owned an old-model automobile that wasn't reliable. She called a neighbor. The neighbors' son-in-law drove Lizzie and her son Mark to Texarkana, to the funeral home where she was shown the girl's body. It was, indeed, Polly.

Mark Moore was a fourteen-year-old sophomore in high school. Dealing with adversity, throughout the Depression, had steeled the family for the unexpected. Polly's death was a loss they would never get over, but they would deal with it without breaking down. After they finished their business in Texarkana, they left for Atlanta to make funeral arrangements. They would remain in Cass County, where the funeral would be.

Ardella Campbell, in whose home Polly roomed, had worked her regular shift as a telephone operator the night before and wasn't immediately aware that Polly wasn't sleeping in her room. She and her mother soon learned that Polly wasn't home. Ardella felt a sense of responsibility for her young cousin's safety and grew agitated. *This isn't like Polly. What has happened?* She wasn't long in learning that the worst had happened.

Lizzie Moore called from Cass County before leaving for Texarkana.

Ardella's best friend, Maurice Richardson, lived right around the corner. Maurice's husband worked nights as a switchman for the railroad. That Sunday morning he had arrived home and gone directly to bed. Ardella, crying on the phone, called her friend Maurice. Polly had been found dead. She had been killed. Ardella choked out the news between sobs.

Ardella didn't own a car. The Richardsons had an old Chevrolet.

"Will you take me out there where they found the body?" Ardella asked.

The two women herded the four children—Maurice's two daughters and a son, plus Ardella's daughter—into the Richardsons' car and drove to the crime scene.

The experience burned into the memory of Maurice's daughter Patti, the oldest of the children.

"It was out in the country. There were trees in the background, but up front was just a great big open field. It looked like a lot of cars had been along there, a one-lane dirt road. A dirt trail only went so far into the field. It was where people had been driving in there and parking, and that's what Richard and Polly did. The car was near the woods. They drove in there and they were parked, and. . . ."

"Well, when we drove up there, there were cars all the way up from where Richard Griffin's car was parked. It was still there. And Mother just pulled right off of [Highway] 67 and in behind that long line of cars. She and Ardella got out and walked down there. They would *not* let any of us children go—at all. Mother said, 'Don't you dare get out of the car!' I did get out of the car, though. I was gonna see what I could see. I saw the car, with people gathered around. I was in the second grade, and so I remember that it was a real tearful thing, and Ardella was very, very upset.

"Mother and Ardella were gone a long time. When they got back to the car where I was keeping my brother and sister and Ardella's daughter, they were grim-faced and tearful—visibly shaken."

The bodies had been removed by then.

"But the car was still there. And the blood was just everywhere. I remember them talking about a great big pool of blood right in front of the car."

The crowd had thinned out by the time Isaac Rounsavall and his son Ray drove unexpectedly upon the murder site. Rounsavall was driving to Highway 67 via the crooked unpaved connections between Highways 59 and 67. The boy saw a half-dozen or so people there, with policemen stationed at the highway to keep others out.

The elder Rounsavall saw Sheriff Presley and got out of the car and walked over to him. Young Ray took in the scene as a curious boy would. The bodies had been moved; the death car remained by the ditch, headed south, framed by rampant honeysuckle. Blood was all over the inside of the car.

Ray watched a young man with a baby girl cradled in his arm, walking about, peering at the ground and all around. About fifty feet from the car, the man suddenly stopped, bent over, the little girl still in the crook of his left arm, and picked up a set of keys. Ray had heard the men say there'd been no keys in the ignition of the Oldsmobile. The man handed the keys to Presley. With a crowd milling around earlier, the officers had not seen the keys, trampled into the soft wet earth by numerous feet.

Later James and Sandy King, en route to one of the few stores open on Sunday, arrived at the intersection of Robinson Road and Highway 67 West. They were in a truck that King drove for a wrecking business. At the highway they saw a crowd milling around on the dirt road across the highway. He turned and passed by a deputy sheriff he recognized. The deputy, Frank Riley, was directing traffic. Towing damaged cars was King's job.

"Is it a wreck?" he hollered.

"No, it's a murder," replied the deputy. He motioned at King. "Come on back. We need to move the car over to the Arkansas police station."

King crossed the highway and backed the wrecker close enough to Griffin's Oldsmobile to hook it to the winch. He hauled it onto West Seventh Street and eastward. Once the Oldsmobile was set down in the alley by the Arkansas police station, the policemen and King pushed it to a space where the fingerprint specialist could go over it.

When King returned to the wrecker, Sandy, who had remained in the truck, shook her head in wonder.

"I don't understand why everybody'd push the car by hand. They just put that many more fingerprints on it!"

Her husband shrugged. Neither of them realized yet that other disorderly crime scenes would eventually follow, obscuring or obliterating potentially crucial evidence.

A physician examined Polly Moore's body and determined she had not been raped—or "criminally assaulted," in the term of the day. But in one of the mix-ups that followed, after the bodies were taken from the scene and given a cursory examination, a hearse conveyed her body late that very afternoon to the funeral home in Atlanta in the next county, so there could be no corroborating autopsy. Griffin's body remained at the Texarkana Funeral Home the rest of that Sunday and the following day.

In addition to the physician's assessment that Polly had not been raped, other evidence supported the opinion. Max Tackett, at the time with the Arkansas State Police but in touch with the Texas side, noted that the victim was still wearing a sanitary pad at the time of death. This fact tended to back up the physician's conclusion. The killer's moving her body from outside to inside the car seems to have been part of a plan to conceal the deaths as long as possible, at least until dawn, by which time he presumably would have made his getaway. Rumors of rape, however, soon spread and persisted for decades.

The Griffin family—Bernice, her son David, and her daughter Eleanor—had finished breakfast and were sitting around the living room reading the Sunday newspaper when a neighbor knocked on the door. Telephones were rare at Robison Courts; the Griffins had none. The neighbor had just heard a news item on a local radio station about a couple being killed. He thought Richard was the male victim. Word eventually reached them that the car had been taken to the Arkansas-side police station, along with some of Richard's clothes, because the fingerprinting equipment there was more reliable.

"We were *stunned*," David Griffin said.

Friends took the Griffins to the other side of the state line. It was Richard's car, all right. They also positively identified the clothing.

The Griffins never visited the crime scene. They didn't see Richard's body until it was at the funeral home. Actually, the murder spot itself was within walking distance from their home in Robison Courts—a long walk but not a great distance. But after identifying the Oldsmobile and his clothing and viewing the body, they'd had a surfeit of tragedy.

Welborn Griffin, Richard's other brother three months out of the Army, was married and living in Dallas. As soon as they could, Welborn and his wife and baby left Dallas by train.

Welborn arrived at the funeral home after midnight. He went inside and found one man on duty.

He identified himself to the attendant. "I want to see Richard's body and see where he was shot."

"I'm sorry, Mr. Griffin," the man said. "I can't do that. The officers told us not to let any family members see where he was shot."

Welborn was astonished.

"I want to know *why* I can't see where my brother was shot!"

Heated words bounced between them, and finally Welborn told him, "Well, I'm going to *see* where Richard was shot. If *you* don't turn the body over, I'm going to turn it over myself! Unless you're big enough to whip me and keep me from it."

Welborn Griffin, like his brother, was strong and well built. His grief and anger reinforced his demand. The man turned the body over and Welborn saw where two bullets had entered the back of Richard's head. He struggled to control his emotions as he stood before his brother's corpse. He saw no exit wound in the front of the head. The bullets hadn't been removed.

He walked several blocks to the Texas-side police station.

"There was a bunch of officers. I told them who I was and began to try to find out something. Well, they give me the runaround. And I tried asking an officer some questions, and this other officer he got in on the conversation and told me that they found Richard's car keys a hundred yards out there in that marsh from where they found the bodies which was just a dirt road. I said, 'You mean a hundred *feet*, not a hundred yards, don't you?'

"'No, it was a hundred *yards*, because we measured it.'

"I said, 'I don't believe me, you, or nobody else can throw a set of car keys a hundred yards.'

"That ended that conversation. I was afraid I was going to really get into a confrontation with him."

Had Welborn Griffin known how the keys were actually found, in the dirt by the man cradling a baby girl, after the crowd had dispersed, he might have sustained his argument. It was an example of how fast facts became distorted as word-of-mouth accounts changed, sometimes radically, and repeatedly.

"I stayed there till near daylight," said Griffin. "About daylight, I went to the cab stand—it wasn't far down there—and caught a cab and went to Robison Courts where my mother and sister and Richard and David all lived.

"They were up. They hadn't slept any all night. It just was sadness, crying, and everything. Nobody could figure out *why*."

In a city in which crime was a constant, the murders left no doubt as to the case's overriding importance. Most of the violent crimes in Texarkana could be connected to something—an unpaid debt, a drunken fight, jealousy, or even racism. But the deaths of Polly and Richard were disconcertingly random. An eight-column nearly inch-high front-page banner proclaimed the tragedy in Monday morning's *Texarkana Gazette*.

COUPLE FOUND SHOT TO DEATH IN AUTO

Accompanying the article were photographs of the two victims, a studio photo of a handsome Griffin and a snapshot of a smiling Polly Moore, with her black-and-white dog, on the front steps of her home while she was in high school. The photo had been found in her purse next to her body.

A justice of the peace executed the death certificates, assessing the cause of death identically in each case: "Gun shot in base of skull."

At work Monday morning, Byron Brower, Jr., noticed that Polly Moore, with whom he had been working as she checked the ammunition trucks, hadn't shown up. He hadn't read the newspaper yet. Others began talking about the murders, and he then realized that the young woman's body he had seen in the car the morning before was that of Polly. He hadn't been close enough to recognize her.

Polly's services were held at the Pleasant Hill Baptist Church Monday afternoon in the little community of Bryans Mill, with burial in the cemetery near where she had been born seventeen years before.

It was late Monday afternoon when the police notified Welborn Griffin that his brother's body was being released. He called the funeral home in Cass County, and two men accompanied him to the police station to acquire the release. When they arrived, they learned of a change in plans. A Texas Ranger was on the way. The body couldn't be released until he arrived.

Welborn Griffin and the undertakers waited in the police station for what seemed an interminable period. He heard two uniformed policemen talking about the antics of two women, both drunk, after the bodies and car had been moved. Blood had seeped out of the car onto the ground beneath. One of the women shoved the other down and tried to push her nose into the blood in the dirt. Welborn didn't know whether to believe it or not. One policeman said the crowd of onlookers had grown so large, later, that there was hardly standing room.

The Ranger—Jimmy Geer—finally arrived at nine o'clock that night.

As the Ranger bounded up the stairs, the officers—Griffin said—"were just like a bunch of little kids with a schoolteacher. They all run up there and tried to talk at the same time, so he jumped up in a chair and started to cussing and told 'em to *shut up!* They did.

"And the first question he asked 'em was, 'When y'all found that car and the bodies, did y'all rope that area off? And secure it until you could make a *thorough* investigation?'

"And they told him, 'No.'

"And I'll tell you the exact words he said. Told 'em, 'Well, if you didn't do that, you destroyed all the goddamned evidence there was!' That's just the words he told 'em, right there."

The room turned chaotic. "They did a lot of talking and I couldn't tell a word that was said, to save my neck." The Ranger created a checklist to ensure that all possible evidence would be collected. Foremost was to retrieve the bullets from Richard Griffin's head, a procedure not done in Polly's case. Eventually Welborn gained a release of his brother's body, and the funeral director took it back to Cass County for services. By that time it was nearly daylight.

That afternoon—Tuesday—Richard's services were held in the Union Chapel church, close to where the family home had been, his grave just inside the cemetery gate. In death, both had returned to Cass County, six miles apart.

Welborn was never satisfied with the response, then or later, from the Texas-side officers.

The town that had two of almost everything and promoted itself with paired images now had an unexpected, unexplained double murder on its hands, one that was not quite like any of the numerous crimes it had known before. But that wasn't apparent at first, and this was likely why the police and rangers at the time were so lax with their due process in the immediate aftermath of discovering the bodies.

From the beginning, the Griffin-Moore case was a huge one, larger than it first appeared. Dozens of well-coordinated detectives—compiling and processing evidence, filing information, interviewing suspects and potential witnesses, scouring the area—would hardly have been overkill. But manpower, or rather the lack of it, was a problem from the start.

Even worse, evidence was sparse. The bullets taken from Richard Griffin's head, the hulls of the bullets, and possibly (or possibly not) fingerprints from the dead man's car—these were the only tangible clues. The bullets that killed Polly Moore had not been removed and had been buried with her body. It was assumed the same weapon killed her as killed Griffin. The cartridge shells seemed to come from the same gun. If the bullets were needed later, her body could be exhumed. If any witnesses existed, it would take energetic, and lucky, digging to identify and locate those.

Although lawmen recognized the case as an exceptional one, residents appeared not overly upset or fearful. The vicious attack upon Mary Jeanne Larey and Jimmy Hollis the month before had faded from most people's memory. People with no connection to either case tended to wonder if the killer hadn't known the couple and executed them out of revenge or jealousy.

In the new case, no suspect could be identified; no motive seemed to exist. Those who knew the victims couldn't provide the slightest information that might lead to a suspect. The verdict of the justice of the peace remained valid: they had died at the hands of an unknown person for unknown reasons.

The morning after his Monday night arrival, Ranger Geer retraced the investigation up to that point, going over the clues presented him and driving to the murder scene where the bodies and Griffin's car had been found, searching for any clues that might have been overlooked. Two days after the crime, it was futile. The milling throng, following on the heels of rain, fatally complicated the officers' work.

The ballistics report from the Texas Department of Public Safety's Bureau of Identification and Records offered the first—and only—solid link to the killer, keyed to the cartridge shells found at the death scene and the bullets extracted from Richard Griffin's body. The murder weapon was a .32 automatic pistol with six lands and grooves with a left-hand twist. It was determined to be a Colt or a similar foreign make. Although veterans had brought back any number of foreign-made guns as souvenirs from the recent war, most likely the gun was American-made and therefore a Colt.

The evidence was assigned the filing label L-11672/0-261, to be maintained for comparison with any other pistol and bullets that might turn up.

This did not mean that there was a definite tie to just any .32 Colt automatic that officers might find. It would have to be test-fired to confirm a fit. It was not an uncommon weapon, but was a relatively small handgun that could be readily concealed—and used—very easily.

(Although investigators found no murder weapon after scouring the brush and surrounding area, coincidentally, more than three years later several little girls did find a pistol a quarter-mile from the crime scene. In October 1949, ten-year-old Marie Barlow and girls her age were playing in an open field of about five acres with tall, knee-deep grass when they came upon a rusted, dirt-clogged pistol. They reported it to an adult, who passed it on to authorities. Was it linked to the 1946 murders? Texas Ranger Stewart Stanley dashed any speculation. It was a .38 caliber Spanish-made revolver. The murder weapon had been an automatic, not a six-shooter, and a different caliber. Lawmen periodically found discarded weapons. Whatever the explanation, it did not fit into the murder case.)

Officers sweated over the mystery. Sheriff Presley and Chief Runnels together posted a $500 reward for information leading to an arrest and conviction, which translates to more than $6,000 today. A year before, a reward of the same size had quickly led to the solving of the Curtner murder. Five hundred dollars was a large amount of money, especially when it might be collected with a few words and an appropriate name attached.

No such information was forthcoming. A motive was hard to pinpoint. Griffin's pockets likely had contained coins or small bills—pocket change—rather than large bills, hardly enough to kill for. This suggested that robbery had been secondary, an afterthought, perhaps even a ploy to throw lawmen off.

At first, suspicions turned toward sex as a motive, that the assailant had raped, or had intended to rape, Polly Moore. No evidence substantiated it. She was fully clothed. A physician confirmed that she had not been "criminally assaulted." There was the possibility that the mysterious gunman had *intended* to rape Polly Moore and that sex *was* a motive but the killer got distracted and changed his mind. But if that had been his intent, why had he not at least partially disrobed her, or assaulted her sexually in one way or another? No connection was made in any way to the earlier beating incident and the female's sexual abuse.

Because the ground had been patted wet by rain, obscuring any car tracks or footprints that may have existed earlier, it was difficult to establish that the killer had driven to the scene, and although it seemed the most likely, it was still possible the killer had walked there. A café and beer joint, Stockman's Cafe, was situated on Highway 67, not far off. If as a pedestrian he had risked exposure, he could have readily ducked into the heavily wooded area nearby and evaded scrutiny.

Almost any theory was possible, because no one knew.

Within four days following discovery of the bodies, officers had taken more than fifty persons into custody for questioning, while chasing down more than a hundred false leads. It was a grueling process with little rest. Three suspects, arrested and questioned because of bloody clothing, explained the stains to officers' satisfaction.

Meanwhile, the Texas Rangers dispatched Dick Oldham to join Jimmy Geer. In a state where the old legend "one riot, one Ranger" was the only recipe needed for success, the force in Texarkana had doubled before a week was gone.

The case remained unsolved into April. More than 200 false tips and leads were followed. One suspect, "a girl from Kansas City," was arrested in San Antonio, 425 miles away. Rangers drove her to Texarkana. Quickly eliminated as a suspect, she had not even known of the crimes.

Mary Jeanne Larey, now living in Oklahoma, learned of the murders. The more she learned, the more certain she was that they were connected to her own night of horror. She was so certain that she took a trip back to Texarkana to talk to officers.

She was convinced that the same man who had attacked Hollis and herself had now gone a step farther and had killed. If they would listen to her, perhaps they could learn something about the murderer.

Her plea fell on deaf ears. Officers again insisted that she knew her attacker and was protecting him by withholding his name. She just as fervently insisted she had not known the man, and that he was a Negro, just as she had asserted back in February, despite Hollis's belief that a white man had attacked them.

Still a bundle of nerves, she returned to Oklahoma having changed no minds.

Officers seemed not to have remembered Jimmy Hollis's prediction three days before the murders that at the next opportunity his assailant would kill. Nor did it dawn on them that a similar *modus operandi* seemed to link the cases, down to the men having to drop their trousers as a means of immobilizing them.

Three weeks passed.

By Palm Sunday, April 14, Texarkanians were gearing up for "Straw Hat Day" and wearing stylish spring apparel. The Sunday edition of the *Texarkana Gazette* featured the first of an Easter series, written by Dr. Tom J. Wilbanks, pastor of the Pine Street Presbyterian Church on the Texas side. At the movies, John Wayne starred in *Tall in the Saddle*, while the Paramount Theater advertised the new RKO Radio production *Deadline at Dawn*. The ad carried a warning:

"A night filled with TERROR."

CHAPTER 5

A BOY, A GIRL—AND A GUNMAN

Before the trolleys shut down in Texarkana in the 1930s, subsequently to be replaced by buses, one route took passengers all the way to Spring Lake Park north of the city limits, where they enjoyed picnic grounds, recreation for softball and other sports, and a relaxing site for all ages. Sue Wilson McCrossen recalled that her Girl Scout troop would *hike* all the way from their gathering point at Highland Park Elementary School about twenty-five blocks from downtown, out Ghio Boulevard and past the city limits to the park. It was three miles each way. They took their lunches. The park was a popular family venue, featuring a dance pavilion along with the eponymous body of water with its own resident alligator. People from surrounding areas visited the springhouse to fill jugs with its water, believed to harbor healthful constituents.

In the park's spacious and wooded bounds, some sealed off from public view by clumps of trees and bushes, young couples traditionally trysted, day or night. To those exploring the park for the first time at night, its winding roads and trails could seem more like a perplexing labyrinth;

to its frequenters they were avenues of graceful respite and abandon. It was a fun place.

Yet, historically, or at least in legend, Spring Lake Park was the backdrop for Texarkana's first known act of violence. In 1541, so the story went, the Spanish explorer Hernando de Soto quelled a mutiny by hanging a soldier from a tree in what was to become the park. Every schoolchild in the region learned the account. Some residents vowed they knew which tree the unfortunate Spaniard had been hanged from—400 years before.

The murders of Polly Ann Moore and Richard Griffin, as violent as they were, set off relatively few alarms among young people in Texarkana. What residents hadn't noticed was that the Griffin-Moore murders had broken the pattern of the past, when a motive was readily apparent, however mundane, petty, or grand it may have been. That had not become apparent in the aftermath of the killings. Nor had officers or the public linked the February beatings to the murders. Consequently what might have been seen as a huge red flag escaped anyone's notice. Violence was the last thing anybody expected as a result of necking and smooching.

Despite the steady crime level in this town, it was still a trusting time. Most encounters were peaceable. Minor troubles almost always led to amicable resolutions. When a man driving an old-model Dodge skidded into C. J. Neighbors's car on the Texas side in the late afternoon of Thursday, April 11, Neighbors saw no reason for alarm. No one was injured. The damage to his car was slight. The other driver was apologetic and friendly. "I'm Smith," he said. "I live on College Hill. Just let me know what it costs." The affable, cooperative man drove off. It was the last Neighbors saw of "Smith."

It was easy to conclude that "Smith" was driving a stolen car. Taking another's car required so little expertise that teenagers could do it. Yet many residents continued to leave the keys in the ignition, both tempting and enabling thieves. Theft wasn't complicated. "Hot-wiring" was almost as simple as turning the key. All you had to do was connect two wires to the ignition to fire the engine. A thief with any experience could hot-wire a car and drive it off in about two minutes. The older the car, the easier it was to steal.

After school on Friday, April 12, James Paul Martin, a junior at Kilgore, Texas, High School, borrowed his brother's shiny Ford coupe and drove more than a hundred miles to Texarkana. His mother had misgivings about the trip. He was only sixteen, his seventeenth birthday three weeks off. She was afraid he wouldn't drive safely enough.

Young Paul had many friends in Texarkana. His father had operated an ice business in the oil town Smackover, Arkansas, where Paul was born. When a more explosive boom opened in the huge East Texas field in the early 1930s, Martin, Sr., moved his business to Kilgore. His wife, loath to live in yet another rough-and-tumble boomtown, chose Texarkana's Arkansas side as the family's new home. Her husband periodically returned to Texarkana. Paul and his three older brothers attended school in Texarkana.

In late 1940, when Paul was eleven, his father died unexpectedly. Inez Martin and her sons moved to Kilgore. The war came. Paul's brothers entered the service. Paul, too young to serve, attended military school in Mississippi the last year of the war, then returned to Kilgore High and worked part-time in the ice plant. That summer, he was to be the plant's night engineer.

His Texarkana friends liked him. One classmate remembered him as "a short boy with the best attitude you ever saw. I don't think he had an enemy in the world. Everybody loved him, and he just loved people."

Upon arrival in Texarkana that Friday, Paul headed to his close friend's house in the same block where he once had lived. He would stay with Tom Albritton for the weekend. As young boys they'd walked all over Texarkana together. They reminisced and made plans for the next day.

High among Paul's plans was seeing Betty Jo Booker. They'd known each other for ten years, since elementary school on the Arkansas side.

Betty Jo Booker, a fifteen-year-old junior at Texas High, was busier than Paul Martin probably realized. A popular girl and a serious student, she also held a part-time job that few others, boys or girls her age, could claim. She played the saxophone in a local orchestra. Jerry Atkins and His Rhythmaires performed at VFW Club dances. Band director Atkins, only sixteen himself, had inherited the band when older musicians went to war.

For her fifteen years, Betty Jo had a packed background, much of it tragic. Her brother four years older—Billy Boy, the family called him—was born with brain damage. He never developed mentally past childhood. He had died in a Little Rock institution when he was sixteen.

Worst of all, her father died young. A personable man, Miller County, Arkansas, tax assessor William Blanton "Boogie" Booker had died in a traffic accident near Shreveport, Louisiana, in 1932. He and others were en route to check on relatives in northern Louisiana after a killer tornado had taken eighty lives. His skull was fractured. He was thirty years old. Betty Jo, not quite three, never had a chance to know him.

Following Booker's death, the governor of Arkansas appointed the widow to serve the rest of the term. Bessie Booker subsequently was elected to several terms.

The following year after her father's death, Betty Jo was crowned Miss Tiny Texarkana at a local pageant. Her mother had a bathing suit of gold lamé made for the occasion. While still a child, Betty Jo took swimming and dance lessons. She performed song-and-dance numbers for civic groups and sang at church. One Christmas she sang all four verses of "Silent Night, Holy Night." She had to stand on a table so the congregation could see her.

Betty Jo became painfully aware of growing up without a father. "Everybody has a daddy but me," she would tell her mother. Once, she suggested, "Let's go downtown and find me a daddy." After four years of widowhood, Bessie married Clark Brown, a salesman for a sand-and-gravel firm. Betty Jo, then seven, was jubilant. "Now I have a daddy!" Her stepfather became the father she'd never known. The two of them would sing together while washing and drying dishes. He taught her old cowboy songs. He was everything she'd wanted in a father. She felt whole again. So did her mother. "Our home was the happiest in the world."

After Bessie Booker Brown finished that term as tax assessor, the new little family moved to the Texas side of town, settling in a pleasant middle-class neighborhood, Sussex Downs.

Betty Jo had played in the Arkansas High band. When she moved, she became a member of the Texas High band. She made new friends in Texas, while keeping those in Arkansas. "Everybody liked her," a classmate said.

During the bitter 1945 football rivalry between the schools, she emphasized that after the game the score would be forgotten. The Razorbacks
and the Tigers tied, 7-7.

The earlier tragedies only strengthened the mother-daughter bond.
To say that they were close merely approximates their relationship. Betty
Jo was all Bessie had left from her early family. The mother adored her
daughter—or, as she put it, "I worshipped her." She maintained scrap-
books documenting virtually every aspect of Betty Jo's life, a consolation
for her double tragedies.

Though not "boy crazy," as her mother put it, Betty Jo dated from time to
time. Herbert Wren, a childhood friend from the Arkansas side, remembered
she was the first girl he ever kissed. Later, on the Texas side, she occasionally
dated Sonny Atchley, drummer for the dance band, and, more often, Jimmy
Morriss, another Texas High student.

As the April weekend rolled around, Betty Jo was unaware how promi-
nently she figured in Paul Martin's plans during his visit from Kilgore.

Paul Martin had in mind taking Betty Jo to the midnight movie at the
Paramount. He didn't spell it out when he called her Saturday morning.
He said he'd drop by in the afternoon. He'd also learned of a slumber
party to which they might drop by.

Paul spent the morning getting ready. He washed and shined his
brother's car. Nearby old friend Herbert Wren was mowing his family's
lawn; the boys waved at each other.

The weather was so pleasant that Betty Jo changed her afternoon
plans. She and Sophie Anne White decided to go swimming. She told
her mother to tell Paul, if he came by. Sophie Anne had already graduated from Texas High and was studying music at the University of Texas
in Austin. Betty Jo spent a lot of time at the White home, a brisk walk
away. Sophie Anne's mother taught Betty Jo piano lessons. When she
was in town, as she was this weekend, Sophie Anne played trumpet in
Jerry Atkins's band.

Sophie Anne drove them to TP (or Texas & Pacific) Lake southwest
of town. Her father was the lake's superintendent. The family swam and
fished there regularly. It was early in the year for swimming, but the large
lake was shallow and the water wasn't cold. The girls enjoyed the brisk

first-of-the-year swim and returned home about four o'clock, invigorated and looking forward to playing for the dance that evening.

While Betty Jo was gone, Paul drove by. Her mother explained that Betty Jo had gone swimming. Paul, who'd known the family for years, lingered and chatted with Bessie and Clark Brown for more than an hour, talking of school and his family's business in Kilgore. As he left, he said, "Tell Betty Jo I'll call later."

He did. He said since he hadn't seen her, he'd pick her up after the band finished playing. She said she would have to modify her own plans but thought she could do it. She had expected Jimmy Morriss, a fellow student, to meet her after the dance. Young Morriss worked late Saturdays in a department store.

She called Morriss at work. "Jimmy, an old friend of mine, Paul Martin, is in town from Kilgore and called me. Do you mind if he picks me up tonight?"

Morriss, like most of the other Texas-side youths, had never heard of Paul Martin. Basically, she was breaking the date, but considering that she'd told him Martin was an old friend, Morriss, a pleasant and agreeable youth, assured her that it was all right with him.

While Betty Jo performed in Atkins's band, Paul Martin and Tom Albritton spent the evening with friends about town. Tom had a date with Ramona Putman. Paul wanted to go to the midnight movie after meeting Betty Jo. He would pick up Tom and Ramona as soon as he fetched Betty Jo. Tom and Ramona would wait on the Albrittons' front porch.

It was a warm afternoon, cooling as night came near, but not expected to hit lower than the mid-forties, enough to wear a coat or jacket. The days were gradually growing longer, the sun setting at 6:45 that afternoon. It would be dark by the time Betty Jo showed up for her stint with the dance band. The moon, which rose that afternoon, would be on the wane and soon gone by time they called it a night. One of the mothers took the girl members of the orchestra to the VFW Club. This night the duty of taking the girls home fell to Ernest Holcomb.

Charlsie Schoeppey was fifteen and a "high sophomore" at Texas High. Her family lived on Anthony Drive in Sussex Downs, across the street from

Betty Jo's family. That night she and her boyfriend, Jim Boyd, Jr., with other couples drove out to Spring Lake Park and parked on a dirt road. Accompanied by car radio music, they danced in the road by the side of the car. It was a great night. They were energetic teenagers, and it was spring, with the end of school a few weeks off. She was in by midnight but then went to a slumber party near where she lived, got little sleep and ate too much junk food. She had to be home in time to attend Sunday school and church.

It was a big night at the VFW, with a big crowd expected. Manager Lacy Lawrence promoted the event by promising to give away eight pairs of nylon hose, with the following ad: WHO WILL BE THE 8 LUCKY WOMEN—ATTEND THIS DANCE & FIND OUT. The same day, a string of four movie theaters—Ritz, Princess, Joy, and Palace, the latter a "colored" site—proclaimed similar promotion tactics. If you patronized one of their theaters, you could purchase a genuine Army steel helmet for only twenty-five cents. Nylons, steel helmets—all readily evoked the recent war and its consumer scarcities.

Emblematic of postwar transitions, the VFW Club's Saturday night dances made it a popular nightspot. During the war the large white frame building had housed the USO Club. A short stroll from downtown, it was even nearer the town's busy, widely known red-light district in the other direction. Lacy Lawrence, a local café proprietor, assumed its management, sold beer, and added a local orchestra of skilled teenagers who had developed during the war—Jerry Atkins and His Rhythmaires. You could dine and dance—and drink beer. "BRING YOUR WIFE/BRING YOUR GIRL FRIEND."

Atkins had started playing in the band when he was only fourteen, too young to drive himself to the gigs. His group was a holdover of the big-band era that had flourished during the war. As older musicians entered the service, Atkins had inherited the band. When the war jerked Texarkana into a twenty-four-hour town, the demand for entertainment grew. Atkins recruited musicians he knew, practically all from Texas High.

Betty Jo Booker was one of four girls in the band. Although the atmosphere at times was rowdy, as customers avidly consumed beer, parental ground rules and Atkins's guidelines made it safe for the girls. Atkins and

Ernest Holcomb, the first saxophonist, alternated in escorting the girls home, with emphasis on their arriving soon after closing time.

Because it wasn't his night to collect the girls, Atkins and his fifteen-year-old drummer, Bailor Willson "Sonny" Atchley, arrived early at the VFW Club to set up the music stands and check out the equipment. Modeled to some extent on Duke Ellington's orchestra with prominent saxophone sounds, the Rhythmaires aimed at echoing the big band sound. With the talented Sophie Anne White joining them with her trumpet, it was a special occasion. Cora Ann Hunt, as usual, accompanied the band on the piano, and Betty Jo on the alto saxophone, Betty Ann Roberts also on the trumpet, with Haskell Walker playing the tenor saxophone, and Sonny Atchley, drums. Most were seniors poised to graduate. Betty Jo and Sonny Atchley had another year of school ahead.

The band began at nine o'clock. The musicians played, the customers drank beer and danced, and never the twain did meet, as if an invisible but impenetrable barrier separated them. Usually the evenings passed without incident; this one was no exception. They played for four hours, with breaks, and nothing much happened.

They played their usual repertoire of melodies, strongly influenced by Glenn Miller's band, featuring such tunes as the standby "Tuxedo Junction," as well as "Along the Santa Fe Train," "At Last," and "String of Pearls," blending nostalgic wartime songs with current popular ones.

Soon after one o'clock the band wound up its gig with the last melody, "Good Night, Sweetheart," followed by the lights-out signal, "Show Me the Way to Go Home." It was well after one o'clock. The musicians began putting away their sheet music and instruments. Getting paid took longer; Atkins had to find the manager and extract the money due the musicians. When Atkins got the money, it was already divided out, cash on the spot; he only had to hand over each one's share. He and Atchley put their instruments in Atkins's car and drove off. It was just another "normal" Saturday night: no beer bottles thrown, the usual wait for the money. Atkins was unaware that Paul Martin had waited outside for Betty Jo. He had assumed Holcomb would take her home.

Atchley was spending the night at Atkins's parents' house. The youths drove to the all-night Goodwin's Cafe to eat breakfast and unwind. At

Goodwin's they talked about the night's work. They were teenagers in a town that never closed, but all-night restaurants were safe, the lights bright and the establishments respectable. They picked up a Sunday paper, browsed through it, and headed to Atkins's home at 2617 North State Line, on the Texas side. Although they'd never paid any attention to it, the house was a half dozen blocks from the room Jimmy Hollis had shared with his brother on the Arkansas side at 3502 State Line, and slightly over a dozen blocks from where Polly Ann Moore had roomed with her older cousin. More than anything else, the proximity of the addresses reflected the city's small size.

Tired from the evening's work, their stomachs filled, pleasantly exhausted, Atkins and Atchley turned in around four o'clock. It was Sunday. They could sleep as long as they wished.

Just as Betty Jo had adjusted her plans to accommodate Paul's arrival, his double-dating plans had to be scrapped. Early in the evening a group of friends that included Martin, his buddy Tom Albritton, and Tom's date Ramona Putman went to a movie, then ate a snack at a café. Later they intended to make the midnight movie at the Paramount. Paul left the group to pick up Betty Jo, not realizing she wouldn't be able to take off early from her VFW gig. Ramona, knowing her mother didn't want her to stay out after midnight, called for permission to go to the late movie. Her mother said No. Tom and Ramona waited at the Albritton front porch for Paul to return with Betty Jo. When he hadn't made it by half-past eleven, Tom walked Ramona home several blocks away. When he returned home, Paul still hadn't shown up. Perhaps Betty Jo hadn't been able to leave the VFW in time; perhaps they had dropped in on the slumber party afterward. It had been a long day. Tom went to bed.

Paul Martin, unaware that Betty Jo would not be able to leave the dance in time to attend the midnight show, waited in his car. He was standing outside when she emerged from the building. Betty Ann Roberts walked to the car with her. It was the first time Paul and Betty Jo had seen each other that weekend. He took her saxophone case and set it on the back floorboard of the coupe. As late as it was, the night was far from over. There remained the slumber party-in-progress of Betty Jo's friends that they could drop in on for a while. Then perhaps they would have a snack at one of the all-night restaurants. But first, before they did anything else, Betty Jo had to drop off her saxophone at home. It was an unvarying routine, whatever else she did after any performance, for her to take her expensive musical instrument home first. On the way to her Sussex Downs home, however, Paul suggested they drive to Spring Lake Park, only a few minutes away from Anthony Drive, and *then* deposit the saxophone. Later they could visit Betty Jo's girl friends at the slumber party. With the weekend slipping away, Paul would be returning to Kilgore in a matter of hours.

He drove the coupe north past the city limits to Spring Lake Park, crossed the Kansas City Southern tracks leading north from the city, and entered the park area. For most teenagers, it was familiar ground. Paul parked. The darkened sky ensured them absolute privacy.

It was a cool evening after warming into the 70s that afternoon. By eleven P.M. while the band still played, the thermometer had dipped to 58. By two A.M. the reading was headed to the middle 40s. People were already talking about the traditional "Easter cold snap." Betty Jo had worn a full-length coat that was comfortable in the chilly night.

After they had been parked for a short while, a car drove up. A man got out and strolled to the driver's side of their car. He spoke in a casual but authoritative tone. He held a pistol in his hand.

CHAPTER 6

PALM SUNDAY HORRORS

When Betty Jo first played the VFW gig, her mother would wait up for her, regardless of the hour. Betty Jo always gave a full report on the evening, down to what she'd eaten and done. In due time, however, Bessie saw no reason to wait up so late and went on to bed before her daughter arrived in the wee hours.

On this Saturday night, Betty Jo still not in, Bessie went on to bed and fell asleep. She hadn't been asleep long when she got up. Betty Jo wasn't in, and her saxophone wasn't where she always left it when she went back out after playing for the dance.

Bessie woke her husband.

"Clark, Betty Jo isn't here. Her saxophone's not here. Something is wrong."

Drowsily, Clark Brown said, "Well, don't get upset. You'll hear from her."

"No," she said, "I'm going to call the police. I'm going to call the hospitals."

"Bessie, don't do that. It will embarrass Betty Jo, and it will embarrass you, if there's nothing wrong. She'll show up after a while and explain."

Bessie couldn't go back to sleep. She turned the matter over and over in her mind. Betty Jo had *never* gone anywhere without letting her know she was going back out. She *always* told her. The break in the pattern troubled her. She imagined all sorts of scenarios. Had she been in an accident and unable to notify her family? The worried mother could find no satisfying explanation for her daughter's not being home or not having called to tell her why. Betty Jo was so dear to her that she didn't know what she'd do if something happened to her. She persisted in asking her husband to make calls.

"Bessie," he said, "something unexpected may have happened and she didn't want to call this late. There is always a first time."

Finally he agreed to call Janann Gleason, who was holding the slumber party. Perhaps Betty Jo and Paul had dropped in there; maybe Betty Jo had decided to stay and had forgotten to call. It would have clashed with her past behavior but was a possibility. But no, they hadn't seen or heard from Betty Jo.

Bessie Brown's alarm heightened. Now Clark Brown joined in her concern. Unknown possibilities invaded their imaginations.

Bessie called Betty Ann Roberts. She was sleeping. Did she know where Betty Jo had gone after the dance? No, she had seen Betty Jo put her saxophone in Paul Martin's car and saw them leave together. That was the last she'd seen or heard from them. She didn't know what they'd intended to do next.

Dawn that Palm Sunday ushered in a wave of troubling uncertainty to Bessie and Clark Brown.

Tom Moores, a prominent farmer who lived on Moores Lane in the Pleasant Grove community north of town, arose as usual at five o'clock. He turned on the radio and dressed. By five-thirty, he was brushing his hair when he heard an unusual sound for that time of morning. It was a gunshot, definitely a gunshot. He listened carefully, but didn't hear anything else. One gunshot. He wondered why anyone would be firing a gun for any purpose at that time of day, on a Sunday morning. He didn't think any more about it. He got ready to check on his large farm in the Red River bottoms.

Shortly before six o'clock, Mr. and Mrs. G. H. Weaver and their young son left their home on Summerhill Road north of town, on their way to Prescott, Arkansas, a day trip to visit relatives. As they cut through along North Park Road skirting the park, they saw a form lying at the edge of the unpaved road. It looked like a human body. As Weaver drew closer, their fears were confirmed. It was the body of a boy, lying on his left side, his head and the trunk of his body on the leaves and grass. His feet and legs jutted onto the dirt road. He was wearing a light-colored long-sleeved shirt, with his arms and hands in front of him, crumpled in death.

Weaver didn't get out to investigate. He drove two hundred yards to the nearest home and told them what they had found, asking that they notify the sheriff's office.

Sheriff Bill Presley and Texas-side Chief of Police Jack N. Runnels, old friends, were together, meeting for breakfast and pre-church coffee, when the call came. They sped out together in Presley's car. They were the first lawmen to arrive on the scene.

Carefully they checked the boy's body, this time protecting the tracks and other possible clues at the scene. They immediately verified that the boy was dead. He could be identified by contents of his wallet: Paul Martin. He had been shot four times. One bullet had entered the back of the neck and emerged through the front of the skull. Another entered through the left shoulder, fired from the back, with the third bullet going into his right hand. The fourth bullet went into his face. Blood was seen on the other side of the road, by a fence, indicating that he might have been shot on one side of the road and crawled across.

Soon other officers, city and county, arrived and with a systematic search combed the area for clues. Not much to find.

Martin's coupe was located abandoned alongside the road parallel to the Kansas City Southern tracks and crossing. The keys were in the ignition. The automobile was about a mile from where his body had been discovered. The car was near the lake and a short walk, across the KCS tracks, to the Spring Lake Park School.

Presley, careful to avoid tracks, studied bushes and brush around the park. At one point he scrutinized a spot in the parking area flanked by bushes. He looked for anything out of the ordinary. He saw a small black object on the ground around the bushes. Gingerly he stepped over and picked it up. It was a date book. He examined it. It had belonged to Paul Martin. He didn't say anything. He unobtrusively slipped it into his suit coat pocket, keeping it to himself for the time being. He also found a used condom not far away but did not bother to retrieve it. Had it been decades later, in the time of DNA testing, he might have done differently, but as it was there was no way to determine who had used it and when or with whom. It was not uncommon to find condoms in lovers' lanes like that one. The date book definitely had belonged to the dead boy. There was no point in alerting the public—or the killer—of his finding it.

None of the officers, and few others in town, even knew that Betty Jo Booker had been with young Martin that night or, for that matter, if *anyone* had been with him. Her status would not be raised until the news of Martin's murder had spread over town and had reached the small group of teenagers who had known that she'd left with Martin.

As the news of the murder moved by radio and word of mouth, lawmen streamed toward Spring Lake Park. Officers soon learned that a girl had been with Martin—her name: Betty Jo Booker. She was missing. Those not searching for clues to Martin's murder were seeking any sign of the girl.

Jerry Atkins was sleeping soundly when the telephone woke him at six o'clock. The family had one phone, and it was closer to Jerry than to his parents. He reluctantly slipped out of bed and stumbled to the phone.

A troubled female voice responded to his drowsy hello.

"Jerry, did you take Betty Jo home last night?"

The wakeup irritated Atkins, still half asleep.

"No, it wasn't my turn. Ernie took her home," he snapped, wondering why anyone would bother him, and risk waking his parents, at that hour.

"Do you know where she went after she left the VFW?" the girl persisted.

"Well, no. Why are you asking me?"

"She was supposed to come to our slumber party, and she never did."

He hadn't known about the slumber party and couldn't fit the facts together in his sleepy state. He seriously doubted that Betty Jo had gone anywhere but home.

"I'm sure she's at home," he grumbled. "Why call me, this early? I'm trying to sleep!"

Atkins dragged himself back to bed.

He seemed to have just dozed off when, two hours later, the telephone rang again.

Even more irked, he stumbled back to the hallway.

Another, different female voice asked the same question as had the six o'clock caller.

"Do you know where Betty Jo went?"

"Well, call Ernie Holcomb! He took her home. I don't know anything about it," he said.

"We don't think Ernie picked her up."

Atkins asked, "Did you check with her parents, Mr. and Mrs. Brown? They live in Sussex Downs."

This time the voice added, "She was picked up at the VFW by Paul Martin, a boy who drove over from Kilgore. They were both supposed to come to our party but they never showed up."

Atkins had never heard the name Paul Martin, had not known that anyone but Ernie Holcomb was to have taken her home. Betty Jo hadn't told him anything about a change in plans.

"What's the big deal, anyway?" Atkins, now more awake, asked.

"We heard a news bulletin on the radio. A teenaged boy was found shot to death at Spring Lake Park," she said. "We're pretty sure it was Paul Martin."

Despite the caller's seeming certainty, Atkins still couldn't believe Betty Jo had gone anywhere with Paul Martin simply because he had never heard his name. In his early-Sunday-morning fog, the whole thing felt distorted and unreal. Atkins, a Texas-side boy, hadn't realized Betty Jo had known Paul Martin since her school days in Arkansas; her move to the Texas side and Martin's move to Kilgore,

Texas, had left that part of her history foreign to him. It just hadn't come up in conversation.

After the second early-morning call, Atkins's parents and his guest Atchley were out of bed and listening to his end of the conversation. They could tell something unusual was going on.

When Atkins reported what he had been told over the telephone, Atchley told him that he'd known Martin was to have picked up Betty Jo after the dance and that she was not going directly home. He hadn't thought to tell Atkins. This shifted their attention to Ernie Holcomb. Had he known of the change in arrangements, or had he, after all, taken Betty Jo home?

Atkins asked the operator to ring the Holcombs' number. Dial phones had not yet come to Texarkana.

The Holcombs' phone rang and rang. No answer.

This raised additional concerns. Atkins called Haskell Walker, another member of the band, and woke him up. He didn't know any more than Atkins did. Hurriedly the youths dressed and, skipping breakfast, walked to the Holcomb residence, only three blocks away.

The automobile was gone. There was nobody home.

They walked back to the Atkins house. They turned on the radio, hoping to learn something. They didn't know what to do. They began calling about town. By then, people were leaving for church or other Sunday-morning activities. Finally they talked with Sophie Anne White and Betty Ann Roberts. Had Ernie taken them home? Did he take Betty Jo home when he collected them? They confirmed definitely that Betty Jo had not left when Ernie Holcomb collected the other three girls and took them home. She had gone with Paul Martin, as she'd told Atchley she would. Prospects grew decidedly grim.

If Paul Martin's body had been found in Spring Lake Park, what had happened to Betty Jo?

Atkins and Atchley were in a quandary as to what to do next. They soon learned that hundreds had already flocked to the Spring Lake Park area to find Betty Jo or her body. They would have joined the search parties, had not the radio newscasts emphasized that people should *not* go there. It would complicate officers' duties. There were too many people there already.

So what *could* they do? Well, there was Betty Jo's saxophone, which she'd taken with her. It could be traced by its serial number. Had it been found? Did the authorities know of it?

Early Sunday morning, a little after eight o'clock, thirteen-year-old Bill Horner's mother sent him to the little general store next to Spring Lake Park Elementary School for a loaf of bread. As he walked into the store, one of the few open at that hour on Sunday morning, he saw police cars driving by, toward the park itself, and away, in both directions. Inside, he asked a woman in the store, "What're all these police doing out here?"

"There's been a killing over there," she said.

A killing, he immediately thought, *and we sleep with our doors unlocked!* This piqued the boy's curiosity. He debated with himself whether he should satisfy his curiosity and walk over to where the activity seemed to be centered, whether he'd get in trouble if he did. He told the storekeeper he would be back, and he left. He crossed the KCS tracks and the wide crossing that lay on the dirt road that ran parallel to the tracks and directly into the park, through the twin guard posts standing symbolically at the entrance. At that point, he saw three men to his right, maybe eighty yards from the crossing up the dirt road between the rail line and the park. He walked there. The three men paid him no attention. He didn't know what he would have said if they'd asked him what he was doing there. One of the men got into a car and drove off. The other two men, dressed in suits and hats as if on their way to church, stayed, looking down at the ground. Nearby a Ford coupe was parked, mostly off the road but partially at the edge of the dirt road. It was headed south, toward town.

"I can't figure out why there're no tracks coming out," he heard one of the men say.

Young Horner's eyes followed the route they were surveying, covering an expanse of leaves, pine needles, and dirt, but not enough that anyone wouldn't have left footprints. They'd found two sets of tracks, one larger and probably a man's tracks, the other set smaller and probably a woman's. One of the men said, "They got out here"—indicating the road—"and they went over there. And where did they go from there?" The tracks appeared to lead from the road over dirt and leaves toward brush, no more than thirty feet from the road, but they had found none going back toward the road or car, as if they had gone to a point, then disappeared. The two men—Presley and Runnels—then got into their car and drove off. They had hardly noticed the boy's presence.

After they left, teenager Horner strolled near where the lawmen had gone, careful not to intrude upon the tracks they had observed. Nor did he want to leave his tracks close to the scene. He realized what they had been talking about. The two sets of tracks pointed away from the road but didn't return. Where had they gone? Why had they ended so abruptly, apparently not returning to the road? He kept walking back and forth, back and forth, trying to see where the tracks had gone but couldn't. "That bothered me ever since I'd seen that," he was to say years later. Where did they go? How did they get out of there? He even looked around to see if there was a vine they might have swung out on—the fictional character Tarzan was strong in the boy's imagination. He stood around, puzzled, trying to reason how it had happened, why no tracks seemed to go back out toward the road. It was as if, he concluded, the owners of the tracks had vanished. There was no evidence that one of the persons had tried to escape the other. They were just plain footsteps.

Had the tracks had anything to do with the case? Had they gone from one car, presumably the one parked by the road—as it turned out, the car Paul Martin had driven—to another car, unknown to the officers? The puzzle seemed unsolvable.

After a while, young Horner walked back home. He had forgotten to buy the loaf of bread his mother had sent him for. He didn't explain where he had been and what he had seen. The rest of the day, and for days afterward, he fretted over the scene. For decades later he would tumble it over in his mind from time to time.

Before Tom Albritton had gotten out of the house that morning, an officer appeared at the door. Paul Martin's body had been found in Spring Lake Park. Hadn't he been spending the weekend with him? The news numbed. He couldn't believe it. Yes, Tom told the lawman, Paul was spending the weekend with him but hadn't come back the night before.

Why would they have gone to Spring Lake Park? Tom was asked. He groped for words. If you had a car, the usual thing to do was to go to Spring Lake Park and smooch, he told the man. It was popular for young people on both sides of the state line.

When Herbert Wren arrived at First Methodist Church, Arkansas, for Sunday school, he learned of Paul Martin's body being found.

Later that morning he and others drove to Spring Lake Park. The pleasant venue was now a backdrop to horror.

"It changed our community overnight," said Wren. "Before that, youngsters never felt threatened or uncomfortable anywhere. Now young people suddenly were in potential danger at night almost anywhere."

Swarms of lawmen converged upon Spring Lake Park as search parties organized to find Betty Jo or, what was more likely by now, her body, unless she had been kidnapped and was, somehow, still alive. The search widened beyond the immediate area where Martin's body had been found and where his car had been parked.

With the crime scene secured, Sheriff Presley drove into town and headed for the First Methodist Church on the Texas side of State Line. He was a member of the Men's Bible Class there. It was a large class; more than a hundred men attended on Sundays, drawn by two popular teachers, Dr. Henry Stilwell, superintendent of Texarkana, Texas, schools and president of Texarkana College, and District Judge Norman L. Dalby, who alternated Sunday sessions. Presley knew the large group of friends would be assembling, and he recruited them to join the search. Grimly he announced the mission, and men spilled from the church into cars headed for the park. It was the easiest way he knew to organize a search party on short notice on a Sunday morning.

In the morning, fifteen-year-old Charlsie Schoeppey was so sleepy that she begged to miss services and stay in bed; her parents consented. Sleep was short-lived. Her father returned soon and explained why he'd come home unexpectedly. Ted Schoeppey had arrived at the church to learn of the tragedy and the need for search parties. He didn't know that his daughter and other youngsters had been frolicking in the park several hours before. He piled into the car with the Boyd brothers—James and George—and James's two sons Jim, Jr., and Jack. All but

George were neighbors of the Browns in Sussex Downs. Jack Boyd sat beside Betty Jo in class. Young Jim Boyd, Jr., had been Charlsie's date the night before; he was returning to the scene in a decidedly more somber mood. The older Boyds chose the Pleasant Grove community to search because they'd grown up there, had played and hunted in the woods as boys, knew every foot of it. They drove the car off Summerhill Road onto a dirt road. They unloaded and fanned out.

George Boyd was the first to see a body behind the trees in rough terrain in a wooded stretch a few yards off the lane.

"Oh, my God, oh, my God," he yelled repeatedly, "there she is!"

He was close enough for the others to hear him. They came running. It was, indeed, a girl's body, fully clothed, her full-length coat buttoned, lying on her back with her right hand in the overcoat pocket. She was wearing a Middie blouse, as it was called, and a plaid skirt, with patent leather shoes. She lay in apparent peace, as if she'd gone to sleep. Amid pine trees and saplings sprouting green signs of spring alongside the dead leaves of winter, the body was covered by noonday shadow while sunlight streamed down several feet away. It was Betty Jo Booker.

Ted Schoeppey and George Boyd stood guard at the tragic scene while the others drove off to relay word to officers at a barricade on Summerhill Road. The road had been closed and manned by lawmen to ward off the curious.

Sheriff Presley was soon upon the scene, setting about to protect the crime scene from any milling curiosity seekers as had contaminated the Griffin-Moore case. The body was approximately a mile from the location of Martin's body and twice that from the coupe they had ridden in the night before.

Betty Jo had been shot twice, once in the heart and once in the head, entering the left cheek near the nose. The angle of the bullets, on cursory examination, suggested the gunman had been right-handed and had faced her as he killed her. It wasn't much of a clue.

The sheriff believed Martin had been killed first, though he acknowledged that it was impossible, at that point, to tell the exact time of the shootings.

From the first discovery of the bodies, the sheriff cited the compelling outward similarities to the Griffin-Moore case. Other evidence would soon back up that assumption. He emphasized, to news reporters and other investigators, that the bodies had not been abused, beyond the bullet wounds. Unlike the Griffin-Moore case, however, no attempt seemed to have been made to conceal the bodies of Paul and Betty Jo. Although the bodies of the first couple had not been hidden, they had been left inside the car where they might be mistaken for weary travelers sleeping, posed inside the parked car in order to avoid or delay their discovery. The new bodies had been left recklessly where they had been killed, Paul's in full view of anyone driving along the road, Betty Jo's in the woods where she had been taken; no effort had been made to hide or bury the bodies. The killer had heartlessly taken their lives as if they had been hunted animals. It was a chilling discovery.

The finding of Paul's body swept through the town within hours. Discovery of Betty Jo's body accelerated the spread of both news and rumors. Almost immediately, as residents remembered the earlier double murder, a state of horror and panic began building. Another young couple had been slain in a lovers' lane, forming a pattern in people's minds that had never existed before, though the Hollis-Larey beatings still hadn't been connected to the pattern. Four deaths in three weeks—exactly three weeks apart, a late-Saturday-night crime—shouted out that something previously unheard of had shattered the pattern of life—and death—in Texarkana.

The Griffin-Moore case hadn't really alerted the public to its personal implications. Now with a second similar one, most residents suspected that the same hand had killed all four. Previous headline murders had been single ones or perhaps a rampage by one criminal on one occasion, then ended. As bad as the Griffin-Moore case was, it had seemed to be an act unlikely to reoccur. The Martin-Booker murders suddenly presented a different face. There was no way to conclude that this was just another murder in a violence-prone region. The known facts, even before they had been collected and ascertained, put the three-week spree in a separate, frightening category of its own.

Added to this, Richard Griffin and Polly Ann Moore, though they had both lived in Texarkana, were not widely known because they had moved there from Cass County. Nor were they as young as Paul Martin and Betty Jo Booker, who had gone to school in the city and had a broad range of friends locally.

That bright and sunny Palm Sunday morning, as young Jimmy Morriss arrived at First Methodist Church, Texas, teenager Ross Perot, who decades later would make his name internationally known, came up to him. Perot told him there'd been a murder of a boy at Spring Lake Park. Betty Jo Booker may also have been a victim. Her escort had been found dead. Officers were looking for her or her body. Perot didn't yet know that Morriss was to have picked up Betty Jo the night before, had her plans not changed.

Deep shock was the only way to describe Morriss's reaction. He vaguely remembered Martin's name from his brief telephone conversation with Betty Jo the night before.

After church, he drove his parents home and then rushed in the family's 1937 Chevrolet to see the Browns. He saw a line of cars parked on Anthony Drive. In his haste to go inside, he put the gear in reverse, opened the door to get out before he realized he hadn't turned off the engine. The car jerked backward before he could remedy the error. Then he went inside and joined the mournful crowd.

Jerry Atkins and Sonny Atchley experienced the worst day of their young lives. They talked with Sophie Anne White and Betty Ann Roberts, who had both been in the band the night before. They soon realized that the Rhythmaires were the last to have seen Betty Jo alive. They needed to tell officers whatever they might know or could remember from the night before.

The radio and word of mouth spread the news that the Texas Rangers were descending upon Texarkana in force. They would want to talk to anybody who knew the victims. The musicians hadn't heard anything on the radio about Betty Jo's saxophone. That led to a guess that it hadn't been found in Martin's car.

About nine o'clock Sunday night the teenagers went to the sheriff's office. Captain M. T. "Lone Wolf" Gonzaullas had arrived that afternoon from Dallas to lead the Rangers' investigation. The four musicians spent considerable time talking to, and answering questions from, Sheriff Presley and Captain Gonzaullas. Right off, they mentioned the saxophone. It hadn't been found in Martin's automobile, making it an important key to the mystery. They described every detail they could recall about the night before and the dispersal of the musicians. Had anything unusual happened at the dance? Did anybody among the customers do anything unusual or suspicious? Did anyone seem to direct his attention especially toward Miss Booker or the other girls? Had anyone followed her to the car? Had anyone loitered near Paul and Betty Jo outside the building? The answers were consistently *No* or that they didn't know. The gap between the couple's leaving the VFW and discovery of their bodies remained a mystery.

The *Gazette* captured the scene in a front-page photograph of Atkins, Betty Ann Roberts, and Sophie Anne White talking to the officers. Gonzaullas, wearing the traditional ten-gallon hat and cowboy boots adorning his crossed legs, sits in profile, dominating the scene, while Presley, in suit and tie with a felt business-style fedora, sits listening in the background. Every face in the picture is grimly serious.

There was no thought of school the next day. Atkins went to the Beasley Music store, where Betty Jo had bought the instrument, and acquired the make and serial number of the saxophone, which was circulated to music stores and pawnshops over several states. By then Atkins had learned that Ernest Holcomb had gone early Sunday morning to Vivian, Louisiana, with his parents to visit his married sister. They hadn't returned until late Sunday night. The Holcomb family learned of the trouble soon after returning to Texarkana, when a Texas Ranger rapped on their door. Holcomb remembered seeing Betty Jo push her saxophone behind the seat of Martin's coupe. Betty Jo had already told him she wouldn't be leaving with him, because Paul Martin was picking her up. He'd not thought to tell Atkins about her change in plans.

On Monday, Atkins went to see Betty Jo's mother and stepfather. Weeks of anguish lay ahead.

CHAPTER 7

RISING TERROR

Tension hung heavily over the town. Four young people had been murdered, almost at random, over a three-week period. Where might the killer strike next?

The death certificates were less revealing than the newspaper reports: "Murdered—Shot to death." The difference in the new case was that the death scenes were not at a single site. Inez Martin, Paul's mother, signed his certificate; Clark Brown, Betty Jo's stepfather, signed hers.

Although results of a medical examination were not made public, it was assumed by many that Miss Booker had been raped before her death. Outwardly, however, there was no concrete proof, although it could not be completely dismissed. She had been fully clothed, as well as wearing her coat on that cool night, indicating she had not been undressed. Sheriff Presley emphasized that neither body had been abused. Considering the almost haphazard manner in which the two bodies had been left, apparently just as they had fallen, it seemed unlikely that the killer would have raped the girl, then had her put her clothes back on before shooting her.

However, one detail in the state's file at Austin, never made public, noted that her vagina displayed bruising. No mention was made of semen or rape, and the bruise could have been caused by a handgrip, or an object such as a pistol barrel, as was done with the female beating victim, or other means. No one but the two earlier victims, however, had connected the beating incident to the murders. There was another note in the same file, however, that indicated she had had her coat off—outside—at some point: a leaf was found between her coat and her blouse.

On the other hand, and more telling, FBI lab results a week later, on April 20, revealed that a swab test of the girl's vaginal passage was positive for male seminal secretion. No foreign hairs were present among her pubic hairs, though they did contain semen. A saline solution wash of the boy's penis ruled out the possibility of intercourse between the young couple, thus leading to the conclusion that her killer had raped her. The evidence was as precise as the science could make it at the time and definite enough to assign blame to an unknown man. In the absence of today's DNA studies, results were unable to tie the event to a specific man.

One phrase alluded to the previous double murders: "Not definitely known if victim Moore had been raped." No data had been presented that she had been raped, which meshed with evidence cited earlier that she had not been "criminally assaulted," as a physician had stated, and that she was wearing a sanitary pad, which may have saved her from that crime if the killer had had rape in mind.

In the same April 20 dispatch, the FBI confirmed that the same firearm—a .32 automatic—had killed all four victims. But, also, three latent fingerprints could not be explained. One found on the steering wheel, while not necessarily that of the killer, was not the owner's print or that of either victim.

No publicity was being released about the bullets and cartridges or the unexplained latent prints—nor that the girl had been raped.

The report signed off with the most disturbing part: *No definite suspect known.*

Despite the lab evidence, a reflective analysis would tend to conclude that the killer was not a conventional rapist who more likely would have sought a lone vulnerable female, although attacks, followed by rape, on couples were not rare. He had, however, eliminated the male first in both cases, which left a lone vulnerable female in his grasp. Betty Jo Booker's killer also had taken care that her body was normally clothed and left in a condition unlike that of many rape-murder victims. The body was not hidden, beyond being left in the woods, and was not desecrated or mutilated. The single bruise appeared to be incidental. In addition, unlike the first double murders, the killer had faced Betty Jo Booker when he shot her, rather than in the back of the head. Although the results were the same in all four deaths, the Spring Lake Park killer had modified his tactics in these small, but possibly important, ways. Why? What was going on?

By Sunday night, six Texas Rangers were on the scene, all under the direction of a seventh, Captain M. T. Gonzaullas. The Department of Public Safety dispatched an additional contingent of four technical experts, along with a technical laboratory, from Austin.

The city grew tense. Hundreds of cars jammed the highway and roads near the park. Rumors snowballed, some wild and without any basis in fact. The girl's body had been abused in unimaginable ways, according to one. The city embraced panic as never before.

Immediately, officers began rounding up anyone who might have been involved, whether transients walking the streets or the objects of tips. Telephone calls poured in. Officers within a hundred-mile radius followed up on all reports, whoever the suspect, whether male or female, white or black, of any age, wherever they might be found. Alibis were checked. Officers toiled through the night.

Residents in the area of the shootings were systematically questioned. Tom Moores, the farmer living near where Betty Jo's body was found, told officers what he had heard at five-thirty that morning. The sound seemed to come from the direction of Morris Lane, he said. This would tend to tie Betty Jo's death to that time. However, Mrs. L. L. Swint, who lived only about two hundred yards from where the body was found, had heard nothing. She hadn't known anything had happened until the hearse passed to collect the body.

Months later, in November, a former resident who'd moved to Broken Bow, Oklahoma, forty-five-year-old Ernest Browning, told of seeing an old-model automobile coming out of the lane around six in the morning. He'd lived at the intersection of a side road and Summerhill Road. He'd heard shots, followed by a car starting. He saw an old-model car drive to Summerhill Road for about a hundred yards, then turn south toward Newtown, a black section of Texarkana. He'd wondered what was going on. It was not quite light enough to tease out the license-plate numbers. He wasn't sure he could identify the driver. The report seemed to tie in with the time and the place. He was described as "the only living witness found to date." Browning saw the car's driver only momentarily early that morning as the man drove out of the lane and passed Browning's residence. The killer had come very close to being identified or his license tag noted, yet had managed to escape again.

When the news traveled to the 3100 block of Anthony Drive, Betty Jo's mother and stepfather were hardly the only ones shocked. The neighbors knew each other and felt closely linked. Floyd Edwards, a teacher at Texas High, and his wife lived in the same block. Directly across the street from the Browns' home, a special agent of the FBI, lived—Horace S. "Buzz" Hallett. Hallett and his partner Dewey Presley (no relation to Sheriff Presley) had already been deep in the investigation of the Griffin-Moore case. Now Hallett had an added, deeply personal motivation for finding the culprit and seeking justice for the little teenager who lived across the street.

On the following morning, a bold eight-column headline in the *Texarkana Gazette* heralded the tragedy.

'TEEN-AGE COUPLE SHOT TO DEATH

The two-column deck head identified the victims in three lines, followed by an assessment of the emotional state of the community:

BETTY JO BOOKER, PAUL MARTIN KILLED IN DOUBLE SLAYING
TENSION GRIPS CITY AS INVESTIGATION LAUNCHED TO SOLVE
SECOND TWIN MURDERS

Large photographs of the teenaged victims accompanied the account. The one of Martin taken four years before, when he was twelve, depicted him boyishly as much younger than his sixteen, almost seventeen, years. In the photo, he is wearing a suit and tie. Characteristically, he is smiling. Betty Jo, in a picture not quite typical of her face and appearing older than her fifteen years, is also smiling. It was a photo she had given her friends in the Delta Beta Sigma sorority. Within a short time, she was to have had her portrait done by local master photographer Nathan Guier when he returned from a conference in New York.

Unlike the funerals of Polly Moore and Richard Griffin, which had been held in neighboring Cass County, the new funerals became citywide events. Hundreds attended—relatives, friends, and others, including the curious and the morbid.

The funerals were held at different times on Tuesday at the Beech Street Baptist Church on the Arkansas side, a church both victims had attended. Martin's services were in the morning, at ten; Betty Jo's, at two in the afternoon. Pelting rain fell throughout the morning service; Martin's mother, heavily veiled, leaned on the arms of her surviving sons as she descended the steps of the church. Martin was buried alongside his father Ruben S. Martin, Sr. and the space that eventually would hold his mother, in Hillcrest Cemetery, just west of the city on the Texas side.

Texas Senior High classes were dismissed at noon for Betty Jo's funeral. The Texas High School choral group sang hymns. Berta Sue Phillips, who had been a classmate of the dead girl, sang a solo. As a long line of teenagers filed by the open casket, it was more than Bessie Brown could stand. She broke down, sobbing. Sightseers trickled in. Watching the mourners file by the casket, Sue Phillips saw a middle-aged woman in a rough homemade dress, who she couldn't believe was related to or knew the dead girl. The woman held a child of three or four by the hand. As they reached the casket, the woman picked up the small child and held her up, for a long moment, so that she could view the corpse, then filed on past. Sue Phillips was horrified. The scene left an indelible, distinctly unpleasant, impression. Betty Jo was buried in Woodlawn Cemetery, on State Line in Arkansas, alongside her father and brother, Billy Boy. She was almost Billy Boy's age at death. The three graves bore mute testimony to the multiple tragedies that had visited the family. Her pallbearers included members of the Rhythmaires band—Atkins, Atchley, and Haskell Walker—as well as Jimmy Morriss and others.

There would be no closure for Betty Jo's grieving mother. Bessie, trying to grasp the tragedy, told a reporter, "I can't understand this." She was convinced her daughter was "an innocent victim of a madman." No one could refute that. She had lost her entire early family.

What would newsmen call the unknown murderer? Editor J. Q. Mahaffey and his staff at the *Gazette* recognized the need for a short term by which to refer to the case. Rather than describe it as "the Texarkana murders," which would not necessarily distinguish it from numerous other cases and would sully any chamber of commerce promotion, City Editor Calvin Sutton saw a solution. "We've got to have a handle for the killer," he told Mahaffey. "How about calling him the Phantom? He has been elusive, like a phantom." Mahaffey couldn't think of a better label, and agreed. "Why not?" he said. "If the sonofabitch continues to elude capture, he certainly can be called a phantom."

Though derivative, it was an effective summing-up, and a term already in popular use locally. The killer appeared, seemingly out of nowhere, left only death, and faded into the darkness, like an apparition. The daily newspaper contained several models. "The Phantom," a purple-garbed avenger, chased and punished evildoers in the comic section, acting, however, in an opposite manner than did this local Phantom. There were the movie, *The Phantom of the Opera*, showing locally, and The Masked Phantom, who had wrestled at the Armory.

From that point on, Phantom it was, a one-word label to serve as a symbol for a murderous plague, and a thuggish killer operating under cover of darkness. Neither Mahaffey nor Sutton realized the significant part this would play in the lasting drama, as the naming of the criminal, and the case, only added to the tension, as well as the mystery.

On Tuesday the local newspaper used the brand for the first time. The afternoon *Daily News*'s front page featured a photograph of Paul Martin's casket being borne down the steps of the church. A five-column headline labeled the case.

PHANTOM KILLER ELUDES OFFICERS
AS INVESTIGATION OF SLAYINGS PRESSED

The morning *Gazette* further fixed the name in the region's mind.

PHANTOM SLAYER STILL AT LARGE AS PROBE CONTINUES

By injecting the manufactured name, Phantom, the newspaper created a melodramatic twist that suggested a battle of wits between lawmen and villain that might have issued from a Charlie Chan or Sherlock Holmes film.

"Texarkana's Phantom Killer continued to match wits with some of the best investigative brains in Texas Tuesday as the investigation of the brutal murder of Paul Martin, 17, [*sic*] and Betty Jo Booker, 15, trudged along methodically and laboriously Tuesday with no break in the case anticipated immediately.

"Texas Ranger Captain M. T. Gonzaullas said that it was one of the most puzzling cases he had encountered in his 20 years of criminal investigation."

It was the birth of an image that would become larger than its reality and invade every person's mind with fear throughout the town. The mystique of the Phantom would only grow.

Within days, what most people and officers had guessed was confirmed: that the two double murders were linked. The *modus operandi* was similar. A ballistics expert at the Texas DPS lab in Austin reported that the murder weapon for Paul and Betty Jo was also a .32 caliber Colt automatic pistol—or foreign make—with six lands and grooves, with a left-hand twist. The Colt was the only American-made pistol that fit the description. This was identical to the bullets that snuffed out the lives of Richard Griffin and Polly Ann Moore. It was clear that the expert thought an American Colt was the gun to seek. A Colt was infinitely more common; any such foreign-made caliber would have been quite rare.

Captain Gonzaullas was not alone in being baffled. The local *Daily News* called it "the most puzzling crime ever committed in Bowie County." That covered a multitude of cases stretching back to the town's boisterous nineteenth-century founding, if not to de Soto's brief visit in 1541.

CHAPTER 8

A LEGENDARY RANGER

f, in 1946, Texas Ranger Captain Manuel Trazazas "Lone Wolf" Gonzaullas had pranced into Texarkana on a white Arabian steed decked out in silver buckles and ensconced in a saddle capable of drawing the envy of Hollywood, along with his usual accouterments of a pearl-handled, gold-and-silver-plated .45 caliber pistol strapped on each hip and, of course, crowned by the obligatory ten-gallon white Stetson, he wouldn't have created any more of a stir than he actually did. By then he was the stuff of movie lore, a legend in his own time. Most of it was true.

The Martin-Booker murders brought him and additional Rangers to Texarkana for an indefinite stay. As the Ranger in charge, he also came to be an official spokesman, along with Sheriff Bill Presley, for the investigation. Gonzaullas soon was regularly holding informal press conferences at the downtown Grim Hotel. He was put up at the Grim for the duration of the investigation, conveniently across from the offices of the *Texarkana Gazette* and *Daily News*. The Gazette Building served as a nerve center for media. Most mornings Gonzaullas held forth "in full bloom," as an

Arkansas officer described it, entertaining newspaper staffers and anyone else who happened to drop by.

He was colorful, in all the term implied, and he was not shy. By 1946 he'd had a variety of experiences that young lawmen today wouldn't have the opportunity to boast about. He worked oil boomtowns, bootleg cases, and mob violence. A devout Presbyterian and regular Bible reader who'd eschewed alcohol his whole life, he relished his cigars and—something he shared with his wife—*legal* gambling. His concept of justice was keyed to the Old Testament's eye-for-an-eye, tooth-for-a-tooth approach in Exodus. A biographer likened him, as far as his law enforcement went, to "a thundering prophet of old who brought down the wrath of God on wrongdoers."

Explaining his nickname, he once told a reporter, "I guess I got that nickname because I went into a lot of fights by myself—and I came out by myself, too." Another quoted him as saying, "I've been in many a fight. Knives, guns, and fists. I won all with His hand on my shoulder."

During his career he was reputed to have killed as many as seventy-five men in the line of duty, some in fierce gunfights in which he beat the odds of survival. He was tight-lipped about it, refusing to cite a number. "That's a gross exaggeration," he commented of the high figure, without correcting it. A biographer eventually reduced the toll to one-third as many, only twenty-five.

He was not a big man, physically, hardly the model for the six-foot-plus Ranger of movie fame, but of average height. He was broad-shouldered, carrying about 170 pounds, with dark hair and with piercing grey-green eyes. He was born in Cadiz, Spain, on July 4, 1891, to naturalized American citizens visiting the country. His father was born in Spain and his mother was born in Canada of German parents. Gonzaullas was the first man of Spanish descent to rise to captain in the Texas Rangers. He grew up in El Paso, across the Rio Grande from Mexico in the far south-western corner of Texas. His intense interest in law enforcement dated at least from the time he was fifteen and saw his only two brothers murdered and his parents wounded in a border raid by outlaws. That was around 1906. He found a role model in Captain John B. Hughes, a tall, rugged Ranger frequently seen on horseback in the streets of El Paso and known as the Border Boss. Young Gonzaullas was determined to follow in his hero's footsteps and, it could be argued, did exactly that.

After a stint in federal service, he rejoined the Texas Rangers in 1927 as a sergeant in Company B and remained until he retired in 1951. Lewis Rigler, one of his men, called him a "very, very intelligent man" who "didn't have much education. Carried a dictionary with him all the time. Looked up words and learned a lot." Rigler praised his work ethic. "He was the last one to go to bed and the last one to eat. Absolutely."

When Gonzaullas arrived in Texarkana, his headline power was assured. He was made to order for reporters, a flamboyant star from Hollywood sent by God (and the governor of Texas). He consistently provided good copy in a case that hardly needed embellishing. He relished his role and rarely disappointed. Women reporters were especially drawn to him, and he to them.

"Lone Wolf Gonzaullas was the best-looking man I ever saw in my life," said editor J. Q. Mahaffey. "He sent my girl reporters back to the office with stars in their eyes. He had them talking to themselves."

He had a sense of the theatrical, knew how to dress, how to pose. Reporters flocked to him like geese in migration, expecting, and usually getting, a colorful and newsworthy quote, whether they printed it or not.

Mahaffey designated sports editor Louis "Swampy" Graves, a recently returned Air Corps veteran of the Asian theater of the war, as the paper's greeter to the visiting press. Graves was on hand when Gonzaullas checked in to the Bowie County sheriff's office for what was to be an extended stay.

"He was wearing sharply creased whipcord trousers with a short jacket, boots with a high sheen, carrying pistols with ivory handles, all crowned with a Stetson," Graves said. "He was a fine-looking fellow with the skin texture of the Spanish, dark hair and eyes, standing about five-ten and weighing maybe 180. Nothing in his appearance to indicate a killer, even on the side of the law. He was personable. It was hard to believe the Ranger had killed anybody, much less the high number cited."

Lone Wolf's imperfections were rarely reported, but fondly remembered, even treasured. Graves enjoyed one such moment.

"Lone Wolf dropped a leather box on a constable's desk and when asked what it contained, he said:

"'A new fangled fingerprint set.'

"'How do you operate it?'

"'Danged if I know!'"

That week, the Texas Department of Public Safety distributed an all-points bulletin. If it produced the hoped-for response, it could lead to an early break in the case by tracing a trail leading to the killer, with evidence no jury could ignore.

SPECIAL NOTICE—WANTED FOR MURDER

WANTED person or persons unknown, for the murder of Betty Jo Booker and Paul Martin, on or about April 13, 1946, in Bowie County, Texas. Subject or subjects may have in their possession or may try to dispose of a gold-plated Bundy E-flat Alto saxophone, serial #52535, which was missing from the car in which the victims were last seen, when it was found abandoned about 1.55 miles from the location of the boy's body, and about 3 miles from the location of the girl's body. This saxophone had just been rebuilt, replated, and repadded, and was in an almost new black imitation case with blue plush lining.

It is requested that a check be made of music stores and pawnshops. Any information as to the location of the saxophone or description and whereabouts of the person connected with it should be forwarded immediately to the Sheriff, Bowie County, Texarkana, Texas, and the Texas Department of Public Safety, Austin, Texas. (Refer our file O-261/997).

In the absence of more tangible clues, officers pinned hopes on finding the missing instrument, which eventually might be traced to the killer.

A twenty-four-hour-a-day investigation became the norm. Every imaginable suspect, or anyone who might have had even the remotest connection to the victims or the case, was taken in for grilling. City police rounded up suspects and herded them into the sheriff's office. Youngsters who had known the victims were questioned. All day and into the night, individuals of all ages and statuses trod the creaking stairs to the second floor on Main Street. Any man with an arrest record or a shady reputation of any degree was hauled in and subjected to scrutiny of his whereabouts on the tragic Saturday night. A dragnet, broad and fine, brought in men and women, black and white, within a radius of 100 miles, some from even farther. No one was exempt from being detained.

A cab driver found himself a major suspect after his taxi was reported in the Spring Lake Park area early that Sunday morning. But his version soon checked out, his alibi firm. The dispatch records, among other evidence, proved he could not have been near the murder scene at the crucial time. He was one of many who were eliminated only after definitely establishing their innocence.

As the weary days beat on, Gonzaullas confided to editor Mahaffey, "Texarkana has more human driftwood than any other town I've ever been in, other than San Antonio or El Paso. You have more petty thieves, more prostitutes, more pimps, more of an underworld than many big cities." It was an eye-opener as a major probe dug deep into the social fabric to reveal marginal denizens of whom most of the town's upwardly mobile people, even prosecutors, were unaware.

Newspaper staffers, local and out-of-town, camped near the door to the interrogation room. Reporters concluded that the lawmen faced a brick wall, despite their voiced hints of optimism. Two former war correspondents arrived in the first wave of out-of-town newspapermen. Wick Fowler represented the *Dallas Morning News*; Charles Boatner, the *Fort Worth Star-Telegram*. They were harbingers of the flood of journalists coming from important papers in St. Louis, Kansas City, Denver, and other distant points.

Fowler, a man of keen wit as well as a hard-nosed reporter, attended a Gonzaullas press conference in the Grim Hotel.

"Wolf," asked Fowler, "what kind of a man is this Phantom murderer?"

"I don't know, Wick, but he's a damned sight smarter than I am!" said Gonzaullas.

"Now, Wolf," said Fowler, "you don't think I came all the way over from Dallas to find that out!"

It was one of a series of anecdotes told at Gonzaullas's expense.

A large delegation of investigative experts soon assembled in Texarkana, including men who had cracked some of the most difficult cases in Texas. Officers reserved little time for sleep. Along with state-of-the-art technical equipment—newly developed car radio equipment and fingerprinting devices—Ranger Joe N. Thompson piloted an airplane to provide faster transportation in tracking down a lead or suspect, wherever that might be.

The sheriff's office was so packed with Rangers and highway patrolmen that at times the atmosphere edged toward pandemonium. There was not even room for all of them to sit down at the same time.

Most of the investigators at one time or another made their way to Boyd's Drugs at Main and West Broad, a half block from the sheriff's office. Boyd's was a popular hangout. That was how Jim Wilson, one of the owners, came to meet Gonzaullas. One day the Ranger sought a private chat.

"Mr. Wilson, we are in dire need of a private place in which we Rangers, alone to ourselves, can meet, out of public view. We need room so we can freely discuss the case and any matters we might bring up. If I'm not mistaken, you have a lot of space in your back storeroom that might serve for this purpose. Would it be possible to use it, so that no one would be aware of our presence? There's a door to the store from the alley where we could enter relatively unobserved."

What they had in mind, Wilson surmised, was an idea to plan operations of their own without the knowledge of other law enforcement officers.

Wilson conveyed Gonzaullas's request to his partners, who readily agreed. They wanted to help however they could, and thought perhaps that enabling this "elite squad" to work in privacy would finally be the key to teasing out the killer's identity.

The heavy large metal back door, to which Gonzaullas now had the keys, opened for freight deliveries from the alley. The Rangers' ingress and egress occurred after the drugstore was officially closed. At those hours virtually nobody was on the streets. The Rangers could slip unobtrusively into the alley without notice. By meeting late at night they would avoid inquisitive reporters.

One of the Rangers' plans, concocted at the backroom meetings, was to set traps for the killer. A Ranger, for instance, would drive into the countryside to a lonely road where lovers might go. The Ranger would have with him a dressed-up female mannequin, luring the Phantom into believing he had another easy pair of victims. The Rangers didn't risk borrowing mannequins from a local store. They had them shipped in, to keep the plan a secret.

With no substantial clues to guide them beyond the pattern of the murders' timing with three-week intervals, other lawmen took a similar approach. A tactic soon developed on both sides of town to simulate parked couples in remote parking sites, disguising lawmen as couples, with one as a woman, hoping to lure the villain into a trap—and a well-deserved fate.

Night after night, lawmen strategically set their traps. Night after night, they failed to net their man. Everyone was tense. Lawmen were virtually everywhere, at all times. The heat was on. The killer was lying low in hiding, wary of attacking again, or had left town. He was no longer assured of killing at random and getting away with it. Immediately after the Spring Lake Park shootings, young lovers were hard to find outdoors at night.

None of the traps worked. Mostly tedium resulted among the trappers, who waited and waited for a phantom that never materialized.

Gonzaullas, who had served in locales where nothing less than martial law had restored order, realized that the Texarkana situation was getting out of hand. The people needed reassurances. He put it forth with dramatic emphasis.

The Rangers, he promised, would not leave Texarkana "until officers apprehend the murderer or murderers of Betty Jo Booker, Paul Martin, Polly Ann Moore, and Richard Griffin."

Those he hoped to impress took his statement to heart. Few ever forgot.

CHAPTER 9

FEAR STALKS BY NIGHT

T he *Texarkana Gazette* ran a daily box recording the traffic toll,
always on the rise. By April 18, the death toll for the year from
traffic accidents had reached fifteen, with forty-six injured. But it
was the malicious, not accidental, deaths in Texarkana that continued
to haunt the community.

While officers doggedly plodded on, frustrated and exhausted, public
tensions peaked. Finally recognizing the Griffin-Moore murders as a
horrifying pattern, residents focused on the three-week interval between
the crimes. When would the killer strike next? In three weeks—again?
And where? Who would be his new victims? Fears generated outrage and
anger. Concerns for personal and family safety rapidly set the emotional
tone of the region. Chaos lurked in the wings.

Fear of the night rose in a way none had experienced before. Few, if
any, window shades remained up. Doors in a formerly trusting community
were locked and bolted. Overnight those who had never owned weapons
bought them or improvised by keeping knives or clubs near at hand.

"People armed themselves and were quick to shoot," recalled Max Tackett, at the time an Arkansas state trooper. "The biggest danger for a policeman was the chance of getting shot by good citizens. It was just risking death to go out then with civilian clothes on."

A visiting hardware salesman told Thomas Pirkey that his Dallas-based company's warehouse had been depleted of handguns and rifles within three days of the Spring Lake Park murders, all going to Texarkana where they immediately sold out.

Nothing was as terrifying as the dark threat of the unknown.

Within hours of the discovery of the bodies on Palm Sunday, the populace approached a rare state of tension. An outcry arose for a curfew and other policies to keep more young people from falling victim. The reward fund skyrocketed overnight, soon reaching $6,425, which is around $76,600 today. Banks, businesses, individuals, veterans and service organizations, and nightclubs contributed as avidly as those striving to meet a United Fund drive goal. Even a lumber company in El Dorado, Arkansas, eighty miles away, kicked in $100.

Safety of young people became paramount in the minds of men and women over the city, especially among those who had children.

With that in mind, John Quincy "J. Q." or "Jake" Mahaffey, the editor of the *Gazette* and by then known among his fellows in national organizations like the American Society of Newspaper Editors and Associated Press Managing Editors, sat down before his old upright L. C. Smith typewriter. That April night he began what would become a steady stream of editorials about the case. This one urged private parental curfews for youngsters. He pointed out the "bad name" the crimes were giving the city nationally. Then he concluded on his opening theme.

"A caution is indicated, 'Keep away from remote dark areas. That is where death awaits you.'"

Within days the entire town appeared to be in consensus about a curfew. Events moved swiftly. The Texarkana Teen-Canteen changed its hours and provided adult escorts to each youth's car. The Paramount Theater cancelled its midnight movie. The Texarkana Ministerial Alliance unanimously adopted a resolution to petition both city councils to close "all public places of amusements on midnight Saturdays." A broad group of Christian leaders, ranging from Methodist to Baptist to Catholic, signed a resolution citing an urgent need to curb juvenile delinquency and what they considered its tragic aftermaths.

A poll reflected a variety of views in the adult community, some of them extremely strong. Roy D. Hopkins, the owner of a feed-and-seed store and father of three children, offered a forceful remedy: "Burn all night clubs, and eliminate every one, as to me there is no such thing as a 'nice' one and eliminate the midnight picture shows that are now in existence. Both are immoral and a menace to our growing children. I believe in a nine o'clock curfew."

It was a scary time for youngsters, especially for those learning how to drive. After the Martin-Booker murders, teenagers felt as if they were being targeted by the Phantom, even more at risk than adults, and the further paranoia brought down upon them by their parents and other concerned—if sometimes agenda-pushing—adults did nothing to assuage the feelings of fear and trepidation

Tom Albritton, Paul Martin's friend, remembered how the city's youths responded to the threat. "If we went anywhere at night, we took guns with us and went in groups, usually to each other's homes. Sometimes we'd go to a movie, but always as a group. There was no parking in cars anymore."

Any suspect could expect the full, undivided attention of his captors until he was definitely eliminated. A man we will call "Sammy" was one who repeatedly proclaimed his innocence while in the shadow of the electric chair. His problem was physical and circumstantial evidence that placed him near where Betty Jo Booker's body had been found. The most damning was Plaster of Paris casts of car tracks near Spring Lake Park that matched Sammy's tires.

Sammy was a black man about thirty-five years of age with a likeable personality and a clean record. He denied knowing of the murders until everyone else knew of them, didn't own a .32 automatic, but the tire tracks seemed to condemn him.

He was willing—eager—to take a polygraph, or "lie detector," test. It showed he wasn't telling the truth. He took it again. He flunked it again, and then failed it a third time. He appeared headed for Texas's Death Row.

Sheriff Presley pondered the matter. Sammy had a fine reputation, was never known to be violent, but when he claimed he hadn't been where the tire tracks proved his car had been on that tragic night, the polygraph disagreed—three times.

Presley didn't believe in charging a man with a capital crime on the basis of circumstantial evidence—alone, even if a failed polygraph test seemed to back it up. He knew Travis Elliott, a Texarkana psychologist with skills as a hypnotist. Why not have Elliott hypnotize Sammy, even if the session couldn't be used in court? It would be kept in strict secrecy but perhaps could offer clarity. Sammy agreed. Elliott agreed.

Elliott explained the process to the sheriff and FBI agent Dewey Presley. A subject in a deep hypnotic trance, he emphasized, cannot tell a lie. The officers were willing to try it.

Elliott privately talked with Sammy, exploring a gamut of topics, putting the suspect at ease and chatting freely as they reached a stage of transference. Then Elliott left Sammy alone in the office and joined the two men outside. As they left for the café downstairs, Elliott told the lawmen, "I can hypnotize him, but you have the wrong man. He has no criminal tendencies." Sammy was well adjusted. He was a normal, stable man with a forthright personality. Not the sort of man who would murder four people randomly, or subject women to a brutal assault.

The sheriff returned with Elliott for the session. Slowly, gradually, the psychologist guided Sammy into a trance. The suspect was counting by threes backward when he went under. Elliott kept him in a state of catalepsy for ten minutes. Then he told Sammy to open his eyes. His first question was the focal one.

"Did you kill Betty Jo Booker?"

"No."

"Do you know who did?"

"No."

Officers knew where Sammy had been at five P.M. of the Saturday of the murder weekend. Elliott hooked into that time and led the suspect forward. Sammy and a friend had made some honky-tonks, drinking beer and a whiskey called "100 Proof." Late that night Sammy took his buddy home, cutting through Spring Lake Park. On his way back, he stopped by the little road to urinate. Then he drove to the west side of the park and waited. His married paramour lived near. He could see the house. The light went out, meaning the husband had left for work. Shortly afterward, Sammy went to the house, talked to the woman. His intentions didn't work out. He went home and to bed. His account was straightforward, without hedging or hesitation.

The hypnotist invited the sheriff to pose questions, which Sammy answered readily.

Gradually Elliott woke up Sammy and assured him, "You'll feel all right and your troubles will be gone."

Indeed, they were. The sheriff and deputies checked the story, corroborated every detail. Sammy had been caught in a lie he didn't believe himself, in a clumsy attempt to conceal a touchy personal affair. Hypnosis had cleared him.

Rumors snowballed, some ensuring an atmosphere of horror. Within days one spread that the female victims' bodies had been viciously mutilated. The girls' breasts, so it went, were chewed up horribly. Another added gnawed fingers to the desecrations. The reports aroused images of a bestial, sex-mad pervert, raising public anxiety to a fever pitch. The rumor mill operated nonstop, day and night.

Rumors continued to swirl so forcibly that Ranger Gonzaullas just as forcibly denied them, insisting that false reports were hindering officers' work. He chided those enabling the rumors.

One account had the killer arrested, another that he had identified himself and confessed, easily refuted. Another: the Phantom had struck again, a third double murder, then a fourth such crime—doubling the death toll.

"Help" tips poured in. Two women volunteered information collected in dreams. Another woman called that a nineteen-year-old woman living in her house had disappeared. All law agencies searched through the night. In the morning she arrived back home, safe and unharmed. The Phantom had missed her, one he apparently hadn't known of.

Nothing slowed the wild rumors, particularly those that a sex fiend was at large, that the girls' bodies had been mutilated. It wasn't true. "There was not any evidence of a warped sexual mind on either of the bodies," said officer Max Tackett. "But because of the wild rumors it seemed to be necessary to sift through any persons who might have had these features—and there were lots of them!"

The rumors only added to lawmen's workload.

Even daylight wasn't a cure for the nerves. Levia Brower, in her fifties, kept a loaded .25-20 rifle handy, prepared for the unexpected. She was by herself in her rural home when a car drove up. She didn't recognize it or know who the driver was. Taking no chances, she raised the rifle to her shoulder and aimed a warning shot near the passenger. The motorist hurriedly motored off. Later Mrs. Brower realized her target had been a neighbor woman who hadn't identified herself quickly enough.

In the middle of the week following the latest murders, Rose Juliette Victoria Mitts, a petite French war bride, stepped off the train at Union Station at State Line and Front Street. Her husband, Roy E. Mitts, joyously greeted her. She hailed from Roussillon, France, and knew no English. Perhaps it was just as well, considering the latest brutal news on everyone's lips. Her husband, fluent in French, translated for her, enabling him to filter the harsh realities. The twenty-four-year-old ex-soldier took his four-foot-eleven wife around town, showing her State Line Avenue and the unique federal courthouse and post office in both states.

Two weeks after the murders, April 27, a Saturday, a rumor swept over the city that a man had been found dead at Twenty-Ninth and Wood on the Texas side. Had the Phantom struck early? Phones busily circulated the account. Police sped to the scene. They found a fifteen-year-old boy in the middle of the street, drunk and passed out, but very much alive. They took him to the city jail and called his father, who hurried down to take him home to sleep it off.

That Saturday night, the first shooting occurred. It was not a killing, nor in the secluded countryside, but in a well-lighted café with witnesses. A man wearing an Army uniform entered a West Seventh Street café and shoved his way into the establishment's dance hall without paying a cover charge. The cashier stopped him. A scuffle ensued. Cleo Wells, thirty-two, a recently discharged member of the Women's Army Corps, joined the cashier in an effort to block the intruder. The man pulled a pistol and fired at Miss Wells. The bullet struck her in the left thigh. The gunman fled. An ambulance soon arrived and took the woman to Michael Meagher Hospital. She was not seriously injured.

One early-Saturday event may have contributed to the rumors that spread so explosively. At four-thirty that morning, a man unloading ice at the Texas-side McCartney Hotel, close to Union Station downtown, found the body of a woman. Mrs. Sue Murray, age sixty-seven, had died from an apparent leap from a fire escape at the hotel. As soon as her death was reported, Chief Runnels, Gonzaullas, and Deputy Sheriff Zeke Henslee rushed to the scene. Their investigation revealed that she was in town, apparently despondent, because her husband, a traffic manager for the Cotton Belt rail line, was being treated for a stroke.

Even this tragic event was soon recycled into a rumor that she had jumped out of a hotel window, falling right at Gonzaullas's feet as he started out the hotel's lobby door. It wasn't like that at all—wrong hotel, to begin with—but at the time accuracy continued to be the earliest casualty of the rumor mill.

Editor Mahaffey, hearing of the matter, was shocked. "This is the damnedest town I've ever seen. Just bodies falling everywhere!"

Two days later, a Monday night, four teenagers failed to return home at night. This set off rumors that four more bodies had been found. Parents notified officers. Patrols spread out. It had been raining. They turned up, safe but haggard. Their car had been stuck in mud in a rural area. They'd had to walk nine miles for assistance to get the car pulled out. It was three o'clock Tuesday afternoon before they were back in town and in touch with their families.

"All four are safe and sound," Sheriff Presley told reporters. "But I'll have to admit that they put some gray hairs in my head today."

By April 23, nine days after the second murders, the seven-millionth serviceman had been discharged.

Two weeks after the Martin-Booker murders, Ruth Bryan Gabour, a reporter at the *Texarkana Gazette*, received a call. The man suggested he was "the Phantom" or at least was privy to special information. He didn't say much, didn't make any threats. He predicted another weekend crime, at the three-week mark. (Everyone else expected it too, or at least feared it.) He suggested they meet at a specific location. Her city editor,

Cal Sutton, ruled that out immediately. The caller gave no hint of his identity. He abruptly hung up. Other reporters also received a plethora of strange calls. She and her colleagues had tentatively deemed it a hoax or practical joke, but there was no way to be certain.

A more recent comment by FBI profiler John Douglas probably sums up the unlikelihood that she had heard from the notorious gunman.

"Killers don't call, and callers don't kill."

City editor Calvin Sutton and Mahaffey worked up ideas to hype the story, ever searching for increasingly lurid and attention-grabbing headlines, giving no thought, at that stage, that in the process they might whip up fears past any reasonable limits.

"We wanted to create something to give an impression of the suspect going up the stairs to the headquarters of the Texas Rangers," said Mahaffey. "There were all these Rangers in town, and they drove every night. I mean, they guarded the city at night. We cut out a shadow that looked exactly like a ghost and took a picture of this stairway up to the sheriff's office and superimposed a shadow, to represent the suspect. It was calculated to send people out of their minds."

And well it probably would have, but for Mahaffey's ruling it out at the last minute. After giving it more thought, he realized the impact it would have.

"People began to circulate rumors as to who the Phantom might be. And every eccentric fellow in town was suspect as the Phantom, and everybody circulated rumors which would grow till everybody was suspicious of everybody else, and that's what triggered the hysteria, and the fact that every time one of these would quiet down, another one would break out. And we certainly played it for all it was worth."

And then some.

While the headlines continued to spin, Betty Jo Booker's chemistry instructor at Texas High left her lab book in place as a somber reminder. Each time her classmates entered the lab, they would remember her fate, a silent memorial to her absence.

As residents grew more apprehensive, the three-week interval between killings stood out. The Phantom had struck in the early Sunday mornings of March 24 and April 14, exactly three weeks apart. If the pattern continued, that meant another rampage on the weekend of Saturday, May 4, or Sunday, May 5. A countdown began.

With April winding down, a new hope flared—actually, the only one of any consequence—in far-off Corpus Christi, Texas, 450 miles southwest on the Gulf coast. A thirty-year-old man, whom we'll call "Charlie Jones," had tried to sell a saxophone to a music store on April 20, six days after the Spring Lake Park murders, and the report finally reached Texarkana on Monday, April 29. Betty Jo Booker's missing saxophone had become an integral part of the case, along with the .32 automatic. Jones, witnesses said, had walked into the store and asked the employee if she wanted to buy "an alto Bundy saxophone." He didn't have the saxophone with him but described it to her. She said she would have to talk to the manager. "What do you have to talk to him about it for? You work here, don't you?" he said. She noticed that he had begun behaving extremely nervous. When she tried to call the manager, Jones abruptly turned on his heels and left, disappearing down the street. The manager reported the incident to the police. That wasn't what led to his arrest, however.

Jones was arrested at a waterfront hotel after he bought a .45 caliber revolver at a pawnshop. When bloody clothing turned up during his arrest, he became a definite suspect in the Booker-Martin case.

The police brought in the saleswoman to identify him. Police didn't find a saxophone. But they did find his bag with blood-spattered clothing.

"Okay, you've got some big explaining to do," a policeman told him.

"It's not a big deal," Jones protested. "I got in a fight in this bar and the guy cut me on my forehead."

Captain Gonzaullas dispatched Ranger Joe Thompson in the state's plane to Corpus Christi. It was late Tuesday, April 30. If Thompson turned up sufficient evidence, Presley and other officers expected to head for the coast.

Weather delayed Thompson's arrival in Corpus Christi.

Presley and others in Texarkana put their optimism on hold. The saxophone hadn't been found.

Meanwhile, the third weekend since the latest killing was only days off, a fact foremost in everyone's mind. If the Corpus Christi suspect turned out to be their man, residents could relax instead of dreading the coming weekend.

The arrest failed to yield much more than very guarded optimism. Captain Gonzaullas, echoing what Sheriff Presley had stated earlier, was quick to dampen expectations. The case against the man grew weaker.

"Everything the man tells us is being checked and double checked, and everything he has told us this far has been found to be true," Gonzaullas told reporters. "He has answered all of our questions without hesitancy, and we are making every effort to find out if he is telling the truth or is covering up. We are convinced that thus far the man has told the truth."

The same day, Governor Coke R. Stevenson notified A. C. Stuart, president of the Two States Telephone Company in Texarkana, of his personal interest in the case.

"The governor told me that he was very much interested in the solution of the two crimes and would keep the Texas Rangers on the case indefinitely," Stuart told reporters.

A week or so after the Martin-Booker shootings, Arkansas Trooper Max Tackett was patrolling the Highway 71 route that ran from Texarkana to Ashdown in Little River County.

At the Index Bridge over the Red River, he stopped a young man in an old car by himself. A man alone in a car was more likely to be stopped than a couple or a car with several people in it. Checking license plates was not as easily done then as it is now. He pulled the man over and walked up to the car. In the back seat the man had a .22 rifle. It was in plain sight, but of course it was no simple matter to conceal a rifle in the car itself. Tackett went through his usual routine. Let's see your driver's license. Where are you going? What are you doing with a gun?

The man answered the questions casually and seemingly straightforwardly. The gun was there, in plain view, because he needed to practice target shooting, and he wanted to find a place in the country where he could practice. With the scare going on, he wanted to be ready.

Tackett studied him carefully and decided the answers were convincing.

"Be careful," he said as he dismissed the man. Having a .22 rifle in the car was as common as anything you could imagine. Almost everyone owned a .22 rifle in that place and time. Tackett gave it no further thought.

By Thursday night, May 2, a thorough investigation of the Corpus Christi man's contentions ended in what officers termed "a complete washout." He had been in a fight, readily explaining the bloody clothing; his alibi was thoroughly checked out. Though he had no saxophone, officers never revealed why he had tried to sell one. Gonzaullas was the first to announce the man's innocence.

If geography, politics, competition, and athletics had divided the two cities, the Phantom scare changed all that, at least momentarily. Soon everybody was united by fear.

Two weekends had passed since the Spring Lake Park crimes. Might the killer be compulsive, seeking victims by the calendar? While no one expected to be off guard in between, nearly everyone anxiously cast his and her eyes toward Saturday, May 4, hoping, praying a pattern would not form, fearful that it would.

CHAPTER 10

MURDER STRIKES HOME

Virgil and Katie Starks had grown up together, had known each other all their lives. He was only a few months older than she. In March of 1946 they celebrated their fourteenth wedding anniversary. The next month Virgil marked his thirty-seventh birthday; Katie would celebrate hers in September.

Childless, they were a comfortable farm family in the Homan community of Miller County, Arkansas, about ten miles northeast of Texarkana on U.S. Highway 67. They had lived there about five years. Native Texans, they'd grown up in the Red Springs community west of Texarkana. That was the same community from which Sheriff Bill Presley had come. They first emerged in the census of 1910 as children. Both were born in 1909—Walter Virgil Starks on April 3, and Katherine Ila Strickland, six months later. They went to school together. Their families owned nearby farms in Bowie County, as they later were to do in Miller County.

Virgil's father, Jack Starks, moved his family to Arkansas in the late 1920s. By the time of the 1930 census, Virgil, twenty-one and single, lived with his parents on the farm at Homan. Katie still lived in Bowie County, twenty and single. That changed on March 2, 1932, when Virgil and Katie, each twenty-two years old, married in Miller County. It was the second union of their families; Charlie Starks, Virgil's older brother, and Gertie Strickland, Katie's older sister, had married earlier and also lived in Miller County. (Later, in the early 1940s, the properties their families had sold in Bowie County were taken over by the federal government via eminent domain to build Lone Star and Red River defense plants for the war effort.)

They lived right on U.S. 67, a major highway connecting Texarkana and Little Rock. The same route threaded through Texarkana and stretched westward to Dallas. Although the Starks farm was ten miles out of Texarkana, Katie, an attractive and personable woman, was not isolated. Family members of both Starks and Stricklands lived in the vicinity. They had frequent visits from nieces and nephews. There is a photograph taken that spring with Virgil and Katie kneeling by the side of their house, smiling into the camera. A small niece is standing, with the assistance of Katie, in front. Virgil kept busy on the large farm—500 acres, in cultivation and for grazing of livestock—and in his welding shop; Katie, in the home and working in the yard. She also actively maintained a broad range of social ties; she had, for example, attended the fashionable bridal shower for Jacqueline Hickerson at the Grim Hotel earlier in the year. They had attended the First Methodist Church, Arkansas, in Texarkana for years and had many friends there, having transferred their membership from the church in Texas. Virgil had a solid reputation as a progressive farmer.

At a time when few rural families had electricity, the Starks home did. They had another rural rarity for the time, a telephone, which was listed in the Texarkana directory: *Starks, Virgil, Welding Shop, Highway 67 North: 5016-W.* He was the only Starks listed in the Texarkana directory. The listing immediately before him, J. T. Starkes, came close. The name immediately following Virgil Starks, and one that must have generated an excess of wrong numbers in the middle of the night from inebriated men, was Billie Starr's at 807 West Fourth in Texarkana, Texas: 3440. Ms. Starr operated a well-known bordello at that address.

Their white frame farmhouse, situated about a hundred feet off the highway, was comfortable and spacious, six rooms and small porches at both the front and back, with a barn nearby. Though set off the highway, one side of the house was in full view of anyone driving along the highway. Shrubbery neatly surrounded the house, in front and at the sides. A screen door at the back was the entrance to a small porch there. As you entered the front, the entrance opened to the living area on the left, a bedroom on the right. The kitchen and dining area were at the back. There was a middle room, an oak-paneled sitting room with an easy chair, the radio, and the telephone with a hand crank ringer on the wall. It comprised around 1500 square feet.

A wooden loading chute facilitated the movement of livestock, and a nearby arena served as a stage for impromptu, informal rodeos. Bought earlier when land prices were still low because of the Depression, it was a major holding of choice land. Cotton was the big crop, then corn and feedstuff. A shop in which Virgil kept his welding equipment and other tools lay nearby. The shop was a frame building with a roof and a dirt floor, with a door on hinges. The barn lay to the left of the shop. Virgil, an accomplished welder, had erected a sign.

VIRGIL STARKS

ELECTRIC, ACETYLENE WELDING

WORK GUARANTEED

Two tenant structures—"shotgun houses"—sat at the other end of the farm. The men there worked on other farms in the community.

Friday, May 3, for Virgil was another long day. At the end, his back was giving him fits again. It had been a mild day, no higher than 75 degrees by midafternoon, cooling down to 63 degrees by eight P.M. Partly cloudy, there had been slight rain, a bit over a third of an inch. The days were gradually growing longer, the sun setting at seven P.M. that day. The moon, which had risen at 7:12 that morning and would soon be setting, was already low in the west and waning.

While Katie put the supper dishes away, Virgil sat in his easy chair in a room in the southwest corner of the house, a heating pad applied to his sore back, as he listened to the radio and read the *Texarkana Gazette*. It was dark outside. Behind his chair, the window shade was halfway down, covering the upper portion of the window, with a section of the curtain draped to one side. Shrubbery outside reached up to the bottom of the windowsill.

Like everyone else, Virgil and Katie had followed news of the Phantom shootings. The Texas cases had been in isolated lovers' lanes, but rural Arkansans hardly felt exempt from anxiety. The case was of more than casual interest to the Starks couple and their relatives in the community. They had lived in rural Bowie County and still had numerous friends and relatives there. The fact that their friend Bill Presley was sheriff and investigating the crimes only increased their interest.

The hottest lead, though, had fizzled.

MAN IN CORPUS CHRISTI IS FREED
OF SUSPICION IN MURDER CASES

The *Gazette* presented a riveting front page. In a bloody uprising, the "most spectacular in the history of federal prisons," convicts, armed with a machine gun and rifles, had killed and held guards hostage at Alcatraz Island federal penitentiary. Trouble at the Rock had erupted the day before, gaining front-page coverage over the nation that would continue for days. Authorities dispatched Marines to the scene. Two guards had been killed, and three inmates, described as ringleaders, were to die, with fourteen wounded.

Virgil reclined in a chair, his back to the window. With the newspaper spread over his lap, he listened to a radio program that he regularly heard on Friday nights.

Well before nine o'clock, Arkansas State Troopers Max Tackett and Charley Boyd drove their 1941 Ford State Police patrol car by the Starks house, en route from Texarkana to Hope, the district headquarters for the State Police thirty miles away. They had to turn in their April expense accounts by ten P.M., or they would lose the entire month's reimbursements, not a trivial amount during a time of tight salaries. Both men, in their thirties, had returned from World War II service in late 1945.

Tackett, thirty-four, had volunteered for the Army in December 1943, and was sent almost directly overseas, where he served in combat zones in Belgium, France, Holland, and Germany. Boyd went into the Navy. Resuming their old jobs, they had hit the ground running, shooting it out with a felon at nearby Fulton during the New Year's holiday.

Traffic was sparse as they drove along narrow two-lane Highway 67. Miles out of Texarkana, Tackett noted an old-model car parked across the railroad track off a dirt road. This was near a road leading to a large stretch of timber called the Big Woods. Patrons of bootleggers at times parked there to await delivery of moonshine whiskey. It was situated on their right as they drove north, maybe a thousand feet past the house on the left. The car was parked parallel to the railroad track. It was headed north, as if it had come from Texarkana. That was about all they could tell of it in the dark.

Ordinarily they would have stopped and investigated. But this Friday night they were racing the clock. Any delay might cost them their expense money. They couldn't afford it.

"Charley," said Tackett, "we don't have time now, but we need to check out that car on our way back."

They mentally marked the spot. They roared on.

Their repayment assured in Hope, they headed back to Texarkana. The weekend had begun, and they expected to be busily occupied. The Texas murders had increased their already-heavy workload.

It was dark outside as Virgil Starks sat with his heating pad on his back, the light on, reading the newspaper and listening to the radio. The window was closed, but the shade was up as he sat with his back to the window.

Katie Starks undressed for bed and, in her nightgown, lay on their bed in the next room. She called out to Virgil.

"Why don't you come on to bed?" It was getting late, for a farm family.

"As soon as this story ends," he said.

A little later Katie heard a noise in the back yard.

"Virgil, turn down the radio a little," she said. "I hear a noise outside."

Whether he heard her or not she never knew.

Minutes later, an intruder wielding a .22 automatic weapon standing just outside the window, eighteen to twenty inches from the pane where he could see the back of Virgil's head, shot twice, pulling the trigger immediately after the first shot, firing through the screen and window, pumping two bullets into the back of the homeowner's head. The killer had to stand back because of the heavy hedge. It didn't take a crack shot to accomplish the feat. A six-year-old child, one lawman later stated, could have hit a target from that distance.

Without making a sound, Starks slumped forward in his chair. The newspaper fell to the floor, his blood spattering it. One bullet went through the heating pad, short-circuiting it.

Katie, in the bedroom, didn't recognize the shots. It sounded like the breaking of glass. Virgil's dropped something, she thought. Wondering what had happened, she got off the bed and hurried into the sitting room. The radio was still on. Virgil was slumped over in his chair, blood running down his neck. A pool of blood had formed on the floor. She saw the holes in the windowpane. She rushed up, lifted his head, and saw he was bleeding and lifeless. Immediately she recognized that he had been shot from outside the window. She turned and raced to the hand-crank telephone on the wall.

The killer remained just outside the window, making no attempt to flee. With the light on in the room, the killer could watch her movements, as he had observed her coming into the room. She could not see outside into the dark.

She never got to use the phone. When she reached it, the killer fired twice more, at her head, before she could start her call. One bullet entered her cheek beside her nose and emerged from behind the ear; the other shot entered her lower jaw just below the lip. The shots crashed through her teeth, scattering fragments to the floor.

She fell to the floor and lay there stunned for a moment, miraculously still alive. Though seriously wounded and in full view of the killer in the well-lighted room, she had the presence of mind to drop to the floor, so that he, outside on the ground, might believe he had killed her and that she lay dead on the floor, but he would be unable to see her and keep shooting at her from outside. In that position on her hands and knees, she inched her way toward the back of the house. She crawled until she thought she was out of view from outside and then went back into the bedroom.

There was a .45 revolver in a dresser drawer. She wasn't sure exactly where it was. Time was moving fast, her needs urgent, and the pain must have been unimaginable. She might waste precious time searching for it. Then other frenzied thoughts surged through her mind. She could find paper and pen and leave a note. Saying what, she wasn't sure, but attesting to what had happened, if she didn't survive. Then she started to the kitchen in the corner room. She opened the door to the kitchen and heard a noise—someone was trying to come in the back door of the kitchen. Just as she entered the kitchen door she heard the man trying to enter the house through the kitchen window, then saw him climbing through a window at the screened-in back porch. All she saw was his leg and knee. He was coming after her! Her only thought was to get away as fast as she could. Her home was no longer a sanctuary.

Terrified, throwing caution to the wind and blinded by blood spurting from her wounds, she ran back, half stumbling, into the bedroom, through a passage way, then another bedroom, and through the living room, frantically flung open the front door and ran pell-mell out of her home into the yard, into the darkness, down the driveway, and headed for the highway. Dressed only in her nightgown, by then saturated with blood, and barefoot, she left a bloody trail in the house. Hardly aware of the rough surfaces her bare feet trod, she crossed the highway, then the railroad tracks.

Oblivious to her condition and dominated by the greatest fear she had ever known, she dedicated all of her energies to escaping. She had to get over to her sister and brother-in-law Betty and Jeff Allen, who lived almost directly across the highway. Approximately two hundred yards away, they were her closest and most obvious sources of protection. Was he behind her? Would he shoot her again? Would he kill her? Her over-riding thoughts were of escape.

She hadn't seen the man at all, only his leg poking through the kitchen window, had no idea what he looked like.

It was the beginning of a night of terror for Katie Starks.

After shooting her, the killer ran along the side of the house and around to the rear of the house and bounded up the steps. Then he entered the screened porch and broke into the house through the kitchen window.

He wasted no time gaining entry. Though his primary goal had become finishing off the only witness, he paused long enough in the house to survey his work before pursuing Katie farther. He stopped for a moment before Starks's body, staring down at what he had wrought with his own hands. Then he headed out of the room to the front. The brief halt may have given Katie a few more minutes' headway. By then, seeing that she had fled, his own thoughts turned to escape. There was no time to search for her in the dark and compromise *his* safety. The hunter could become the hunted—fast—if things went awry, and they had.

Upon reaching the Allen house, Katie's expectations were dashed. There was no light in the house. She stumbled to the front porch, called out, and knocked on the door, frantic with fear. No response. No one home. She was farther from help than she'd realized.

She was not the sort to give up without her strongest effort. The Praters! she thought. Somebody must be home there. She stepped carefully off the Allens' front porch and, her struggle for survival overcoming her fatigue, started running toward the home of A. V. Prater, whose house was about fifty yards from the Allen home.

Reaching the Praters' home, she knocked on the door and called for help. She was bleeding profusely and feeling weaker by the second.

The family was home. Prater rushed to the door, switched on the light, recognized Katie immediately, and seized his rifle and fired it from the front porch into the air to signal neighbors. Elmer Taylor heard the shot and rushed to the scene.

"Bring your car, Elmer," Prater yelled at Taylor. "Mrs. Starks has been shot!"

They rushed her to Texarkana, to Michael Meagher Hospital just east of the state line. Easing Katie in the front seat and the Praters and their baby in the back, Taylor lost no time in covering the ten miles. Katie turned to the driver and handed him one of her dislodged teeth, this one with a gold filling, which she had clutched in her hand during her escape, for safekeeping. She had spat it out into her hand. Katie slumped forward in the front seat, in a semi-conscious state during the entire trip to the city. She had been losing blood the whole time. Her nightgown was soaked. Several of her lower teeth had been shot out. They drove into the

Emergency entrance to the hospital. Taylor and Prater jumped out of the car to get help.

Rushed into the hospital, she gained true sanctuary for the first time. A physician scurried in. The bullet striking her right cheek had emerged from behind the left ear. The bullet to her jaw had broken the lower jaw and lodged under her tongue. It was a miracle she was even able to talk. While the doctor was amazed she hadn't bled to death, even more striking was that her pulse was normal, no evidence of shock. These indicators boded well for her prognosis. She was whisked into the operating room. Although in critical condition, she was no longer in the dark, barefoot and bleeding, with a cold-blooded gunman on her trail. Her husband was dead, but she was safe in a hospital with physicians and nurses to care for her. Nothing was assured, but now she had a chance to fight for her life, with proper medical assistance.

Troopers Tackett and Boyd had crossed the Red River bridge and were back in Miller County when the call came on their patrol car's radio. They'd already passed the Starks home, about five miles from the Red River bridge, on their way back to Texarkana. The old model car they'd intended to check was gone. Tough luck. We should have stopped then, they agreed.

The police radio message was somber. A shooting at the home of Virgil Starks on Highway 67. Starks dead, Mrs. Starks critically wounded. Another murder! Tackett turned the car around in the middle of the highway and stomped the accelerator. He and Boyd were the first officers on the scene.

He remembered the old-model car they'd seen parked in the vicinity of the Starks home. He worked it over in his mind. That must have been the killer's car. It was a disquieting revelation. They had passed around the time of the shootings or shortly afterward. From that moment he believed they had missed an opportunity to either prevent the murder or to apprehend the culprit. They never changed their opinions. The driver of the car, they were certain, had shot the Starks couple.

The lights were still on in the farmhouse. The troopers went inside, guns drawn to be sure. Mr. Starks was slumped over in death in the blood-soaked chair. The first things they saw were a blood-stained floor and muddy footprints. Smoke filled the room where Starks's body lay, stinging the nostrils. Starks's armchair smoldered from fire caused by a short-circuit of the electric heating pad. The victim's blood soaked into the chair and onto the floor. The body, however, was not burned, while smoke swirled all about and from between his legs. Within seconds they ascertained that Starks was beyond help.

They had to work fast. Numerous other officers would be converging on the death house in a very short time. They had only a few precious minutes in which to rope off the house and surrounding area in order to preserve any possible clues that specialists might find. In accepted police procedure, they began carefully isolating possible clues in the house.

Their efforts were almost for naught. Minutes later the house and grounds were inundated by lawmen from both sides of the state line, some from as far as thirty miles away. Everyone raced to the scene as soon as the emergency message went out. "Hundreds of officers," said Tackett, in a bit of exaggeration, swarmed in. They couldn't control the outsiders and, according to Tackett, the incoming officers "stomped out all possible evidence."

Soon it would be impossible to preserve any important clues the killer may have left behind, as lawmen got in each other's way.

Chaos and poor liaison continued to characterize the investigations.

Early Friday evening, Sheriff W. E. "Elvie" Davis, a stout forty-five-year-old cigar-smoking veteran lawman, was sitting with Chief Deputy Tillman Johnson discussing what the weekend was likely to bring. Davis, former police chief on the Arkansas side who had started out as a rural schoolteacher, had been elected sheriff in 1938. Though a good speaker on the stump, he was shy in many ways and dodged reporters, usually assigning that duty to his chief deputy.

Johnson had just returned to Texarkana and his old job on May 1 after receiving his discharge from the Army. He had been drafted in January 1944 as a private and sent to Camp Chaffee, near Fort Smith, Arkansas. He advanced fast, became a tech sergeant and acting first sergeant of his outfit. He was to recall later, "I got shot at more at home in Miller County than I did in the Army!"

In the Army, Johnson often went home on weekends and had kept up with the Texarkana murders. Davis, like his counterpart in Bowie County, sported a small staff—seven in all, including the sheriff and the jailer—to cover the entire county.

When the city desk sergeant called on Friday night, Johnson answered the phone. Davis, Johnson, and Deputy Bill Scott left immediately for the Starks farm.

"By time Elvie and I got there it was a three-ring circus," said Johnson. "It was a carnival. There were already a lot of people, including officers, around when we arrived. Max and Charley were there. The city police were already there. Buzz Hallett and Dewey Presley from the FBI were there. Neighbors had started pouring in.

"The house was wide open. Soon people were tromping all over. I tried to seal off the scene, but by then much had probably been lost."

Scurrying about outside, Johnson first sought to cordon off the crime scene with whatever material he could find. He located some telephone wire around the house and stretched it around to keep the curious at bay. The word had gotten out; soon people began collecting, gawking. Other lawmen began arriving. The sheriff's men left the inside of the house to the FBI agents to the extent they could. Outside, Johnson found hulls from the bullets used to shoot the couple and saved them as evidence. Three empty cartridge hulls from a .22 caliber gun were collected.

Immediately a blockade was thrown up on U.S. Highway 67 for several miles both northeast and southwest of the murder scene. Several men found in the general vicinity were picked up for questioning. Occupants of cars believed to have been in the area at the time of the shootings were also picked up.

While the other officers rushed about the house and grounds, Johnson and Bill Scott headed west from the house, to see if anyone in the community knew anything. They knocked on the doors of neighbors. They briefed them on the crimes. The neighbors were horrified. They could imagine no possible motive, knew no enemies that Starks may have had. His reputation was excellent.

There were a lot of hitchhikers around Texarkana; anybody out of the ordinary automatically qualified as a suspect. They would sort them out later. Time was of the essence. Better to detain an innocent man tempo-rarily than to let the guilty one slip through.

Several men in the general vicinity were picked up. Tenants lived some distance behind the Starks house. In each of the two houses there were two men, who worked on the nearby farms, and their families. Without ceremony Johnson and Scott seized the men, to question them later. It was no time for calm reasoning. If anyone even faintly qualified as suspect, he was held.

There was no way of knowing from whence the killer had come or where he had gone. Within hours deputies arrested a dozen men, took them to jail for safekeeping until they had time to check out their stories. Over the weekend three men remained in lockup. It didn't mean they were strong suspects; they had only been near enough to the Starks home to justify rounding up.

Johnson and Scott didn't go inside the Starks house that night. But just about everybody else did.

Sheriff Davis headed for Michael Meagher Hospital to question Katie Starks.

Officers inside the house found a scene of rural tranquility violently and abruptly shattered. The dining-room table was covered with material and patterns that Katie Starks had been using to cut out a dress. Money in the house was not bothered. Katie's purse lay on a bed in full view, containing both money and jewels. Nothing seemed to be missing from the house, with no evidence of ransacking or burglarizing. This did not necessarily mean the intruder hadn't intended to rob the house and its owners; if so, his plans apparently had gone awry the moment Katie ran to the telephone. From that point the killer apparently concentrated his efforts on eliminating her and, that failing, on escaping himself. If he had simply wanted to kill Starks, and nothing else, he had ample time to shoot and run immediately. But he had lingered until she had appeared.

They found what some believed to be the killer's bloody footprints on the linoleum floor. He had gone into the sitting room, apparently inspected Starks's body, then stepped into a pool of blood nearby. The *Texarkana Gazette* that Starks had been reading lay on the floor, splattered with blood.

The killer's lingering by his victim's body, while Katie was fleeing, pointed toward his desire to survey the product of his work, like a boy checking out an animal he has hunted and killed, not to be sure it was dead but to examine the result of his sport and handiwork

Three clues remained. The killer had dropped a red flashlight outside in the hedge beneath the window from which he took aim. He had probably set it down on the ground when he'd aimed the weapon, then forgot to retrieve it when Katie's entrance threw him into a panic. The .22 bullets and shells were collected. The bullets were .22 caliber but too battered to identify definitively. The cases apparently came from an automatic or semi-automatic weapon because of the closeness of the holes in the window with each pair of shots, believed to be from an old model .22 Colt Woodsman. The gun was unlikely to have been a pump or bolt-action rifle, which would have created a different shot pattern. Based on their accuracy, many officers felt the shots came from a rifle, but they couldn't be sure it wasn't a .22 pistol, instead. The bloody footprint only provided an approximate clue but helped track the killer's steps—and were the first concrete physical markers the killer had left behind thus far.

The flashlight along with the tracks provided the first tangible clues in the six weeks of murder. The flashlight would be checked for fingerprints. It was a two-cell light with a black barrel, red-rimmed around the glass. It wasn't much, but it was more than had been left behind in the earlier cases.

Was the shooting connected to the earlier ones in Texas? Miller County Sheriff Davis hedged his comments. Not definitely, for a different gun was used, a different caliber. But he didn't close the door on the possibility.

"It is possible that the killer is one and the same man."

The flashlight was turned over to the FBI agents. Fingerprints weren't likely to be found on the flashlight itself, but hopes rose that a print might turn up on the batteries therein. Agents Hallett and Presley walked carefully through the house. Although it might be difficult to match definitively with a shoe, the man's track in Katie's bloody path was hard evidence. The track seemed to be about a size 10. The retouched shoe sole apparently had been loose and had been sliced off about the place that a man would cut it off in order to half-sole it. The corner of the cut-off sole had folded back, leaving a triangular imprint.

Footprints appeared to have gone out the front door, down to the edge of the highway. He apparently had run about two hundred yards along the highway, crossed to the other side, and continued beside the railroad tracks a quarter mile away, where Tackett and Boyd had spotted the parked car. Making a plaster cast of the track in the house was out of the question because of its condition, so Hallett took the next best step. He cut out that portion of the linoleum floor as possible evidence.

There were so many people tracking in and out of the house, however, that some wondered whether the track belonged to the killer or to one of the men arriving to investigate. There was no way to be certain. Tillman Johnson, for one, was uncertain that the track belonged to the killer.

The evidence was sent by plane on Monday to FBI headquarters in Washington, where they had been promised priority attention.

Texas Ranger Captain Gonzaullas appeared at the house, even though it was in Arkansas, minutes after receiving the call. On the scene he forcibly vented his emotions. "This is an outrage! I only wish the jury that will try this man could see this house as it is now. This woman possessed tremendous moral courage."

He viewed the heavy trail of blood Katie had left in her wake and added, "It is beyond me why she did not bleed to death."

Bowie County Sheriff Presley, getting the report, sped across the state line as fast as he could to the Starks home. The fact that he had known both Virgil and Katie as they had grown up added to his shock. He walked through the house of death, shaking his head.

"This killer is the luckiest person I have ever known. No one sees him, hears him in time, or can identify him in any way."

The news spread rapidly through the community and to the families of the victims. When Virgil's father, Jack Starks, learned of the tragedy, he drove to the home of his other son Charlie Starks and his wife Gertie. Jack Starks told them that Virgil had been killed and Katie seriously wounded and was in the hospital.

They all drove to the scene of the shootings. They arrived as the funeral-home attendants were carrying Virgil's body away. They talked briefly with officers and neighbors, then headed to the hospital for the long vigil for Katie.

J. Q. Mahaffey left the *Gazette* late. There'd been the usual work to be done on the Sunday edition, some of the pages going in early. As he drove up to the house in Beverly Addition on the Texas side, he saw his son, John Quincy, standing on the porch.

"Daddy," the boy said, "Mr. Sutton called that he did it again!"

"Who did?"

"The Phantom. He did it again."

Mahaffey immediately drove back to the newspaper office and soon afterward sped to the scene of the latest shooting.

As soon as he reached the Starks home, he saw Tillman Johnson.

"Tillman, what can you tell me about what happened?" Mahaffey asked.

"I don't know, J. Q., I just got here. I don't know any more than you do. When I learn something, I'll let you know."

He asked Mahaffey to stand back, as they were combing for evidence. The editor stepped back immediately. Subsequently Johnson found the .22 long-shell cases.

They didn't see each other again that night. Minutes later, Johnson and Bill Scott began scouring about the farm, picking up anyone who might have been in the area.

Officers at Arkansas's Cummins State Prison rushed bloodhounds to the scene. Dogs traced two trails to the highway. They ran a trail from the house to the railroad tracks and up to a point where tire tracks were found. Apparently one of the trails had been used to reach the house, the other to flee. The trail was lost at the highway. Bloodhounds are not always as accurate in their tracking as might be desired, and there was no certainty that these were on the right trail, for they had no known scent of the killer to follow, no piece of clothing. The flashlight, which must have been handled by a gloved hand, was not helpful.

Worst of all, by the time the bloodhounds arrived on the scene, a multitude of tracks and scents complicated their work. Men milled around, inside the house and outside on the grounds.

Working with the track the dogs were able to pick up, though, the killer had apparently crossed over the highway, gone down the railroad tracks, and escaped, probably by a car he had parked nearby. This scenario coincided with Tackett's belief that the parked car he and Boyd had seen in the shadows was the gunman's.

As soon as they could drive from Little Rock, a contingent of State Police supervisors arrived. By 6:30 A.M., Lt. Carl Miller was jotting notes in a neat hand to file a detailed report with precise measurements, citing distances from ground to window, how far apart were the bullet holes in the window. Apparently the gunman had not changed his stance outside, judging by the horizontal closeness of the two sets of bullet holes. The lower holes, through which Starks had been shot, were 32 inches from the floor; the upper holes, through which Katie was shot, were 42 inches from the floor. The policeman extricated one bullet in the north wall 56 inches from the floor. From the numbers it could be readily seen how Katie had saved her life by dropping to the floor where the assassin could not get a third and fourth shot at her.

In addition to the bloody footprint found on the kitchen floor, a similar footprint was found near the driveway entrance to the yard, about fifty yards from the corner of the house. Four tracks were lifted between a cottonwood tree and a willow. Those found near Starks's welding sign suggested the killer had gone first to the shop, possibly looking for something to steal, before walking toward the house. Casts were made of the prints; but it was problematic, because of the indistinct condition of the tracks, whether they could be used to accurately match a shoe or boot.

Tire tracks across the highway and railroad line, where Tackett and Boyd had spotted the car, showed that a car had turned around at that point, in order to get back onto the highway. It was not possible to tell which direction the car had taken on the highway. Judging by where the car had been parked, it probably had come from the direction of Texarkana. Where it went after the shootings could only be guessed. Had it continued, north, toward the Red River, or had it returned toward Texarkana?

Gazette city editor Calvin Sutton, who had dubbed the killer the Phantom, arranged with the Associated Press's Dallas bureau to be ready in case another murder occurred. Bill Barnard was in the AP office that night.

"When the Starks murder happened, I dictated the story to Bill over the phone straight onto the A [i.e., national] wire, off the top of my head, and he shot it to the puncher.

"In the movies or on television, the reporters go out and solve these things, but nothing was further from any of our minds. We grew up a lot in that time, believe me."

The next morning, a Saturday, the *Gazette* heralded the fifth murder in six weeks with heavy 96-point black Gothic capitals, more than an inch high.

MURDER ROCKS CITY AGAIN;
FARMER SLAIN, WIFE WOUNDED

The biggest manhunt in the region's history continued with renewed energy and greater urgency, as befitted the biggest crime-news story to hit a town that before then had known everything else.

CHAPTER 11

NOBODY IS SAFE!

As Lt. Miller of the Arkansas State Police worked in and around the house the following morning, Chief Deputy Sheriff Tillman Johnson began about two hundred yards away, near where the suspect car had been parked the night before.

A fence almost directly across the highway from where the car had been parked divided Starks's land from his neighbor's. It was about a thousand feet from the fence to the house. Johnson strode across to the fence line. A portion of Starks's land had been plowed, then dampened by rain, about a third of an inch the previous day. Johnson checked the plowed ground from the edges, looking for any sign. Along the fence row a long, narrow strip of grass provided a firm buffer between the fence and the plowed land.

He walked on the grass while studying the plowed ground. About a hundred feet from the highway, he found what he was looking for—footprints crossing the plowed field, in the direction of the house. He felt sure he'd found the killer's route. He'd come directly from across the highway where Tackett and Boyd had seen the parked car. The man had taken that route so as not to be seen from the highway.

Recent plowing, along with the rain, had left the soil soft and in rows. Johnson stepped carefully alongside the tracks, following them without going close. None of the prints was ideal, though one was better than the others. It would be difficult to match, but he thought it possibly was a boot print with the heel worn on one side. He couldn't be sure. The condition of the soil precluded making a precise model.

He followed the tracks across the field. They ran in only one direction, toward the house and outbuildings. Johnson, calm and cool in most situations, suddenly grew excited. These were definitely a man's footsteps. He felt certain it was the killer's path.

It appeared the stalker had risked the softer soil of the plowed ground in order to avoid being seen by a passing car on the highway. He had first headed straight for the house. This would have taken him near or into the welding shop where Starks frequently worked.

The gunman had a flashlight, which would have facilitated inspection of the shop. Although there had been some rain earlier, the plowed ground wasn't boggy, though definitely softer than the grassy strip. Johnson, six-foot-one and weighing almost two hundred pounds and wearing cowboy boots, didn't bog down at all but walked easily across the plowed field. Once he'd crossed the field, the killer could have wiped the mud off his shoes by dragging his feet over the yard and continued on his way.

After entering the grass of the yard, the tracks couldn't be traced farther. Finding no tracks around the house, Johnson looked for tracks leading back to where the car had been parked. None crossed the plowed field in the returning direction. Apparently the killer had fled over the yard and crossed the highway and the railroad track to reach his car.

As for the strip of linoleum with a bloody shoe print sent to the FBI lab, no identification ever resulted. Johnson, for one, was never convinced that it was the killer's footprint. Too many men were milling around inside and outside the house that night. Almost any of them could have left the print. But those across the plowed field, imperfect as they were, had to belong to the killer, Johnson reasoned.

The tracks were distorted. Mud further blurred the evidence. Two plaster casts were made of the imperfect tracks. One track looked like a walking boot with a heel worn off on one side. But they couldn't take the cast and make a positive. It would be difficult to prove that a given boot or shoe had made it. The ground was too soggy. Only one thing was certain: the killer had muddy or damp footwear, whether he had washed them off or discarded them.

"You just couldn't get a good plain track out of it," said Johnson. "Mine looked the same, going along beside it. But it did put us into the idea that the man in that car had walked down to the house. We couldn't track him anywhere else.

"We found some tracks leading from the house, but whose they were, we couldn't determine. We couldn't know they were the same person's.

"It appeared that he would have gone across the railroad tracks and then gone back to his car. There was a lot of grass and water and it was wet through there and you just couldn't tell much about it."

Officers found several cigarette butts near where the suspicious car had been parked, indicating that, if the butts had been left there by the killer, he—or they, if anyone had been with him—had smoked them while waiting to ease across the highway. He may have arrived before it was fully dark and waited till darkness so that he could explore with impunity. There was also the possibility that someone dealing with a bootlegger had smoked the cigarettes, but it was another suggestive clue and, if true, indicated that the Starks home invasion was a premeditated, carefully calculated crime, whatever may have been the major motive for this or any of the other murders.

An approximate layout of the murder scene followed this rough map.

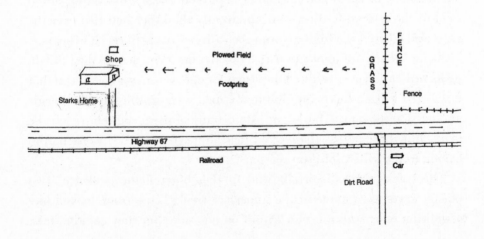

Howard Giles, son of Arkansas-side Police Chief R. Marlin Giles, served with the Navy in Washington, D.C., as a fingerprint specialist. At war's end, he was assigned to Europe to help identify German Storm Troopers, using fingerprint records. He was there for about six months before discharge, after which he joined Texarkana's Arkansas-side police department. Just after the Booker-Martin murders, he took over from Bryan Westerfield, who had filled in during the war. As it happened, he was in place when the Starks murder occurred and was sent out that night to collect any fingerprints he could.

On Monday after the shootings, with Katie still in the hospital in serious but improved condition, more than five hundred persons attended solemn funeral services for Virgil at the First Methodist Church, Arkansas. More than sixty of the mourners were relatives of the couple. The Reverend Edward W. Harris, who earlier had railed against the "criminal element" in Texarkana, conducted the services.

"This tragedy is the third of its kind that has struck our community," the pastor said. "Each of us in a community way more than in the usual manner feel a sense of kinship with you in the sorrow you feel today," he said to Mr. and Mrs. Jack Starks, parents of Virgil Starks. "It is a sorrow that weighs upon every home in this community."

He expressed, for the family, confidence in officers and newspaper people, and all others "who bear the responsibility in the community for ending the reign of terror."

Somber faces in the audience at times were streaked with tears.

On Tuesday morning, Sheriff Davis had a long talk with Katie Starks in her hospital room. She was in reasonably good spirits, considering what she had been through. She told the sheriff again that she hadn't seen the man who shot her. She said she had started to get a pistol, but her vision had been so obscured by blood that she couldn't be sure where she was going. By then she felt she was going to be killed. She wanted to leave a note before she died. But instead she decided to flee as she heard the intruder rip the screen from the back window, whereupon she flung caution to the winds and ran out of the house as fast as she could.

The Arkansas State Police's forensics lab in Little Rock confirmed that the .22 caliber gun that killed Virgil Starks was an automatic or semi-automatic weapon. But the bullets were in too rough a condition for them to concretely determine if they came from a rifle or pistol, as the men who collected the bullets initially feared. If the bullets indeed came from a rifle, it was a common weapon that almost every family in the county owned.

It possibly was of foreign make, the ballistics expert said, but in his opinion it was a .22 Colt Woodsman. The weapon in the other four murders had also been a Colt, but a .32 caliber. "I think this is what you're looking for." It resulted in a search for the death gun by locating and firing hundreds, starting in the Homan community. Only if the gun itself was found could a definite identification be made.

Dr. C. L. Winchester, a veterinarian serving as coroner, an elected position, signed Virgil Starks's death certificate. The stated cause of death was no more revealing than it had been in the deaths on the Texas side.

"Gun in hands of unknown person."

Suspects were in short supply. As in the earlier murders, a clear motive was elusive. Starks's reputation in the community was solid.

Weeks later, the FBI lab returned the killer's flashlight to the Miller County sheriff's department. The technicians hadn't been able to find prints on the flashlight or its batteries. It was a heartbreaking report. It did, however, mean that they were dealing with an experienced criminal who had wiped off fingerprints or used gloves, an organized killer who had arrived at the crime scene determined to leave no clues.

The color and design of the flashlight was fairly uncommon, to the point that one like it could be identified, a two-celled flashlight with the tip of it red. Tillman Johnson checked every store in Texarkana. Only one store carried the brand, and the storekeeper didn't remember selling that particular one. Johnson took the flashlight to J. Q. Mahaffey at the *Gazette* and asked if he would run a picture of the flashlight on page one. Mahaffey went to the publisher and owner, Clyde E. Palmer, who agreed to do so.

The *Gazette* also agreed to send a photograph of it, in color, over the Associated Press wire. The incident remained fixed in city editor Sutton's memory for years afterward.

"The *Gazette* ran the first spot color photograph in the United States, of the flashlight left at the Starks home," Sutton said. *"Editor & Publisher* magazine credited us with having been the first to do it. It was not a true color picture. We used two cuts, one of the shiny part of the flashlight, and one of the red handle."

The *Gazette* ran a four-column photo ran on page one.

HAVE YOU SEEN THIS TWO-CELL FLASHLIGHT?

THIS IS A PICTURE IN DETAIL OF THE FLASHLIGHT FOUND AT THE SCENE OF THE STARKS MURDER. THIS IS A TWO-CELL, ALL METAL FLASHLIGHT, BOTH ENDS OF WHICH ARE PAINTED RED. THREE RIVETS HOLD THE HEAD OF THE FLASHLIGHT TO THE BODY OF THE LIGHT. THERE HAS BEEN ONLY A LIMITED NUMBER OF THESE LIGHTS SOLD IN THIS AREA. IF YOU HAVE OWNED OR KNOW OF ANY ONE WHO OWNED ONE OF THESE LIGHTS, REPORT AT ONCE TO SHERIFF W. E. DAVIS, MILLER COUNTY COURTHOUSE, TEXARKANA, ARK. YOU MAY BE THE ONE TO AID IN SOLVING THE PHANTOM SLAYINGS.

Nothing came of it.

The killing of Virgil Starks gave the case a new level of urgency. The Starks case increased the tension that the murderer still had not been caught, and brought in political figures. Congressman Wright Patman, a powerful U.S. representative who lived in Texarkana, Texas, made contact with FBI Director J. Edgar Hoover and Attorney General Tom Clark, securing promises that priority would be given to the Texarkana needs.

The governor's office in Little Rock beefed up the State Patrol contingent in the Texarkana area, assigning ten troopers to Miller County.

On the Texas side, Ranger Gonzaullas announced the arrival of a powerful mobile radio transmitting station—"one of the best in the country." Ten more Texas DPS patrol cars, each with two men in it, arrived, equipped with three-way radio sets. Within the week, a Teletype machine in the sheriff's office connected Texarkana with major law-enforcement offices all over Texas.

Texarkana had gained, albeit by dubious means, what very rarely happened—focused attention from both state governments, no longer a stepchild of two states.

The Texas crimes had already spread caution across the state line, especially after dark. On the night of May 3, Leslie Greer, campaigning for Miller County tax assessor, and his wife attended a fish fry and foxhunt in the rural southern part of the county. When two youths rode up on horses, the group went on alert. Alice Greer fetched her husband's antique .45 revolver from the car, readying it for action. The young horsemen turned out to be harmless local residents, but the culture of fear only continued to grow with the latest murder.

"Regular" crime continued at a lesser pace. On Sunday night, May 5, two days after the Starks shooting, a 1941 Chevrolet coach was abandoned in the 300 block of West Broad, near downtown. It bore Louisiana license plates. It remained there for several days before police towed it to the station. Its owner was Joe Morgan of Shreveport. He was notified and went to Texarkana to retrieve his property. He said it had been stolen from him on Saturday, May 4. Phantom fears had slowed other crimes but hadn't halted car theft, a seemingly endemic practice.

Rumors surfaced in the Starks case as they had in the earlier murders, threatening to dominate the investigation. Many of them assumed that a different criminal had perpetrated the latest one. Similar rumors had afflicted the Hollis-Larey beatings, even the Griffin-Moore murders, that a jealous suitor was to blame. That they were all unproved hardly slowed them. In the Starks case, rumors eventually embraced almost every variant possibility, without a shred of basis. An angry man wreaking vengeance on Virgil Starks hardly would have stopped shooting after firing only two shots that obviously had killed him. In so-called crimes of passion, the anger is so open, so volatile that the killer may confront his victim in broad daylight and shoot and shoot and shoot, usually until he is out of bullets. He also would have shot and run. No evidence was ever presented to prove any of the rumors. The loose talk also unjustly assailed the integrity of the victims.

Several distinctive features of the Starks case argued for its being a continuation of the earlier serial killings in Texas, rather than a grudge slaying or a crime of passion.

One of the case's strangest aspects feeds into the argument. Despite the widespread terror over the region, Starks sat in a chair by a window with the shade up, at night with the light on inside, dark outside. Anyone could see inside; he couldn't see outside. Clearly Starks displayed no fear of the "Phantom" or anyone else. He obviously lived in less fear of the serial killer on the Texas side than did all of the others in his community. He might well have been the only one in the region so vulnerable.

Tillman Johnson believed Starks might have felt protected by virtue of his house being close to a relatively busy major highway, the main route from Texarkana to Little Rock, too public for the killer to risk. And, of course, it was in Arkansas, not Texas—a fact that failed to calm most Arkansans that fateful night.

The light could be easily seen from the highway. For an impulsive, or compulsive, killer the temptation may have been more than he could resist. The Phantom, by then, whatever his level of intelligence, realized lovers' lanes were more dangerous for him now, as they were now full of disguised officers setting traps in an area already teeming with lawmen.

Going by the tracks that Johnson had found, the killer appeared to have gone first to the welding shop, perhaps seeking a piece of equipment he could steal and sell. A thief would have done that. This also would have coincided with the noise Katie had heard outside. A man intent solely on assassination wouldn't have bothered to check out a welding shop before hurrying to settle a score.

That said, the man may have intended to steal or rob, but he also came to kill. If he had not, he wouldn't have been armed. He saw Virgil Starks's light from the highway. He parked away from the house. He got out of the car with his .22 and flashlight. The flashlight indicated that he needed it to look around, in the shop or anywhere else, for items to steal. The gun suggested a more violent intention. If theft had been his only goal, he wouldn't have needed a gun.

The killer must not have lived in the community or known much about it. He seemed unaware that the Starkses had a telephone—until Katie ran to the phone to call. A gunman with murder in mind, and thinking clearly, would have cut the phone line—if he'd known there was one. This argues for the view that a stranger did it. Rural telephones were so rare at that time that everyone in the rural community would have known who had one.

If he'd known of the phone but for some reason neglected to disable it, he arguably would have shot Katie as she came within range while near Virgil's body. His first action did not come until she turned from the body and lifted the receiver and started to crank the mechanism to reach an operator. Then he shot her and broke into the house to finish her off. He may have gloated at her horror upon finding her husband dead, then panicked when he saw how fast the alarm could be spread and expedite his capture. If he could not kill the witness, he must escape, as soon as possible.

Had he killed Katie, no one would have known until the next day, much as had happened in the two Texas double murders. Based on this, his target was not only Virgil Starks but everyone else in the house. He would have had time to see her, watch her, then go inside and kill her up close at his leisure, much as he had done to his earlier victims. The phone, suddenly entering his perception, thwarted him. What may have seemed to be an easy mark at an isolated rural home became a dangerous boomerang. He didn't have time to search for valuables, even to take Starks's wallet or money.

Furthermore, if the killer had been someone known to the Starkses, with a grudge against Virgil, he likely wouldn't have lingered to see Katie and possibly be recognized. If he didn't know them, he'd have less fear of recognition—he was a stranger, after all, and one who intended to leave no witnesses.

After she fled, he didn't know where she was or where she'd gone. He ran to his car. His actions indicated that he wasn't familiar with the locale. If he'd known the Starkses and the community, he would have known where the other houses were and where she might have gone. But he was in the dark, in more ways than one—he'd also lost his flashlight.

Might it have been a "copycat" killing, a term that did not arise for decades? Unlikely, for the killer would run even greater risks, if he had a known motive. He then might be charged with the Texas slayings also.

As was to be emphasized later by Max Tackett, each of the Texas victims had been shot two times, as if the killer believed no more was needed to wipe out a life. Paul Martin had been shot four times but only twice at a time, the fatal series coming only when the killer, afterward, apparently saw that the boy was still alive from the earlier two shots. In Arkansas, the gunman had shot Starks two times, then Katie twice. He could have shot either more times but had not. A similar mentality seemed behind all of the crimes.

A parallel to the Griffin-Moore murders was that Starks also was shot almost point-blank in the back of the head, execution-style. The killer seemed to know it was the surest way to kill, not a difficult conclusion to reach but one that suggested knowledge gained through experience.

If the earlier murders were crimes of opportunity, the Starks shootings could be seen as continuing the pattern. The Starks home provided the easiest target he'd had. Similarities that appeared to link the cases were several: couples only as victims, killing or disabling the male first, two shots at each victim (except for Martin, killed in two series of two shots each), an automatic weapon, vulnerable victims at night, use of a flashlight in at least two, possibly all, cases.

A strong flashlight was a part of the gunman's equipment in at least two of the cases, the Hollis-Larey beatings and the Starks shootings.

Though the caliber was different in the Starks case with a different gun, an automatic was used in the two double murders and probably in the beatings. The same .32 automatic killed four victims, a .22 automatic rifle or pistol in the Starks case. Knowing that the police were looking for a .32 automatic warned him to dispose of it, while a .22 rifle or pistol wasn't suspicious—until May 3.

Arguments seeking to derail the one-killer theory pointed out that a different weapon was used in the Starks slaying, that the victims were at home in a house and not in a secluded lovers' lane, and that the victims were older. But the argument only deflects, rather than refutes, the position that the same man did it all. The distinctions were superficial. He obviously would change his weapon to a more common, less conspicuous caliber. By then, he had a more restricted cast of potential victims from which to choose. Where else but in a home could the killer find a couple at this point, now that all the lovers' lanes were being watched? Thousands locked their homes tight and shielded their windows after nightfall.

Lovers' lanes were too hot to explore. He had to hunt his game in a safer venue.

Additionally, the Starks killer appeared to be an experienced burglar, suggesting that he had committed a range of other crimes in the past, perhaps as a career criminal. He broke into the house as surely and swiftly as an old hand. He hadn't needed that skill in the previous crimes. He also seemed to know the rural roads on the Texas side better than in the Homan community, suggesting that he had moved from his accustomed base of operations in Bowie County to a less familiar rural Miller County.

If the killer was a different one, settling a grudge against Starks, why did he linger just outside the window after he had shot Starks dead until Katie entered the room—to eliminate a witness? She had not witnessed the shooting. The shooter had not seen her until she entered the room. He could have shot and run and escaped before she appeared. What had he waited for, to see what she looked like? A grudge-holder would have known both Starks and his wife and what she looked like.

Did he shoot her to keep her from telephoning to spread the alarm? Undoubtedly. But if he had been a man who lived in the community he would have known the Starkses had one of the few rural telephones. He could have cut the phone line before he fired. The fact that he did not argues for his not knowing about the phone or knowing the couple. Everyone in the community knew of the telephone. A rank stranger would not have.

Officers never developed any evidence to implicate *anyone* who knew Starks. They thoroughly checked out every suspect. The Starks shootings were as motiveless as the earlier ones.

In the final analysis, a logical marshalling of the facts gave greater credence, and a preponderance of evidence, to the same hand's having committed all four incidents.

The Texas Phantom, whoever he might be, in all likelihood also was the Arkansas assassin.

Vexing times took different forms over the nation. In Georgia the Ku Klux Klan—"for white gentiles only"—burned five crosses on top of Stone Mountain as white-robed, masked Klansmen made their first public statement since Pearl Harbor. The Associated Press reported that seven hundred Klansmen initiated five hundred new members into the secret organization, with a thousand wives and children of the new members brought in by five chartered buses. The Georgia group was described as the "mother Klan" of all American KKK organizations.

The week after the Starks shootings, another body turned up, near Ogden, Arkansas, about sixteen miles north of Texarkana in adjoining Little River County. The body was mutilated, having been run over by a Kansas City Southern train. A Social Security card identified him as Earl Cliff McSpadden; an employment card gave Shreveport, Louisiana, as his home. His brother in Dallas identified him as a transient oil-storage-tank builder. The family had not heard from him since May 3. His letter of that date bore a Texarkana postmark.

The question immediately rose in lawmen's and residents' minds: Was he murdered and his body set on the train track to cover up the crime, or had he been struck by the train and killed instantly? Opinions differed. The coroner, Dr. Frank G. Engler, empaneled a jury that returned a verdict coinciding with his own conclusion that McSpadden had died "at the hands of persons unknown." Dr. Engler believed McSpadden had been stabbed to death elsewhere and his body placed on the tracks to conceal the crime and perhaps make it *look* like an accident or suicide. The coroner said that although the body had been mangled, there were no bruises indicating that the man had fallen from a train. He cited a deep wound two inches long on the left temple, deep enough to have caused death, and cuts on the hands indicating the dead man had struggled with an assailant armed with a knife. He said McSpadden had been dead for at least two hours before the body was placed on the tracks, that there wasn't enough blood around the wounds that caused the death when the body was found. The left arm and leg had been severed. A freight train had passed the Ogden station at five-thirty that morning. Blood was discovered on the highway a short distance from where the body was found early that morning.

Little River County Sheriff Jim Sanderson strongly disagreed. He felt sure that the train had killed him without help from anyone else. He believed the death was accidental. He felt "absolutely certain" of it and considered the matter closed.

By then, any suspicious death in Texarkana was likely to gain widespread attention, fueling the rumor mill with a new frenzy of speculation. Few believed this death was connected with the earlier murders, though. It simply did not fit the profile.

Forty-seven officers, most of them special deputies, patrolled secluded lanes. None would be quoted, but the *Gazette* reported that "general sentiment of the majority [is] that the motive for the murder was one of sex mania."

An unnamed officer said, "I believe that a sex pervert is responsible." Off the record, one said he thought that in the first murders Griffin's pockets had been turned inside out in an effort to conceal the real motive.

In most minds, sexual assault, despite evidence to the contrary, was accepted as the chief motive. The news article built upon that existing belief.

"A diabolical killer," the story began, "believed to be a sex maniac, who blasted the peace of a modest farm home into a nightmare of blood and horror Friday night, remained at large Saturday night and it was feared he might strike again at any moment, at any place, at anyone."

On Sunday after the murder, three weeks since Betty Jo Booker and Paul Martin were shot to death, an eight-column, inch-high, all-capitals headline on page one of the *Gazette* proclaimed:

SEX MANIAC HUNTED IN MURDERS

A three-column picture of Katie Starks in her hospital bed, her head swathed in so much bandaging that she was unrecognizable, commanded a portion of the front page under the headline.

The prison riot at Alcatraz, tagged as "the most spectacular in the history of federal prisons," which had ended in the deaths of the convict ringleaders and two guards, with fourteen wounded, remained on page one but was swept from the main headline into a one-column story.

The Texarkana headline verified the suspicions and anxieties of thousands. Panic knew no bounds.

What type of man was responsible? The unknown factors promoted his mystique, making kings of rumors. The *Gazette* began looking for an expert who might offer insight. Two days after the Starks shooting, staffers found their man—Dr. Anthony Lapalla, a psychiatrist at the Texarkana Federal Correctional Institution.

Dr. Lapalla offered meager solace to a populace already up to their necks in fear. He predicted that the murderer was planning "something as unexpected as was the murder Friday night of Virgil Starks and the attempted murder of Mrs. Starks." He believed the same man had committed all of the crimes. "He may lay low for awhile, but eventually he probably will commit another crime."

He pegged the man to be about middle age, with a strong sex drive, a sadist. Such persons—intelligent, clever, and shrewd—Dr. Lapalla said, often are not apprehended.

Dr. Lapalla's theory held that the murderer knew at all times what was going on in the investigation and realized the outlying roads were being constantly patrolled. That would explain why he had struck the Starkses in their home instead of waylaying persons on the roads.

Basing his theory on case histories of similar criminals, he noted that such criminals often divert attention to a distant community, causing people to believe the crimes are unrelated, or else he may overcome his desire to kill and assault women.

Dr. Lapalla doubted the man had ever been confined in a mental institution. He also doubted he was a war veteran because such "maniacal tendencies" would have been observed while in the service. The killer wasn't necessarily a resident of the area, despite how well he seemed to know it. He could have come from another community but acquainted himself with the local situation before beginning his killing spree.

"This man is extremely dangerous, with a tremendous impulse to destroy," Dr. Lapalla emphasized. "He works alone, and no one knows what he is doing because he tells no one. He might be thought of as a good citizen. He probably has reasoned that the only way to remain unidentified is to kill all persons at the scene of his crime."

Although several black men had been picked up by then, Dr. Lapalla felt certain a white man was to blame.

With the unknown factor gnawing insidiously at every mind, Dr. Lapalla's insights soothed few nerves and only brought into the open old hidden fears. The Phantom could be anyone! Residents wondered about the man across the street, the respected businessman, the minister's son, or some returning veteran perversely reacting to his combat trauma.

Satisfied that the February beatings had been the early work of the same man who had attacked and killed other couples, J. Q. Mahaffey dispatched a reporter to Frederick, Oklahoma, to interview Mary Jeanne Larey, the young woman beaten in February. The editor contracted with Paul A. Burns, a printer, entrepreneur, and pilot, to fly Lucille Holland there. Burns's 65-horsepower, two-place side-by-side Luscombe Silvaire had a three-hour range and he expected to reach Frederick, Oklahoma, before dark. A stout headwind, however, slowed the plane significantly. He had to stop once to refuel, then land at Frederick in the dark after buzzing the field to bring the airport manager out to train car headlights on the field.

The teenaged Mary Jeanne insisted that the February 22 attack on her and Jimmy Hollis was the first in the series of crimes committed by the Phantom. She was sure of it beyond any doubt. She still did not understand why officers didn't believe her when she told them the man was black, an assessment with which Hollis had disagreed. But, she added, Texas Ranger Joe Thompson had flown to Frederick after the Martin-Booker murders and questioned her again.

"I believe now that the officers connect all of the crimes," she said.

She was trying to lead a normal life, but for the first time in her life, her aunt said, Mary Jeanne was "extremely nervous" and would neither sleep in a room alone nor go upstairs by herself. "And in her dreams," wrote Holland, "Mary Jeanne sees her attacker almost every night."

The following morning, Holland's story dominated the front page.

**MARY JEANNE LAREY DECLARES
MAN WHO ATTEMPTED TO ATTACK
HER ON FEB. 22 WAS PHANTOM**

A week after the Starks shootings, the traffic death toll remained stuck at fifteen. None had died from traffic in May, with thirty-one days since the last death. A total of fifty-six had been injured for the year, three in May. Gunshots had claimed more lives than traffic accidents over the past two months, a dramatic turnabout. The Phantom, competing with thousands of motorists, seemed to be winning the death game, hands down.

A current movie title featuring Richard Arlen reflected the rising tensions, titled *The Phantom Speaks*.

CHAPTER 12

A MEDIA INVASION

have arrived in Texarkana, the home of the Phantom killer. I have talked to a newspaperman named Graves. I am quartered at the Grim Hotel, and the hair is rising on my neck."

Kenneth Dixon, a popular columnist for the International News Service, wrote the most widely quoted lead about the Phantom case. A master of suspense like Alfred Hitchcock couldn't have produced a more tantalizing opening. It took an outsider like Dixon to see anything unusual about the landmark hotel or the surname of a respected local family.

The 250-room hotel, a source of civic pride, eight stories high with a rooftop garden, was named for the Pennsylvania-born banker William Rhoads Grim, dead since 1925.

Dixon, a veteran war correspondent who'd covered the European theater, arrived in town by bus from Kansas City. Most of the incoming news people used bus or train service, if they were beyond easy driving range. Sports editor Louis "Swampy" Graves escorted Dixon to the hotel, across the street from the newspaper office. Taking care of out-of-town reporters was a major assignment.

No other story had ever brought so much attention from the national news media. Reporters checked in from New York, Los Angeles, Chicago, and Miami. "They were intrigued not only with the Phantom and the Texas Rangers sent here by the governor," said editor Mahaffey, "but they were gripped by the mass hysteria our headlines had created in the city during March, April, and May."

Incoming news people added another dimension to the developing chaos. Mahaffey, serving as liaison, as he put it, "between the invading press and the local community," was to see more than he'd expected. "I didn't have to worry about the phantom killer," Mahaffey said years later. "I had a staff of pretty fair newspaper hands who were taking care of him—and in spades. My problem was the horde of newspaper and radio people that came to town from the big cities."

He subsequently reported his experience to his peers at the American Society of Newspaper Editors in Washington. "The mass media descends upon Texarkana," he said, "and all hell breaks loose. If some of the reporters and photographers sent to us had not been so old I would figure they were your rankest cubs. They had very bad manners, couldn't hold their whiskey, and they made passes at my girl reporters!

"One young squirt from one of the Western papers had the audacity to complain to me about the fact that he wasn't making much time with my girl reporters. He seemed to be totally unaware of the possibility that the girls were being true to me." The audience laughed.

Because of the preponderance of female reporters Mahaffey hired during the war, fellow editors called him "The Phil Spitalny of News-papers," referring to the director of the popular "All-Girls Orchestra" of that time.

Many reporters, he complained, weren't content merely to cover the murders but wanted "desperately" to become a part of the story, perhaps even solve the case themselves.

"The mass media proceeded to get themselves into all kinds of trouble. Two of them had a fight in the corridor of the Grim Hotel and got jugged for being drunk and disturbing the peace. Another was picked up for drunk driving. The officers found another in a parked car with one of my girl reporters—the one that was *not* being true to me. They said they were laying a trap for the Phantom. A likely story!"

Bob Carpenter of the Mutual Broadcasting System in New York City had arrived in Texarkana before INS reporter Ken Dixon, eventually doing a coast-to-coast broadcast hookup. The Blue Network, as it was also known, covered 315 stations in the nationwide broadcast.

Time and *Life* both sent a reporter and photographer. They sought several types of pictures: a long shot of Texarkana, Texas; long shot down "Fatal Lane" ("as it is now called") with Texas Rangers and officers from both sides simulating the investigation around the murder site at Spring Lake Park; three or four pictures of the victims, "being held so that camera can make the Closeup of the gruesome condition"; Captain Gonzaullas—"and his staff who have been placed in charge and to coordinate the search for the phantom killer . . . Gonzaullas giving instructions to the men, in front of a State Police Map—laying out the block system. . . . Whatever else Captain Gonzaullas can suggest that would help the buildup to a Dramatic Story. . . ."

All the reporter and photographer—and local cooperating officers—had to do was fill in the blanks.

A trumpeting headline in *Life*'s June 10, 1946, issue proclaimed to the world what the local residents already knew.

TEXARKANA TERROR
SOUTHERN CITY IS PANICKED BY KILLER
WHO SHOOTS ACCORDING TO SCHEDULE

The article described the city as "tight in the grip of mass terror." A two-page spread recounted the five murders, commenting that after the latest shooting "housewives in mounting hysteria were barricading themselves inside their homes and rigging up homemade alarms of pots and pans and string which their husbands kept tripping over. Friday passed, then Saturday and Sunday, without a murder. Texarkanians breathed a sigh of relief. But it was a small one. The Phantom was still at large."

The article did not exaggerate. One of the accompanying photographs shows a woman with two little boys leaving their imposing two-story brick Georgian-style home to stay at the city's downtown Hotel Grim during her attorney husband's absence from the city. The woman was Mrs. Janet Sheppard Arnold and her sons, ten-year-old Richard S. Arnold and four-year-old Morris S. "Buzz" Arnold, each of whom later would become a federal judge. Eventually Richard and Morris Arnold served together on the Eighth Circuit Court of Appeals based in St. Louis, Morris appointed by a Republican, Richard by a Democrat. Each was to be mentioned as a possible Supreme Court nominee. She was the daughter of the late U.S. Senator Morris Sheppard (D-Texas); her husband, the prominent attorney Richard L. Arnold. Each morning they would return to the family home. Less affluent residents bolted their doors, nailed down their windows, and cowered in the dark, sleeping fitfully, praying for the dawn, greeting each new day with eyes red-rimmed and puffy. If the man of the house was out of town, his family spent the night with relatives or neighbors. What there was of a tourist business dried up. Travelers didn't want to spend the night in Texarkana with the Phantom still at large.

The city was under siege by both print and radio media. Colonel Homer P. Garrison, director of the Texas Department of Public Safety, telegrammed Captain Gonzaullas:

UNIVERSAL NEWS REEL COMPANY IS SENDING CAMERAMAN JIMMY LEDERER TO TEXARKANA TO MAKE SOME BACKGROUND SHOTS. ANY COURTESY EXTENDED TO HIM WILL BE APPRECIATED.

Gonzaullas's boss in Austin need not have worried that his man would snub a newsreel camera likely to further burnish the reputation of the colorful Ranger force. Gonzaullas had had many years of experience in dealing with the press and radio and relished it. An Associated Press reporter—among others—quoted Gonzaullas, his eyes bloodshot from lack of sleep, as saying of the Phantom, "I'd give that fellow two shots at me if I could get one shot at him!" He wasn't likely to have the opportunity. The Phantom didn't go in for dramatic Old West high-noon showdowns. He preferred the dark, with unarmed and unsuspecting victims.

Sensationalism whipped the flames of fear. Much of the rank speculation was simply false, including an out-of-town news report that a "sex
maniac" had mutilated the female victims' bodies, had dabbled his
hands in blood, neither of which had happened but which many in the
town believed. Locally, gunshot and prowler calls turned out to be cars
backfiring or a prowling cat thrashing about in a garbage can. A more
hopeful local rumor had the killer in jail, guarded by Texas Rangers with
submachine guns. Reporters, as well as the public, were caught up in the
frenzy. Nor were veteran newspaper people immune to the scare they had
helped generate. Mahaffey himself, a veteran at covering gore-and-guns
stories, personified the reality of a region on edge. He could hardly sleep.
One Saturday night, a pounding at his front door brought him face to
face with a dreaded crisis.

"Let me in there! Let me in there!" came a man's raucous shouts.

Aroused from a light sleep, Mahaffey and wife Ruth exchanged tense
looks. They left their bed without another word. He grabbed his son's
baseball bat. "Who's there?" Mahaffey called out in a quavering voice
from the kitchen. "Get away from that door!"

It was a false alarm, but a heart-thumping one. The instigator turned
out to be a harmless meandering old drunk, lost and confused, looking
for his home. The drunk was lucky. A man armed with more than a baseball bat might have blown him away first and not given him a chance to
identify himself and assuage fears.

The Phantom story spread to far reaches of the globe and to Texarkana's
servicemen overseas. Joe Forgy, with the Army of Occupation in Germany,
read about it in *Stars and Stripes*. Don Preston, a soldier stationed in
Luxembourg, learned of it in another national magazine. Henry Jackson,
with the Navy in the Far East, saw a Texarkana dateline heading the story
in the English-language Shanghai *Evening Mercury*. Marines and sailors
found details in other international and West Coast newspapers.

Texarkana was on the map, for a reason nobody wanted to brag about.

Uplifting events, with crowds, offered welcome respites. Bluff, hearty
Charles B. Driscoll, syndicated columnist of "New York Day by Day," flew
into town for several festive days capped by a speech to a sold-out audience. By then he'd read of the local bad news in New York newspapers.

As if to dispel residents' jitters, he said, "New York papers just would not go to press at all if there were not at least five murders a day." His friends in the Big Apple had warned him of the risks in Texarkana, but he shrugged it off. "These Texarkana crimes will soon be solved and the guilty person apprehended." His optimism failed to infect the crimes' investigators.

Tension radiated throughout the region, as far as a hundred miles or more.

In Lewisville, Arkansas, in another county, Sheriff Ocie Smith Griffin received calls almost every night from those who insisted they'd seen the Phantom. Even his daughter Jo, home from college, joined the Nervous Nellies. One night while sleeping peacefully in her upstairs bedroom, she was awakened by a noise. She thought it came from their old wooden garage. Peering out, she saw a man headed for the garage. She raced downstairs and alerted her father. "The Phantom is in our garage!" Unconvinced, he finally agreed to shoot the Phantom so all could get some sleep. He opened the front door and shot into the sky. In the next instant, the sheriff's car, which had been parked in the garage, barreled out, into a deep ditch. Two men jumped out and sprinted to the woods. They were trying to steal his car. After Jo saved his automobile, Sheriff Griffin stopped calling her a Nervous Nellie.

Twice as far off in Texas, Phantomania also took its toll. The Amerson family out of Mt. Pleasant, sixty miles from Texarkana, felt vulnerable when the father worked a night shift at a refinery. Concerned over her seven children, Mary Amerson draped quilts over the windows, propped a chair under the doorknob. Nobody stepped outside after dark. In Little Rock, 165 miles away, Dottie Morrissey recalled, people were "scared to death" of the Phantom.

As panic continued unabated, Mahaffey became convinced that something—anything that might work—had to be done to reduce the mounting hysteria and foster stability. Radio was king of the airways. Everybody tuned in. Why not let a major authority figure provide reassuring words to the community? Who better to deliver the message than Lone Wolf Gonzaullas? Mahaffey arranged for an appearance on Radio Station KCMC, the Voice of Texarkana, situated upstairs in the *Gazette* Building. He would frame the questions to the legendary figure, leading to a soothing effect on their listeners, who would realize that safety encircled them.

Soon after the introduction, the editor eased into his pivotal question.

"Captain Gonzaullas, what would be your advice to the people of Texarkana who are so frightened at this time?"

He settled back in his chair, a benign smile brightening his face, to admire the famed lawman's thoughtful, steadying observation that Rangers and other lawmen had the situation under control, were on guard twenty-four hours a day, and could assure them that the killer would not, could not strike again.

"Well," said Gonzaullas, "my advice would be for everyone to lock up their houses as tight as they can and to oil up their guns and see if they are loaded or get 'em a double-barreled shotgun. Put them out of the reach of children. Do not use them unless it's necessary, *but if you believe it is, do not hesitate to shoot!*"

Mahaffey's smile faded faster than it had appeared. It was the exact opposite of what he thought would have come out of Lone Wolf's mouth. A fresh wave of hysteria whisked through the studio. He quickly changed the subject.

Mahaffey soon confirmed what he had already suspected, that the notoriety of the case, hyped to a great extent by the local press as well as by those from out of town, was doing great harm to his city, from the virtually complete disappearance of the tourism industry, to a drying up of night entertainment, as well as nervous daylight shopping. Flashy journalism, coming from a variety of directions, had created a stigma and exacerbated fears.

At the annual meeting of the Associated Press Managing Editors that year, an editor from New England inspected Mahaffey's badge and said, "Oh, Texarkana! One of the survivors, I presume."

Another editor friend from the East called Mahaffey one day and began his conversation, "Hey, Jake, anybody still alive down there?"

CHAPTER 13

LAW AND DISORDER

Without a clue of any kind these men have been called upon to solve one of the worst tragedies that has struck the south in many years. These men are working day and night."

The Time-Life instructions for the story, though dispatched from far-off New York, framed the plight of the investigators as accurately as anyone could have.

Indeed, "these men" were doing exactly that, with a variety of results, not always up to the expectations of a terrified public.

A culture of fear, fanned by the media, enveloped the region. The citizenry girded as for war. Weapons and blinds sold briskly. By the Friday after the Starks shooting, there were no window shades and few Venetian blinds left in Texarkana stores. One store manager said sales of blinds were up fifty percent over normal. Other customers frantically bought grilles for windows, window sash locks, screen door hooks, night latches, and other protective devices. Classified ads documented the emergency: *Watch dogs wanted. Watch dogs for sale.*

"Texarkanians were nervous and jumpy," reported the *Daily News*, the *Gazette*'s afternoon sister paper. "In their minds most of them pictured the killer as a sex fiend with an insatiable lust for blood."

Police busily responded to calls from widely scattered neighborhoods and remote locations. Reports of gunshots in the night often turned out to be backfiring automobiles. Delivery boys like Hayden Coe dreaded going out after dark but had no choice. Dortha Hale Stone lived with her married sister; for safety, five slept in the same room. Her brother-in-law kept a gun inches away. Bill Blocker was one of hundreds who tried to buy guns. His long-barreled .38 Special was back-ordered and arrived too late to do him any good. When Jim Boyd, Jr., took Charlsie Schoeppey to the Texas High prom in May, they and other couples were escorted in and later out by officers, with a warning: "If you go out to eat after the dance, go to Two States Coffee Shop." Open around the clock, with police usually present, it was a safe public venue.

Only dawn brought relief—until the next night.

Few behaved as if immune, but residents of one house on County Avenue in Arkansas stood out. Curtains on the large picture window were never pulled at night. You could see the occupants walking to and fro, while their neighbors hovered behind tightly bolted doors and darkened windows. Either they felt safe, when thousands did not, or they simply had not succumbed to the hysteria that cloaked their neighbors. They were in the tiniest of minorities.

Uneasy residents bombarded the police with prowler calls. Most complaints were readily explained and nonthreatening, but each one had to be checked out. One call seemed to be the real McCoy—two bodies in a front yard on County Avenue, a well-traveled street. Policemen, brandishing guns, closed in on two Hereford heifers. Somehow escaped from a cattle truck downtown, the cattle had plodded along till they decided to bed down for the night. Residents seeing white faces in the dark on the lawn had assumed the worst.

Other incidents were less easily explained. On the Texas side one Saturday morning, a stranger approached an eleven-year-old girl on the sidewalk. He offered to take her home. She ignored him and kept walking.

He drove away. Police advised parents to warn their children to steer clear of all strangers. It was a sensible policy.

Suspects turned up in almost every city, no matter how far off. Four days after the Starks shootings, a white gunman at Kilgore, Texas, over a hundred miles away, forced a black motorist to drive him to Lufkin, another East Texas town. He brandished two pistols and claimed to be the Phantom killer. Releasing his victim, the gunman apparently stole a car and escaped. Captain Gonzaullas wasn't impressed. He didn't think the Phantom would boast about his crimes or let his victim go.

Ultimately, more than a thousand suspects—1,300, by one count—were checked out and dismissed. Numerous enough to populate a small village, the detained or sought men often had little in common: an escaped prisoner of war in Arkansas; a knife-wielding assailant in Oklahoma; a carnival worker from South Dakota arrested in Oklahoma City after buying a bus ticket to Texarkana; a number of war veterans interrogated for various reasons.

The dragnet spread. A twenty-one-year-old Air Corps veteran in Los Angeles feared he might have been involved. He had been in Texarkana, had been in a coma, but was soon cleared.

Murders elsewhere earned scrutiny for any similarity to the Texarkana crimes. When a young couple was shot to death in Fort Lauderdale, Florida, a connection appeared likely. The murder weapon was a .32 automatic. The MO was the same as the Texas double slayings, in which a .32 Colt automatic with six lands and grooves and a left-hand twist was used. The Florida murder weapon, though, was a .32 *Savage* automatic with six lands and grooves and a *right-hand* twist. Close, but no match.

Officers received offers of "help" on every hand: written, telephoned, even telegraphed, and mostly going to Gonzaullas. One man with "psychic powers" quoted thirteen chapters from First Corinthians before promising to lower an "orantal boom" on the killer if lawmen would donate the "bounty." None provided tangible leads that officers could take to heart.

Certain legal activities registered a marked decline. In Miller County's May 22 report, only three couples applied for marriage licenses, with four of the individuals from out of town, half of those from other states.

Only one divorce suit was filed in the period: Peggy Tresnick vs. Stanley Tresnick. The couple had married in 1944. The soldier husband, from Pennsylvania, had gone overseas and had never returned to her after the war. She claimed desertion.

Crime, unlike legal filings, persisted. Early on Friday, May 24, three weeks after the Starks murder, J. E. Andrews from the Texas side parked his 1941 Chevrolet two-door sedan in front of the State National Bank just on the Arkansas side downtown. It was 8:45 A.M. When he came back a half hour later, his car was gone. Early morning. Downtown. Broad daylight. The gall of the two men who had tried to steal the sheriff's car was not in short supply amongst thieves, who perhaps even felt emboldened with law enforcement so distracted with their hunt for the Phantom.

As the case remained unsolved amid a tense populace, lawmen became a target of citizen scorn. Officers weren't trying hard enough, some believed. Aware that officers of all jurisdictions frequently collected for meals and coffee at a popular downtown café just under the sheriff's office, one cynic predicted, "If the Phantom ever walks into John's Place, they'll catch him!"

Another critic late one night strolled into the café crowded with pistol-totin', Western-bedecked lawmen. He took one look and hooted:

"Ten thousand dollars worth of cowboy boots and big white hats—and fifteen cents' worth of brains!"

He was fortunate to escape arrest for public drunkenness.

As befitted the most colorful lawman with the highest profile and a take-charge personality, Ranger Captain Gonzaullas generated the largest share of anecdotes, many of them, never publicly revealed, unlikely to enhance his image.

Editor Mahaffey termed Gonzaullas "my principal headache."

"He didn't have time to hunt for the Phantom—he was too busy giving out interviews and trying to run the *Gazette*," said Mahaffey. "All the other officers working on the case became rather jealous of Lone Wolf and complained bitterly every time his picture appeared in the paper."

Newsman Graves, who perceived Gonzaullas as warmhearted and sincere ("It was hard to believe he'd killed twenty or so men"), agreed that the Texarkana assignment was not the best use of his abilities. "He was not a detective," said Graves. "He was better on horseback and shooting."

Tillman Johnson, the Miller County chief deputy, held a similar view. "Whenever Gonzaullas came down the stairs from his hotel room, he called for the press. He was a showman, and he had a reputation for being a killer. So the press all followed him.

"He didn't do any real police work himself. He'd get in that car and ride around, ask a lot of questions about what the other officers had found. Then he'd release it to the press like it was his information. After a while, some officers got to where they wouldn't tell him anything."

One day while the investigation was at white heat, Bill Presley was driving on the Texas side with Gonzaullas. Tillman Johnson and Max Tackett sat in the back seat.

After they had discussed several angles to the case and some current suspects, Gonzaullas suddenly said, "I'm not going to leave Texarkana until we solve this case!"

Johnson ("I was kind of a smart-ass back then"), fully aware of the slow, nonexistent progress of the case, piped up from the back seat. "Have you bought you a home here yet, Captain?"

The long silence that ensued told Johnson he was in Lone Wolf's doghouse from then on.

As a veteran of gun battles, Gonzaullas knew how to prevent an ambush. Although he was never shot in the back in Texarkana, his preparations weren't always flawless. He never realized that Dorothy Blanchett, agent for Texas Air Lines in the Grim Hotel lobby, kept a .45 revolver in her desk drawer each time he held news briefings a few feet in front of her. He was safe, but only she knew why. Keeping the weapon handy was standard, having nothing to do with the murder case, but to protect receipts paid the airline.

Another day as he was walking down Pine Street near the *Gazette*, pleasantly chatting with reporter Ruth Bryan, she surreptitiously slipped her hand to his pearl-handled pistol, gripped the handle, gingerly lifted it from its holster, and presented it to the astonished Ranger, a playful prank its victim was loath to advertise. Fortunately for his public image, these anecdotes never saw print, nor did they diminish the magnetism he exerted on young reporters. He continued to be "good copy."

Resentment toward Gonzaullas boiled over in the days after the Starks murder. J. Q. Mahaffey was at the Miller County sheriff's office, talking with trooper Max Tackett, when an urgent telephone call came. Following the shooting, the Starks home had been put off limits. But just now, a neighbor reported seeing strange lights in the farmhouse.

Tackett dashed to his car, Mahaffey close behind. They sped to the scene. As police cars converged on the farmhouse, Tackett got out, joined by three other policemen. As Mahaffey crouched behind one of the police cars, unwilling to test anyone's aim, Tackett and the patrolmen, guns drawn, fanned out toward the house.

Tackett yelled out, "WE'VE GOT THE HOUSE SURROUNDED. YOU MAY AS WELL GIVE UP. COME OUT WITH YOUR HANDS UP!"

The front door to the house opened slowly, tentatively, and a head, bedecked by a large white hat, cautiously peered out.

"Hold your fire!" came a man's voice.

Mahaffey stood up from behind the car to see Lone Wolf Gonzaullas himself emerge, accompanied by a female photographer from *Life* and *Time*.

"What are you doing here?" Tackett asked, more than a little peeved.

"I was just reenacting the crime for her," replied the Ranger, rather sheepishly, "and she was taking some pictures." The flash bulbs accounted for the strange lights seen in the house.

Tackett exploded with exasperation. He turned to the editor and shouted at the top of his voice, for the benefit of all within earshot, *"Mahaffey, you can quote me as saying that the Phantom murders will never be solved until Texarkana gets rid of the big city press and the Texas Rangers!"*

The minor league Texarkana Bears became a major beneficiary of the troubled times. Fans could forget the Phantom for a few hours, find safety among thousands, and be entertained. Owner Dick Burnett offered a bonus: hard-to-find beer, out-of-state Griesedieck, from St. Louis. A talented club kept the fans excited—southpaw Jinx Poindexter, who had pitched for Connie Mack's Philadelphia A's; fireballer Vallie Eaves and power hitter Vernon "General Gawge" Washington, both former Chicago White Sox players; and Bit McCulloch, Hal Simpson, Hal Van Pelt, and Gabby Lusk. Cold beer, hot baseball, cheering people all around you: the games drew more than at much larger Little Rock. Once the game was over, people seemed reluctant to head home.

Summer brought a cautious return to "normal." On June 17, eight were injured in a car collision in Miller County. Two days later, the heralded Louis-Conn rematch at Yankee Stadium ended with Joe Louis keeping his heavyweight title by knocking out challenger Billy Conn in eight rounds. A series of weddings followed in the Texarkana area, some with links to the murders of the spring: Robert M. Hollis (beating victim Jim Hollis's brother) and Lorraine Fairchild (with whom he'd double-dated that terrible night); Howard Giles (the new Texarkana, Arkansas, finger-print specialist) and Ossie Jean Mote; Eleanor Bernice Griffin (Richard Griffin's sister) and Jesse Alva Proctor; and Bill Blocker (who'd bought a new revolver that arrived when the worst was over) and Wanda Ann Wood. Additionally, Peggy Tresnick, nee Stevens, who had sued her soldier husband on grounds of desertion, received her divorce on June 27. The spring's traumatic events had claimed their victims and left long-lasting scars, but life was still moving on.

Stakeouts designed to nab the Phantom became mostly dull exercises in which tedium dominated, but a few patrols produced the unexpected.

One night deputy Tillman Johnson, a tall, cool sort of man who himself had been shot at in the line of duty, was patrolling with trooper Charley Boyd and came upon a couple parked on the Sugar Hill Road north of town. Johnson got out and walked up to the car. Boyd remained in the police car to cover Johnson. The couple cuddled in the back seat of the parked car.

Johnson identified himself and proceeded to lecture them. "There's a killer loose. Aren't you scared to be parked out here at night?"

"You're the one that ought to be scared, Mister," said the girl. "It's a good thing you told me who you are. I was ready for the killer."

She'd held a .25 caliber pistol on him all the time.

Finding lonely, isolated sites for stakeouts was no problem. The rural environs of Texarkana abounded with them.

One dark night, Bill Presley and two colleagues drove an unmarked coupe onto a dirt lane branching off Highway 67, a few miles west of town. It was a perfect setting for a love-struck young couple seeking privacy—or for a would-be killer stalking them. They parked the car with two store dummies inside, propped snugly by each other to simulate cozy sweethearts. The officers slipped into the grass and bushes nearby and quietly waited. All were heavily armed. Presley clutched a submachine gun. They waited. And waited. And waited.

About an hour later, a car turned off the highway onto the dirt road. It moved slowly, then on past. Yards ahead, it stopped. It had run into a dead-end, as the officers knew it would. The suspect car turned around.

"We've got him now!" Presley whispered excitedly to the others.

As the car moved slowly back to the set-up, the officers as one rose up, pointing guns. "Get out, with your hands up!" Presley shouted.

The car stopped. Out came the driver and two women, visibly shaken.

The driver, his hands hoisted as high as they would go and his lips twitching, identified himself, his wife, and another woman. One woman's legs were quivering. They were lost.

It was the nearest officers came to capturing anyone that night.

The day-and-night routines exhausted officers. None slept soundly or long. Sheriff Presley, like many others, slept in his clothes an hour or two at a stretch. Usually an immaculate dresser, he once went a week without changing clothes. One day, while talking to a friend in Boyd's Drugs, he tried to explain the status of the investigation.

"Well, we've had a lead or two, but so far we—" The sheriff's words trailed off in midsentence. His eyes fluttered and closed. He slumped.

"Grab him. Bill's gone to sleep!" his friend yelled as he reached out.

Feeling hands upon him, Presley's red-rimmed eyes opened, surprise upon his face.

"Every day just wore you down," summarized Howard Giles, the Arkansas-side fingerprint specialist.

Meanwhile, technology forged ahead. Local residents learned that on January 1, 1947, dial telephones would come to Texarkana.

As promising as telephone technology appeared, it lagged far behind what was to come. The same was true of forensic science. Today's crime labs make those of 1946 seem primitive by comparison. On all fronts in Texarkana, lawmen struggled. They lacked the tools available today in a major case. No computerized fingerprint searches. No refined ballistics techniques. No advanced fiber and blood analyses. No standardized crime-scene protocols to be followed without exception. No psychological and criminal profiling that the FBI and other agencies have developed to an art and science. No depth of knowledge of serial-killer behavior that has accrued over the years; it took a while to realize that they were dealing with a serial killer. Most of all, DNA studies were far in the future.

Serial murders are perplexing under any circumstances, even today. But without the advances made over the past six decades, officers too often faced a wall. Had they benefited from today's science, especially DNA, they might well have broken the mystery to everyone's satisfaction.

That said, lawmen themselves made miscues that even today would jeopardize their hard work. But if they'd known what investigators now know routinely, through training and application, they might have avoided those blunders. They might have, for instance, ordered autopsies on all the bodies, possibly disclosing evidence unseen by eyes alone, even latent fingerprints on victims' bodies. For one thing, a proper autopsy would have recovered the bullets from Polly Ann Moore's body. It wouldn't have revised the cause of death, which was obvious, but other data might have surfaced. Certainly autopsies would have provided more details as to sexual abuse or rape, though FBI records do document that in the Booker case. With today's DNA science, the semen found on her body could be compared to the DNA of any major suspect who might be arrested. At the time, there was no medical examiner to study the bodies, though a physician did ascertain that Miss Moore had not been raped. Only justices of the peace ruled the cause of death. DNA evidence also could have been collected from the cigarette butts left near the car parked across from the Starks home.

Officers, often with an assist from good citizens, muddled the picture. This was especially true in the Griffin-Moore case. The crime scene, already compromised by rain, was left unprotected, to be trampled by the feet of the morbidly curious. Compounding the matter, no care was taken to isolate Richard Griffin's car from being touched by the gawkers;

police themselves pushed the car by hand, adding their own prints and possibly smudging or erasing suspect evidence.

In the Martin-Booker murders, the crime scene was preserved somewhat better, but the distance created its own problem. The search for Betty Jo Booker's body, though necessary, may have destroyed other evidence such as tracks.

The Starks case, despite initial efforts to seal off the house and yard, soon presented a muddled crime scene. Mostly visiting lawmen did what gawkers had done in the first Texas slayings. Even the bloody footprint saved by the FBI agents probably wasn't that of the killer. Too many men had passed through the house and grounds. The tracks in the plowed field probably were those of the killer but were too squishy to compare to a shoe or boot.

Today's improved ballistics science might establish whether the .22 bullets at the Starks home came from a rifle or a pistol, possibly narrowing the search.

Without a fingerprint identification or an eyewitness, the investigation then, as it would today, boiled down to human information. No valid confession was likely. Hordes of people offered their suspicions, which landed their targets in custody temporarily, but none really qualified as an eyewitness. One man did see the killer's car speed away from the Spring Lake Park murders. Unfortunately the car had been too far away in the dim dawn to make clear the license plates or the driver's face.

The best human information came from the Hollis-Larey case, though the victims disagreed on crucial features of the criminal. Officers refused to connect the case to the murders until months later. Without some sort of human information, especially a degree of eyewitness evidence, investigators were likely to continue to grope in the dark.

They didn't know where to look for the killer or what he was like. They could only persist without letup and pray for a lucky break.

CHAPTER 14

BEHIND A SERIAL KILLER'S FAÇADE

If serial killers gloat over their misdeeds, they almost never do so publicly, and rarely to other individuals. Doing so would betray them. To risk exposure would court severe punishment. Although they may be proud of what they've done—frustrating the police, terrifying the public at large—and revel in their notoriety, their crimes are so monstrous that they will go to any length to thwart detection.

Mostly their efforts will be aimed at keeping a low personal profile to avoid arrest and denying culpability, much as might any lesser criminal. This is not to say that some may not taunt the police, once they believe they can safely do so. A few grow so arrogant as to dare lawmen to find them or learn their identity. And some few, once captured and facing certain punishment, may agree to cooperate with their captors by revealing their actions, usually in hopes of evading a death penalty.

On those rare occasions when a serial killer does talk of his exploits (most, but not all, serial killers are male), some of the mystery recedes. Those moments have been infrequent, but revealing. One classic example is that of Alexander Pichushkin, a Russian convicted of killing forty-eight individuals and attempting to kill three others. The thirty-three-year-old former supermarket worker was called the Chessboard Killer; he placed coins on the squares of a chessboard as a way to keep a running total of his victims. He lacked only No. 64 when police apprehended him, indicating even more deaths than he was charged with.

He killed his victims in Moscow's sprawling 6.6-square-mile Bittsa Park, promising vodka to those he lured there. He smashed their skulls with a hammer or threw them into sewage pits after getting them drunk. Most of the victims were men, many of them homeless. When the killings accelerated in 2005, the public panicked. Pichushkin later said that police had stopped him repeatedly for identity checks but had let him go. He was finally arrested when officers found his name and phone number on a piece of paper in his last victim's apartment, a woman who worked with him. At first he denied any connection with her death. Then police presented subway surveillance camera footage showing them together, and he confessed and led police to bodies of other victims. "As we were heading to the park and talking," he said, "I kept thinking whether to kill her or to take caution. But finally I decided to take a risk. I was in that mood already." Three men survived being thrown into sewage pits, and one was able to identify him.

Calm and aloof, Pichushkin said he had first killed a classmate in 1992 when he was eighteen. Though questioned in that case, he was never charged. The Bittsa Park murders began about a decade later.

When sentenced to life in prison—the first fifteen years to be in solitary confinement—Pichushkin's words to the court, as quoted by the McClatchy News Service out of Moscow, documented the heights of grandiosity he had ascended as a result of his crimes.

"I have now been detained for 500 days. All this time, my fate has been decided by a huge number of people—cops, lawyers, prosecutors, judges, jurors," he said. "In my time I myself have decided the fate of sixty people. I was an executioner. I decided myself who would live, and who would not. I was almost a god.

"For me, a life without murder is like a life without food for you. I felt like the father of all these people, since it was I who opened the door for them to another world."

He emphasized that he never robbed his victims. "I don't need junk, even if it's very valuable. I'm only interested in human life. That's more precious than anything. I took the most valuable thing."

No one would argue his point on the value of what he'd taken. His grandiose assertions offer little insight into *why* he had killed so many or why he would have taken more lives had he not been apprehended. His words do tell us how at least one serial killer felt about his "accomplishments." By indirection we may gain a glimpse into the inner workings of a mind that *needed* this feeling of god-like power.

The granting of life or death is a basic, primitive expression of power. In the lives of serial killers, the delivery of death affords a sense of power they don't publicly or legally have. This, in turn, suggests a perceived need for control or power that comes forth in extralegal means on a one-on-one basis. Whether an individual death stands as a symbol for revenge or anger upon a larger segment of society, or as a surrogate for other individuals, may not be readily determined. But in any instance, the killings are likely to continue until some event—arrest, accident, death, institutionalization, intensive surveillance, retreat to a new location—intervenes.

Compared to Pichushkin's numbers, the Phantom's toll was paltry—only five known dead, three injured. To each victim's family and friends, however, the pain was as great, as deep, as anything experienced by survivors of Pichushkin's murderous impulses. Just as important, in comparing the tolls in Moscow and Texarkana, the small American twin city was relatively harder hit. Moscow, an industrial center and the Russian capital, with a population of well over 10 million, was at least 200 times larger, even though the Moscow killer restricted his malefaction to a portion of the city that was in his "comfort zone."

Did the Phantom, like Pichushkin, also feel god-like as he shot his innocent victims? Probably. He demonstrated his power. He made headlines (or vice versa). An entire community feared him. He was known, albeit by his moniker, nationwide, even abroad. His name, as "the Phantom," was on everyone's lips. Policemen sought him futilely. He had committed perfect crimes, attesting to his skills and brilliance. He had outsmarted the smartest. He was "almost god-like." In 1946 he must have felt what Pichushkin, thousands of miles away, did sixty years later.

If Pichushkin gave us a quick glance inside his mind, he left vast areas yet to be explored when it comes to trying to understand the psychology of a serial killer. Fortunately we don't have to rely solely on a Russian serial killer's courtroom outbursts for a peek into the inner workings of this peculiarly perverse pathology. The past several decades have generated a vast amount of data that dispels much, but far from all, of the mystery.

What, exactly, is a serial killer? Clearly Pichushkin qualified. So did the Texarkana Phantom. How do they differ from other killers of multiple victims—the spree killer and the mass murderer?

These questions were addressed in a three-day symposium sponsored by the FBI in San Antonio in 2005. Participants included 135 subject-matter experts from ten different countries on five continents. Serial killers may be found anywhere in the world, in many guises in many cultures.

For purposes of law enforcement, a definition was adopted.

"The unlawful killing of two or more victims by the same offender(s), in separate events."

An older description, cited by FBI agent John Douglas and others, classified such a killer as "someone who has murdered on at least three occasions, with what we call an emotional cooling-off period between each incident. This cooling-off period can be days, weeks, months, even years. Occasionally, it is only hours. But the important consideration is that each event is emotionally distinct and separate."

The Phantom case fits either definition.

With the spree killer, there is no cooling-off period.

The mass murderer kills four or more at one time and place.

Douglas, known to millions via television, has called serial killers "the most bewildering, personally disturbing, and most difficult to catch of all violent criminals." Because they're motivated by more complex factors than other criminals, their patterns are more confusing. But they have three intentions in common: manipulation, domination, and control.

Douglas and others categorize the killers by how they behave at the crime scene—whether they are organized, disorganized, or a mixture of the two types.

The *organized offender* takes measures to protect himself from suspicion and arrest. He is careful. He often moves the body from the death scene, postponing its discovery and giving him time to distance himself. He often has an uneven work history. Though sexually inadequate, he is socially adept, which may help him catch his victim unawares. His intelligence is average or above average.

The *disorganized offender*, on the other hand, may become impulsive under stress and leave the murder weapon or other evidence at the scene. He is, in a word, sloppy—disorganized. He also tends to be sexually incompetent. He claims to be heterosexual but seems to be ignorant of sex and may have sexual aversions. (A psychiatrist in another analysis has ascribed a fluid sexuality to serial killers, enabling them to function as either heterosexuals or homosexuals.)

The *mixed offender* exhibits characteristics of both types, blending organized and disorganized behavior.

The Texarkana killer demonstrated both organized and disorganized features. He moved the bodies of Richard Griffin and Polly Moore into the car so they would not be discovered for hours; Betty Jo Booker's body also was left in a wooded area. He left no fingerprints. He was prepared, taking a gun and, at least twice, a flashlight to the scene. These fit into the organized category. But he also exhibited spells of disorganization: he left Paul Martin's body in plain sight, and he left the flashlight outside the Starks home.

These patterns would earn him a *mixed* label, tending toward *organized*.

Though categories tell us the *types* of serial killers, they do not offer much of a profile fitting a certain perpetrator.

The first profile of the Phantom killer came in early 1946—from his first victim, Jimmy Hollis, who from his up-close encounter pictured the assailant as a young white man, not over thirty, and desperate. It wasn't much to go on and officers ignored it, but in time other analyses supported his view, as professional insights contributed additional patterns. The government psychiatrist Dr. Anthony Lapalla made valid points months later that are hard to fault. Unfortunately, he confirmed the public's worst fears by suggesting that the killer could be virtually *anyone*.

Twenty-five years later, in 1971, three Texarkana psychiatrists provided comments based on public information then known. Dr. James H. Thomas, the only one who'd lived in the area during the murders, believed the Phantom was a psychopathic personality or sexual deviate or both. He doubted the killer was a war veteran, because his warped personality would have been detected and rejected. Dr. Russell Walling, another psychiatrist, agreed that the man probably was a psychopathic personality, devoid of conscience. "They don't have feelings of anxiety, except when they are apprehended. Then they become very anxious," he said.

A third psychiatrist agreed with the psychopathic, or sociopathic, designation. Dr. Luther White, who'd taken his residency at Massachusetts General Hospital, cited the criminal's rage as probably mostly directed against women, that he was angry at his mother and fearful he'd be punished severely by his father if he didn't live up to expectations. He doubted the killer had raped his victims or, if he had, he thought he had done it only once. "When women become manifestations of the person's mother, sex becomes incest, in a sense, and therefore forbidden," he said.

Dr. White established the killer's age as well into his twenties or older—"old enough to have experienced failure vocationally and in his masculine role. He felt inadequate as a man. I think he had failed a lot up to that. A successful person would be less likely to commit such a crime." Dr. White also concluded that the killer was insecure in confronting people and needed a weapon, with his victim at a disadvantage, as happened.

He estimated the killer's intelligence as low average, even a bit below average. "It doesn't take much of an IQ to get in trouble." He believed the killer had had prior criminal experience, possibly had learned police tactics in jail, and also took pride in being tough.

These views, of course, were at best preliminary, delivered by professionals who did not specialize in forensic medicine, dealing with limited information about the case.

In recent decades, profiling, as well as explaining, such criminals has developed into a refined science. Experts can now delve much deeper into the behavior, patterns, and motives of serial killers as well as other murderers. From this reservoir of research we can draw a better likeness of such offenders, though still far from knowing the last word on the subject.

Serial murders are relatively rare, amounting to less than one percent of all murders in a given year. But while the number of serial killers is relatively small, the social impact of sheer terror in a large population is beyond measuring.

Overall, it is risky to generalize what type of person a serial killer could be. Some may be dysfunctional loners; not all are. As the 2005 FBI symposium put it, some *seem* to be normal, with families and jobs. They may blend in. "Many serial killers hide in plain sight within their communities." Nor are they all white males; they come from all racial groups. (One expert, criminologist Jack Levin, has estimated that seventy-five percent of serial killers act alone, while one fourth have an accomplice.)

Not all serial killers are sexually motivated. Other motivations—anger, thrill, financial gain, attention seeking—may play strong roles. In serial murder, motive is difficult to isolate. The killer may have more than one motive or may develop other motives as he adds to his deadly toll. Focusing on a motive doesn't necessarily lead to a prime suspect. Anger repeatedly turns up in psychological assessments.

"Regardless of the motive," the 2005 consensus statement reminded, "serial murderers commit their crimes because they want to."

In most homicides, the killer and victim know each other. This enables the police to round up suspects in a timely manner. But in serial murder, the killer and victim rarely know each other. The term once used, "stranger killings," remains descriptive. The killer benefits by having strangers for victims, making it much more difficult for police to track him. It could be anyone. As Northeastern University professor of criminal justice Jack Levin observed in another setting, "Most serial killers—especially those who manage to stay on the loose—target strangers. The last thing they want is to be connected back to the people they victimize." This also partially explains why serial killers don't usually kill those they associate with, even if those people may already harbor vital information about them, may even have been witnesses or confederates. Harming their associates could directly draw attention and possibly lead to arrest.

"Most serial killers have very defined geographical areas of operation," experts at the FBI symposium agreed. "They conduct their killings within comfort zones that are often defined by anchor points (e.g., place of residence, employment, or residence of a relative)." Sometimes they go outside the comfort zone either to avoid arrest or when they've grown more confident and move to new territory.

In either case, according to John Douglas, driving around may become a habitual pattern. As the killer scouts out the territory, he familiarizes himself with landmarks and potential sites for his practices. (In Texarkana, that seemed to be lovers' lanes.) When he drives at night, he considers himself hunting, a night hunter stalking human game—in this case, couples.

A serial killer may be compulsive when he decides to kill, even before he has selected or happened upon his victim, but his compulsion is obviously under his control and conscious decisions. Otherwise he might commit his crimes, night or day, with witnesses or in venues likely to attract attention. His crimes are usually carefully planned. Though he may be impulsive, he is ready when opportunity appears.

Even if he claims his victim in a moment of opportunity, the serial killer has spent time working out the crime in his mind, through fantasies and planning. He usually seeks a special category of victim (as did the Phantom), vulnerable individuals at a time and place when the killer can maintain control. After a cooling-off period of days, weeks, or months, he will strike again. As the FBI's Robert K. Ressler and associates put it: "He thinks he will never be caught, and sometimes he is right."

Other findings seem to apply particularly to the Starks shootings. Specialists have concluded that some killers may change their *modus operandi*, or MO, thus confusing the police into believing a later crime is not related to the earlier series. The killer may use a different gun or switch to a knife or other weapon, anything to suggest a different person is to blame. James Alan Fox and Jack Levin point out a parallel possibility: "It is also commonplace for them to branch out to more respectable victims as they become convinced that they are smarter than the police and will never be apprehended."

This feeds into the copycat belief, which as Helen Morrison has pointed out is "very common in serial murder cases." Many persons feel such horrible crimes couldn't be committed by the same person, that others must have been involved in some of the cases. This resonates in the Starks case—where the killer used a .22 instead of a .32 and invaded a home and not a lovers' lane—because many people believe a killer always strikes in the same way. "The victims indeed may be similar, but the way of killing varies somewhat," said Morrison.

The making of a serial killer, the experts concluded, involves "a complex process based on biological, social, and environmental factors." The biological predisposition and psychological makeup must combine at "a critical time in their social development. . . . The most significant factor is the serial killers' personal decision in choosing to pursue their crimes."

Psychopathy turns up frequently in the discussions. The psychopath, or sociopath, mixes charm, manipulation, and intimidation to achieve his selfish ends. His charm is superficial, while he exhibits a grandiose sense of self-worth and is a pathological liar. He feels no guilt or remorse, shows no empathy for others. He seeks stimulating behavior, is impulsive, lives off of others, pursues no realistic life goals. He probably had behavior problems in childhood as well as juvenile delinquency.

Somewhere along the line of development, the serial killer came up short, to the detriment of society. His conscience didn't develop at a critical time. He felt he could do as he wished, so long as he was not caught, without regard for morals, laws, or social pressures. It's the story of the bad seed—frequently with exacerbating factors.

Yale developmental psychologist Paul Bloom believes a serial killer is likely the result of a developmental defect—a genetic accident, which then is exacerbated by environmental factors. The "accident of genes," as he put it in an Associated Press interview, may leave a person more likely than others to become a serial killer but is far from being the sole explanation. He cited genetic differences in people's empathy and compassion and how much they care about others. This includes their ability to control violent rages. "I'm sure a serial killer is somebody who has the genetic short end of the stick. Then you toss in certain environments. Your typical serial killer had a very unhappy childhood. There's some evidence that people who turn out to be psychopaths, even murderous psychopaths, have the short end of the genetic stick." But, he added, there is a multitude of environmental factors to consider as well.

When criminals are sociopaths, they commit crimes without a feeling of guilt or of any sympathy for their victims and victims' families. But all sociopaths aren't murderers, least of all serial killers, just as all murderers aren't sociopaths.

A serial killer may have no conscience or a weak one.

"The behavior of a serial killer after his capture provides some insight into his level of conscience," write James Alan Fox and Jack Levin. "Genuine sociopaths almost never confess after being apprehended. Instead, they continue to maintain their innocence, always hoping beyond hope to get off on a technicality, to be granted a new trial, or to appeal their case to a higher level."

In 1988 Robert Ressler and associates, after studying thirty-six sexual murderers in depth, drew a number of conclusions that seem to relate to many other killers, including serial killers. All but seven had killed more than once. The crime held a symbolic significance to the killer, a finding possibly of importance to the Phantom case. There were sexual concerns, implied in the Phantom case. All of these factors were spurred on by fantasies turned into reality.

Characteristics of the killers included lying, living with fantasies, school failure, poor work habits, and a preoccupation with family and personal problems. The killer had followed a long and active fantasy life that featured violent thoughts and fantasies. Before the first killing, many of the fantasies revolved around murder. Afterward, the fantasies focused on improving the murder technique, to do the next one better than the first. Their thought patterns began early in life and continued amid social isolation, functioning as an escape mechanism. As inner stress grew, the crucial step was acting out his fantasies. Thought preceded the act. The killer sees nothing wrong with what he has done, leading researchers to a conclusion that "these men murder because of the way they think."

A central question persists: Why did the Texarkana killer specialize in attacking and killing couples? Petty robbery hardly explains it. Holdups were common at the time, netting a wide range of proceeds; some in early 1946 may even have been committed by the Phantom. One of the females was raped but not others. If sex or robbery was not a primary motive, what was?

The eminent psychiatrist Dr. Shervert H. Frazier of McLean Hospital, affiliated with Harvard Medical School, in a telephone conversation during which he was supplied the basic facts of the Texarkana cases, stated his opinion that the killer was troubled by a relationship in his life, one he could not enjoy. Resentment builds up. Revenge is deep in his heart. His violent reaction toward unknown couples serves as a way of getting even for his own perceived emotional injury. Seeing couples parked or at home reminds him of his lost or shattered relationship. He feels the couple is happy. He knows that he, the shooter, is not. He aims to even the score, symbolically. Though he is attacking strangers, they symbolize, in his mind, what he has lost and whom he blames. They become surrogates upon whom to inflict his vengeance. (Dr. Frazier grew up in Marshall, in northeastern Texas.)

Though not discussed during the telephone interview, Dr. Frazier authored a paper in 1975 that seems to fit into the Phantom case, even though he was referring primarily to adolescent murderers and not serial killers. At the time, Dr. Frazier was psychiatrist in charge of the McLean Hospital and professor of psychiatry at Harvard. "Murder is a process—not an event, but a phasic development," he wrote, pointing out that the killer's self-concept is deficient, leading the criminal to wreak vengeance not on his primary target but on a stand-in for his fury.

Dr. Frazier's paper explained that "the acting out becomes a desperate attempt at mastery, an attempt that fails. The murderer has a learning deficit that is reminiscent of the behavior of toddlers for whom each act is a new event, an attempt to learn about the self." Still speaking of adolescent murderers, Dr. Frazier wrote that with a deficient self-concept, the killer encounters confusion, resulting in a disorganized action pattern.

Dr. Frazier found defects in the early socialization of many murderers he had studied. The individual becomes unable to respond to emotional cues, presenting defenses that are inadequate to cope with stresses. The resulting depression leads to acting out by unleashing rage at some substituted figure of authority, which may have been the object of an earlier anger.

"To the early adolescent, external causes are very important. The person who gets killed is substituted for the intended person."

To go beyond what Dr. Frazier wrote and build upon his findings, we may speculate that a violent inner drama precedes the murders and may continue even after he has "settled the score" with surrogates. What, specifically, is the relationship that spurs him to take others' lives? It could be any relationship in his life, in or out of his family. His victims may represent parental or authority figures who displeased him or a love relationship in which he lost out to a competitor, perhaps one in which he was spurned. Possibilities are endless. His perceptions may not appear realistic to an objective observer, but to him they are paramount. They are the cause of his unhappiness and lack of success. In the Phantom case, he was poisonously resentful of the male victim, whom he killed first, and in some instances, purposefully humiliated by forcing him to pull down his pants. He may have been less angry with, or may have entertained mixed emotions toward, the female. He also seemed to take some pains to conceal her body, rather than carelessly leaving her in open view. He did not desecrate her body, suggesting some degree of respect toward her. The ages of his victims would not reflect an exact comparison with those with whom he was "getting even." They could be younger or older. He simply found a couple approximating those he despised.

By choosing strangers for his vengeance, the killer demonstrates his inability to deal directly with those he deems to have treated him unfairly. He is afraid to confront that person face to face, though he harbors cold anger and resentment and yearns for revenge. The ultimate revenge is to destroy. The best—perfect—model for the victim in such a case is a stranger. Neither knows the other. By killing the selected stranger the perpetrator has exacted his revenge, albeit a step removed from his primary target. On the face of it, there is no motive, unless one erroneously assigns robbery or another act as a motive, making it increasingly more difficult to identify the culprit. Thus, murder of surrogates.

Once he has destroyed the victim or victims, he is emotionally appeased—for the time being. Other elements may enter in, including possible addiction to the rush, the excitement and power he feels in the act of killing other human beings, but he is also acting out a drama of revenge, driven by deep-seated anger that may have persisted for much of his life. While he may savor his peak moments of murder and escape from the police, in time fantasy isn't enough. When triggering, or stressor, events occur, he sets out to kill again, to regain that feeling of excitement and power he has experienced no other way.

In every instance, the Phantom found his preferred victims: vulnerable couples isolated, at night, helpless before a man with a gun and no scruples.

Other psychological considerations may relate to the Phantom's behavior.

"Serial killers may be compensating for the inferior role they were forced to play during childhood. Killing gives them everything missing from their otherwise drab, dreary, and mundane existence," wrote Jack Levin, who also attended the FBI symposium. "Rather than be just an ordinary person with ordinary talents and ordinary abilities, serial killers see themselves as becoming supermen who cannot be stopped by the police or the FBI. . . .

"Taunting law enforcement is one way to feel powerful. Another is to spread fear and terror throughout a community, if not an entire nation, and become infamous in the process."

He added: "They want to be given a moniker—a notorious name—that will ensure that their evil deeds are permanently embedded in our collective memory, that they become a household word. . . . The press often complies by creating a moniker that is widely known—Son of Sam, Hillside Strangler. . . ."

The media-dubbed Phantom became a household word as he spread terror over the Four States Area, with his "achievements" heralded over the nation.

Once started, can serial killers stop killing? Most, perhaps, may be compelled to continue, while some few do stop. The BTK killer in Wichita, Kansas killed from 1974 to 1991, then did not kill again, all the way to his arrest in 2005. He'd found substitutes for murder, apparently legal activities that somehow better channeled his needs.

"It is not that serial killers want to get caught; they feel that they *can't* get caught," said Dr. Levin.

Should a serial killer evade capture, will he continue to kill? The consensus is that he probably will, barring physical disability or, possibly, aging factors that would limit such high-energy crimes.

Most authorities seem to agree that the sociopathic killer cannot be rehabilitated and once incarcerated should never be released. The offender failed to develop a conscience at the critical age and never will. Whatever his intellectual potential, he will never grow emotionally into a normal individual who is "safe" enough to re-enter society. And often, the more intelligent psychopaths will be able to discern what psychiatrists are looking for and feign the appropriate results.

"There is no realistic way to rehabilitate a sadistic sociopath who has made a career of killing," writes Jack Levin. "A forty-two-year-old repeat rapist or murderer doesn't suddenly develop a conscience. He may find religion, shed tears, say all the right things, but chances are, he is no more remorseful now than he was when he raped or killed for the pleasure of it."

Applying the varied data and observations of a number of experts, ranging from FBI specialists to academics to clinical psychiatrists and psychologists—mostly compiled over the years since 1946—a tentative profile can be drawn of the Texarkana terrorist. He probably would be an obscure, angry, ineffectual, cold-blooded loser, a sociopath; white, at least twenty-five years old, of average intelligence and probably sexually inadequate; from a dysfunctional background, and a stranger to his victims, not a veteran of the recent war; a local resident familiar especially with the Texas side roads, who spent a lot of time driving.

If he had experienced a string of failures, he, like Pichushkin decades later, had taken human life but remained a free man, undetected. He had committed perfect crimes. He had terrorized a region. Everybody feared him. They trembled at the mention of his pseudonym.

He was The Phantom, publicized by the media and known from coast to coast. He was somebody at last!

CHAPTER 15

AN ACCIDENTAL BREAK

Texarkanians, still occasionally jittery from the spring horrors, began to settle down. No new double attack had occurred. Three weeks, the anxiously awaited interval, passed without incident, then a month, then six weeks. If the Phantom was on a strict schedule of shooting every three weeks, something had shattered his timing. Had he moved his operations elsewhere? Maybe. Was it just too hot for him in Texarkana? Residents hoped so. They were grateful for the Texas Rangers and other lawmen covering the area. Anything to keep the hometown terrorist from striking again.

Slowly the case faded from the front pages. Summer came with its usual sultry oppression in an era when air-conditioning was a rarity displayed only by a few downtown businesses like Kress, the 5¢-10¢-25¢ store. As the weather heated up, a few brave souls dared to open their windows at night. Most used hand fans to temper the sweltering temperatures.

Tentatively the two sides of Texarkana eased back to what passed for normal. Couples resumed necking in lovers' lanes, albeit more guardedly.

The traumatic spring still burned deeply into the collective and individual memories. Couples kept their ears open for the odd sound, any movement outside their car. Crime and assorted violence continued much as before the Phantom's intrusion, but none conveyed the raw terror that the serial murders had precipitated.

Veterans resumed their interrupted lives, seeking jobs, entering college on the GI Bill of Rights. Lawmen continued their weary work. The Phantom may not have killed since early May, but he remained free. The search was still on, but there was a sea change: time to relax, if uneasily, and get on with life.

Trooper Max Tackett, like other lawmen in the region, had his hands full dealing with routine. He had returned from the Army in late 1945 and almost immediately found himself, with his fellow trooper Charley Boyd, in the middle of the headline shootout in nearby Fulton, Arkansas.

Tackett felt a personal responsibility for not having checked out the parked car near the Starks home the night of May 3. He believed he and Boyd would have caught the killer red-handed or possibly prevented the crimes. From then on, he was to pursue any hint of a clue.

Before the Starks murder he had observed a pattern of criminal activity that neither he nor others fully understood, but which he found intriguing.

While examining car-theft files for the Texarkana area, one day he compared thefts with the dates the cars had been reported stolen and when automobiles were abandoned, presumably by the thief or thieves, or recovered. Zeroing in on the dates of the Texas crimes, he correlated some of the car thefts with those weekends. Nothing unusual about car thefts. What stood out, almost like a blaring railway signal, was a connection that hadn't been reported.

On every night of the assaults and murders, he noted, a car had been stolen in Texarkana, and a previously stolen car was abandoned. Why? Perhaps the man who had stolen the car had used it to leave town, then had returned. Why had he returned? Were these all the actions of one man, or were they coincidences that involved several men? If one man was responsible for all of the weekend thefts, Tackett couldn't assign a reason to the actions. Had the thief simply tired of a particular vehicle?

Or was it part of a plan, not keeping a hot car long enough for it to be recognized by police? Tackett found it difficult to dismiss the relationship. It justified watching closely.

His next challenge raised the question, why not a coincidence? With old cars wearing out and customers waiting for new models, car theft wasn't likely to recede. Coincidence was possible, but he couldn't dismiss the pattern so easily. *Why had the cars been stolen?* Obviously, for transportation. But why steal another and abandon the previous car? The thief might simply have wanted to drive a different, perhaps better, car, or he had another reason, known but to him, for ditching the old car. Tackett felt certain there was more than the surface indicated. The matter rarely strayed from his mind.

In the latter part of June, Tackett received a routine assignment from his district supervisor at Hope. Rather than an intriguing mystery to solve, it was cut-and-dried. Jim Mays, an old farmer who lived near the new dam that was being built near Murfreesboro, a small town in Pike County, had called the state police about a man who hadn't paid his rent. The old man was angry with the deadbeat. Several weeks' rent money was worth complaining about.

The district director asked Tackett to see the farmer, who was a good citizen in the community. Tackett knew the area well; he had grown up at Glenwood in northern Pike County.

Tackett called on the farmer, who had taken down his errant tenant's car license number. The man drove a light green 1941 Plymouth sedan. Its Arkansas license number was 61-917. His name was Youell Swinney. Tackett commiserated with the farmer, promised to start right in on the search. His quarry had previously lived in Texarkana; at the time, he reportedly lived at Delight, in a picturesque part of southwestern Arkansas near Murfreesboro and about sixty-five miles from Texarkana. At the time, construction of the Narrows Dam near Murfreesboro was under way, also not far from Delight.

He reported the license number to the Hope office so that Milton Mosier, the state's identification specialist, could run a check on it. The results of the license-plate check transformed the routine deadbeat complaint to another level. The car had been stolen the night of March 24, the weekend of the Griffin-Moore murders, from Wayne O'Donnell in Texarkana, Arkansas, while O'Donnell was visiting inside the Michael Meagher Hospital. Its driver was still operating it under the same license plate. Now Tackett was dealing with a felony.

He, and other officers to whom he passed the information, failed to locate Swinney. He interviewed members of his family in Texarkana. They couldn't help, either. He hadn't been seen for a while. The family had no idea where he was and couldn't track his movements.

Some time later, the car was reported in the vicinity. Late one night Tackett, Charley Boyd, and deputy sheriff Tillman Johnson drove up the highway between Ashdown and Allene where the car had been sighted. They sat in the State Police car at an intersection, waiting, hoping to spot the car. They never saw it.

A larger lead emerged, with other parts of the puzzle gradually falling into place, when the five-year-old son of one of Swinney's family members remembered a habit of his older relative. The observant boy described a parking lot in Texarkana.

"He always leaves the car there," the boy said.

Tackett checked the lot. Comparing the stolen car and license number with the others there, he found no match. But if the boy was right, the car would turn up eventually. Trooper Boyd periodically drove by the lot, looking for the stolen Plymouth. One day in late June he spotted it, compared the license tag, and surreptitiously began a stakeout.

Boyd's patience paid off. When a tall, slender woman in her early twenties appeared and claimed the car, Boyd stepped out and arrested her. But the man he sought wasn't to be seen.

Her name was Peggy Lois Stevens Swinney. It was her wedding day. She had just returned from Shreveport, Louisiana, she said, where she and Youell Lee Swinney had married a few hours earlier. She was twenty-one years old and had been a resident of Texarkana, Texas. Boyd took her to the Miller County jail until her consort could be found—and impounded the stolen car. She found temporary housing in a cell on the west side of the fourth-floor jail.

They had missed their major quarry, but they had the next best, his wife (of a few hours) and the hot car he had been driving. The dragnet had tightened. Tackett and Boyd felt it was now only a matter of time before they also had him in custody.

The arrest of Peggy Swinney paid dividends, even if she had no idea where her husband was by then. They had been together when he sent her for the car, she said, but now she had no idea where he might be. She could tell officers about his habits. She had no picture of him but could describe at least some of his behavior. For one thing, he hid—or at least spent a lot of time—in theaters during the afternoons. When he stepped out to smoke, he always stood where he could watch all the other people, presumably to make a getaway if he needed to do so.

They didn't know what Swinney looked like, but other officers knew the name. He was a "police character," a man with a record who had been in various kinds of trouble over the years. It wasn't an unusual profile for a car thief. A period of watchful waiting—and searching—ensued. It was the afternoon of Friday, June 28.

Peggy Lois Stevens Tresnick Swinney was born May 17, 1925, in Breckenridge, Texas, an oilfield boomtown. According to the 1930 census, the Stevens family lived in Stephens County, Texas. Breckenridge is approximately seventy miles west of Fort Worth. She had two older sisters, an older brother, and a younger brother. Other siblings were born in the 1930s.

In 1944, when she was nineteen, she had married Stanley Tresnick, a twenty-one-year-old soldier from Pennsylvania. A justice of the peace performed the ceremony in the Miller County courthouse. It was a fragile marriage, at best. Less than three months later, Tresnick shipped out for overseas. She never saw him again, and apparently neither expressed a need to resume the relationship after the war. In early 1946, while she was in the Texas-side city jail for a minor charge of public drunkenness, she met Youell Swinney, who had gone there to get another woman out of jail but instead encountered Peggy.

She had been together with Swinney since soon after that. In May she filed suit in Bowie County to dissolve the matrimonial bond with Tresnick, charging desertion. The final decree came on June 27, 1946. She was twenty-one.

The next day, June 28, Swinney drove Peggy seventy-five miles south to Shreveport, Louisiana. On the marriage license issued in Caddo Parish,

Swinney gave his birthplace as Arkadelphia, Arkansas, and his age as twenty-nine. Both parents—Mrs. Myrtle Chaffin of Texarkana, Arkansas, and Stanley C. Swinney of Montgomery City, Missouri—were listed as living. He gave his occupation as "bookkeeper."

Apparently the clerk misheard or Swinney gave the wrong information, citing Breckenridge, *Kansas*, rather than Texas, as Peggy's birthplace. Her occupation: "none," her parents, both of Texarkana, Texas. She acknowledged that she had been previously married, to Stanley Tresnick, but was now divorced.

Legally they were man and wife. Their honeymoon trip was a short one back to Texarkana, their married bliss lasting no more than a few hours.

Atlanta, Texas, a town of about 5,000, approximately twenty-three miles south of Texarkana in neighboring Cass County, was a quiet little town in the pine tree belt amid rolling green hills. It lay on U.S. Highway 59 that goes to Houston—or if you turn east at Atlanta onto Highway 77, you are about fifty miles from Shreveport, if you choose the Texas, instead of Arkansas, route.

On Monday afternoon, July 15, oilfield worker Hibbett Lee had the day off and, as was his custom, was hanging around Atlanta, shooting the breeze with anybody he might find. He especially liked to chat with Homer Carter, the town marshal who was The Law in Atlanta, a "tush hog" who had earned respect over the years with his no-nonsense approach to order in his town. White-haired, stocky Carter always kept a Roi Tan Perfecto cigar in his mouth, chewing on it between words. He took it out to eat and at bedtime. If you didn't see the cigar, well, maybe you'd better take another look to be sure it was Carter you thought you were seeing.

His visit with Mr. Homer finished, Hibbett Lee sauntered over to Ed Hammock's car lot just a block away. Cleon Partain was helping out there and had his own cars, and Lee thought he'd check on what was going on. The lot was only one block off Highway 77, the route coming from Shreveport into Atlanta. If you went through Atlanta you'd see the lot.

Lee had barely stepped onto the car lot when a new Plymouth drove up. He stopped to take a look. New cars were something to behold. Everybody wanted one.

A tall, slender man, dressed neatly and wearing a white shirt and tie, stepped out of the car and walked toward Lee. Wiry, lean, and tanned, Lee dressed casually, with a big hat, cowboy boots, khaki shirt and trousers, good Texas garb for a man used to working outside.

The stranger approached Lee. "You buying cars, Mister?"

"I don't work here," said Lee, hooking his head toward the nearby little office; "somebody there can help you. Mr. Partain."

By then Cleon Partain was headed their way.

The newcomer glanced about the lot. He was interested in selling his car.

Partain knew the car business and was a shrewd trader. You didn't get many chances to buy a slightly used car. He sized up the man.

"It's a good car, drives real good, low mileage. I haven't had it long, just broke in good, but I can't afford to keep it. Lost my job and I need the money."

"It's a good looking car, all right," agreed Partain. "It got a lien on it?"

"No, it's all clear."

Partain looked it over, inside and out. It was clean looking inside with some dust outside but still shiny. A car like this would sell fast. He could find a buyer almost immediately.

Partain was wary. He didn't find many people willing to sell a new model like this. As he inspected the car carefully, he realized it had been on the road. There was a thin veneer of dust on its exterior. In the car business you came to know the type: a smooth, assured-talking fellow whose story didn't quite satisfy. The man wasn't from Atlanta, not even Cass County. Partain knew every face in his area.

"You got your title?" Partain asked as he studied the man's face.

The question didn't faze the man. "Sure. I didn't bring it with me, but I can take care of that. I'll get it to you."

Partain looked at the car again, this time memorizing the Texas license number. The number wasn't one normally seen in eastern Texas.

"I better not make an offer on it today," Partain said. "Tell you what. Find the title and maybe we can work out something."

The stranger eyed Partain coolly, without emotion, and nodded.

"I was just driving by and thought I'd see if we might do business."

The man got back into the Plymouth and headed toward Texarkana.

"Hibbett, we're not going to see that guy again," Partain said. "Run over and tell Homer I had a suspicious fellow tried to sell me a new Plymouth. Didn't have a title to it. Never saw him before. I got a feeling he's got a hot car."

Lee jogged over to Homer Carter's office to relay the message, with the license number on the piece of paper Partain had handed him. Carter radioed the Texarkana police to be on the lookout for a suspected car thief driving in from Atlanta. The Atlanta police station maintained radio contact with the one local patrol car and with stations in Texarkana and Shreveport.

"I'm coming to Texarkana and I'm bringing a man with me who was there when this joker tried to pull this stunt."

As Carter and Lee motored toward Texarkana, they speculated on their suspect. A man trying to sell a car without a title would alert a legitimate dealer, which is what had happened. Hibbett Lee might not remember the features of the man, but he would recognize the car if they found it parked along the road or at a filling station en route to Texarkana.

By time they reached Texarkana, Carter had his answer. The car had been stolen in Pampa, in the far-off Texas Panhandle. Partain's hunch was validated. By then, patrol cars circled all around downtown Texarkana and on the main thoroughfares, searching for the car. Officers felt they could at least keep the man inside the small city, then narrow the search to a few areas. As one officer said, "We could bottle this town up with five cars."

Carter drove to the Miller County sheriff's office where Tackett maintained a small office. Carter's old friend Johnson was out on a whiskey-still bust in the county. Tackett, in uniform, listened as Carter and Lee described the situation. Carter hadn't seen the man and Lee wasn't sure how to describe him, beyond the fact that he wore a neat dress shirt and a tie and was tall. Not enough, really, to go on.

Tackett's mind flashed back to the man he'd sought for the unpaid rent which, in turn, had become a stolen car case.

"I think I know who you're after," Tackett told them. The fugitive was still around, he believed, driving yet another stolen car. What he knew of the man's behavior fit the man who had appeared in Atlanta. If they caught him now they would solve two car-theft cases, instead of one.

Tackett had never seen the man, and Hibbett Lee didn't remember exactly what the man looked like. Tackett observed how distinctively Lee was dressed: cowboy boots, big Western hat, thick belt buckle—easy to remember.

Tackett said to Lee, "You wouldn't recognize him, but he'd recognize you! He doesn't want to see you again. Tell you what we can do. You go into a number of public places we'll pick out. I'll follow at a respectable distance. We may be able to find our man, because he'll do all he can to avoid you."

Tackett rushed home, pulled off his uniform, put on a truck driver's garb, work khakis and an old floppy hat, ordinary work clothes he wore when he wanted to blend in, and hurried back to join the pair from Atlanta. By the time he returned, Tillman Johnson had arrived from his rural assignment. He drove the men downtown where they could initiate their plan. Then he would patrol around, looking for the stolen car or any sign of action.

The plan was simple. Lee would saunter into the places they selected. Tackett, so as not to be associated with him, would keep a respectable interval but close enough to observe any reactions Lee's entrance might cause. He would look for a man to make a fast move when Western-bedecked Lee and his flashy cowboy boots strode in.

It was a hot July afternoon. A steady flow of traffic and pedestrians gave the downtown area a lively picture. They entered a couple of businesses. Lee went in, trailed discreetly by Tackett, slouching along. After making sure nobody had reacted, Lee went back out, Tackett well behind.

Next they headed for the Arkansas Motor Coach station just off Front Street, by the popular Jefferson Coffee Shop and across from always-busy Union Station and the rail yards.

As Lee went through the door and stepped forward as if going to the rest room, Tackett scanned the waiting room.

Most of the people hardly noticed the colorfully dressed Lee, but suddenly a man in a white shirt standing by the wall turned on his heels and dashed toward the back of the station. *That's our man!* Tackett told himself. He gave chase, running as hard as he could. The passengers, startled, peered questioningly about. Some stood up, to see what was going on.

The stairwell was empty as Tackett lost sight of the man. Tackett pulled his concealed pistol and climbed the stairs two steps at a time. There was but one place left for him to go—the fire escape. Tackett slipped through the opening and found the man crouched there. Tackett pointed his pistol meaningfully.

"Please don't shoot me!" the tall young man said, his anxiety level soaring. He held up his hands. His eyes showed a touch of terror.

"I'm not going to shoot you for stealing cars," Tackett replied as he frisked his prisoner. He found no weapon.

"Mister, don't play games with me. You want me for more than stealing cars!" And then he added, "I will spend the rest of my life behind bars this time."

Slightly winded, his adrenaline still pumping from the chase, Tackett registered the remark without comment. He marched the man back to the waiting room, where Lee and Carter stood. Meanwhile, Johnson was driving about the Union Station area. As Tackett came out of the building with his prisoner, Johnson was parked in the street. Tackett hustled the man into the car, with the Atlanta pair in the back.

The prisoner settled in the front seat, between Johnson and Tackett. By then he appeared calm, as you'd expect a veteran thief to be. They hadn't driven two blocks when he suddenly turned to Johnson and blurted out, "Mr. Johnson, what do you think they'll do to me for this? Will they give me the chair?"

"They don't give you the electric chair for stealing cars," said Johnson.

"Hell, I know what you want me for. It's for more than stealing cars! You don't electrocute someone for stealing cars."

Nobody had mentioned anything about the electric chair. Johnson frowned. *What brought all that out of him?*

The captive persisted. "Do you think I could be lucky enough to get out in twenty-five years?"

"Oh, you won't get much," Johnson said. "Maybe five or ten years."

Puzzling as it was, the comment didn't mean much to Johnson and the other men. Though they couldn't forget what he'd said, they hadn't questioned that he was more than a garden-variety hot-car artist. The unusual replies came so unexpectedly, so reflexively, that the words wedged in their minds. They had a prisoner to hustle to jail, then get to their other duties. They knew they had a car thief, but what, exactly, did he mean? When one of the men asked what he'd meant, he clammed up. Within minutes, he was a different man, giving nothing but perfunctory answers. He was cool, even cold, with no affect. He became a textbook exhibit of noncooperation.

After he reflected on it, Johnson realized that the prisoner hadn't reacted as an ordinary, innocent person would have. Based on his own experience, Johnson had found that if the arrested person was not guilty, he would have demanded, in outrage, "What have you got me for?" The prisoner hadn't. Instead, to Tackett upon his capture and later in the car, the man had made his statements impulsively, displaying a high degree of anxiety.

By sheer coincidence, the event was recorded for posterity. When they arrived at the Miller County sheriff's office on the first floor of the Miller County Courthouse, a photographer just happened to drop by. Within minutes of the arrest, Ted Dougan with a click of his lens recorded a lasting impression. The photo can be found in the photo section of this book. Dougan often dropped by the office; this day he had no real reason to do so or for taking the picture. He just lined up six men and took their picture. Dougan mostly took school pictures, and sometimes pictures for the sheriff's office. Five in the picture are hard-looking men. One is in a state trooper's uniform; that's Charley Boyd. Chief Deputy Johnson, in khakis, stands next to him at the edge of the photo; he also wears a badge and has a pistol strapped on his hip. Three others are in khakis, tough guys who might have been rounded up in a raid. The tall, neatly dressed man in a white shirt with delicate stripes and tie, with a cigarette in his hand, could have passed for a plainclothes detective who had designed the raid. Few persons unaware of the circumstances would have picked out the prisoner.

The khaki-clad men were Tackett, Carter, and Hibbett Lee.

The well-dressed young man in the middle, standing between Boyd and Tackett, was the freshly nabbed fugitive and alleged car thief, Youell Lee Swinney.

Minutes later, Johnson booked Swinney and guided him, via the elevator, upstairs to the jail on the fourth floor of the massive old concrete block building. The county kept cells on both the fourth and fifth floors, depending on the number of prisoners at a time. Women's cells were separate from the men's. Peggy Swinney was in one. If the fourth floor became crowded, deputies would walk the women up to the fifth floor. Sometimes a trusty assisted the jailer in feeding or checking the prisoners.

The newlyweds resumed their interrupted honeymoon behind bars, in separate cells, in a town hardly noted as a resort center.

CHAPTER 16

INCRIMINATING REVELATIONS

s Tackett, Johnson, and Boyd discussed Youell Lee Swinney's intriguing arrest reactions with Miller County Sheriff Elvie Davis, their questions rapidly congealed into firm suspicions. Had they apprehended someone other than a common car thief? Obviously their prisoner thought so. "You know you want me for more than stealing cars!" He had impulsively tipped them off, believing they knew more about him than they did. And why would he ask if he might get the electric chair? Or ask if Johnson thought he might be lucky enough to get out in twenty-five years? These were questions even a novice thief would not have asked. Inexperienced youths knew a stolen car wouldn't land them on Death Row or even close to a quarter-century in lockup. This man, approaching thirty, was no beginner.

Most of all, he was asking these questions of authorities in Arkansas, as if he were concerned about a matter related to their jurisdiction. But this concept did not readily come to mind as the officers wrestled with the larger picture.

Tackett wasted no time applying his observations about the spring's car-theft pattern to Swinney. Was he the one who had stolen, then abandoned, those cars on the murder weekends? Swinney was barely in his fourth-floor cell before officers began avidly expounding theories. Swinney had placed himself high on the lengthy list of suspects.

Was this the lucky break they had hoped for?

Soon, though, Swinney started to talk, sparingly and guardedly, but never again about the topics he had blurted out to his captors that afternoon. No, he told them, the only thing he had ever done was drive a car he didn't realize was stolen. That was all he meant, he said, if he said anything at all.

Any stolen car in Texarkana automatically interested the FBI because of the likelihood it had crossed the state line in violation of the federal Dyer Act. The FBI was notified of the arrest and entered the case almost immediately. Three days later FBI Special Agent J. C. Calhoun sat down with Swinney in the sheriff's office and questioned him about the cars he may have stolen. By then Swinney had had time to think over what he intended to say. He readily, almost eagerly, incriminated himself in felony theft, documenting that he'd violated the Dyer Act as well as state laws. He admitted having possession of stolen cars.

Agent Calhoun stuck to the car thefts over which his agency had jurisdiction. He led Swinney through his background. The prisoner claimed to have finished high school at Texarkana, Texas. That would have been at Texas High, if he was telling the truth, and the date would have been 1934 or 1935, a contention later proved to be incorrect. He said he and Peggy Lois Tresnick had married in Shreveport. He was registered, he said, for Selective Service in Miller County, Arkansas.

Swinney then cited three stolen automobiles that had been transported in interstate commerce.

CAR # 1: He stated this offense occurred about February 1946. "I stole a red Chevrolet coach, about a 1941 model in Texarkana Texas, near the First Baptist Church. My wife (who was not my wife at that time) had been told to wait, as I was going to get a car. She was not told how I was going to get it."

(This apparently was the automobile belonging to Luther McClure, taken in early March, not February, across from the First Baptist Church.)

"I drove to my mother's home in College Hill in Texarkana, Arkansas." (This confirmed he had violated the Dyer Act by driving across the state line.) He picked up Peggy and they drove to Hope, then back to Texarkana before heading west. They picked up hitchhikers en route to West Texas. "Near Lubbock I told Peggy the car was stolen, and said that we had better get rid of it." He told the couple riding with them to drive the car to Beaumont, Texas, and to deliver it to a man there. He'd made up the recipient's name.

CAR # 2: "In about April, 1946, a man I knew in the Texas penitentiary met me in Texarkana, Texas, at which time he had a green Hudson sedan, about a 1940 model. I do not recall his name but he was about 25 years old, 5 ft 8" tall and weighed about 155 lbs. He said that he had stolen this car near the Swann Motel in Texarkana, Arkansas. He was afraid to keep it and gave it to me. I drove this car with Peggy to Dallas, Texas, Oklahoma City, St. Louis, Missouri, Little Rock, Arkansas, and to Texarkana, Arkansas, where I abandoned it."

CAR # 3: He also assigned original blame to another, claiming he had purchased it from a man whose name he didn't recall. "A man I know only as Chuck, with whom I served in Leavenworth pen sold me a 1941 Plymouth sedan about May 1946 for $900.00. I paid him $150.00 in cash. He told me that I could locate him at the White House Cafe near the railroad station and pay the balance, or a part of it, in two or three weeks. He is about 40 years old, weighs about 170 pounds, is 5 feet 11 1/2 In. or 6 ft tall, is a white man of dark complexion. Peggy and I drove in this car to Shreveport, Louisiana, Dallas, Texas, San Antonio, and back to Dallas and I had tried to locate Chuck, without success. I then told Peggy that I felt that the car was stolen. We were married at Shreveport, Louisiana, and came to Texarkana Texas, where Peggy was arrested. I was a block away and saw her picked up and stayed away."

Not only did his admissions facilitate documenting his hot-car record; they also provided some insight into his behavior. The FBI agent remained skeptical of Swinney's account of how he came to possess cars 2 and 3, which on the surface appeared to have been constructed in such a way that identifying the men to whom he claimed he'd turned over the Hudson and the Plymouth would be difficult, if not impossible.

Swinney had readily implicated himself in a federal crime, of transporting a stolen car across a state line. This could qualify him for less harsh federal time, rather than a state prison. By then he was a connoisseur of correctional facilities, having taken jolts in both state and federal prisons.

His statement also revealed how close Charley Boyd had come to arresting Swinney along with Peggy in the lot where the car was parked. Swinney, like an old buck sending the doe ahead, should there be hunters near, had sent Peggy as his "doe" to make sure the coast was clear. The coast hadn't been clear. So he had run away.

With Swinney and his wife in jail cells across the fourth-floor space from each other, it was possible for one to shout or yell at the other, communicating in primitive fashion when officers weren't around. The sheriff's offices were downstairs and much of the time there was no deputy or jailer on hand to monitor the prisoners' words. A quieter way, avoiding the ears of other prisoners, was to pass notes. There was always the possibility of a note's being intercepted, so the writing had to be couched in guarded language.

It didn't take long for the couple to attempt to pass notes. By the time of Swinney's arrest, officers had had two and a half weeks in which to fire questions at Peggy. She had talked, but hadn't provided any significant revelations. Once he was arrested, however, things moved swiftly. Swinney immediately became a hot suspect for some, if not all, of the Phantom killings. Suddenly anything Peggy said took on a greater importance.

When a lawyer visited her, on behalf of her family, he informed her that Swinney was being held for murder. An officer sat within hearing distance.

She immediately exclaimed, "How did they find it out?" Then she stopped, realizing she had said more than needed.

A brief "correspondence" began between the couple. Eventually their written words made their way to their keepers.

Peggy wrote, alluding to something the officers hadn't previously known. "I haven't mentioned anything about the watches or ring." Tackett noted the sentence and filed it for future reference. Some watches had been stolen in Texarkana, Texas. Was that related to what she wrote? Or was it a euphemism for something else?

Her note prompted a reply from Swinney that ended up in the state police files. The heat was on. Neither prisoner had any concrete knowledge of how much the lawmen knew.

Swinney wrote to "Dear Peggy" in an easily readable handwriting.

"I never expected to have you write me the things you did. As I told you they are trying to make you hate me and peggy [sic] you know as well as I do that you have not did anything and should not be in jail and I dont know what has come over you or what you have heard but whatever it is it isn't so as I thought you loved me more than to write me the things you did. I believe that you will be released soon and I had hoped you would write me and come to see me. Peggy don't believe that stuff you have heard about. You can read my statements to the FBI and see for yourself just what I have said. I told them that your statement was correct and I did not add anything to it. If you told everything you knew and everything we did [since] February. Now honey think this over and you will see that I am right. Honey let me hear from you about this because you know how much I love you and how much you mean to me. Let me hear from you. Honey everything I said was written down by the F.B.I. and ask them to let you see the statement. Answer right back. All my love, your husband, Lee."

His note was carefully crafted. It was clear that he was anxious about what she had told officers. He wanted her to read his statement to the FBI and tailor her remarks to parallel his. He wanted her to get out of jail so that she could visit him and he could talk directly, and confidentially, to her. He'd revealed nothing that might point to any connection with murder or to a contradiction of any alibi he had given.

Like Peggy, he had no way of knowing what, or how much, the lawmen knew, nor the extent of evidence they might marshal against him. He did know one thing for certain: if Peggy talked freely, his case would be severely compromised. She had been with him, knew more about him over the past several months than anyone else. She had the information the officers wanted.

A few days later, more substantial evidence appeared—the promise of an eyewitness. Peggy Swinney surprised officers, suddenly announcing, "I'll give you a statement." Whether she was driven by anxiety over how much officers already knew or whether she was determined to relieve her own mind, she was "ready."

Events soon relegated the stolen car to a lesser, but integral, status. The prospects of nailing a serial killer now took center stage.

Over two days, July 23 and 24, she gave three formal statements that Chief Deputy Johnson typed as she spoke. Her statements did not jibe perfectly, but overall, her words fit into a pattern. At long last, hers was the kind of human information they so sorely needed, the prospect of an eyewitness.

PEGGY SWINNEY'S STATEMENT # I

Ten minutes after eleven o'clock on the morning of Tuesday, July 23, she began the first statement. She told how she was in the Texarkana, Texas, jail in late January or early February when Youell Swinney went looking for another woman ("some girl"). They talked through the window, she upstairs in the jail, Swinney in the alley. He apparently paid her fine, probably for a misdemeanor like drunkenness or vagrancy, to secure her release.

Her first date with Swinney began on the afternoon of Thursday, February 14, Valentine Day. They met at the Lone Star Sandwich Shop, a beer joint in the 100 block of State Line on the Arkansas side. They spent the evening with a sailor and his girl friend. The next morning they went to his sister and brother-in-law at 220 Senator Street on the Arkansas side. This was a pattern to be repeated over the next several months. That week Swinney obtained a job at Mid-South Supply Company, a business on the Texas side downtown.

The statement was aimed at establishing a time line with which to determine specifically where Swinney had been over the course of the spring. Certain events stood out, but none of them pinpointed where Swinney was at crucial times on the nights of February 22, March 23, April 13, and May 3. She related events by days of the week, rarely providing the exact date.

Tillman Johnson later went over the statement, which he had typed single-spaced on three long legal-sized pages. In the margins he noted the dates to which each mention referred. The dates would have to be tentative and, sometimes, approximate. Nonetheless, Peggy Swinney was beginning to fill in the blanks.

Her account provided Swinney no alibi for the night of February 22. She was with his sister, she said, and he wasn't there the night on which Jimmy Hollis and Mary Jeanne Larey had been held up, attacked, and viciously beaten.

On the 26th, Swinney took Peggy back to her mother's on Richmond Road, outside the city limits on the Texas side. This location was no great distance from where the February 22 beatings had occurred. The following Sunday, Swinney rented an apartment on the Texas side. They remained there a week, until she left him after "a fuss."

During this time, her friend Dorothy R— tried to locate her by telephone, calling all over town, to tell her Swinney was looking for her. Later, when Dorothy did get in touch with Peggy, the friend told her that Swinney had a .32 caliber pistol.

Two days later, Peggy was sitting with another man in a café near Union Station when Swinney appeared, walked directly over to them, and struck her. Swinney told her companion that he meant to have her "even if he had to kill somebody to do it. Swinney took me away from him."

The forcibly reunited couple then went to his sister's, where they stayed until Saturday, when they went to a second-rate hotel. The following day they went to a movie, afterward to his mother's home for the day. That night after walking downtown by himself, he returned with a red Chevrolet two-door sedan.

(If this was the red Chevrolet that Swinney told the FBI he had stolen near the First Baptist Church, her or his memory of the date and time was off.)

The next day, they headed west, beginning a series of trips that continued for months, establishing a pattern of driving great distances in stolen cars, picking up hitchhikers, ferrying passengers from one city to another. She corroborated his account of driving to Lubbock, where he turned the car over to the hitchhiking couple for them to deliver to a fictitious man in Beaumont. Swinney and Peggy hitchhiked back to Texarkana.

Moving to Saturday, March 23, the night of the Griffin-Moore murders, while they were in a second-run theater he left for two and a half hours, until eleven P.M. after which they went to his mother's house for the night. Her version left him with unexplained hours but seemed to cover him for the later period when the murders occurred.

He was gone most of the next day and that night. Subsequently they returned to the hotel. She told him she wanted to go to her mother's home, angering him. He slapped her in the face with a towel.

"He started to telling about a girl who testified against him in taking her rings. He told me that he had killed the girl for it."

His claim that "he had killed the girl" seems not to have been followed up by officers, perhaps because they viewed it as a threatening lie used to intimidate Peggy.

From that point on, she cited a series of trips taken over several states in stolen automobiles. He stole a Hudson automobile in Robison Courts, the subdivision in which Richard Griffin's family lived. Days later they drove to Dallas, almost always short of funds, and began driving in conjunction with Mack's Travel Bureau, a travelers' exchange developed during the war. They busily traversed the region, taking strangers to a variety of destinations. Using Dallas and Texarkana as hubs, they transported passengers to San Antonio, Oklahoma City, El Paso, New Mexico, Lubbock, St. Louis, Austin, and Shreveport. They would spend a day or two in Texarkana between trips, then return to the road. When they went to a movie or were in a motel room, he would absent himself for hours while she waited.

She told of picking up a painter in Dallas, en route to Louisiana. Swinney ran into a city bus in Dallas and kept going. At Longview, Texas, the painter went into a liquor store. Swinney drove off without him, keeping the man's clothes he'd left in the car. They then spent "about two days" at her mother's.

The "about two days" she said they spent at her mother's coincided with the April 13 weekend of the Martin-Booker murders. Though she hadn't elaborated, she had documented that Swinney was indeed in Texarkana that Saturday.

The initial statement stamped uncertainty onto Swinney's whereabouts on February 22 and parts of March 23 and had blurred over April 13-14, except that each time he was in Texarkana.

Skipping past the weekend of the Martin-Booker tragedy, she enumerated their travels in a stolen Plymouth.

From Dallas they took passengers to New York City, a trip of four days and nights each way. They stayed only forty-five minutes in New York before turning around and heading back. Back in Dallas, they drove to Oklahoma City, San Antonio, Wichita Falls, and other Texas points. Their final trip, with Memphis as the destination, ended at Hope, Arkansas, thirty miles from Texarkana, where they dumped a sailor headed for Memphis and went instead to the little town of Antoine where Peggy's sister lived.

This brought them to Thursday, April 18, the day before Good Friday, four days after the bodies were found at Spring Lake Park. The day after Easter Sunday, Swinney and Louis Lamb, Peggy's brother-in-law, applied for work at nearby Murfreesboro on road construction close to a new dam site. They roomed with the Lambs.

On Friday afternoon, May 3—the day of the Starks murder, Swinney and Peggy's sister quarreled over the money Swinney owed for his and Peggy's board. He left in a huff.

"He went to Antoine and told all the men that had been riding with him to work that he was going to Texarkana and would not be able to haul them to work anymore. Then we went to Delight and got a room at the Delight Hotel. We left my sister's to go to Delight about six P.M. We arrived at Delight, got the room, and went up to it. Swinney was still mad. Swinney left and drove the car away. In about five hours, or sometime after midnight, Swinney came back into the room. I saw that he was fully dressed. Swinney undressed and got into bed with me."

They arose that morning—a few hours later—at five A.M., had breakfast, and went to the job site where her brother-in-law was working, left there at nine, and returned to Delight to find a place to live. They found a room at Jim Mays's residence, two miles east of Delight, and the next day moved their meager belongings there.

Again—this time with a greater and even more suspicious gap—she had failed to provide Swinney with an alibi for the Starks shootings. She had, however, guided officers by saying he had gone to Texarkana that night and had been gone long enough to commit the crimes, all without involving herself. She had also documented his anger that afternoon. She claimed she wasn't with him but was at the Delight Hotel during the hours in question. Her omissions raised a string of red flags.

Swinney went back to work on Monday, May 6, and they stayed at the Jim Mays residence for the next two weeks, running up a bill which Swinney never paid and about which, eventually, Mays complained to the State Police. They left Delight on Sunday, May 19, slightly over two weeks after the Starks murder, and returned to her parents' home.

The following day, a Monday, they drove to Nashville, Arkansas, for a movie Swinney was eager to see—*Jesse James* (1939) in the Howard Theater. The fictionalized, glamorized version of the outlaw's legend starred handsome Tyrone Power. Swinney drove sixty miles each way to see it.

If they'd been in Nashville a week earlier they could have seen, at the same theater, Chester Morris as Boston Blackie in *The Phantom Thief*, a title tailor-made for the times and the region.

That week they left the Four States Area and drove more than five hundred miles to Waynoka, a town of about three thousand in northwest Oklahoma near the Oklahoma Panhandle. Swinney took a job on a railroad maintenance crew for the Atchison, Topeka and Santa Fe. He rented a room for Peggy. He stayed at a camp for the workers during the week.

At Waynoka, Swinney was up to his old ways.

One Sunday, she said, Swinney took a carload of Mexican workers in his car, took forty dollars from one and, in all, eighty dollars from them. She saw him take the money. They remained in Waynoka for about three weeks, during which time Swinney stole "a bunch of clothes" from a hotel there.

They returned to Texarkana and stayed with his sister until June 28, the day she married Swinney in Shreveport, after which she was arrested.

Tillman Johnson witnessed the statement. Peggy read it, said it was accurate, but would not sign. She told him that Swinney threatened to kill her if she talked to officers. Johnson recognized she was scared to death of Swinney. "I should have put it into the statement, which I didn't," he said later.

It was a beginning. She'd implicated Swinney in several felonies—thefts, armed robbery—but not murder. What stood out, however, was that she had placed Swinney in Texarkana on each of the pertinent nights, without providing him an alibi.

PEGGY SWINNEY'S STATEMENT # 2

The next afternoon Johnson sat her down for a second statement that delved deeper and produced more incriminating revelations.

"Sometime during the middle of April—it was only two or three days after the Booker-Martin murder, Lee Swinney and I were at his sister's on Senator Street. We were in the back room alone. We were discussing the murders in Texarkana. I asked Lee who killed these people. Swinney told me that it was someone with a brilliant mind, someone with more sense than the cops.

"He then told me that he had better come to town and get rid of it. I ask him what he was talking about. Swinney then told me that he had the saxophone that was taken from the Booker-Martin car. He said that a man gave it to him. After this conversation we came to town and Swinney carried me to the Joy Theatre and left me there. He was gone about one or two hours. He came back to the theatre and got me out. Before I went to the show, Swinney had only about two dollars and fifty cents. When he got me out of the show Swinney had about twenty-two dollars in all."

Then she reverted to April 13, the night of the Spring Lake Park killings. In early evening they arrived in Texarkana from Dallas. After eating steaks at a café, they went to a movie at the Joy Theatre. Before the film was over, they drove to the Stockman Hotel just outside the city limits on the Dallas highway and drank several bottles of beer. (This was a short distance from where the Griffin-Moore murders had occurred three weeks earlier.) From there they moved to Drivers Café, inside the city limits, drank beer till closing time, then bought four bottles to take with them.

On a Saturday night, last calls for beer in Texas would have been one o'clock in the morning.

They drove about town for a while, then Swinney headed for Spring Lake Park. They found several cars parked on the road in the park. Swinney drove close to a dairy, where they stopped. They drank the four bottles of beer, after which Swinney left her in the car alone. After he was gone for about an hour, she heard what sounded like gunshots. Hours later he returned, as dawn was breaking. He drove out of the park area at a rapid rate of speed.

She observed that his clothes were wet to his knees, damp to his waist. Before they left the park, Swinney stopped at a parked coupe and removed a large black case and put it in the trunk.

"I asked Swinney what he was doing, getting something out of that car. Swinney replied that a friend told him to come out there and get it."

En route to her mother's early that morning, Swinney stopped and changed clothes in the woods. Near her parents' home they drove to a locked pasture gate. Swinney ignored the lock and took the gate off its hinges at the other end. They then drove into the pasture and parked in the woods. Shortly before dark they drove to the gate. A man on horseback, who owned the property, met them there. He threatened to have them arrested. "Swinney told him that if he did he would sure get him after he got out of jail. The man let us go on."

This time she had placed Swinney on or near the scene of the Martin-Booker murders but nothing more. Each time she spoke, she seemed to edge closer to the kind of eyewitness evidence the officers sought.

PEGGY SWINNEY'S STATEMENT # 3

The same date, shortly after ten o'clock that night, she produced a meatier version, complete with details she had skirted around in her first two statements. Johnson always had other witnesses present when he took her statements. This time Sheriff Davis, Tackett, and Boyd joined the session. Along with some modifications, she offered the kind of specific details she earlier had studiously avoided. It was as if she previously had wanted to divulge all but was held back by some unseen hand, such as Swinney's threats.

Repeating her account of their arrival from Dallas and drinking beer at the two cafés the night of April 13, she said they left the Drivers Café at closing, drove about town and then to Spring Lake Park.

"He told me that he was going out to the park and rob someone that we would find in the park. He told me that he was not going to work as long as he could get money from someone else."

They drove through the park and took a road away from the lake.

"We had passed several cars parked along the road in the park. We passed one car which was a coupe. Swinney pointed the car out to me and said, 'The people in that car should have some money.'"

The coupe was parked on the gravel road outside the park along the railroad track. It was a few hundred yards from the gate to the park.

"We drove about two hundred yards past this coupe and Swinney stopped our car. Swinney told me that he wanted me to go with him to rob the people. We both got out of the car and walked back toward the coupe that we had spotted. Swinney had taken a gun from the car seat. This gun had been laying in the seat between us while we were driving toward the park. Swinney had the gun which he told me was an automatic in his hand as we walked back toward the parked coupe. We walked up to the coupe and the couple were in the car talking. We walked up on the driver's side of the car.

"Swinney had the gun in his right hand and I was standing on his left side. Swinney told the couple to get out of the car. The boy in the car asked us what we wanted and who are you to tell me to get out of the car. Swinney told him to get out of the car or he would show him who he was.

"The boy got out of the car on our side and the girl got out on the side away from us and walked around the front of the car to where I was standing. Swinney told me to search the couple. I did not search them and told Swinney I was not going to. Swinney told the couple that if they did not hand over everything they had that he would kill them. The boy had his hands up and begging Swinney not to kill them. The little girl was begging me to make Swinney stop and not kill them.

"Swinney got mad because they would not hand over their stuff and I would not search them. The little girl and I were standing near the front of the car. Swinney was standing several feet from the side of the car and to my right. The little boy was standing in front of Swinney about four to six feet. Swinney had the gun pointed at the boy. He shot him two times and the boy fell to the ground. The little girl and I began to scream. I told Swinney not to kill him. Swinney told the boy that he ought to shoot him again. The boy did not say anything that I heard after the shots were fired and he went to the ground.

"After the boy fell to the ground, shot, Swinney bent over him and went through his pockets and took his billfold and what money he had. I saw him then put the boy's billfold back into the boy's pocket after he had taken the money out of it. While this was going on, I was holding the girl and she was crying."

Swinney told Peggy to keep the girl while he got the Plymouth and returned. He backed up to the coupe and ordered the girl into the stolen car.

"The girl got into the front seat of our car. She got into the car and Swinney then picked the boy up and put him into the back seat. Swinney told me to get into the car. I told him that I was not going to get into the car. He told me that he was going to kill me. Swinney then told me to get into the coupe and be sure not to touch anything so that I would leave fingerprints. Swinney had a glove on his left hand. It was a brown cotton glove.

"He held the door of the coupe open for me with the glove hand. Swinney then got into the Plymouth car of ours and drove north on the gravel road toward the dairy back of the Spring Lake Park. It was just breaking day when Swinney drove up beside the coupe with our [car] headed toward town, the same way the coupe was headed. Swinney got out of our car and came to the coupe and with his gloved hand opened the door for me to get out. He then looked into the coupe and found a large black leather case in the car. He put this case into our car in the trunk. Swinney told me that he had tried to get some from the little girl and she would not let him have it and that he killed her. I ask Swinney what he did with the bodies and he told me that he put them where no one would find them."

Swinney drove into the park area. His clothes were bloody. He changed clothes in a restroom near the springhouse and washed his hands in the spring.

They drove to a café on the Arkansas side and drank coffee. They then drove near her parents' house on the Texas side and parked on a side road in the woods. They slept in the car until that afternoon, then went to her parents' house. When her parents walked to a bus stop near there to go to town, she said, "Swinney got scared that they were going after the law." He followed them to the bus stop and talked to her father, who assured him they didn't intend to call the officers.

Swinney and Peggy drove to a lane near the parents' home to a gate.

"The gate was locked. Swinney took the gate loose from the hinge side of the gate; he did not bother the lock. We drove into the pasture about a quarter of a mile from the gate and parked the car. We then walked back down to my mother's house and hid in some woods near the house. We were close enough that we could watch the house to see if the law came here. We stayed here until almost dark and went back to the car. Swinney made me wait and let him go to the car first to see if there was anyone there. We got into the car and started to drive out. We were stopped by some man on a horse who told us that it was his land and he threatened to have us arrested. Swinney told him to have him put in jail but he would get him when he got out of jail.

"I ask Swinney what he did with the gun that he killed the two kids with in the park. He told me that he did away with it at the same time he did away with the bodies."

They then left the pasture and headed for Swinney's sister's home for a short stay, then back to her mother's house where they spent the night and the following day, a Monday. That night they left for Dallas, stopping at almost every town in between. About ten or fifteen miles east of Dallas Swinney drove onto a side road.

"Swinney got out of the car and took the clothes out of the trunk of the car that he had on the night he killed the couple in Spring Lake Park. These clothes were khaki pants and shirt. They had a lot of blood on them. Swinney put paper under the clothes and set them afire. We stayed there about two hours burning the clothes, as they were hard to burn. Swinney made sure that every part of the clothes burned. He said that he wanted to be sure that they were all burned up so the officers would not find them."

In Dallas they picked up a man at the travel bureau and took him to Tyler in east Texas. They registered under "A. J. White" at a tourist court that night and returned to Dallas the next day.

Again Peggy refused to sign. She said Swinney would kill her if she did.

By her word she'd been an eyewitness to Swinney's shooting Paul Martin and had implicated him in Betty Jo Booker's murder. Yet parts of her third account, while more detailed than her first two statements, blurred over some of the events and were not clear about Paul Martin's death; he was shot, in all, four times, whereas she had cited only two shots. Was her memory impaired—she'd drunk a great many bottles of beer that night—or was she holding back something?

One of her sentences seems to have gone unquestioned by officers: "Swinney told me that he had tried to get some from the little girl and she would not let him have it and that he killed her." He may have told her that, but it raises questions. If Swinney were interested in sex, it wouldn't have mattered whether the helpless fifteen-year-old schoolgirl would "let him have some" or not. He was a strong, hardened man with a gun. He could have done as he wished, easily could have raped her whether she fought back or not. The lab evidence was that he had raped her, though not in the way that a conventional rapist might have. This indicates he didn't want Peggy to know and thus lied to her. But if Peggy's version was accurate it may suggest sex was not a driving force, at least not the main factor. In the final analysis, his dominant goal was to destroy.

The next time Peggy gave a formal statement four months later, her responses would be recorded by a polygraph.

Events moved swiftly. The next day, Miller County Sheriff Davis took Peggy to Dallas. They spent the day trying to locate the site where she claimed Swinney had burned his blood-spattered clothing. The search failed. The several sites she thought might be the one never revealed evidence of a burn. Either her memory was defective or her story was not true. Dallas detective Will Fritz interviewed her and concluded she wasn't telling the truth. Then she refuted her earlier claim and admitted that Swinney hadn't burned any clothing near Dallas.

Things fared better when Texas officers questioned her and took her to the crime scene at Spring Lake Park. She guided them to the graveled road and walked directly to where Paul Martin's car had been parked.

"That's where the little boy and girl and the car was parked."

She told how she had gone into the clump of woods nearby. This explained the woman's heel tracks that officers had found exactly there. She gave an account of the teenagers' final hours.

The Bowie County sheriff asked, "Did you see Swinney take anything out of the boy's pockets, besides his wallet? Did he take anything else out?"

"I saw him take some papers or stuff."

"What did he do with it?" Presley asked.

"He took it and threw it over in those bushes over there," she said.

After she was back in the car and out of hearing, Presley pulled a small datebook from his coat pocket, displaying it so all could see.

"I've had this ever since we made our first investigation at the scene the day the bodies were found. It's Paul Martin's datebook. I've kept it in my pocket, and I found it right where she said Swinney threw it."

He'd preserved the evidence, unknown to anyone else, to keep the newspapers from getting hold of it or others learning he'd picked it up, to keep the killer from knowing of it. The one piece of physical evidence, not known to any of the others until that moment, which Peggy had not known he possessed, strongly supported her claim that she had been where she said she was and that she was telling the truth. It tightly linked Swinney to the crime scene. Although Peggy sometimes wove confusing accounts, the general contours of her statements meshed with the known facts. Lawmen believed she edited her comments from time to time to minimize her own role in the killings, in order to insulate herself from the most serious criminal charges that might be levied. There also was a sense that she jumped about in her versions, reflecting mental or emotional instability. Johnson put it two ways, in the folk vernacular. "Her bread wasn't brown. The elevator didn't go all the way to the top."

Tackett believed she knew a great deal more than she revealed. "If the full truth be known, Swinney would be in the electric chair, and Peggy would be sitting in his lap."

The datebook was a compelling piece of evidence. The problem was, officers needed Peggy's testimony to verify the connection, and there was a catch.

As Swinney's wife, they couldn't force her to testify against her husband. The Texas law was firm on that point. The couple's trip to Shreveport on June 28 had erected a powerful roadblock not readily removed.

Peggy Swinney cooperated in a variety of ways. She even submitted to hypnosis. The hypnotist, Travis Elliott, who'd hypnotized "Sammie" and exonerated him, put her in a trance in a room of people that included her parents and other "reliable people" such as a prominent physician, several lawmen, and a prosecutor. She talked freely. Texas Ranger Stewart Stanley, concerned about corpses found along Texas roads, questioned her about passengers Swinney had transported. She told of one man Swinney had picked up. When they stopped by the roadside, Swinney and the man walked away from the car to "take a leak." The other man never came back. That was as far as she went about the other deaths. In the Texas roadside cases, people had gotten robbed and were slain, with their belongings missing. Swinney was suspected, for he robbed and stole clothing, but nothing was proved.

Her three statements, while yielding new insights, also contained inconsistencies. Sheriff Presley, for one, citing the Texas-side murders, said some of her details were incorrect. Officers acknowledged, though, that flirting with the electric chair herself, she had a vested interest in modifying her story from time to time.

A steady stream of investigators bombarded her with questions. Although only the three sessions recorded by Tillman Johnson were reduced to print, other revelations were as intriguing, also implicating Swinney. In every instance, she placed him in the general locale of each crime, while leaving him without an alibi.

FBI agent Horace "Buzz" Hallett told his neighbor Bessie Brown, Betty Jo Booker's mother, what Peggy had recalled about the first double murders. Swinney returned to their motel room that night with blood all over him, she said, and "just *laughed* about what he had done" and got away with. This fit the facts, as for the bloody clothing, for Richard Griffin's blood almost certainly spurted all over his murderer.

Max Tackett remembered another instance. "She made the statement that he came in, the night of the death of Virgil Starks and the shooting of his wife, to the place where they were staying, and he had blood all over him. She said he wiped the blood on a towel and put it under a mattress in the room. Sometime later we found the towel there."

Tackett did not make clear whether the blood came from Swinney or someone else. The technology of the time was imprecise. There is no record that it was tested, nor an explanation of how Swinney would have had so much blood on him. Had her memory failed her, mixing up an earlier incident with that one, or had she simply misstated?

While Peggy managed to place Swinney on stage, or at least in the vicinity of the crime scenes, she herself was always somewhere else, except in the Martin-Booker case, according to her version. In the Spring Lake Park slayings, she minimized her role to that of an imperiled observer who had no choice in being there. What officers seem to have failed to recognize, and to pursue with vigor, was that while she claimed no alibi for Swinney, she had none herself, either. If she wasn't where she claimed to be, was she with him on each occasion?

Of the several incidents, she singled out one, the Martin-Booker case, in which she was an eyewitness. Why had she seized upon this one, when she could have just as well maintained silence, as did Swinney? From all indications, the park murders troubled Peggy deeply. The victims were young teenagers, children, really. She referred to them as "the little boy and the little girl." Despite her fear of Swinney, these killings in which she was in close contact may have inspired her readiness to talk in the first place. Betty Jo Booker's mother said an officer, probably an FBI agent or Captain Gonzaullas, had told her of Peggy's reaction that fatal night. "She said that she held Betty Jo while he killed Paul, and she said that she felt so sorry for Betty Jo, but if she hadn't been scared to death of the man she would have let her go."

Being on the scene of any of the crimes would have haunted any normal person. The evidence suggests that Peggy herself was basically not a criminal. Whatever she may have thought of the other victims, these were children, fifteen and sixteen, just kids. She was up close with them and perceived them as young innocents who hadn't harmed anyone, who deserved to live. The experience must have pushed her to the breaking point by time of her arrest. It was as if she wanted Swinney to be held responsible for that night of horror.

There may have been another factor at work. Her telling of the Texas crimes might deflect attention from the more recent Starks shootings, as it did, and get her, and Swinney, out of Arkansas's custody. But nothing was likely to suppress the terrible memory of the little girl and the little boy at the mercy of a pitiless criminal enforcing his whims with a pistol. Her fears soared even with Swinney behind bars. It wasn't a certainty that he would remain a prisoner, although she seemed willing, even intent, to help keep him there.

As she poured out her memories, Peggy from time to time gave the impression she was living a kind of Bonnie Parker and Clyde Barrow adventure. In 1946 the exploits of the bank-robbing outlaw couple of the 1930s was still fresh, especially in Texas. Bonnie and Clyde had met their fate in a hail of bullets on a north Louisiana road in 1934, only a dozen years earlier. Dallas, their home base, was also a second home for the Swinneys.

Like Bonnie and Clyde, Peggy and Lee Swinney traveled the country, eluded the law, and had all kinds of adventures. If Peggy felt she was a latter-day Bonnie Parker, with Swinney her Clyde Barrow, she could make the case, part of the way. Swinney had taken her to places she'd never been before, would never have seen—St. Louis, Oklahoma City, San Antonio, even New York City. It was a heady, if fearful, experience. Constant movement. New places. New people. She'd never seen anything like it.

Although Bonnie and Clyde killed people, it was in the course of a bank robbery or during flight from the cops. The Phantom killings were cowardly, in the dark, with the unarmed victims unable to strike back. Swinney had never displayed such boldness as to rob a bank. By comparison, his stickups were petty stuff.

Swinney had spent enough time in the Texas prison system to hear inmates spin yarns about Clyde Barrow and his gang. In a way, he could compare his own feats to Barrow's. He had a special interest in outlaws. He'd driven 120 miles, round-trip, to catch a movie about Jesse James. Now, if Peggy's statements were true, Swinney possessed his own brand. He was the Phantom, in his mind a brilliant successor to Clyde Barrow and Jesse James, finding his notoriety under a code name.

Peggy was aware of the darker side that generated mixed feelings. Swinney killed with little thought and never in a running gun battle with the police. He'd threatened to kill her if she talked. Her fears took the edge off any glamour she might have gained from the relationship. This set her apart from Clyde Barrow's mate. Bonnie Parker took an active role and exhibited no fear of her man. Peggy, according to her own view, took a passive, often reluctant, stance as Swinney's companion. Moreover, Tillman Johnson suspected that Swinney manipulated Peggy, using her as bait in their travels to lure men whom he robbed.

Tackett made a comment that has not been corroborated by any other source, which was that Peggy had a venereal disease and Swinney did not, indicating they had no sexual contact. If true, that would fit into Johnson's theory that she was "bait" to attract men into Swinney's grasp and little more.

Whatever the details of their relationship, it was, for Peggy, exciting but risk-laden. When she looked at the downside of their life together, it was very, very far down, as deep as down can go.

CHAPTER 17

THE PRIMARY SUSPECT

Youell Lee Swinney at twenty-nine was no stranger to jails.

His criminal record stretched as far back as 1929, at least, when he was twelve years old. By 1946—seventeen years later—he was an ex-convict several times over. At the time of his arrest in July he'd been out of the Texas penitentiary barely more than six months, having made it back to Texarkana in time for Christmas, 1945. He'd served time in reform school, two state penitentiaries, and federal prisons in Oklahoma, Georgia, and Kansas. His résumé was impressive, in a negative sense, highlighting a variety of crimes ranging from theft, burglary, and counterfeiting to strong-arm robbery. This was the first time he had been held as a suspect in a murder case.

Born February 9, 1917, in Arkadelphia, Arkansas, Swinney appeared in the census of 1920 as a member of a family residing in Redland Township, at New Edinburg, Cleveland County, in southern Arkansas. The father and head of household, Stanley Swinney, was a thirty-two-year-old Arkansas native and a Baptist minister, at New Edinburg

U. S. Post Office and Court House, Texarkana, Texas, Arkansas

UNITED STATES
POST OFFICE AND
COURT HOUSE

TEXARKANA, TEXAS

TEXARKANA, ARK.

Man in Texas and his Ass in Arkansas

IB-H1388

A popular postcard in Texarkana in the 1940s.

LEFT: Jim Hollis in 1947 after his beating the year before. *Courtesy of Diana Burris.*
RIGHT: Mary Jeanne Larey a few years after the incident.

The Rythmaires on the VFW bandstand in 1946, with Betty Jo Booker playing the saxophone second from left.

Betty Jo Booker. *Courtesy of Grace Guier.*

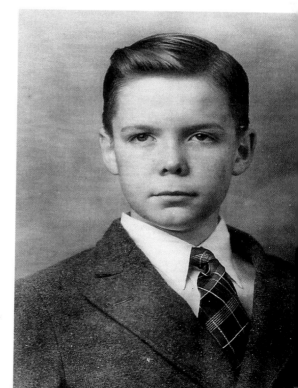

Paul Martin as a younger boy. *Courtesy of the Tom Albritton Collection.*

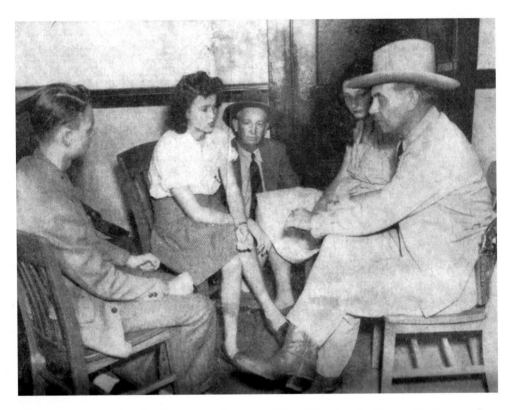

This photo appeared in the *Texarkana Gazette* in 1946 following the Martin-Booker murders. From left to right: Jerry Atkins, band leader; Betty Ann Roberts; Sheriff Bill Presley; Sophie Anne White; and Texas Ranger Captain M. T. "Lone Wolf" Gonzaullas.

TOP AND BOTTOM: Paul Martin and Betty Jo Booker's bodies at the crime scene. *Courtesy of Tillman Johnson Collection.*

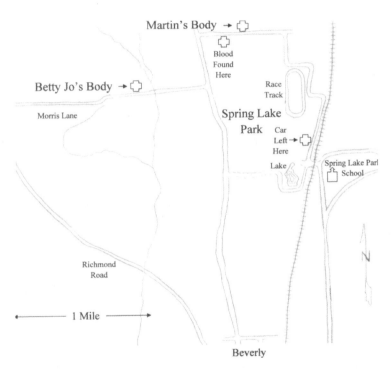

Map of the Booker-Martin crime scene. *Courtesy of Andrew Lusk.*

Richard Griffin in his Navy uniform. *Courtesy of the David Griffin Collection.*

Polly Ann Moore, in the last photo taken of her. *Courtesy of the Mark Moore Collection.*

Texas Ranger Captain M. T. "Lone Wolf" Gonzaullas. *Courtesy of the Tillman Johnson Collection.*

James M. Hollis as a college graduate.
Courtesy of Peggy Francisco.

Newspaper editor J. Q. Mahaffey.
Courtesy of Prudence Mackintosh.

Bowie County (Texas) Sheriff W. H. "Bill" Presley. *Courtesy of Billie Edgington.*

As the pressure mounts on the unsolved murders in the spring of 1946, Sheriff Bill Presley (in felt hat) is flanked by Texas Rangers and Texas state troopers en route to the Sheriff's office in Texarkana. *Courtesy of the Billie Presley Edgington Collection.*

TOP AND BOTTOM: Inside the Starks' home, May 1946. In the top image, note the two bullet holes in the windowpane, through which two shots were fired per hole, indicating that an automatic weapon was used. The curtain was open. The bottom image shows the wall crank phone where Katie Starks tried to call for help but was shot. *Photos courtesy of the Tillman Johnson collection.*

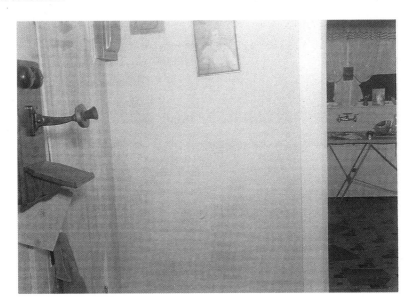

Youell Swinney mug shots, (left) entering the Texas Prison system in 1944 for robbery by assault, (right) re-entering the Texas prison system for larceny in 1981. *Photos courtesy of Texas Dept. of Corrections.*

GAZETTE   SATURDAY, SEPTEMBER 23, 1972

nciary hearing is completed

their recommendations concerning parole for Swinney from the Board of Pardons and Paroles.

All five declined to discuss their recommendations for the hearing transcript, citing that the information had been held by court decisions to be privileged.

However, both Cooksey and Nunn discussed their recommendations for a bill of exceptions, which was to be filed separately with the hearing transcript.

The Board of Pardons and Paroles, when considering prisoners for pardon or parole, seeks advice from the district judge of the court in which the prisoner was convicted, from the district attorney and from the sheriff of the county in which the conviction occurred, whether or not they held the office at the time of the conviction. The board is not bound by the recommendations.

Judge Nunn is the current Fifth District judge, while Cooksey and Rachel serve as district attorney and sheriff, respectively. Judge Line and Judge Jones both served as district attorney.

Both Cooksey and Judge Nunn said that they had opposed Swinney's parole because they were not convinced he had been rehabilitated after his habitual criminal conviction.

Cooksey said that he was opposed to parole for convicted habitual criminals.

In addition, Judge Nunn said that he received a letter from Swinney saying to "don't dare" oppose his parole. Judge Nunn said he had never heard of Swinney before receiving the letter.

Swinney later denied he had written such an order to the judge.

Both Cooksey and Judge Nunn denied Carter's question asking if the reason they opposed Swinney's parole was because several local officials had told them that they believed Swinney was involved in several murders in the Texarkana area in 1946.

Both men admitted they had heard the allegations, but added that it was not the basis of their reasoning in opposing Swinney's parole.

FBI agent Hallet had previously testified that Swinney was under investigation by local officials concerning five deaths in 1946. He added, however, that no charges were ever filed against Swinney in connection with the deaths.

The transcript of the hearing, along with the bill of exceptions, will be transcribed and sent to the Court of Criminal Appeals, which will then rule whether to grant Swinney's request for the writ of habeas corpus.

Judge Nunn estimated it would take from 90 days to six months for the transcript to be completed and sent to the appeals court.

Swinney, who has been held at the Bowie County Jail at Boston for about two weeks, will be returned to the Texas State Penitentiary at Huntsville to await the appeal court's ruling.

Youell Swinney, foreground, leaves County Building, escorted by Deputy Sheriff E.M. Watts. (Staff Photo)

LEFT: Peggy Swinney. *Courtesy of the Robert Stevens collection.* RIGHT: Youell Swinney at his 1972 Evidentiary Hearing, as covered in the *Texarkana Gazette.*

Tillman Johnson and Max Tackett, with Byron Johnson, Tillman's son. *Courtesy of the Tillman Johnson Collection.*

The arrest of Youell Swinney, July 15, 1946, Miller County, Ark., sheriff's office: left to right, Miller County chief deputy Tillman Johnson, Arkansas State policeman Charley Boyd, suspect Youell Lee Swinney, Arkansas State policeman Max Tackett, Atlanta resident Hibbett Lee, Atlanta city marshal Homer Carter. *Courtesy of the Tillman Johnson Collection, photo by Ted Dougan.*

MILLER COUNTY SHERIFFS OFFICE

W. E. DAVIS
Sheriff

TILLMAN JOHNSON
Chief Deputy

W. H. SCOTT

Deputy

Lawmen of the Miller County (Arkansas) Sheriff's Office. *Courtesy of the Tillman Johnson Collection.*

Tillman Johnson (left) and Mark Moore, Polly Ann Moore's
brother, reflect on the murders. *Courtesy of the author.*

apparently on a preaching job. The mother, Myrtle Looney Swinney, was also thirty-two; she'd been born in Georgia. Youell was two years old, the fifth of five children with two older brothers, two older sisters at that time. The census was taken on January 3. The following month Youell would be three.

Over the years, the elder Swinney moved about frequently, at various times living in Bodcaw in Miller County, Arkansas, in Stamps and Eureka Springs in Arkansas, in Texarkana (both sides of town), and Oak Cliff in Dallas. He attended college, Ouachita Baptist, in Arkadelphia for one semester. That seems to have been when Youell was born there.

Youell exhibited troubled signs early in life. Essentially he fell through the cracks of society in a rocky family environment. "I know he was in trouble all the time," a niece—older brother Cleo's daughter Joyce—said, keyed to family memories she'd heard. Swinney Sr. struggled with alcoholism. His daughter-in-law Winnie, Cleo's wife, later assumed the task of getting him sobered up on Saturday night so he could preach on Sunday. At the time, the two families lived nearby in College Hill on the Arkansas side of Texarkana.

Neither parent gave Youell much attention. It was as if he was unwanted. "His mother and daddy didn't care," Joyce said. "I hate to say that, but it's true." Swinney Sr. reputedly was a ladies' man. Cleo, the eldest son, eventually assumed a role of responsible adult, helping rear his younger siblings. While holding a job, he also grew a vegetable garden, raised hogs for meat, kept a milk cow and beehives, all to feed the large family. His parents' behavior created a sore spot for at least some. "They wouldn't even let us call them Grandpa and Grandma," said Joyce. "We had to call them Mr. and Mrs. Swinney."

Youell's favorite in the family became his older sister-in-law, Cleo's wife Winnie. She was kind to him and became a mother figure. She and Cleo assumed a major role of supporting the younger siblings as well as their own children.

In 1926, by which time two more daughters had been born and the family was in Texarkana, Arkansas, Stanley Swinney sued Myrtle for divorce. She answered with a motion seeking alimony, suit money, and attorney fees. The case came before the Miller County Chancery Court on

November 6, 1926. Following depositions from Swinney's relatives, the judge granted an "absolute and complete divorce" for Stanley from Myrtle "on grounds of personal indignities such as to render his condition in life intolerable." Stanley paid the court-directed attorney's fee for Myrtle. Custody of the children proceeded. By then, the older son and daughter were grown and gone and two girls younger than Youell had been born.

Stanley Swinney received custody of Youell, nine, and two daughters, twelve and seven. They were to live with him for the full nine months of each school year. Myrtle had visitation rights. During the three months of summer vacation Myrtle, if she wished, could have them with her. The court awarded Myrtle custody of a son, fourteen, and a daughter, three. Stanley would have visiting rights and pay fifty dollars each month for support of those in Myrtle's keep.

Subsequent reports were that Youell moved about from one place to another over the years. It may have been soon after the divorce that Youell, just a boy, was living with his grown brother Cleo in the College Hill neighborhood of the Arkansas side of Texarkana and got into trouble, possibly for the first time. Unknown to Cleo and his wife, the boy Youell broke into a neighborhood store and stole candy and chewing gum. Money was scarce; when Cleo's wife saw the boy eating candy and chewing gum, she wondered how he'd gotten it. He denied doing anything wrong. Cleo had a small barn behind the house. Suspecting the treats had been stolen, Cleo searched the barn for contraband and found Youell's cache. Cleo, a hardworking man when jobs were scarce, wanted nothing to jeopardize his good reputation. He reported it to the police. It probably was Youell's first burglary. Because of his age and the small value of the loot, the boy was given a harsh admonition and let go.

What is certain is that Youell's arrest record started at an early age. With the store burglary for candy not appearing on the police blotter, his first recorded criminal act, so far as can be ascertained, came a few years after divorce had split up the family and left him shifting from one domicile to another.

On September 25, 1929, Youell Lee Swinney became the subject of a front-page story in the *Texarkana Evening News*, with lurid headlines almost as sensational as those later tracking the Phantom story. As a juvenile, his name didn't appear in the story, but a matching of his name on the Bowie County district court docket with details in the newspaper article leaves no doubt that he was the boy described. It was, in effect, his official debut in crime, and a media splash. What experiences or nether connections may have prepared him for that moment, we have no way of knowing; his family life documents that his boyhood was anything but normal. He was a troubled boy by then, as the following news headline from the *Evening News* revealed:

TEXARKANA CHILD RACKETEER GANG DISCLOSED AS 'FAGANS' ARE SOUGHT

Three boys were held in the Bowie County holdover jail on Main Street after their arrest for theft and possession of stolen goods. Youell, at twelve, was the oldest; the youngest, only eight. If the reporter and editor were to be complimented for recalling the plot of *Oliver Twist*, the spelling, of Dickens's child manipulator Fagin's name, only missed by a letter.

"Three boys, the youngest eight and the oldest twelve," the *Evening News* reported, "nonchalantly gazed through the bars of the Bowie county holdover jail Tuesday while officers searched for other members of an alleged band of child racketeers who made smoking and spending money through sale of stolen property to a junk shop in the city.

"Two other youths, believed by county officers to have been the brains behind the theft combine, were the objects of a search. Officers expressed a belief that they were the 'Fagans' of the organization, using the children as their cats' paws.

"The three were arrested as they attempted to escape from the yard of a warehouse owned by the electric company near the Texas viaduct. An employee caught them in possession of bars of brass. He took them to police headquarters.

"'Some older boys told us they'd give us six bits if we'd sell the brass for them,' one of the lads told county officers."

The newspaper added: "The three youths seemed little worried by their imprisonment Tuesday or by the prospect of possible terms in the state reformatory should Judge [George W.] Johnson so decree."

Because juvenile records are shielded from public view, the disposition of young Swinney's case was not available. However, in the 1930 census, taken just a few months later, Youell's name is missing from the household of his father, in whose custody the judge in 1926 had placed him. This raises the probability that he was temporarily residing elsewhere when the census taker came. The census showed Stanley Swinney and his new wife Bessie, nee McKinsey, a church pianist, in Bowie County with four children—three daughters from his first marriage and a son from the second, but no Youell. Piecing together data from other sources, he may have been in a Texas reformatory.

In 1930, Myrtle married John Rudolph Travis, and they resided in Texarkana, Arkansas. Family lore labeled him as a mail-order husband, following Myrtle's ad that lured him from California to Texarkana with his two small children. The liaison was short-lived. A few years later she filed for divorce, which was granted in an uncontested case. In 1936 she married J. H. Tackett, "a very good old man" ten years her senior. He died. By 1946 when her son Youell was arrested, she had remarried again, to Carl Chaffin, in Texarkana. Stanley Swinney, following his second wife's death, was living in Missouri with his third wife, nee Nella Dorcas Fitzgerald.

Although the father, Stanley Swinney, had received custody of Youell, the boy seems to have spent some time with his mother and, later, stepfather. Years later, Youell complained that his stepfather had been abusive to him, but there is no proof of it extant nor of which stepfather he meant. Most likely he referred to his mother's second husband, his first stepfather, because of the age when he would have been most sensitive to such behavior.

According to Swinney family informants, there was more to the story, that neither birth parent was supportive in his younger years. One account has it that on one occasion in Eureka Springs, Arkansas, Swinney Sr. forced Youell to remain outside while the rest of the family ate dinner inside the house. In this version, Youell pleaded with a sister that he was starving and begged, "Can't you get me a biscuit or something?" These observers have it that both father and mother "virtually disowned" him as a boy and youth, with the father treating him harsher, the mother less so.

Swinney's rap sheet, compiled by the FBI, grew lengthy as his encounters with the law stretched forward.

On February 19, 1932, ten days after his fifteenth birthday, he was arrested in Texarkana, Arkansas, for burglary and larceny at a school building. According to a niece and nephew, this was the College Hill Elementary. This resulted, based on his prison records viewed in 1971 in Huntsville, Texas, in his being sent to the reformatory for boys at Pine Bluff, Arkansas, a fact confirmed by family members.

His next brush with the law came on January 4, 1935. The U.S. Secret Service held him for possession of and attempting to pass counterfeit nickels. Luck held for him. The charge was dismissed because of his being a juvenile—he was seventeen, a month shy of eighteen—and the "minor character" of the coins, five-cent pieces. But three months later, on April 3, 1935, he was picked up for investigation by the police in San Antonio, then released. A few months later, July 24, Texarkana, Texas police arrested him for possessing counterfeit coins and turned him over to the Secret Service. He was sentenced to two years in federal prison and taken by U.S. marshals to El Reno, Oklahoma. When he was conditionally released in 1937 at age twenty, he had lost fifteen days of good time for prison violations.

He was soon back in custody. In 1937, picked up by the sheriff's office in Monroe, Louisiana, for counterfeiting, he returned to federal custody. The following year, he escaped from federal marshals, for which he was assessed three years and eighteen days in the U.S. maximum-security prison at Leavenworth, Kansas. Imposition of sentence was deferred till his term at Leavenworth was completed; he was ordered to report to the court at the expiration of his current prison sentence. In 1939, the twenty-two-year-old Swinney was given three years for counterfeiting and escape from the U.S. marshals. He was lucky again, to receive a conditional release, but authorities sought him soon for violating the conditional release by failing to report and an alleged robbery. He was arrested in November 1940 for parole violation by the sheriff's office in Shreveport and held for U.S. marshals.

By then his life was an old, recurring story: arrested for a variety of crimes, including felony theft, with a record of raising money through counterfeiting, then sentenced, getting out early, escaping from federal custody, as well as violating conditions of his probation.

At some point during these years, he claimed to be married to a woman he lived with in Hobo Jungle, a neighborhood next to College Hill on the Arkansas side. A search of county records turned up no such union or a divorce dissolving it, apparently making his claim fictive.

His criminal career shifted gears in late 1940. In December he was arrested and charged with grand larceny—automobile theft. According to the indictment, on November 19 in Texarkana, Arkansas, he stole Dr. J. W. Burnett's new 1941 Master Deluxe Chevrolet Coupe, valued at eight hundred dollars. Although Swinney's counterfeiting activities had netted him federal prison terms, this felony bought him into the Arkansas state judicial system as an adult for the first time, eligible for the harsher confines of the state prison.

Prosecuting Attorney Dick Huie worked out an agreement with the defendant to plead guilty in exchange for a three-year sentence. On February 11, 1941, Circuit Judge Dexter Bush, accepting the plea of guilty and the agreement, pronounced sentence.

The bleak legal wording spelled out the outcome.

"On this day comes the State of Arkansas, by its attorney Dick Huie, and comes the defendant hereto in proper person and by attorney and enters his plea of guilty to the crime of Grand Larceny and prays the mercy of the court and the court after due consideration fixes his punishment at a term of Three Years in the State Penitentiary for Grand Larceny."

Though the record asserted that an attorney represented him, no lawyer's name appeared on the instrument. Decades later, this would become the major focus of contention of whether an attorney had been present or not.

Swinney was just a few days shy of his twenty-fourth birthday. It was his first state conviction since his juvenile days.

Swinney remained behind bars when the United States entered World War II in December 1941. Less than three years after his conviction, he was released into wartime America—but only briefly. In August 1943, when he left the state prison, the sheriff's office in Little Rock detained him as a federal parole violator. That took him to federal prison in

Atlanta, Georgia, to complete his counterfeiting sentence and for his earlier escape.

On April 12, 1944, he was discharged upon expiration of his sentence, only to be seized the next day in Monroe, Louisiana, for parole violation, the specific reason left unclear in the records. The incident resulted in an extension of his probation, with supervision extended for five more years, until 1949.

His in-and-out status with federal authorities made his name familiar to U.S. marshals, but he was soon back in a state court, now Texas, where his boyhood escapades had begun.

In August 1944, he faced a charge of robbery by assault, or strongarm banditry, in Texarkana, Texas. He pleaded not guilty. The jury found him guilty as charged. Judge Robert S. Vance sentenced him to five years in the Texas state penitentiary. He remained in the Bowie County jail at Boston, the county seat, until his transfer to the state penitentiary at Huntsville in November, when he acquired his new identity, Offender # 103738. He had entered a new phase, convicted of a violent crime. His release date would be 1949, the same year his federal probation had been scheduled to end, before the new state conviction.

Swinney was one of three prisoners arriving from Bowie County the same day. The other two had been convicted of burglary. Swinney was the oldest and the only one sentenced for a violent personal crime. The others were seventeen, drawing a two-year sentence, and twenty-two, assessed nine years on multiple counts.

Swinney's processing into the Texas prison system provided one of the most detailed impressions of him up to that point. He was twenty-seven years old. He had two juvenile sentences and four adult convictions behind him. Physically he was five feet eleven inches tall, weighed 166 pounds, with blue eyes, brown hair, and a fair complexion. He stated he was a Baptist. He wore size nine shoes.

The most intriguing part of the citation referred to "Marks on Person" that the clerk entered.

"Vaccination scar. Tattoo of skull and heart with letter Revenge, lower inner left arm. Cut scar left side upper lip, cut scar at side of eyebrow."

He used tobacco. His habits were "Temperate"—the same self-assessment that all other inmates invariably told the clerk.

Swinney answered "Yes" to his ability to read and write—a claim many convicts of that day could not make. He said he'd completed nine and a half years of school. In light of later information, he appears to have stretched his claim by several years, possibly in hopes of getting assigned an easier job. He cited an occupation as an office clerk and that he could type. He had served time before. He knew which skills helped avoid hard labor.

As for being an ex-serviceman, the space was left blank at a time when the U.S. was fighting some of its bloodiest battles overseas.

The tattoo on his lower left arm was the prisoner's most distinctive physical feature. It combined a drawn heart and skull with letters spelling a word that left no confusion as to its meaning: *Revenge.*

Whatever circumstances led to his ordering the tattoo, the results strongly suggested anger sufficient to distill his feelings into a single, unambiguous word. It was as close as one was likely to peer into Swinney's inner turmoil.

His mug shots, frontal and side views, at the time of this incarceration reflect a boyish face with a head of dark hair coming to the collar at the back with long sideburns, and a prominent Adam's apple. He is fairly good looking. He is staring sullenly into the camera.

Of the three from Bowie County who took the long ride together to the state prison that November 1944 day, Swinney was the first of the three out, after serving slightly more than a year of his five-year term. The seventeen-year-old, sentenced to two years, was discharged in July 1946. The twenty-two-year-old, with a nine-year sentence, escaped in 1947, was recaptured the next day, and was finally released in 1950.

Swinney, on the other hand, spent approximately thirteen months of his five-year sentence in prison. He left the prison gates on December 22, 1945, in time for Christmas. His family, led by his minister father, successfully petitioned for clemency to the Board of Pardons and Paroles to secure his early release, which put him back on the streets with a checkered background of criminal activities and an incarceration record that few others had. His prison report had credited him with two years' service. Prison officials noted he had been "courteous and respectful, performing his duties in a diligent and conscientious manner."

He signed a conditional pardon receipt on December 21, accepting the conditions "that I conduct myself in all things in an exemplary manner" and report to his parole board or face revocation and return to prison.

However, there was more to it. A further condition of the parole was that he be released to the custody of the U.S. marshal in Shreveport. If he should fail to comply, the parole could be revoked, returning him to prison.

He was free, with stout strings attached, as he returned to his rough-and-tumble hometown and the uncertainties of a tumultuous postwar society.

By that time, Swinney had established a pattern of functioning poorly in the free world, serving time for infractions, escaping from federal marshals, violating parole, repeatedly counterfeiting and getting caught, while violating state laws of felony automobile theft and robbery by assault, steadily progressing from lesser to larger and, eventually, violent behavior. Despite the long list of convictions, he had been remarkably lucky. By serving much less than the full terms, he had escaped the full consequences of his actions.

Max Tackett, for one, set out to investigate Swinney in depth. The state police files soon bulged with his reports. By the end of July, he had compiled a substantial stack of interviews aimed at documenting Swinney's activities and possible culpability.

He followed the pattern of stolen and abandoned cars he'd observed earlier, starting with the Plymouth sedan stolen from Wayne O'Donnell.

"This car was stolen Mar 24 1946 between 7 and 9 PM, while parked in front of the Michael Meagher Hospital, in Texarkana Arkansas, by Youell Swinny [sic]. It was recovered in possession of his wife at a parking lot in Texarkana. She was arrested by Officer Boyd June 28 1946."

The date, March 24, was the evening after Richard Griffin and Polly Ann Moore were found dead that morning. It seemed reasonable that their killer would want to replace the car he'd driven, in case it had been seen and identified, with a different one.

Tackett questioned O'Donnell about the car's interior and contents. O'Donnell said there may have been a pair of cotton gloves in the car, that there was a torn floor mat in the front of the car but no mat in the rear. His description of the seat cover was identical with that in the recovered automobile.

Tackett speculated: "The fact that the Booker girl was a close friend of the O'Donnells and knew their car well enough to have recognized it in any situation. This girl may have recognized this car and that could have been the reason for the killing."

It was true that Betty Jo Booker's parents and the O'Donnells were friends, and she might have recognized the car.

There was another piece of possible evidence, a pair of shoes that another family member contributed. They had belonged to Swinney. They had been put away while damp and mildewed until they seemed to be brown but actually were a dark tan. Tackett failed to match the shoes with plaster casts taken at the Starks crime scene, but the muddy tracks necessarily were distorted and exposure to water and subsequent drying also had affected the shoes. However, the shoes' having been soaked at one time suggested he had washed them or waded in a creek to get, say, blood and mud off of them, which would fit in with the killer's tracks across the wet plowed field at the Starks residence. By any measure, the tracks at the crime scene were inexact and hard to match with anybody's shoes.

The condition of the shoes made it difficult to compare precisely with other tracks. The tracks in the plowed field were almost impossible to measure because of the soggy nature of the soft earth. Furthermore, the tracks inside the house were never definitively assessed to be those of the killer. They were believed to have been, by some, but others had their doubts. Deputy Tillman Johnson said, "I never in my mind could be certain they were made by the killer. There were too many men walking around in the house. I felt that possibly one of them had made the tracks. But I'm positive, in my own mind, that the tracks in the field were made by the killer."

The shoes became a possible link of Swinney to the crime scene. Tackett's reports covered Swinney's activities from several directions:

- Interviewing Luther McClure, whose 1941 red five-passenger coupe was stolen on March 3 at his home in Texarkana, Texas, he learned that there were no gloves, gun, or ammunition in the car when stolen, and nothing was left in the car, once recovered, to tie anyone to the car. The car was returned from Beaumont to Texarkana by the insurance company.

- Carl Chaffin, Swinney's stepfather, stated that Swinney and Peggy had been at his house on College Hill on Friday, March 8, and stayed until the following Tuesday, March 12. He believed Swinney had stolen his .38 caliber pearl-handled Smith and Wesson revolver.

- Swinney admitted he had taken the pistol and pawned it at the New York Pawn Shop on West Broad Street for twenty dollars.

- Swinney's sister, Maxine Whetsone, while looking through his clothing at her rural home where he had stayed briefly in May, found a shirt with the name STARK on it. She mentioned it to her husband, Wade Whetsone. A quarrel immediately arose. Her husband said he'd "always believed that Swinney was the guilty man in all of these Texarkana murders." Her husband took the shirt to the police. She didn't know how long it had been in Swinney's possession.

    The shirt was to become a major piece of evidence almost immediately.

- Peggy's mother was interviewed about the painter's clothing from Swinney's stolen car. She said Swinney had tried to leave it but her husband had put it back in Swinney's car. She described the clothing as a clean suit of one shirt and one pair of white overalls and a dirty suit of one shirt and a pair of dirty white overalls. Both had paint stains on them. Tackett was unsuccessful in having Texas officers search the house.

Tackett's shoe-leather detective work turned up suspicious factors but no hard evidence, unless the shirt marked STARK could be linked to the crime.

It didn't come to mind immediately, but after a while Tackett's thoughts returned to the man with a rifle he'd stopped at the Index bridge over Red River. He kept turning it over in his mind. That had been many weeks before. Since then he'd stopped and questioned probably hundreds of men. The more he thought about it, the surer he became that the man had been Youell Lee Swinney. He soon persuaded himself he had stopped the Phantom killer that afternoon. If the man was going from Texarkana, as he obviously was, on his way to Delight, Arkansas, or some other Arkansas venue, Highway 71 was one of the obvious routes. Driving was one of Swinney's pastimes; he knew all the roads and back roads in the region. If he wanted to stay away from Texas, where the heat had grown intense, he would concentrate his driving in another area, across the state line in Arkansas. Living in Delight, he could go to Texarkana via either of two routes, Highway 71 or Highway 67. Highway 71 crosses the bridge at Index; if he took Highway 67 he would pass Virgil and Katie Starks's farmhouse, situated right off the highway. The circumstances fit, and Tackett decided that, in fact, he had stopped Swinney that week before the Starks murder and had been conned into accepting the explanation for the rifle in the back.

He didn't mention this to others. It would serve no purpose. There also was the chance that the man hadn't been Swinney, and that this was potentially a case of psychological projection. The encounter had been brief and weeks before. But the thought nagged at him.

If, indeed, that had been Swinney and he had used the rifle at the Starks home, what had he done with the gun? There were no reports of his having a rifle. Did he heave it into the Red River as he crossed the bridge several miles away from the crime scene, or into some other waterway between there and Delight? It was all conjecture, with not one iota of definite evidence. There was, furthermore, the possibility that a pistol had been used in the Starks murder.

SWINNEY'S STATEMENT

Tackett took Swinney to the state police district offices at Hope. Swinney gave a statement beginning with February 23. This would have been the Saturday night *after* the Hollis-Larey attacks, and the Arkansas officers may have confused the dates, thinking they were questioning him about events of February 22. From time to time, the Friday night crime was mixed up with the Saturday date, February 23, in other accounts. At any rate, Swinney, skipping any mention of February 22, offered his version.

"On the night of Feb. 23, 1946, Saturday night, Peggy Stevens and I and Jess Roberts went to Chaylors Night Club in Texarkana, Arkansas. I had a quarrel with Peggy and slapped her. Peggy got [Clarence] 'Fats' Anderson [a bouncer] to come back to our table and quieted it down.

"We left Chaylors place and went to Stockman Hotel. Jess Roberts was with us. While at Stockmans Hotel I had trouble with Peggy and Jess Roberts took it up and Took Peggy and left me at the Stockmans Hotel. We're riding in Jess Roberts car this night. They left hotel bout 11 P.M.

"After Peggy and Jess Roberts left me at the Stockman Hotel I walked down to the apartment where Peggy and I had been staying."

Their room was at 1904 West Sixteenth Street, in the Rose Hill neighborhood on the Texas side. Three blocks away, on West Seventeenth Street, Police Chief Runnels and Deputy Sheriff Riley lived, totally unaware that the suspect and his girl friend had lived near them briefly.

"On the same night," Swinney's statement continued, "Jess Roberts threw rocks through the window of Mr. [Garland] Wells [i.e., his landlord] window. I later paid Mr. Wells for the damage. I left my room and went to 220 Senator St. where my sister lives. I slept in room that night alone."

The statement contained a number of interesting aspects. Tackett believed that Swinney's statement dealt with the night of the Hollis-Larey beatings, a Friday rather than Saturday night, despite the date on the statement. If Swinney is relating his experience of Saturday, February 23, it is much less germane to the investigation, for it would be the night following the Hollis-Larey assaults. If, on the other hand, the actual date was confused and the relevant night was Friday, February 22, a quite different scenario unfolds.

First, an angry situation built up at Chaylor's nightclub to the point that Swinney slapped Peggy, a violent act. The altercation was "quieted down" only when the bouncer intervened. Later at the hotel, according to Swinney, Jess Roberts took Peggy's side of the argument and took her away from Swinney, leaving Swinney by himself at the hotel. Swinney had no car at the time. Swinney said Peggy and Roberts left at eleven o'clock. Selecting that particular time, if accurate, would provide an alibi for the Hollis-Larey case, for on Friday night that was about the time the attacks took place. If, however, the quarrel at the Stockman's Hotel took place earlier, it would have left time for Swinney to steal a car and drive out to the Richmond Road area where the attack occurred roughly around that time. Swinney said the couple left him "about eleven P.M.," an approximation open to interpretation.

The Stockman's Hotel was situated outside the city limits on Highway 67 West, or West Seventh Street, near where the Griffin-Moore murders were committed approximately a month later. If, as he claimed, he walked back to the West Sixteenth Street address where he and Peggy lived, it would have taken him at least thirty minutes, probably more, to cover the distance on foot. And after that, he went to his sister's house on the Arkansas side, all the way across town, where he spent the night "alone." This distance would entail a very long hike, not impossible, but highly improbable. He, being alone, had no documentation of where he was at the times he claimed.

Tackett held to a theory that the altercation with Roberts inflamed Swinney and inspired him with revenge. He was known later that spring to have stolen a car at Robison Courts, a short walk from the Stockman's Hotel. It was an area with which he was familiar. In fact, at one point, a nephew remembered, Youell and Peggy had lived in Robison Courts. It is not clear when this was, for the nephew was a small boy at the time. Robison Courts was much closer than the room on West Sixteenth Street, and anyone could have walked the distance of a few blocks within a matter of minutes.

The February 22 attack occurred in the general area where Peggy's parents lived. Tackett believed Swinney stole a car soon after his quarrel with

Peggy and Roberts and drove out Richmond Road looking for them, guessing Roberts was taking her to her parents' home. Seeing a car parked on a side road, he turned off his lights and drove in, parked, and walked in on the couple, believing them to be Peggy and her boyfriend. Tackett's theory was potentially valid. Although presumably Swinney carried no flashlight with him, he could have found one in the stolen car or could have driven to his room on West Sixteenth, retrieved a flashlight, and taken off on his quest.

Swinney's last previous conviction had been for robbery by assault, which fit snugly with the action that Friday night, and the gunman, according to both Hollis and Larey, was a man filled with rage, which must have accurately described Swinney's emotional state at that hour. If at some point he realized he had come upon the wrong couple, he hardly would have offered an "Excuse me!" and quit the scene. Tackett's theory might also account for the vicious abuse the criminal had inflicted upon the female victim, as an act of vengeance upon Peggy for her part in rejecting him. The gunman apparently believed he had left Hollis dead, which would have paralleled Swinney's feelings toward Roberts, whom he had feared confronting in person earlier. With the comfort of a gun, he held the upper hand, and wielded it.

Whether Tackett's theory explained the evening or not, several items stood out in Swinney's account. He had no alibi other than his own claims for his whereabouts from the time Roberts and Peggy left his presence. No one corroborated his claims. His statement seemed to be given in the context of the attack night, as he carefully crafted the events to provide an alibi for the crimes. Had he been referring to the following—Saturday—night, it would not have mattered at what time they parted company or even what had taken place.

There was, furthermore, the fact that this particular statement was given to the Arkansas state police on July 30, five months after the evening in question. By that time, the events themselves would hold supremacy over exactly which date and time the events had occurred. The emotional memory, if it was strong enough, would stand out more forcibly than a particular date.

Most of all, Swinney presented no supported alibi to account for himself during the minutes a man and woman were being assaulted.

The next portion of Swinney's statement to the state police contained his version of his movements in April. He cited his itinerary but dwelled on no details. His account covered the critical weekend when Paul Martin and Betty Jo Booker were murdered, but mentioned only that he and Peggy had stayed at her parents' home. This version conflicted radically with what Peggy had said earlier. The one thing they both agreed on was that they were in Texarkana that tragic weekend. He offered no specific information about the rest of the spring, as he retraced his movements ending in Antoine later in April.

The interrogation then turned back to March and the weekend of the Griffin-Moore murders. He abandoned a stolen Hudson sedan and they spent the night at a motel. The next day they rented a tourist cabin where, he claimed, he spent the night with Peggy. Earlier he'd roamed about town on foot, then joined Peggy at "about" eleven P.M. This would have placed him with Peggy when the Griffin-Moore murders occurred.

"Spent rest of night in cabin with Peggy. Spent all day Sunday in the cabin. About dark on the 24 March I left Peggy in the cabin and went to town. I stole a 1941 Plymouth sedan near a church downtown."

Again, he had presented a shaky alibi for the hours during which Richard Griffin and Polly Moore were murdered. Peggy was his alibi, and earlier she had given a different account of the evening.

Then after dark he stole a car, which he used to leave town. He did not hesitate to admit the car-theft felony, in fact, seemed almost eager to confess it.

Essentially, he had confirmed that he'd had the opportunity to commit all of the Texas-side crimes, by virtue of having been in Texarkana without a solid alibi on any of the occasions.

When questions zeroed in on the murders, Swinney was never forthcoming. He wouldn't discuss them. "Man, I wadn't here," he'd insist, even though it was proved that he was. "I didn't have nothing to do with it." Repeatedly he denied everything but stealing cars.

CHAPTER 18

TIGHTENING THE NOOSE

A rmed with statements from the prisoners, Tackett and cohorts interviewed a series of witnesses keyed to Swinney's actions while at Antoine, Arkansas.

- Kelly Caldwell: "On Friday, May 3, 1946, I was at a café in Antoine. Youell Swinney came by the café about dusk dark and told me that he was going to Texarkana and asked me if I wished to send any word to my brother who lives in Texarkana. Peggy Stevens was with Swinney. He turned and drove down the street and turned toward Prescott road and out of sight."

- Leonard Hare: "On Saturday, May 4, 1946—I am positive of this date because it was the Saturday following Virgil Starks's death in Texarkana—I saw Swinney and some woman who I presumed to be Peggy Stevens come into Antoine from the cut-off road leading to the Delight and Prescott road. They turned and passed directly in front of my house and entered Highway 26, which is the main Delight and Antoine road. It was just breaking daylight when I saw them. I had seen the two of them several times and knew it to be Swinney and the car he had been driving."

- Clyde Lamb: "Lee Swinney, Louis Lamb, and myself went to Murfreesboro, Arkansas, on Friday or Saturday 19 or 20 of April to see about a job. The following Monday we went to work. Everett Lamb, Louie Lamb, and Jack Barton rode with Swinney to work and back, a distance of about seventeen miles. Rode with him until May 3. This was last day."

- Everett Lamb: "Swinney told me that he was going to Texarkana late in the afternoon of May 3, 1946, and that he was not going to work any more on the Murfreesboro job, as he had no place to stay, and that we would have to secure rides with someone else. All the time that I have known Swinney at Antoine he has told me several times that he was going to Texarkana and he would leave the job. On one occasion I had to catch a ride from work to home because Swinney had left the job and was not there to carry me home."

  Tackett entered a note: "Everett Lamb stated that Swinney told him that on one occasion he was stopped and checked by the police near Texarkana in connection with those murders."

- Jack Barton: "I rode to and from work with Swinney in his car. On one occasion Swinney tried to sell me his car, but I could not buy it. I loaned Swinney fifteen dollars at one time, but he paid me back. I left a pair of cheap white cotton gloves in Swinney's car; they had a blue cuff. Swinney talked once to me about going squirrel hunting and asked me if I had any guns. He said that he might be able to get one from Louie Lamb.

"I believe that Swinney went to Texarkana every Saturday that he was in this part of the country. I remember only Saturday that Swinney did not leave town. On one occasion I saw Swinney arranging his trousers and I glimpsed a large roll of money folded in the middle fastened in some way to his underwear in such a way that it was held in place by his belt, this was about a week or maybe less before he left here for good.

"Swinney told me that at one time he and his wife were parked near Texarkana and a policeman came up to the car and told them that they were in danger and might get killed by the Phantom Killer.

"About dusk dark on Friday, May 3, 1946, Swinney came to my house and told me that I would have to get another ride as he was leaving the job and going to Texarkana. However, I believe that on Saturday morning, May 4. 1946, I rode to work with Swinney. I am not sure Everett Lamb rode or not."

• Mrs. Louis Lamb: "My sister Peggy Stevens and Youell Lee Swinney arrived at my house on Wednesday before Easter Sunday which is the seventeenth day of April, I think. That was the first time I had ever seen Youell Lee Swinney. We went to Hot Springs on Easter Sunday. On the following Monday Swinney and my husband started working at Murfreesboro, Arkansas. Swinney and Peggy boarded at my house until May 3, 1946.

"Immediately after Swinney and my husband arrived home from work on the afternoon of May 3, we engaged in a quarrel concerning some board money due me. I asked Swinney and Peggy to leave. I left and went to a neighbor's home and when I returned they were leaving. This was shortly before dark. My husband told me that he saw

Swinney and Peggy in the car in Antoine about five A.M. Saturday morning, May 4."

The witnesses filled out the picture that had Swinney leaving abruptly following a quarrel with Peggy's sister, going to Texarkana the evening of Friday, May 3. He and Peggy were seen the following Saturday morning back in the Antoine area, and they were in Nashville at noon that day, having the car repaired. He was known to have gone to Texarkana almost every weekend. On the critical Friday evening he had headed toward, then back from, Texarkana, which would have taken him by the Starks home, in an emotional state hardly conducive to calm behavior.

Equally intriguing were Swinney's comments that, while parked near Texarkana, a policeman had warned him and Peggy that the Phantom killer was loose and they were in danger by parking there. They had been perceived as potential victims of the killer, because they were a couple. He had told this account to two men, Everett Lamb and Jack Barton. Considering the tenor of the times, it's almost certain that if Swinney had been alone he would have been taken into custody and investigated, as was many another man by himself during that time. Most of all, his car, which was stolen, would have been checked out, leading to his arrest.

Peggy was his shield, his "cover." Her presence must have protected him on more than one occasion. Little thought seems to have been given to the possibility that the Phantom might have had a girl friend or wife. If policemen had taken the license number, a check would have revealed a stolen car.

The faded khaki work shirt found among Swinney's clothing immediately became a focal point of the investigation. The laundry mark wasn't Swinney's. The shirt was faded. On the collar a dim mark, STARK, had no S on the end of the name but was close enough to the slain man's surname to raise suspicions. Most laundry marks did not spell out the owner's full name unless it was quite short. It made sense to believe that STARK was the mark for STARKS. It was too close to be ignored. The old laundry mark could be seen with the naked eye but all of the letters weren't clear. To satisfy any doubts, Sheriff Davis sent the shirt to the FBI lab for confirmation. Under a black light the full laundry mark was verified.

In the shirt pocket they also found fragments of metallic matter that could have come from a welding shop.

On July 21 the FBI sent a Teletype message to its Little Rock office.

MR. VIRGIL STARKS. VICTIM OF MURDER. DEBRIS FROM POCKETS OF TAN SHIRT FROM SUSPECT CONTAINS MAGNETIC METAL SLAG BALLS, SIMILAR TO THOSE IN GRINDING AND WELDING OPERATIONS. HUMAN BROWN HAIR FRAGMENTS ALSO FOUND. SUGGEST KNOWN HAIR SPECIMENS FROM STARKS AND FROM SUSPECT. QUANTITY OF SAND ALSO FOUND. SUGGEST SAND SAMPLES BE SUBMITTED FROM STARKS RESIDENCE FOR COMPARISON.

[J. EDGAR] HOOVER

Starks was long buried by then, with no hair samples available. Had DNA testing been a reality, positive data probably could have been obtained, but that technology would be decades in the future.

Tackett and Johnson took a dozen pillboxes to the Starks farm and collected samples at random. The welding shop had a dirt floor. The two men scooped up shavings, soil, and slag from different parts of the shop. They sent their collection to the FBI lab.

The report came back that the metal fragments in the shirt were "matching and similar" to those in the Starks welding shop. This was good evidence, but it didn't go far enough.

The shirt was almost identified by the surviving victim. "This shirt was taken to Mrs. Starks," said Tackett, "and she said, yes, that was her husband's shirt and she pointed to a place on the front of the shirt where she remembered personally repairing it.

"But on reflection the next day or so she said she couldn't be sure. She knew it would mean death for the suspect, based on her identification of the shirt, and she said she could not positively identify it. The name was spelled STARK instead of STARKS, and any woman would have repaired a damaged place such as that on her husband's shirt."

Johnson then took the shirt to the three laundries in town. At the third one, Nelson-Huckins, a leading laundry on the Texas side, the manager acknowledged it was their mark. It belonged to one Billie Starr, madam of a well-known brothel several blocks away. All of the whorehouses were situated in Texarkana, Texas; the Arkansas-side police didn't tolerate them.

Armed with the shirt and the laundry's assessment, Johnson headed for the Star Club at 807 West Fourth Street in Texarkana's notorious red-light district. Billie Starr's bordello was housed in a long, one-story dormitory-style building at the bottom of the street and across from her major competitor, Fannie's. He rang the bell at the front door of the white frame structure and waited. He waited a long while. Finally, the proprietress appeared in a robe, unsmiling, and asked him what he wanted—at that time of day, her expression implied. He told her briefly without disclosing the heart of his mission.

"I can't see you right now, Mr. Johnson," Ms. Starr said. "I was in bed. We work late. You woke me up. You'll have to wait till I get dressed."

She ushered the chief deputy into the parlor.

When she reappeared, she had her makeup on and her hair combed. Johnson held the rough khaki shirt up for her inspection, explaining that the laundry records showed it had her code on it.

She handled it gingerly, inspected it with an imperial glance, and sniffed.

"We don't have customers who'd wear shirts like this!" she said haughtily. Handing the shirt back to him, she dismissed the subject.

Studied closely, each letter of the word STARK was more faded than the one preceding it. A quick glance might overlook the terminal K. Years later, when it was too late to be of practical use and the laundry records no longer existed, Johnson realized that the man at the laundry, with a cursory look, must have missed the K. Seeing only STAR, he immediately recognized Billie Starr's mark, and had assumed it was hers, or at least one of her clients'. Johnson felt he had come close to tying the shirt to Starks. If a laundry already had a mark for STAR, it would assign a different mark to Starks, the most logical way being to simply add the next letter, K. Johnson worried about this, but by then there was nothing more he could do.

If the shirt did belong to Starks it was easily explained how it had come into Swinney's possession, linking him tightly to the crime. Swinney frequently stole clothing. If he'd been at the scene that night, looking for something to steal, he would have entered the welding shop, flashlight in hand. The shirt was oversized for Swinney but would have fit Starks, who was brawny and muscular. A work shirt would have been as useful as any other item. At a time when Swinney was employed as a laborer, its utility would have been obvious.

Katie Starks, hearing a noise in the back yard, had asked her husband to turn down the radio. This would have coincided with the intruder's coming from the welding shop. Minutes later the shootings began.

Tackett compiled a detailed chronology of Swinney's whereabouts from February 22 until deep into May, based on information from Swinney and Peggy. There were gaps for days when data were not available, plus the timeline was based primarily on what Swinney and Peggy had told him, subject to error and variations depending on memory and motivation. It did, however, establish their presence in Texarkana during the Texas-side crimes and in the vicinity the night of the Starks shootings. Although details of their lives in a portion of May were not clear, a new phase began in May when they left Delight, winding up in Waynoka, Oklahoma.

Waynoka, a railroad center of three thousand in northwestern Oklahoma, is not far from the state's Panhandle. Hundreds of miles northwest of Texarkana, Waynoka was a short drive north to the Kansas line. Swinney found work with an extra gang on the Atchison, Topeka and Santa Fe, a leg of which operated from Wellington, Kansas to Amarillo, Texas. Waynoka was an important stop on the line.

Swinney later contended that he only worked there three or four days in the latter part of June and the first part of July—clearly untrue, for he had been in Shreveport on June 28, getting married. Peggy said he had worked there about two weeks versus just a few days. Tied to other accounts from people in the area, her statement seems to be more accurate. He put her in the Commercial Hotel at first, a reasonably priced lodging where railroad people stayed. Later they stayed at private homes.

In late August, Tackett typed a note referring to a stolen car.

"The gray Dodge sedan, used by Swinney when he stole the clothing in Nashville, Ark., from the sailors, has been located in Salt Lake City, in possession of two sailors, who claimed that a strange man gave it to them to use. The subjects and car at Salt Lake City at this time."

Two days later he had an even more interesting report, about Swinney's behavior in Waynoka.

"The FBI of Dallas, Texas, has received information from some officer of Waynoka, Okla., that a Negro man purchased a pistol from a stranger, believed to have been Swinney. The Negro later shot up the railroad camp near Waynoka where he was employed and was fired by the foreman the following day. The pistol was taken from him by the foreman on the night of the disturbance but given back to the Negro on the following morning when he was fired.

"The pistol or Negro have neither been located at this time. I have been told by the local FBI agent that the office at Dallas, Texas, is attempting to locate the Negro and pistol.

"The information that we received here is 'That the pistol in question was a .22 caliber automatic pistol."

That would have fit the caliber of the gun that killed Virgil Starks and wounded his wife, Katie.

The search was on for Harry Woods, alias Lawton, who had obtained the gun from Swinney. Woods had been a cook in Extra Gang #1, but the records weren't clear as to which foreman was over the gang at that time, as each of them had worked in that capacity at one time or another near Waynoka.

Tackett drove to Dallas, chasing down claims Swinney had made that would have established partial alibis. Swinney had told Texas-side officers that he could prove he wasn't in Texarkana the night of the Martin-Booker murders, because he had been involved in a minor traffic violation in

Houston that day, for which a Texas highway patrolman had issued him a warning ticket. Tackett had the highway patrol office in Dallas check with Houston authorities. "We ascertained that no such ticket was ever issued to either the name Swinney or to the license numeral on his car."

Swinney had claimed to Arkansas officers that he had a minor accident with a city bus in Dallas that day, presuming to establish an alibi. Tackett called upon the Dallas Police Department, the Dallas County sheriff's office, and the Dallas city bus officials. None of them found a report of the claimed bus accident. The company running the city bus service, Tackett said, "stated that under no circumstances would their driver have failed to report even a minor fender bumping."

Swinney said that he frequently made trips for Mack's Travel Bureau at 708 Commerce Street in Dallas. "Upon checking there," reported Tackett, "I located a former operator of the establishment who knows Swinney, but who would offer no assistance in checking on him. He was very unfriendly to any policeman. The bureau only keeps the signatures of the people who ride with them for a period of one month at a time, for the purpose of maintaining their own books. At the end of that time the cards with the signatures are destroyed.

"Swinney and his wife stated that on April 13 they picked up an old painter at Mack's Bureau in Dallas and contracted to take him to Shreveport. They claim that he got out of the car near Longview, Texas, and that they brought his clothing on to Texarkana, arriving about dark on the evening of April 13. Upon checking at the travel bureau, there was no record of this man and no one apparently remembered him."

Sergeant O. D. Morris of the Arkansas State Police's criminal division wrote the Atchison, Topeka & Santa Fe's superintendent of special services in Amarillo about Swinney, noting that he was being held for Virgil Starks's murder. He mentioned a supervisor's statement that Harry Woods, alias Harry Lawton, working as a cook on gang #1 at Heman, had purchased a pistol from Swinney. A special agent for the railroad investigated.

"I drove to St. Vrain and talked to Mr. [Albert] Calloway; he stated he seen a gun, a .32 or .38 caliber which he thinks was a Colts make, in the possession of Harry Woods, that Woods told him he bought from Swinney.

He also stated there was two guns in camp, one a .22 automatic, which he never seen but talked to Jim Snapp, who *did* see this gun.

"Calloway also stated this man Snapp seen Swinney give his wife a gun to hold on a man whose name he does not know; then Swinney whipped this man with a chain; is possible this gang can be located at Plains, Texas."

A crucial statement began to fill in the blanks of Swinney's activities. Albert O. Calloway, a relief section foreman for the railroad, was foreman of gang #1 at Heman, Oklahoma. One evening he watched a dice game between members of a work gang. Harry Woods, another employee and the cook, also was watching the game after going broke. Woods pulled a pistol from his pocket, either a .32 or .38 caliber automatic, a Colt, and tried to borrow money. Calloway didn't see anybody lend him money. Calloway asked him where he'd gotten the gun. Woods said he bought it from "the bootlegger." Calloway later learned "the bootlegger" was Youell Lee Swinney.

"I also know that Swinney had a .22 automatic in his possession as he was trying to sell it," stated Calloway. "I never did see the gun, but a man, Jim Snapp, now on gang #5, seen the .22 pistol and told other boys that they could buy it.

"This man [i.e., Jim Snapp] also seen Swinney have his wife hold a gun on a man who was working on gang #13, and Swinney then took a chain and whipped this man. I don't know who the man was that was whipped."

Peggy's version was that Swinney held the gun, a shotgun he'd rented, and made her whip the man. This would reverse the role the other witness had assigned her, her account protecting herself by claiming she had no choice but to comply while Swinney held the gun on both her and the whipped victim. The conflicting version made her more of a collaborator, suggesting that Swinney derived deep pleasure from beating the man himself while ensuring that his victim couldn't fight back.

The incident reminded officers of the savage Hollis-Larey beatings.

It became difficult to trace witnesses who had seen and told others of the events. The extra gang laborers didn't stay on the job long and were reluctant to provide information to officers. Turnovers were fast. Some worked a few days or a week or a month, often using "flag," or fictitious, names.

The report concluded: "It seems that Swinney had two or more pistols while working on this gang and that you might be able to pick them up for ballistic examination."

An excellent suggestion, easier said than done.

The string of circumstances implicating Swinney steadily mounted. Swinney, taking Peggy with him, had fled Arkansas and Texarkana for western Oklahoma soon after the Starks murder. Desperate for money, he had done what he rarely did—he took a job at hard labor, far off from Texarkana. This suggested that he was feeling the heat following the Starks shooting. He needed to get away—far, far away.

If he'd had nothing to worry about, he could have remained in the Texarkana area, his comfort zone.

A pattern had formed. The spat with Peggy's sister over unpaid board money—a triggering mechanism—had stirred his anger. The Starks shootings followed—within hours. He'd gone to Texarkana. On the way back, a prosecutor could postulate, he had seen the un-shuttered light from the Starks home with Virgil Starks's silhouette by the window. He parked across the railroad tracks from the residence, waiting for darkness to deepen. Indications were that Peggy was with him, for he rarely, if ever, went anywhere without her. His car was parked heading north, away from Texarkana and toward Delight, where he later claimed to be.

If he'd only intended to steal from Starks's shop, he wouldn't have needed a gun. Being armed indicates that he intended to use it, possibly to kill the stranger by the window and anybody else in the house.

All circumstances pointed toward him. He had no alibi. The couple at the hotel in Delight refuted his claim there. Statements added up to place him near the scene and in a sour mood.

Then there was his marriage to Peggy after months of rambling around together with hardly a care to legitimize their relationship. She had filed for divorce from Stanley Tresnick after the Texas murders had thrown the area into turmoil. The day after her divorce became final, he hustled her to Shreveport for an impromptu courthouse wedding, suggesting that he was in haste to gain legal control of her so she could not testify against him, a maneuver that succeeded by mere hours.

Ironically, if an unpaid debt had led to his trip to Texarkana on May 3, another deadbeat episode—not paying rent due Jim Mays—had led to his eventual arrest.

Tracing and locating the .32 and .22 automatic pistols Swinney had been known to possess proved to be a major frustration. Harry Woods, the extra gang's cook, could not be found. The Santa Fe Railway special agents were unable to locate Woods. The chief of police in Denver reported that Woods had no criminal record there. The draft board in Denver described Woods as born in Mart, Texas, in 1894 (making him fifty-two), five feet six, 150 pounds. His wife's name was Hortense.

Harry Woods, however, seemed to have vanished, taking with him the suspect weapon that might have tied Swinney to the Starks murder.

Carl Miller of the Arkansas State Police summarized the status of the Swinney couple. His report included several relevant points, indicating the certainty with which Arkansas authorities suspected Swinney's guilt. His treatment of Swinney's brief Waynoka experience thickened the plot.

FBI agent Dewey Presley also followed Harry Woods's trail. Woods had quit the work gang at Hoover, a small town in West Texas. The foreman of the extra gang at Heman confirmed that Woods had purchased the .22 automatic pistol. Records verified that Swinney was employed from May 13 to June 3—close to Peggy's contention.

Meanwhile, Peggy was still talking. She told Tillman Johnson that while they were in Waynoka, Swinney bootlegged whiskey. At one point, she said, officers got wind of his illegal activities and seemed to be chasing them.

"Swinney got out of the car and ran off to hide," Johnson reported. "There was another man in the car, name unknown, and they—Peggy and this man—drove off with the whiskey in the car and hid it out in the woods. They sat in the car for awhile and the man tried to get her to have an entercourse [sic] with him. She refused and later told Swinney about it. It made Swinney mad and they drove over toward Woodward, Oklahoma, where he rented a double-barreled shotgun and returned to the camp at Heman where the man worked. Swinney tried to get her to go into the camp and bring the man out and she refused. He went in and came back to the door of the cook shack and told her to bring the shotgun. She took it to the door and went back to the car. Swinney brought the man out and made him get in the car and then drove off down the road and into the woods on a side road. They got out of the car and Swinney held the gun on the man and made her whip him with a short chain."

Johnson wrote at the end: "Peggy states that there were several men in the cook shack when they drove up to get the man, that she was sure they knew what was going on. Swinney did not report back for work after this and they left that night."

Johnson added, as if an afterthought, "Peggy states that she stole the wrist watch from a Mrs. Williams in Waynoka."

Tackett prepared a sheet listing the assaults and murders by date, commenting on Swinney's whereabouts on each date.

First, the Hollis-Larey beatings: Swinney and Peggy occupied a room at 1906 West 16th Street, only about three miles from the crime scene.

Second was the Griffin-Moore case: "Peggy was in Miller Court (proven) and Swinney was seen at 9 P.M. on Broad Street, walking alone. He cannot account for his time from there on."

Third, the Martin-Booker murders: "Swinney states he was at Mr. Stevens' house that night. Stevens (i.e., Peggy's father) denies this, but states he was there early the following morning."

The Starks shootings: "Swinney and Peggy state they were in Delight, Arkansas, in a hotel. They are unable to describe the room. They were seen at about 5 A.M. following morning coming into Antoine from the Prescott road. The people who operate the hotel state they sold a room to a couple about midnight or after."

Every one of the notations placed Swinney near the scene of each crime. Witnesses disputed his claimed alibis.

In a separate set of notes, Tackett compiled a list of suspicious or potentially incriminating factors connecting Swinney to the crimes.

Upon his arrest, Swinney said, "I will spend the rest of my life behind bars this time."

Swinney asked Johnson, "Do you think that I could be lucky enough to get out in twenty-five years?"

When car stealing was mentioned en route to the jail, Swinney remarked, "Hell, they don't want me for car stealing. They want me for something more than that." Yet he subsequently claimed all he ever did was to steal cars.

When a lawyer told Peggy Swinney that her husband was being held for murder, she exclaimed, "How did they find it out?"

"A maroon Chevrolet figured in one of the Texarkana killings. Swinney took a maroon Chevrolet sedan in March. He used it and gave it away to two hitchhikers (in Lubbock) who promised to deliver it to a man in Texas for him. He gave them a fictitious name. He and Peggy hitchhiked back into Texarkana, Texas. If the car hadn't been very hot he would not have gotten rid of it and hitched to Texarkana."

"Peggy Swinney said that Swinney had her whip a man with a piece of chain in Waynoka, Oklahoma, while in a jealous rage. He held a shotgun on him. This might indicate that he was the man who brutally whipped the man and woman in Texarkana, Texas, February 22."

"All of these killings came after Swinney got out of the pen."

"According to all the people talked to yet Swinney was in Texarkana or the vicinity at the time of each killing."

"R. E. Whetstone, Swinney's brother-in-law, stated that on the morning following the Griffin-Moore killings, Swinney showed up at his house in the early morning in a very nervous state and after a while went to a bed and pulled the sheet over his head and slept the entire day."

On the Sunday morning very early after the Booker-Martin killings, Swinney showed up at Stevens's home and drove into the woods and remained nearly all afternoon.

Members of the Stevens family had expressed their belief that Swinney killed those people.

His brother-in-law Whetstone stated that he thought Swinney killed the people.

Swinney told his wife, "I will be blamed for all these killings in Texarkana."

Swinney was in a hotel at Delight, Arkansas, at 5 A.M. the morning after Starks was killed.

Swinney had always stolen clothes every time he had a chance. He had a suitcase full of clothing at the time of his arrest. Virgil Starks could be the owner of the shirt found among Swinney's possessions with the word STARK on the back of it. Mrs. Starks stated that she thought it might be one of Virgil's; it was the right size.

If those who had seen Swinney up close were correct, then Swinney had perpetrated the murders. They added to a web of circumstantial evidence that kept the focus on Swinney.

Officers never placed Swinney in a police lineup, where survivors Hollis or Mrs. Larey—if they had been induced to return to Texarkana—might have identified him, or possibly heard him speak. That incident, in darkness, would have made facial identity difficult, particularly if he actually did wear a mask. As for his voice, it was doubtful that any voice, in a normal tone, would have matched the rage-filled demands made by the February attacker.

Time was running out for holding Swinney without a charge. By then, members of his family had hired lawyers and proposed strategies for setting him free. Miller County had a felony theft charge, for the stolen cars, almost certain to gain a conviction. There were several car-theft cases, on both sides of the state line, for which there was solid evidence. But a felony theft wouldn't net him more than five to ten years, putting him back on the streets again.

Officers felt certain they had their Phantom. Peggy's statements were damning. But she could not be compelled to testify against her husband, and she refused to do so. She repeatedly emphasized that she was scared to death of him. Without her testimony, could a murder conviction be won?

The question haunted officers, inspiring them to explore all possible remedies. The goal, they agreed, was urgent: to take Swinney off the streets, with no expectation of release.

But could it be done?

CHAPTER 19

MOUNTING PRESSURES

A s summer edged toward September, Texarkana bustled with activity. Veterans scrambled for scarce local jobs; some hired on at the still-functioning defense plants or left home to seek employment wherever they could find it. Others, especially unmarried veterans, crammed into Texarkana College on the GI Bill of Rights. One of the student veterans was David Griffin, Phantom victim Richard Griffin's younger brother, back from the war in Europe. Overnight the two-year college experienced growing pains as it registered its largest enrollment since its founding in 1927, necessitating use of temporary buildings.

New, pleasant excitement gradually supplanted the spring horrors. The fact that no similar crime had been committed since early May offered guarded hope that the cycle had ended and life could resume as before. The public knew nothing of Swinney's arrest and interrogation as the major Phantom suspect. With the murder pattern halted, the spotlight had faded from the Texas Rangers and Lone Wolf Gonzaullas, who had been constant reminders of the case's unsolved status.

Most officers believed that with Youell Swinney behind bars, the Phantom's reign of terror was over. They remained tight-lipped about it. No charges had been filed. It was uncertain how the case would be handled, and they did not want another media maelstrom on their hands that could potentially harm their efforts to prove that Swinney was the murderer.

By the end of summer, the entire army of lawmen had entered a relaxed mode. The Texas Rangers quietly eased off, without the fanfare that had heralded their arrival. Captain Gonzaullas concluded, on July 23, as for the Texarkana assignment, "it would not be detrimental to this investigation or cause a recurrence of said crimes if we reduced our forces to a minimum on this assignment." On August 15, he made it plain and direct in a memo stamped CONFIDENTIAL, which he distributed to stations in Dallas, Stephenville, Clarksville, and Waco. The two-page, single-spaced letter spelled out the rationale for the shift of personnel, without revealing the specific reason or mentioning the name of the suspect in Arkansas custody.

Important
Special Attention

In order to conduct other assignments by the Rangers' limited personnel and budget, he said, "and due to the present status of the investigation," it was time to reduce the force in Texarkana to a minimum. He assigned only two Rangers at a time in Texarkana for the remainder of August, then only one for September. After that, Ranger Stewart Stanley, stationed at Clarksville sixty miles away, would keep tabs on the situation. Occasionally thereafter, Gonzaullas would have a Ranger drop in, to make his presence known.

"At this time," he emphasized, "I wish to call your attention to the importance of keeping strictly confidential the contents of this letter and our future plans for handling this investigation."

The orders, secret and never disclosed publicly, were clear to those receiving them.

The Rangers had been called off.

The Phantom no longer threatened.

The Siege of Texarkana was over.

If the residents at large had known this, they would have organized a gigantic spontaneous celebration, the likes of which the city had never known.

And, possibly, a lynching party.

Thirty miles away, in Hope, Arkansas, William Jefferson Blythe was born on August 19, coming into the world as unheralded as the Texas Rangers' drawdown in Texarkana. He would become William Jefferson "Bill" Clinton, elected forty-six years later as President of the United States. By that time, one of his future 1992 opponents, third-party candidate H. Ross Perot, was a sixteen-year-old student at Texarkana's Texas High School.

Totally veiled from public view, officers wrestled with how to deal most effectively with The Man They Said Was the Phantom.

Taking a serial killer out of circulation was the surest way of stopping his crimes. The overriding issue was far from simple: how to keep Youell Lee Swinney off the streets, not just for a mere handful of years that an ordinary felony conviction would ensure, but for a much longer stretch, for life, if possible. The more officers learned about him, the more convinced they were that he was the "Phantom" with a mystique of its own, far beyond what a wanton murderer deserved.

Peggy was the officers' wild card. Her statements told more than enough to be certain Swinney had killed, at the very least, the youngsters Paul Martin and Betty Jo Booker. Her testimony in that case should be sufficient to gain a conviction. With that case solved, ballistics evidence would link the Griffin-Moore murders.

She faced her own problem in the Starks case. She isolated Swinney as a likely suspect while claiming she was in a Delight hotel during the hours when Swinney was in Texarkana. The operators of the hotel shredded her alibi. The couple did not arrive until midnight or later, they insisted. Statements by this reliable couple left Peggy also without a credible alibi. When Swinney drove to Texarkana, going by the Starks home, she must have been with him. The cigarette butts by the site where the killer's car had been parked indicated that more than one person had been there. Swinney wasn't likely to go anywhere, especially at night, without her.

One point officers were to make over and over was that once Swinney was arrested, the murders stopped. Suggestive, but not proof. The Phantom, if he were not Swinney, could have departed for other hunting grounds. No murders elsewhere fit the pattern exactly, but it still did not rule out the possibility that the Phantom had moved elsewhere.

There still were substantial barriers to his successful prosecution. The murder weapons hadn't been recovered. Swinney had possessed both a .32 automatic and a .22 automatic pistol, but he had gotten rid of both and to men who had not been traced.

Without Peggy's testimony, the case would have to be built around circumstantial evidence, a higher bar for the prosecution. Officers had to make a case—rapidly—or risk letting slip the best opportunity yet for solving it. They had him off the street; now they must keep him off. The mechanics of doing so were uncertain. There seemed to be no foolproof method to achieve it. If the prisoner was in jeopardy, his captors also faced a crisis.

A new complication arose: Swinney's father and those of the family whom he rallied—or browbeat—in support. Vowing to save his troubled son from the clutches of the law, one way or another, the Reverend Stanley C. Swinney marshalled a vigorous offense as he fired off letters and telephone calls to offspring and lawyers. Now pastoring the First Baptist Church in Montgomery City, Missouri, where he lived with his third wife, the father Swinney concentrated his pressure on his son Cleo, who lived in Texarkana. He also attempted to field a legal team, repeatedly insisting that Youell was completely innocent and guilty of no crime at all—an absolute denial. If all else failed, he claimed that his connections at high levels in Arkansas would ensure an appellate victory. He journeyed to Texarkana, where he had once lived, to see his wayward son and consult with family members.

In a flurry of correspondence he directed strategy, often contradictory, always aggressive, sometimes bellicose, and self-justifying. He repeatedly spelled out the gravity of Youell's situation as an innocent man about to be railroaded, as if by a kangaroo court. From Missouri he wrote his son

Cleo that he wanted a lawyer in El Dorado, Arkansas, Claude E. Love, to look into Youell's case; he urged Cleo, "Please do this at once." "At once," often heavily emphasized, was an admonition he habitually incorporated into his summons. He was in bed, he explained, taking "heavy sedatives to keep me going." He made a plea that was to be duplicated over the coming months, in a variety of guises and emphases. "If something is not done at once they will kill him and my life would be worthless if they should because I know he is innocent and those people down there and everywhere would have no respect for any of us if we stood by and let those bandits swear his life away which I am convinced they will do if they can." He also repeatedly invoked self-pity, asserting he was ready to sell his furniture (which he seems not to have done) to raise funds for Youell's defense, while asking his son and daughters to contribute money. If he sought a loan, he said, he would have to explain why he needed it and that would ruin him. He continually insisted that Youell was an "innocent boy" at risk of being "cruelly killed."

The lawyer Claude Love eagerly accepted the defense assignment. "Perhaps we may be able to help them understand the 'Sixth Commandment,'" the lawyer wrote, seeming to apply the commandment, "Thou shalt not kill," to the accused man's captors rather than to the crimes officers believed he had committed.

Each new Stanley Swinney letter to Cleo frantically emphasized urgency—"something must be done AT ONCE today"—as he felt "the boy's life is at stake" while he himself was "definitely convinced that he is innocent." He directed Cleo to either get the trial postponed or get Youell turned over to federal jurisdiction, where he would fare better. Meanwhile, he continued, he had appealed to members of the Arkansas Supreme Court, where he intimated he had an ally, for a chance to convict some of the lawmen for malfeasance of office. To start the ball rolling, he ordered Cleo to get Love "at ONCE." The absentee father's orders were easier hurled than carried out.

To one daughter he confided that he had a friend at the state's highest court, should a conviction be appealed, but she must keep it quiet. "A life is at stake," he said, adding his familiar order, "PLEASE ACT AT ONCE." But she must not reveal what he had said of his friend in a high place.

"BURN THIS LETTER BY ALL MEANS," he wrote, or his best source of information would be closed. "Tell Youell all will be well."

He bombarded his son Cleo with complaints and orders, ranging from wheedling to demanding. He claimed, on the basis of no evidence that he provided, that Youell was being beaten and starved to death, causing "the poor innocent Youell untold suffering" and creating a "very precarious condition." At this point he brought in the name of a man, W—, as his substitute candidate for the Phantom, accusing him of trying to harm Youell and asserting that the man would be "brought to justice." There was never any indication his charge had any substance as the minister unleashed tirades and directives in manipulative efforts that waxed and waned. It was anything but pleasant for Cleo, who was becoming the true martyr in the matter.

Despite the elder Swinney's tactics to protect Youell from the law's grasp (which also would inflict a stigma upon him as the father), there is some evidence that there was a lack of affection between the two. A nephew of Youell recalled a family experience, earlier noted, in which Youell, outside and hungry, was refused entrance to his father's house while other family members ate dinner. This indicates, contrary to the elder Swinney's claims, that the relationship between them was hardly what the surface indicated, and perhaps this was all due more to the elder Swinney's fear of the damage his reputation would suffer from having the Phantom Killer for a son, than any real affection for Youell himself.

On the morning of Thursday, October 24, while Swinney and his wife remained in the Miller County jail, P. V. Ward, while repairing a barbed-wire fence in a marshy area bordering Morris Lane north of the city, spied what looked like an old discarded suitcase. It was almost buried under a pile of dead leaves and underbrush.

"Mack," he yelled at his companion J. F. McNief, "go call the law! Here's the Booker girl's saxophone. I know that's what it is."

Soon afterward Police Chief Jack Runnels, Deputy Sheriff Zeke Henslee, and two city policemen arrived. The leather lining and wooden framework of the case had deteriorated; pieces fell to the ground while being placed into a box. Sheet music probably used at the April dance was still in the case. A selection, protected in a plastic folder, was "The Song of the Navy," along with an orange-and-white Texas High School emblem.

The discovery came about 140 steps from where Betty Jo's body was found, on the opposite side of Morris Lane.

At the sheriff's office, Clark Brown, Betty Jo's stepfather, identified the case and the gold-plated (now tarnished) Bundy E-flat alto saxophone bearing serial number 52535. The case's plush blue lining had rotted from exposure to the elements during the previous six months. Spring foliage and water had concealed it. By fall, plants and underbrush had thinned out and leaves had turned brown, helping to reveal what search parties had never seen.

The only chance of there being a latent fingerprint would depend on whether the killer had opened the case and touched the instrument with an ungloved hand.

No fingerprint was found, but police could relax their monitoring of pawnshops and call off the nationwide search for the instrument.

One day in late October—Max Tackett recounted, though he wasn't present and learned of it afterward—the recalcitrant Swinney was being interrogated in the sheriff's portion of the courthouse. Deputy Sheriff Bill Scott, a wiry but tough veteran lawman in his forties, lost his patience after a series of evasive answers about the Starks case. He seized a nearby leather razor strap, which deputies used when they had to shave at the office, and advanced toward the prisoner. He impulsively whacked Swinney, who flinched and suddenly blurted out, "My God, don't hit me with that bat, Mister! Take that bat away and I'll tell you all about it, exactly how it happened."

The "bat" he referred to was a strap with which prisoners at some Arkansas and other prisons reportedly were whipped in those days. Swinney's reaction strongly suggested he'd known the sting of such a beating, probably in the Arkansas penitentiary. He gave the impression that he felt he was about to be worked over and wasted no time in trying to ward it off, even at the cost of self-incrimination.

(A niece, Joyce Swinney Ward, years later remembered seeing "stripes" on her uncle's back, scars from whippings he'd sustained in either an Arkansas or Texas prison. This would explain his reaction to Bill Scott's brandishing the "bat" that day in jail.)

About that time—Tackett's account goes, there being no eyewitness reports, all participants by then being dead—Sheriff Elvie Davis arrived in the room. Davis, a compassionate man, never tolerated mistreatment of prisoners. The lawmen knew a confession compelled by force wouldn't stand up and would work against them. Scott was fully aware of this but had reached the limits of his patience that afternoon. Many officers believed Swinney was on the verge of talking anyway and that this minor event had only accelerated the tendency.

"We're not going to hurt you," Sheriff Davis told Swinney. "I knew your daddy. Let's sit down and talk about it."

Swinney said, "I don't want to talk here."

That was fine with the sheriff, but Swinney rapidly changed his mind. That was all right with Davis, too. He had another plan.

Davis had several concerns. "Elvie was afraid of a lynching," recalled his chief deputy Johnson. "At the same time, he didn't want to mess that case up by getting a confession whipped out of Swinney."

"We'll take him to Little Rock to State Police headquarters and let them keep him up there and get the confession out of him," Davis told his deputies.

A new method, the so-called truth serum, or sodium pentothal, a hypnotic, was beginning to gain public attention. The theory behind its popular name was that the drug relaxed inhibitions and the patient felt free to speak candidly of any and all matters. It wasn't admissible as courtroom evidence and was, actually, in the early stages of its application. Physicians at the state hospital had worked with the State Police on some cases of which Davis had heard. Davis believed interrogating the suspect in Little Rock under the influence of "truth serum" might be the best way to handle the matter. It would protect the prisoner from a possible lynch mob, should the news leak out, while producing a confession.

Davis told Swinney. "We'll take you to Little Rock."

Swinney, hearing the sheriff's words, visibly relaxed.

There is no other evidence that Swinney was ever whacked or threatened with the "bat," Tackett's narrative being the only known source. Swinney never complained or claimed it had happened. The report, though suggestive, likely is accurate.

By late October, arrangements had been made for legal representation for Swinney in Texarkana. Youell's older, hardworking, law-abiding brother Cleo had enlisted local attorneys Paul J. McDonald and Ted Goldman for onsite counseling while Claude Love became available from El Dorado. J. F. McVey attempted to monitor and direct proceedings from Missouri.

A defense strategy began to evolve: use insanity as a means of easing Youell away from the shadow of Arkansas's electric chair for the Starks murder and possibly also for the Texas murders. In this as in other moves, Cleo Swinney took the brunt of the spate of instructions steadily flowing from Missouri.

The attorney McVey wrote Cleo to get an affidavit from Youell's mother attesting to any insanity on her side of the family and anything else that could demonstrate that the son was suffering from a mental disorder. "I understand that he may have been injured at birth, and later on when he was in the Reform School. If she knows of these things, put them in." Pastor Swinney himself declined to admit any mental infirmities on his side of the family, while pressing his ex-wife to document deficiencies in hers. He did, however, execute an affidavit for the lawyers, addressing it to the director of the Arkansas state hospital, in which he cited four points related to son Youell's unsound mind: an injury at birth, a history of insanity on his mother's side, an injury as an inmate in the Arkansas state reform school when another inmate struck him with a stick of wood in the back which caused a spinal hemorrhage, and his own personal observations which convinced him that Youell was not normal and was of unsound mind.

The minister also urged Cleo to secure another lawyer and to contact the top criminal defense attorney, Elmer Lincoln, in Texarkana. Contacts with Lincoln were made but without a follow-up that would have paid a retainer fee. By this time Cleo was already paying the local lawyers seventy dollars a month, not an insignificant amount on a workingman's pay.

The elder Swinney presented a new scenario for the Texarkana murders that would eliminate his son as a suspect and guide the investigation into an entirely different direction. "McVey is still greatly interested in running down the Phantom killer and both of us believe W— and one other are the men. The killer will be arrested some day and people will be greatly surprised who it is or rather who they are."

A parting note dealt with Youell's defense: see that he pleads not guilty by reason of insanity, and request the judge to appoint him counsel at the state's expense.

Attorney McVey, following a brief trip to Texarkana, flailed out in several directions. He criticized the Texarkana defense lawyers and wrote to a friend in Illinois, whom he described as a "federal officer," claiming that Youell Swinney was innocent of everything except taking a car and that he suffered from a form of insanity related to his obsession to drive a car. He was "satisfied" that the prisoner had killed no one. He failed to document his conclusion or to elaborate on his discovery of a new psychological category, insanity with a need to drive (after stealing) a car.

The correspondence made clear that the family was fully aware why Youell was being held, suggesting a large serving of denial, with a side dish of paranoia, by the prisoner's father.

On October 29, Swinney's team—McVey and the local firm of Goldman and McDonald—filed a petition for writ of habeas corpus in the Miller County Circuit Court. They sought an immediate preliminary hearing or release.

Judge Dexter Bush ordered Sheriff Davis to bring Swinney before him.

On November 1, prosecutor Lyle Brown presented a motion to dispatch Swinney to the state hospital in Little Rock for observation. Judge Bush granted the motion, agreeing that there were "reasonable grounds for believing the defendant mentally incompetent." The next step was to deliver Swinney to the State Hospital for Nervous Diseases.

With neither side aware of what the other was thinking, the sheriff's plans coincided with efforts by Swinney's father and his lawyers to dispatch Youell Swinney to the state hospital to assess his mental status.

Both sides had seen their wishes fulfilled—for the moment.

The following morning before daylight, Johnson, Tackett, and Charley Boyd drove Swinney to Little Rock. The prisoner had not carried out his promise to tell "exactly how it happened." He'd clammed up. Tillman Johnson soon had misgivings. He felt officers had been making progress. Even without Scott's provocative gesture, Johnson felt they'd made headway. Swinney had no way of knowing what the officers knew. They had him in jail and they were questioning him intensively about the Starks case, as well as the other crimes. Because he was in custody in Arkansas, his blurting out implied he was ready to talk about the Arkansas crime. The incident provided a further insight into how Swinney responded in moments of stress and high anxiety, adding to his other "almost" confession when arrested.

The spell was broken. The process of breaking him down, potentially leading to a confession, had been interrupted. A different persona took over. On the drive to Little Rock, he would have time to ask himself how much evidence they really had on him. If they had to take him to the state hospital, then perhaps they didn't have all they needed. His resistance returned.

"If we'd have kept him here in Texarkana," said Johnson, "I think we would have broken him. He was close. That was one bad mistake we made," he said, referring to the decision to send him to Little Rock.

Swinney's old responses returned. "He was very unemotional. He was cold," said Johnson.

Johnson sensed that Swinney now believed he couldn't be convicted. Why would they take him to Little Rock, if they already had a strong enough case against him? Swinney knew his own attorneys had planned an insanity defense, but the move to commit him had come from the State.

The hospital casework began for Swinney in his first commitment to a mental institution. He replied to questions regarding his past, detailing his time in reform school at Pine Bluff, Arkansas, at age seventeen for burglary of a school, the divorce of his parents when he was a small boy, his frequent moves after that. At seven a fall from a swing rendered him unconscious, he told hospital attendants, and at eighteen he remained bedfast for two weeks after being run down by a cart. However, he said he'd had no memory lapses, dizzy spells, drug problems, or venereal disease. The rest of his family displayed no criminal tendencies or alcoholism.

He claimed he wasn't guilty when sent to the penitentiary in Texas and was not guilty of the present charge, that he knew nothing about it. He cited his June 28 marriage to Peggy. As he reeled off his record, he committed several errors involving time. He said he'd been paroled, not mentioning it was conditional, in 1944 for strong-arm robbery—1944 was the year he was sentenced, not released, which was late 1945.

His denial of guilt in his previous incarcerations constituted a sweeping claim he would have found impossible to sustain.

Sodium pentothal was eventually administered intravenously. The procedure backfired. The physician inadvertently gave an overdose, and the patient passed into a deep sleep. Swinney said nothing. "Truth serum" had flunked the test.

(In the years since, so-called truth serums have been rejected as an interrogation technique, research finding that although the drug, and those like it, may lead to a relaxing of inhibitions, it does not prevent lying and may even lead to fantasies and a mixing of fact and fantasy. More recently it has been classified as abusive and condemned as an interrogation tool.)

The experience dampened any optimism about cracking a case that lawmen felt was practically solved, and they were no closer to finding a way to keep Swinney in custody for the long term.

Meanwhile, officers fared better with Peggy Swinney. A developing technology—for which enthusiasm was as high as it had been for "truth serum"—promised to put her on record in a dramatic way. She was willing to waive extradition and be interrogated while connected to a polygraph, or "lie detector," machine. That would mean a trip to Austin, the state capital, for a session at Texas's Department of Public Safety.

The year before, Glen H. McLaughlin, chief of DPS's crime lab, had gone to Chicago to learn to operate the machine and interpret its recordings. The DPS purchased a Keeler polygraph soon afterward. He was to use it with several persons during the course of the Phantom investigation. But Peggy, whom he remembered as a "strawberry blonde," was the one with whom he had the best results.

On schedule, Bill Presley and Max Tackett drove Peggy the 350 miles from Texarkana to Austin. They arrived in the early afternoon.

The session produced two statements: one, a verbatim interrogation in a Question and Answer format, the second, a narrative statement much as Tillman Johnson had compiled in Texarkana.

McLaughlin questioned her alone, the machine registering her blood pressure, respiration, and electrical currents as checks on her anxiety and possible deception. Presley and Tackett watched from an adjoining room through a two-way mirror. They could watch her; she could not see them and, presumably, was unaware that they were observing the interrogation.

For the record, McLaughlin led her through routine matters of her personal background. Then he dipped into her memories of the case. He kept a map of the Spring Lake Park area nearby. Letters marked specific sites.

"Now if you will, tell me where you were on April 13," McLaughlin began.

Her narrative statement, boiled down to its essence, came to this:

"On April 13, 1946, Youell Swinney and I left Dallas about noon and drove to Texarkana, Texas. We were driving a Plymouth sedan. I think it was a 1941 model. We got to Texarkana about 6:30 P.M. and went to a show. We went to the Joy Theatre. We got out of the show about 8:30. When we went to the show, Swinney left me for about thirty minutes. When we came out of the show, we went out and drank some beer until the cafés were closed, and then we fooled around town and about 3:30 in the morning Swinney took a notion he wanted to go out to Spring Lake Park and rob somebody.

"We drove out to the park and drove around until we saw where a car was parked. There was a couple in this car. Swinney and I got out of our car and Swinney told the couple to give him what they had. Swinney made me get in the car and I got in the back of the car with the little girl. Swinney got in the front of the car with the little boy. I think the car was a coupe, but it had some sort of a seat in the back.

"When I got in the car, I moved the saxophone case off of the seat so that both the little girl and I could sit down back there. Swinney drove the car, which was the couple's car, around to the place [north of the park]. He stopped the car and we all got out of the car. Swinney shot the little boy. He took the billfold out of the little boy's pocket; I think he took it out of his left hip pocket. He took some money out of the billfold and put the billfold back in the little boy's right hip pocket. We then got back in the car, Swinney, the little girl, and I. We drove down [the road] and turned around, and when we got back [to where the little boy was shot] we saw that the little boy had gotten up and had gone across the road and was now on the left hand side of the road and Swinney got out and shot the little boy two more times.

"Swinney then drove on up [by the park] and stopped the car. He made me stay in the car and he and the little girl got out and walked down the road in front of the car. I don't know how long they were gone, but it seemed like about 30 minutes. They came back in our car. Swinney got out and took the saxophone from the couple's car and put it in our car. Swinney then drove on around past where the little boy was shot on down to the Summerhill Road, and then on around to [Morris Lane].

"He stopped the car there, and made me get out of the car. I walked on down the road in front of the car. I heard the little girl begging Swinney not to do something. Swinney got out of the car with the little girl and they went across the fence on the right hand side. I started back to the car and when I got back to the car, I heard Swinney shoot two times. Swinney came back and got in the car. I got in the car. We drove [away] and turned around, then drove back to [Morris Lane] and Swinney stopped the car and threw away the saxophone case. He got out of the car and threw the saxophone on the right hand side of the road. He threw it over the fence; I think there were some bushes there. Swinney took the saxophone because he was going to pawn it. Then he decided it was too hot."

(Peggy's recall of the saxophone's disposal meshed almost exactly with the facts of its discovery, the details of which she had not been informed. The obvious conclusion was that, whether or not she was reliable on other points, she obviously was present at the time of the park murders, with her statement an unassailable refutation of any claim Swinney might make.)

"We drove on down to the Summerhill Road, turned right, and went on to a restaurant and got something to eat. We then drove out on the Hope highway, on the Arkansas side, and turned off on an off road and spent the day out in the country on an off road. About dark, we came back in and went to Swinney's sister's house, in Texarkana. I don't know the exact address. We spent the night at Swinney's sister's house and left the next morning. The gun that Swinney used was a black automatic, a .32."

(Her statement that they drove out on the Hope highway, which would have been the same one on which the Starks couple lived, differs from her earlier statements that they went to her mother's house that day. Whether these were foibles of memory or whether she intentionally changed her story is not clear.)

She continued: "After we got in Swinney's sister's house, I saw Swinney put the gun in his coat pocket and hang the coat up in the back room. I saw Swinney shoot the little boy two times on one side of the road, and two times on the other side of the road. I didn't see him shoot the little girl, but he and the little girl went across the fence together and I heard Swinney shoot two times, and then Swinney came back to the car alone."

At the end she attested to the truth and accuracy of what she had said.

Then she wrote, in longhand:

"Swinney told me if I ever said anything about it He would kill me,"

She first wrote "anything about this," then drew a line through "this" and substituted "it."

The way she ended her sentence, with a comma instead of a period, seemed to leave dangling whether she had finished writing her thoughts down or not. Her capitalizing He, meaning Swinney, like a deity, created another question.

Under her handwritten coda she signed her name: "Peggy Swinney."

It was the first time she had signed a statement. Did she tell the truth? McLaughlin subsequently concluded that he believed she was being deceptive and holding something back. "I thought she had some involvement, that she had some additional information."

Aside from the polygraph, another tool has been developed in more recent years to help investigators figure out whether or not people they are interrogating are telling the truth. Mark McClish, the lead instructor on interviewing techniques at the U. S. Marshals Service Training Academy from 1991 to 1999, developed the Statement Analysis® system to test truth and deception during criminal interrogations. McClish's book on the technique is *I Know You Are Lying: Detecting Deception Through Statement Analysis,* and his system is based on the principle that deceptive persons' words will betray them. "A person cannot give a lengthy deceptive statement without revealing that it is a lie," said McClish. "People will always word their statement based on all their knowledge. Therefore, their statement may contain information they did not intend to share. Even though people may want to withhold information, they will give us more information that what they realize. The key is to listen to what people are telling you and to know what to look for in a statement."

The author applied McClish's methods and then McClish himself examined the statements. Several points may be made that tend to bear out McLaughlin's suspicions of evasion on Peggy's part while supporting her veracity in other areas. As McClish argued, a suspect may tell the truth but not the whole truth. It is the interrogator's responsibility to search out weaknesses in the story: look for events out of order, pay attention to time references and missing periods of time, while checking for words and phrases suggesting deception. Did the suspect answer the question? Cross out any words? Use unnecessary words? Use an "internal dictionary" that hints of a change in language? The pronouns are important. So are verb tenses and the order of events and the breakdown of the account.

As for time, Peggy left several hours unaccounted for. She didn't tell how long they were on the road from Dallas to Texarkana, nor whether they stopped en route. This may not be a major concern, for that trip by car in 1946, over a narrow two-lane Highway 67, took about half a day of ordinary driving. The impression is that Swinney parked her in the Joy Theatre for a purpose. Based on his previous record, the implication was that he had business to take care of alone, suggesting he intended to rob someone. After that they went out on the town, drinking beer until closing time. On Saturday night on the Arkansas side, closing time was midnight; in Texas beer sales continued until one o'clock in the morning. They seemed to have several beer-drinking haunts on the Texas side. This would mean they left the last beer joint around 1:15 or 1:30 A.M. There is a two-hour gap from closing time till they entered Spring Lake Park. What happened during the two hours? Were they just driving? Possibly. Swinney liked to drive. Did he look for someone to rob? Also possible, for that is what took them to the park. It's possible that her sense of time was off and that they went to the park earlier than 3:30. She had been drinking a lot of beer and may not have remembered well.

Her selection of pronouns is interesting. She commonly used "we" to represent Swinney and her, as if their actions were joint, or cooperative, ones. It was "our" car, even though a stolen one. She identifies with Swinney as if a part of him or joined to him. Yet on that April night they were not married.

One of the striking portions of her statement is her precise memory of which hip pocket Swinney took Paul Martin's billfold from (the left) and which one in which he replaced it (the right). This constituted a close observation of the scene *at night*, a detail that many individuals would have missed, especially amidst something so violent and chaotic. She does not mention the datebook that Bill Presley found in the brush and which she later acknowledged Swinney had tossed away.

Sequence seems to be wrong in one instance, when Swinney and the girl returned in "our" car to where Peggy was waiting. Then Swinney got out and took the saxophone from the couple's car and put it in "our" car. She said she was waiting, alone, but her out-of-order telling may suggest she was there, on the scene, and witnessed the act, instead of learning of it later. On the other hand it may simply reflect the order in which McLaughlin phrased his questions to her and how her answers were combined in the statement.

When it comes to implicating herself as an eyewitness, she consistently states that she had no choice but to obey Swinney. Officers knew she was deathly afraid of him. But she does testify that she saw him shoot Paul Martin four times, enough of a statement to sink Swinney's case, were she to repeat it under oath in a courtroom. On other issues, she emphasizes that Swinney "made" her get out of the car, or he forced her to stay. She walked down the road; she heard the little girl begging Swinney. Then she starts back to the car when she hears two shots that ended Betty Jo Booker's life. The question arises whether Peggy was telling the truth totally, even whether she might have been with Betty Jo Booker when she died.

It is strange that Peggy did not know Swinney's sister's address in Texarkana. But if she intentionally disavowed that knowledge, there is no obvious benefit to her.

Assuming she told the truth, albeit the partial truth, a review of the way Swinney made Peggy stay in the Martin car, while he herded Betty Jo down the road, later returning in "our" car, indicates that he couldn't afford to leave the girl in Peggy's custody, for fear she would escape, bringing an end to his nocturnal game. Betty Jo was already a witness to Paul Martin's murder, which implied that he had no intentions of letting her live.

But, following Peggy's version, if she had somehow been found near Martin's body by an officer while he took Betty Jo in to the words, such a discovery would have injected disarray into the criminal's plans. If Peggy had been caught there, in the Martin car, and arrested, it would have incriminated Swinney. This raises a question: did he really leave Peggy by herself?

At the end of the interrogation, McLaughlin asked, "Is there any other thing about the happenings of that day or that night, April 13th, and the morning of April 14th, that you remember and want to add to this now?" She had replied, "No." It was a compound question, offering her a choice. Was this all she remembered? Probably not. Did she want to add to it at that time? Almost certainly she had answered that part sincerely and truthfully. She was unlikely to volunteer any more, without being goaded.

What didn't she tell? Probably quite a lot. There is a hint that something was going on past her surface reactions, when she edited the coda at the end of her statement, that Swinney had threatened her if she ever told about "this." She'd crossed out "this" and wrote "it" over the deleted word. Evidently there was a significant difference, in her mind, between "this" and "it." What was it? Did the two words mean different things? Did "it" refer to a crime she hadn't described?

A reasonable explanation might be that "this" referred to the events in Spring Lake Park that night, while "it" encompassed a larger picture, that of their entire series of adventures together that spring and summer, perhaps all of the crimes committed. Might "it" have referred to the Starks shootings? What about the other murder and the beating? No one can say with certainly what she had in mind, but it was important enough for her to change her mind about the first word she used and correct it. Considering the volume of words she had poured out to officers after her arrest months before, this seems to have been the first time she had modified a word in a specific statement, and it was such a slight deviation that it was hardly noticeable at the time.

The handwritten note contained another item that is more susceptible to analysis. In speaking of Swinney she capitalizes in her own handwriting the pronoun He, representing Swinney, as one would a deity. Was Swinney like a god to her? The Devil, of course, also receives capitalized attention.

There is one more tantalizing detail. At the end of her note she placed a comma, not a period. She left no doubt she was making a comma, the tail is so long and definite. It was as if she was about to extend her remarks—about what?—and then thought better of it and stopped. She apparently was never questioned about it.

A close examination of her final statement while attached to the polygraph machine tends to lead to the opinion that she told the truth as she remembered it but not the whole truth. Her account of the night Virgil Starks was killed was never brought up on the Texas side. Her willingness to deal with the Spring Lake Park murders may be interpreted as being her way to get attention off the Starks case and, in fact, out of Arkansas's jurisdiction. It also may have reflected her horror, and a troubled mind, over the deaths of a couple who were, actually, children. Officers in Austin had not questioned her about the Larey-Hollis beatings, assuming she was not present, or the Griffin-Moore murders. In their quest to nail down Swinney's complicity and crack the case, evidence on one double murder was seen as sufficient. Once she provided them with a statement on that headline case, they believed, probably correctly, that they had what they needed from her. They could always pursue other cases later.

Mark McClish, the originator of Statement Analysis®, reviewed the author's foregoing conclusions, essentially agreed, and then reviewed the statement himself, as well as Peggy's July 1946 unsigned statements. In the process he added comments that offer further enlightenment—all in 2013, decades after she had made the statements. His analysis obviously came long after the fact, much too late for officers to use; his work does provide an expanded insight into the fruits of the interrogation.

McClish zeroed in on references aimed at further testing her reliability.

As for her account of Swinney's disposal of the saxophone, McClish commented: "We must remember that nothing happens in a vacuum. There will be other things going on besides the incident itself, which will enter into the statement. Her mentioning that she 'moved the saxophone case off the seat in the back' so she and the little girl could sit down is an example of this. This additional information indicates it is a truthful statement. A deceptive story is usually very simplistic."

When Peggy responded to her interrogator's question as to whether she had more to tell, McClish pointed out, "By saying 'No,' she is not saying nothing else happened that she has not told them. If that was the case, she should have said, 'No. That is all that happened' or 'No, I have told you everything I remember.' By simply saying, 'No,' she may be saying there is nothing else that she wants to add even though she has more information."

By drawing a line through "this" and replacing it with "it," McClish noted, she may have revealed a hidden motive. "While the word 'this' indicates specificity it also indicates closeness; the word 'that' indicates distance. By using the word 'this' she is showing closeness to the murders. She may have realized what she was saying and changed the word to 'it' which is a more distant way of describing the situation."

As for punctuating her sentence with a comma instead of a period, McClish clarified: "We end a thought by placing a period at the end of a sentence. The missing period is an indication she purposely stopped writing. She may have more information to share but chose not to."

Her choice of language also proved to be revealing. "The pronouns 'we' and 'us' always indicate there was a partnership between the participants," wrote McClish. "We may not know how much of a partnership existed, but it does mean two or more people did something together." This suggests the possibility that she cooperated in the killings or was at least more than a terrified witness.

McClish's additional comments on the November statement focused on details of language that ordinarily are overlooked but which may reveal a subtext of their own in the mind of an expert.

He cited her account of the evening of April 13: "*We got out of the show* about 8:30. When we went to the show, Swinney *left* me for about *30* minutes. *When we came out of the show*, we went out and drank some beer until the cafés were closed, and then we fooled around town and about *3:30* in the morning, Swinney took a notion he wanted to go to Spring Lake Park and rob somebody.'"

McClish's comment: "She states they 'got out of the show about 8:30.' At this point in her statement, we believe the two of them are no longer in the show. In the next sentence, she backs up in her story and talks about going to the show and Swinney leaving for 30 minutes. If a story is coming from memory, it should flow in sequential order. This out-of-order statement indicates she may not be drawing this portion of her story from memory.

"The word 'left' when used as a verb indicates sensitivity in the statement. She may have withheld some information about what was going on at this point in her statement.

"The number 'three' is a liar's number. When deceptive people have to come up with a number they often choose the number. It should also be noted that when a person is unsure of a number, they use the number three. We have two references to the number three: '30 minutes' and '3:30 in the morning.'

"'*This* car was parked at the place labeled on the map which I drew.'

"The word 'this' can indicate specificity but it also shows closeness. She could have said, 'The car was parked . . .' which would show some distance. However, she used language that places her close to the car. In the Q & A, she refers to it as 'that car.' 'Swinney *made* me get in the car . . .' 'He *made* me stay in the car . . .' 'He stopped the car there and *made* me get out of the car.' She used the word 'made' but does not tell us how he made her do something. 'I don't know how long they were gone but it seemed like about *30* minutes.' She may be deceptive or as she stated she does not know how long they were gone which caused her to use the number 30. 'I *started back* to the car and when I got back in the car, I heard Swinney shoot two times.' The word 'started' means a person began an action but did not finish it. It is odd she used this word because she tells us that she did make it back to the car. A better statement would have been to say, 'I walked back to the car and I heard Swinney shoot two times.' Earlier she said, 'I walked on down the road.' Now, she does not use the word 'walked' but used the word 'back.'

"All of her verb tenses were in the past. Since she is recalling what happened, we expect her to use past tense language. Deceptive people will sometimes unknowingly use present tense verbs if the story is not coming from memory. She also used strong tone verbs such as 'told' and 'made' versus soft tone verbs such as 'said' and 'asked.' In this type of statement, we would expect to see strong tone language.

"A truthful person will be consistent in his language. If he views a firearm as a 'gun,' he will always call it a 'gun.' He will not suddenly start to call it a 'pistol' because to him it is a 'gun.' Deceptive people will sometimes use synonyms because they are making up the story and not following their personal dictionary. A change in language indicates deception unless there is a justification for the change. In her statement, she consistently uses the words 'gun,' 'billfold,' 'car,' 'little girl' and 'little boy.' She does not use any synonyms to describe these things or people."

McClish also found her statements taken by Tillman Johnson to be generally reliable. "She appears to be truthful in her unsigned statements given in July. She does use the word 'pistol' one time which is a change from 'gun.' It may be Swinney called it a 'pistol' and she adopted his language, which frequently happens, when two people are interrogated together.

"She used the present tense verb 'ask' when she stated, 'The boy in the car ask us what we wanted.' Her use of the word 'ask' may be due to poor grammar skills and not necessarily deception." (It also may have reflected Johnson's interpreting a slurred "asked" as "ask" or even a typographical mishap, for the statement was not tape-recorded.)

McClish continued: "As we saw she did contradict herself several times. She said that she watched the girl while Swinney drove their car to where the couple's car was parked. In November, she will state that Swinney and the girl drove the car back.

"After shooting the boy, she states, Swinney picked him up and put him in the back seat. She does not mention this in her November statement."

Summarizing his overall opinion of the statements, McClish concluded:

"After reading the documents, I believe Peggy Swinney is telling the truth in regards to Youell Swinney killing Paul Martin and Betty Jo Booker. However, everyone edits their statements. No one is going to tell us every little detail. Even a truthful person will only tell us what he thinks we need to hear. Therefore, as pointed out, in her statement there are some things she has not told the police. For example, she stated, 'Swinney told the couple to give him what they had.' However, she never states what, if anything, they gave to Swinney. There are other areas [where] she has withheld information and may be trying to minimize her involvement."

Prosecutors now had two *signed* statements from Peggy that implicated Swinney in the murders of Paul Martin and Betty Jo Booker. Like a savings account they could be stored away and held in reserve if all else failed. There were two possibilities: She might change her mind about testifying. And should she divorce Swinney, she could be called as a witness whether she agreed or not.

The signed statements constituted an ace in the hole, should a trump card be needed in the future.

Three days after the interrogation in Austin, Peggy appeared in the Miller County Circuit Court, charged with grand larceny as a partner in Swinney's car theft. Basically it was a holding tactic, to keep her in the clutches of the law as an accomplice. She was essential to the developing strategy.

She pleaded not guilty

The following day—November 26—Judge Dexter Bush ordered Swinney discharged as a patient in the Arkansas State Hospital and returned to Texarkana. Four days after that, Swinney's attorneys—J. F. McVey, Paul McDonald, and Ted Goldman—filed a petition for writ of habeas corpus. This resulted in his being formally charged with grand larceny involving the theft of an automobile. A few days later, in early December, he entered a plea of not guilty. These maneuvers enabled the county to continue holding him but raised the possibility of his making bond on such a charge.

Another local lawyer, William E. Haynie, served as a contact for Swinney.

Meanwhile, Cleo Swinney visited his brother Youell in jail and found him well taken care of, seeming to refute what their father had claimed earlier. There is no evidence that Youell ever complained, even once, about having the "bat" used on him.

After Youell was arraigned, his brother Cleo telephoned attorney McVey that Youell, as instructed, had pleaded not guilty to grand larceny for stealing a Plymouth. McVey complained about the local representation, charging that Goldman had tried to get Youell to confess to the murders. No evidence supports his contentions. McVey then turned his attention to his favorite substitute, a phantom Phantom, W—, whom he had never seen, classifying him as "psychopathic, possibly praecox with a saddistic [*sic*] complex." He instructed attorney Love immediately to seek a change of venue "swearing both against the Judge and the inhabitants of Miller County and any other County in which any of these crimes occurred."

McVey said he was getting a picture of W—, his candidate to replace Youell as the Phantom, as well as to try to get "a statement from the wife of the first man that was killed, if possible, and to warn her to be very cautious as we have reason to believe that its [*sic*] possible that an attempt maybe [*sic*] made upon her." He seemed confused about the victims and the murders. Presumably he had in mind getting Katie Starks to make a statement that would fit in with his theory of the criminal while ruling out Youell, at the same time setting off alarms that Katie was still at risk from his candidate for the slayer of her husband. He also urged Cleo not to share the information with Youell's attorneys in Texarkana—another strange defense tactic.

McVey's barrage of letters left the impression that he was flailing about on all fronts at once. He reported to Cleo that he had made contact with the Arkansas governor, Ben Laney. "The fight is just beginning," he insisted, adding: "I will leave no stone unturned to see that justice is done." He included a bill of $16.60 for his phone, telegram, and postal bills. "All this phoning was rather expensive."

CHAPTER 20

A QUIET "SOLUTION"

P rosecutors and officers on both sides of the state line had pondered how they might overcome the possibility of Peggy's continued refusal to testify. Sheriff Presley in Texas, for one, was opposed to charging a man in a capital case on circumstantial evidence alone, without eyewitness or strong physical evidence such as fingerprints or other laboratory data. He later told Henry Slaton, a highway patrolman, that he had no doubts about Swinney's guilt in the Texas slayings. Even with circumstantial evidence, he believed, the suspect could have been convicted and given the death penalty. But the sheriff didn't want to send any man to his death on circumstantial evidence alone.

During his stint in office, Presley had to convey prisoners to Huntsville whom juries had dealt death sentences. "Not a one of them could read and write," he said. That knowledge further convinced him that only an airtight case bolstered by more than circumstantial evidence should be required if the death penalty might be invoked. With emotions as high as they were surrounding the Phantom murders, a death penalty might be won merely on a charge, with slight evidence. He believed he had the right man for the crimes but didn't think that was the right approach, and he wasn't alone in that stance. Some Arkansas officers agreed.

The goal became to devise a way to take Swinney out of society for as long as possible. An obvious route would be a life sentence as a habitual criminal, a Texas law used on other hardened violators, of which Swinney clearly was. But Arkansas had no such law. There was enough hard evidence, including thefts to which Swinney had admitted to the FBI, to earn him a string of sentences in state and federal jurisdictions. Eventually, however, he would be freed and back on the streets. None of the officers or prosecutors working the case wanted that to happen.

Texas, however, did have a habitual criminal act. If Bowie County could win a conviction for any of the easily proved crimes Swinney had committed, with his record of previous convictions he would be an apt candidate for a life sentence under the act.

No one articulated it publicly that what they proposed was parallel to how the government had nailed gangster Al Capone in the 1930s. Unable to prove Capone's guilt in murders they were certain he had ordered, government prosecutors convicted him of tax fraud. That took him out of circulation. A similar fate could be woven for Swinney, his captors believed. The overriding goal was to take him off the streets, and keep him off. Rather than risk a murder charge going awry, they felt they had a sure way to accomplish it. Texas's habitual criminal act, it could be argued, was designed for a case like Swinney's. (In more recent history in the South, men believed to have murdered civil rights activists similarly were convicted of violating the victims' rights, more readily proved.)

Sweating it out under the threat of Arkansas's electric chair, or at the least a long sentence in its relatively harsher prison system, Swinney could see the advantages of a transfer to Texas, so long as it was not for a murder charge. At a time when Swinney's attorney McVey was trying to set up roadblocks to Swinney's further incarceration, Texas and Arkansas officers agreed that, considering the differences in state law, Texas jurisdiction would fit more snugly into their intentions. Extradite him to Texas and try him for a felony under the habitual criminal act.

The first step was to secure an extradition order. That document, once accepted by Arkansas authorities, would pave the way to move the prisoner across the state line. Sheriff Bill Presley drove to Austin, the state capital, early on the morning of December 3 to present the request to Texas Governor Coke Stevenson. It was a long 350-mile drive on two-lane highways threaded through small towns. By afternoon, the sheriff had his signed papers from the governor and headed back to Texarkana.

The following morning, December 4, Presley and others headed for Little Rock to complete the legal process. Getting wind of the plans, Love called Arkansas Governor Ben Laney, giving a brief history of the case and pleaded for at least forty-eight hours in which to oppose the move. The governor "half-way" promised Attorney Love he would postpone the matter till December 9, according to Love's take on the conversation.

He didn't hear back from Laney, however, and on the afternoon of December 4 Governor Laney granted extradition. Swinney was placed in the custody of Sheriff Presley and taken across the state line to Bowie County. The Texas jurisdiction had played an ace that trumped anything Swinney's father and lawyer might present: in addition to other charges in Texas, Swinney was a parole violator, having violated terms of his 1945 conditional parole, an undeniable fact.

John Frederick, McVey's "federal" contact, grew so indignant at the governor's decision that he promised to take the matter to FBI Director J. Edgar Hoover, U.S. Attorney General Tom Clark, and Texas Governor Coke Stevenson. There is no evidence that he followed through. An hour after his conversation with McVey, however, Frederick did call the county attorney in Bowie County—Maxwell Welch, who would become district attorney in January, succeeding Weldon Glass who had not run for reelection—who, he said, promised him two things: Swinney would get a sanity hearing and since he had been on parole he would be sent back to the Texas penitentiary as a parole violator with perhaps added time because of having stolen a car in Texas. He did not say, however, how much additional time would be added or if they intended to try him as a habitual criminal. It's possible Welch was not aware of transactions under way in the D.A.'s office in which he was soon to perform.

McVey warned Cleo, as he so often did, to beware of moves by Youell's captors, "as there is some possibility that Texas may drop all charges and turn Youell loose. If this happens [Miller County Sheriff Elvie] Davis will, of course, try to send him to the penitentiary in Arkansas as a habitual criminal, and if there is any possible way we want to keep him out of Arkansas until we can prevent this at least from happening, it would be best in my opinion." He believed Sheriff Davis and Judge Bush might try to lull Swinney into believing charges had been dropped, and then proceed. "We cannot relax until Youell is clear of all charges." Whether the Feds would take action, he didn't know. "They could, but if they are convinced that he is not of sound mind they may not do anything about it." At that point he broke off and began castigating his whipping boy suspect, W—.

It was a large—and fantastic—order for a defense lawyer, considering the facts arrayed against the defendant, who had already admitted to several thefts. McVey obviously didn't realize that Texas, unlike Arkansas, had a habitual criminal act and was not likely to drop charges after it had gone to so much trouble to extradite him.

If Youell and his father appeared to be dysfunctional and keeping the rest of the family under continual strain, there was ample documentation.

Although Swinney probably decided Arkansas didn't have a strong case against him in the Starks murder, he could never be sure. As far as he knew with certainty, he still might be tried, found guilty, and electrocuted. He knew they were holding him for "more than stealing a car," as he had blurted out that fateful July day.

Fear of the unknown, which had once terrorized the region, now turned on Swinney. Did Arkansas have the goods on him? Well, probably not a strong case. But what did they have? Were they still making a case, compiling more evidence? They had something, and they had been grilling Peggy, and what had she said?

He didn't know Peggy had spilled the beans on the Booker-Martin murders. By then, he was not anxious about that. He was in Arkansas custody. The Starks case was fresher, leaving him more anxious. The prospect of serving time in Texas on a car-theft charge had its appealing side. He remembered how tough it was in Arkansas's penitentiary where he had served time at Tucker Farm in the early 1940s.

Swinney also was in the crossfire of conflicting legal advice. His father and McVey came forth almost daily with strategy, some of it the opposite of previous policies. The prisoner counseled with his attorneys near at hand. When a deal came, it had to be considered. Once extradition loomed as a reality, there seemed to be little choice.

Tillman Johnson remembered that a deal had been offered, through Swinney's lawyers, to go to Texas and be tried for car theft under the habitual criminal act. He named William Haynie as the attorney who had negotiated for Swinney. He recalled that Swinney had jumped at it. A deal carried the welcomed prospect of getting out of Arkansas and from under the shadow of its electric chair and into Texas and some sort of certainty of life. Granted, it was prison life; he could deal with that. He'd done it before. And he'd always gotten out long before his sentences ended.

It was a good deal that he welcomed with relief, Johnson believed.

Texas officers, once he had been extradited from Arkansas, took Youell Swinney to Mt. Pleasant, sixty miles west, in Titus County. If word somehow slipped out that Bowie County authorities were holding the major Phantom suspect, it wasn't hard to predict that vigilante violence might follow. Lynchings were far from rare in Bowie County and Texarkana-area history. Bill Presley vowed to take no chances over how an angry citizenry might react. He remembered the last lynching in Texarkana, while his predecessor was serving as sheriff, and he was adamant that one would never happen during his watch.

Usually he took prisoners to nearby Cass County for security purposes. This case, however, was the biggest that had ever confronted Bowie County. Neighboring Cass County was too close. A lynching party wouldn't have far to go; besides, two of the Phantom's victims, Richard Griffin and Polly Ann Moore, had come from Cass County. The feeling and tensions were as high there as anywhere else. Presley called Aubrey Redfearn, then winding down his tenure as sheriff of Titus County. Would he take a special prisoner for him temporarily? Redfearn would be glad to accommodate a fellow sheriff. Presley and a deputy hustled Swinney over to the jail one block off the town square in Mt. Pleasant. It was far enough away that the prisoner should be safe. Officers remained tight-lipped, intending that nothing should reach the public about their captive.

On December 9, Youell Swinney wrote a postcard to a sister, giving as his return address "c/o County jail, Mt. Pleasant, Texas."

"Trust you have my letter of a couple days ago. Geneva send me some money & a change of clothes at once. Get in touch with Mr. McVey at once. You, Joe & Cleo come to see me at once."

His repeated admonitions of "at once" could hardly have failed to remind the others of the father Swinney's time-centered demands, suggesting the source of Youell's appeals to urgency.

While Swinney remained in custody in Mt. Pleasant and Peggy in Miller County, a new rumor erupted that threatened to undo the carefully concealed plans of Texarkana officers. A one-column story on December 10, datelined Dallas from the Associated Press, came close to making public what was believed to be a well-guarded secret.

'GOOD SUSPECT'
IN PHANTOM CASE

In Dallas, Ranger Captain "Lone Wolf" Gonzaullas told reporters that officers had a "good suspect" in the case, good news indeed. He said he and Sheriff Bill Presley were working on some "good stuff that has not definitely been eliminated." He didn't say where the investigation was being made, nor would he name the suspect. "Too many times good leads have turned into duds," he said.

The report went on to put Gonzaullas's quote in context. "Widespread rumors of an early break in the five Texarkana murder cases have been heard in the past two weeks," the AP story continued. "Reports have been heard from such widely separated cities as Austin and Midland."

A Texarkana reporter pursued the local angle, leaving the reader to wonder what was going on. "In Texarkana, Sheriff Presley said he had nothing definite in the case and did not feel he could make any statement that would enlighten the public any more than those which he had already issued. He said he knew of nothing of significance to report at the time."

The final paragraph of the story stated the current status of the case.

"Although the reward fund set up for the capture or information leading to the capture of the person responsible for the killings has been dissolved and residents of the Texarkana area have become less nervous, interest still is high in the case and officers continue their probe of what still remains an unsolved case."

Whether Gonzaullas's tip, or leak, to the press was intended to renew media interest in the case or whether he hoped to be the first to signal a break was not clear. Almost immediately, to those who knew anything about the case, it became obvious that lawmen were practicing poor coordination. Others were puzzled.

The "good suspect"—undoubtedly Gonzaullas was referring to Swinney—evaporated overnight. The next day, the local sheriffs joined together to discredit the Dallas-based story.

PROMISING LEAD IN
PHANTOM CASE PROVES DUD
PRESLEY AND DAVIS SAY EXTENSIVE
QUESTIONING OF COUPLE UNAVAILING

The story quoted Presley and Davis as saying "the latest and most promising lead" had "fizzled out and the officers were no nearer the solution of the puzzling crimes than they were months ago." It was an emphatic slamming of the door on the "good suspect" story. The report went on to say that officers of several jurisdictions had been "working day and night trying to validate the story of a woman that her husband had slain Paul Martin and Betty Jo Booker, a teen-age couple, after robbing them of a small sum of money.

"The woman's statement followed so closely the known facts of the case as deduced by the officers that they were almost positive she was telling the truth and at one time were almost at the point of announcing a break in the case," the quotation continued. "Subsequently, however, the woman repudiated her story completely and said that neither she nor her husband had had anything to do with the slayings.

"The investigating officers, however, refused to dismiss the pair as suspects in the case and about 10 days ago the woman was taken to Austin where she was questioned extensively. The man later was taken to Austin and was also questioned at length."

The *Gazette* quoted the officers as saying, "However, our investigation, after all was said and done, has disclosed that the woman was not telling the truth and that on the night Paul Martin and Betty Jo Booker were slain, these two, the man and the woman, were asleep in an automobile under a bridge near San Antonio.

"We will continue to check clues on the killings and will question all persons against whom there is any suspicion."

It was clear, despite the statement, that the officers did not believe they "were no nearer the solution than they were months ago." They still held Swinney and his wife, in separate jails. If they were the couple mentioned who were supposed to have been sleeping in a car under a bridge in south Texas, then the officers were trafficking in misinformation, doctoring their statement to discount the rumors already circulating and to calm down the potential public uproar likely to ensue if a full disclosure came forth. The news story was basically accurate except for two things: the Swinneys did not sleep under a bridge near San Antonio the night Betty Jo and Paul were murdered, and Peggy's statement still stood. Both Swinneys were known—proved—to have been in the Texarkana area during the murders. She was taken to Austin, but no records reflect that he had been taken as well. Swinney was to remain behind bars and looking forward to a trial date. The story served the purpose for which it had been designed, to spike the rumor and prevent the premature exposure of Swinney as the major suspect in the crimes for which he hadn't yet been charged.

The inadvertent announcement of the "good suspect" in the midst of delicate negotiations came close to negating months of hard investigative work and legal maneuvers.

Back in Missouri, McVey continued to push his contention that the Phantom was someone other than Youell Swinney. His candidate was the same W— he had mentioned before. McVey wrote Cleo Swinney that he knew of two "suspicious characters around here," one, he said, fitting the general description of W—. He passed on his suspicions to the local sheriff, but the "suspicious characters" suddenly left town. The next night a man he did not see, but who also fit the description, inquired in town of the Rev. Mr. Swinney. Later in the afternoon while S. C. Swinney was at the post office, "this man"—whom he also didn't see—rattled the door of the Swinney home, then ran when Mrs. Swinney went to the door. Swinney's daughter (and Youell's sister) insisted that W— was in Louisiana at the time, but McVey persisted in his belief that the man was in Missouri.

Stanley Swinney joined in with McVey in flailing out at W—, who he claimed, without evidence, was in Montgomery City with "a St. Louis killer" presumably stalking the elder Swinney. It was a pattern, tinged with paranoia and denial, that was to persist.

McVey remained suspicious. Cleo sent McVey a newspaper clipping that the reward fund had been dissolved. McVey wrote back for him to be on guard. "I am confident," wrote McVey, "that it has not been dissolved and that it has been increased considerably in the past month or two." By then John Frederick had called McVey to report his conversation with Maxwell Welch, soon to be Bowie County's district attorney, who promised "that he would see that there was no crooked stuff or Third degree pulled off."

A few days later, Frederick called McVey, reporting on another talk with Maxwell Welch. Welch assured Frederick "that Youell would be given every consideration; that he would never be indicted for murder, and that the only thing that Texas had against him was the car theft and parole violation, and that it was in view of this fact that he was a parole violator from The State of Texas that the Governor released him to Texas over our protests."

On December 19, Peggy Swinney was released on her own recognition by the Miller County Circuit Court. She had cooperated. This was her reward, freedom for the time being. If things went well, she would never return to jail.

On the Sunday night before Christmas, Max Tackett and Tillman Johnson narrowly escaped death when a seemingly routine traffic stop escalated into a brief but bloody gun battle on Highway 67 East near Fulton, Arkansas. When the last shot was fired, Tackett lay critically wounded and their two prisoners dead. Tackett and Johnson had arrested a white man and a black man as suspects in the theft of a truck. Tackett assembled the two men in the police car to take them to jail in Texarkana, with the white man in front, the black man in the back seat. Johnson, following behind in the stolen truck, saw the police car slow and roll toward a culvert. He got out and sprinted toward the car. The white man held a .38 caliber revolver, later determined to have been stolen from a hardware store in Texarkana, to Tackett's stomach for several seconds. The officer twisted his body and the bullet went into the side of his abdomen. Powder burns scorched his clothing where the bullet had entered.

"This man has a gun—watch out!" Tackett yelled out.

The white man jumped from the car and began firing at Johnson. At close range by then, Johnson seized the man's wrist, turning the gun toward the ground. The man kept firing, the bullets going into the ground. Johnson pulled his own pistol and emptied it into the man, who fell dead to the ground.

Johnson looked into the back of the police car, where the black prisoner was scuffling with the wounded Tackett. Tackett managed to pull his own gun and shot the man in the head, killing him instantly.

Johnson then entered the police car, with the wounded Tackett sprawled in the seat and the dead man's body on the floor, and drove at top speed to the emergency room at Michael Meagher Hospital.

City officers rushed out to the bloody scene, finding the white man's body. Nearby in the gravel, they found a flashlight, still shining.

Tackett recovered, once more reminded of the hazards of "routine" police work. It had been almost a year since the December 31, 1945, gun battle at Fulton when Tackett was fired upon five times before he and State Policeman Charley Boyd killed the ex-convict bandit initiating the shootout.

During this period, the elder Swinney struggled with his own personal crises. A Seconal addiction, which he attributed to his physician's prescription during a previous hospitalization, kept him on the verge of "going to pieces" each time he faced withdrawal. Overshadowing his drug dependency, he lost his livelihood as pastor of the First Baptist Church in Montgomery City when deacons learned of his son Youell's record and reputation. Church members knew nothing of the Seconal addiction, but they didn't want a pastor whose son had served time in the penitentiary. The minister wanted to relocate, to a Southern church, if possible, believing there such a situation would not be a taint.

In mid-January the minister wrote Youell of the deacons asking him to resign. He assured Youell he would work to get him released—even if he got a life sentence, he would serve less time than he had previously. He also enclosed a self-explanatory letter from Texarkana defense attorney Elmer Lincoln. Lincoln offered to take Youell's case for a fifty-dollar retainer and a nominal fee to defend him, and start work on the case. The odds were that Lincoln, knowing only the father's version, failed to realize the full nature of the case. The Reverend Swinney did not follow through. He appeared to have a less expensive remedy in mind. He advised his son that, the prosecutor being inexperienced, he should not try to defend himself and not ask for court-appointed counsel. Just plead Not Guilty and any conviction would be overturned.

The minister insisted, to his son Cleo, that a lawyer would get Youell off with a light or suspended sentence. Later in the month he changed his mind, saying Youell should plead Not Guilty by reason of insanity, contradicting his earlier advice, no doubt to the bewilderment of the recipients of his directives.

On January 13, 1947, the Bowie County Grand Jury for the Fifth Judicial District convened in the stately 1890s courthouse in the county seat, Boston, in the west end of the county and indicted Youell Lee Swinney for felony theft. His bail was set at $7,500, a large sum for the time.

Bowie County could be called the County of Three Bostons. Within miles of each other in the western end there were Boston, Old Boston, and New Boston. The county seat was in just plain Boston, consisting of one square block on which the courthouse and jail were set. Decades later, the seat was moved to New Boston.

The indictment, prepared by the new district attorney, Maxwell Welch, accused Swinney of stealing, on March 3, 1946, the automobile belonging to Luther McClure, valued at five hundred dollars. The grand jurors also noted Swinney's previous convictions, August 28, 1944, in Texas for felony robbery by assault, and his February 11, 1941, Arkansas conviction for grand larceny.

Witnesses before the grand jury included Luther McClure, the owner of the stolen car, FBI agents Horace Hallett and J. C. Calhoun, and J. B. Como, deputy sheriff in Beaumont.

The foreman of the grand jury, G. Ross Perot, a Texarkana cotton broker, signed the indictment. Perot's teenaged son, H. Ross Perot, was a senior at Texas High.

There is no extant documentary evidence that Swinney and his defenders cut a deal with authorities, but numerous lawmen have attested that such a negotiation did occur. Each side had a goal: the authorities wanted to keep Swinney behind bars, Swinney wanted to escape the electric chair. Several officers have asserted this as a fact, though not written on any public document that exists. Tillman Johnson, the last lawman to die, repeated the same story. In essence, Swinney was offered the opportunity to be transferred to Texas and be tried for felony theft under the state's habitual criminal act, for which a conviction would likely mean a life sentence. But whatever sentence he received, it would not be death. Anxious over his fate in Arkansas, according to this version, Swinney was eager to accept the transfer and plead guilty in Bowie County. The details, the oral recapitulation goes, were worked out by members of Swinney's family and his attorneys in Texarkana. Some of the events that followed tend to bear out this account.

While the shadow of the Phantom's deeds hung over the town like a Halloween wraith, Swinney's name had never appeared in print or on the radio. Only lawmen and members of his family knew the reason he was being held. Even though he made the front page of the *Texarkana Gazette* on February 11, 1947—two days after his thirtieth birthday—his name appeared almost as an afterthought, as better-known local police characters, notably Maxie Lott and Johnny Orr, Sr., hogged the headlines. Even then, it was only a one-column story at the bottom of the page.

Maxie Lott was to be tried as part of a $150,000 stolen-car ring in Bowie County. The previous week, Johnny Orr, Sr., had been sentenced in Upshur County to five years in the pen for car theft. Swinney's name didn't appear until the sixth paragraph of the eight-paragraph story, a tiny recognition in a dim spotlight.

"Cases besides Lott's scheduled for trial this week include: Youell Swinney, Texarkana, felony theft; Harry Spahler, Gregg county, forgery and attempt to pass forged instruments."

The object of the nationwide manhunt had been reduced to a brief, obscure sentence shared with another alleged felon.

The jury list for Swinney's trial consisted of twenty-three potential jurors. Twelve of the first thirteen were chosen. Gus Looney was elected foreman. Coincidentally, Looney had the same surname as Swinney's mother's maiden name. They were not related.

Under state law at the time, theft of property valued at fifty dollars or more constituted a felony.

FBI agent Buzz Hallett watched the proceedings closely, from beginning to end. He had a special interest in the case. Not only had he investigated the series of murders, he and his wife Frances lived at 3104 Anthony Drive in the Sussex Downs subdivision of Texarkana. Betty Jo Booker's mother and stepfather Clark Brown lived at 3105 Anthony Drive, directly across the street. He committed to memory every detail as he sat quietly in the courtroom.

The defendant appeared without an attorney. Judge Robert S. Vance, a highly competent jurist, asked him if he had an attorney and then if he wished to have an attorney appointed by the court. Swinney replied that he did not and wished to represent himself. The judge again asked if he wished to have an attorney appointed. Again Swinney said he wished to represent himself. This tends to confirm the unofficial story, that he had agreed to plead guilty, whether he had a lawyer or not. It also coincided with one, out of many, advisories from his father to let them proceed without his having a lawyer. His father's various strategies had included pleading not guilty on the basis of insanity but hadn't advised him to refuse court-appointed counsel, only to let them convict him without a lawyer.

The judge next asked the prisoner, "How do you plead to the charge as read?"

"Guilty, your honor."

Judge Vance rejected the plea, explaining that in a proceeding under the habitual criminal act, the defendant was not allowed to plead guilty.

"I am entering a plea of not guilty in your behalf," the judge said.

That exchange was to remain burned into Agent Hallett's memory the rest of his life. He didn't think it mattered who represented Swinney, for the evidence of the stolen car made for a cut-and-dried case. Luther McClure testified to having the car stolen.

Prosecutor Welch introduced Swinney's signed statement to the FBI, in which he said that he and his wife drove the Chevrolet the day of the theft, March 3, 1946, to Hope, Arkansas, and then to Wichita Falls, Texas, and from there on to Lubbock, Texas. He admitted picking up three hitchhikers on the trip. At Lubbock he gave a note to one of the hitchhikers, asking him to drive to car to Beaumont, Texas, and deliver it there to a man who turned out to be nonexistent. As evidence, the deputy from Beaumont, J. B. Como, testified to recovering the car and finding a wartime tire-ration card in the glove compartment that bore the name Luther McClure. Como identified Swinney from a description given by the hitchhiker. Prosecutor Welch had no difficulty sealing the case for the State. He then introduced previous convictions that included a three-year sentence for felony car theft in Arkansas and the five-year term for robbery in Texas, for which he was paroled after eleven months.

Welch indicated that Swinney was implicated in the theft of at least five automobiles; he was being tried for only one.

Swinney attempted to cross-examine witnesses with unimpressive results. The clincher was his criminal record, which was extensive enough to prove the prior convictions quite readily. The term "three-time loser" was made to order for Swinney. The prosecutor felt he had an airtight case.

As his own attorney, Swinney chose not to put himself on the witness stand, certainly a prudent move. Judge Vance's charge to the jury underscored very strongly that his failure to take the witness stand should not be considered in deliberations. The judge also emphasized that the burden of proof was on the State, that the defendant was presumed innocent until proved guilty beyond a reasonable doubt; and if any doubt remained, he should be acquitted.

The rest was up to the jury, and the decision wasn't prolonged. No mention was made at any point about murder or the Phantom case. The focus remained strictly on the lesser, but multiple, felonies.

Within an hour, the foreman, Gus Looney, orally and in handwriting delivered the verdict:

"We the Jury find the defendant guilty as charged in the indictment."

The jury also found the defendant Swinney's conviction to be the third felony conviction as pursuant to Article 63 of the Texas Penal Code, thereby enhancing the punishment. The jury recommended life in prison. The habitual criminal act was a threat held over repeat offenders at the time. A violent crime such as murder was more likely to net death or perhaps ninety-nine years, amounting to longer even than "life."

The following morning, the *Gazette* reported the proceedings in a modest one-column story on page 1, surrounded by larger headlines on other events.

YOUELL SWINNEY, EX-CONVICT, GIVEN LIFE IN PRISON

HABITUAL CRIMINAL ACT INVOKED
AFTER CONVICTION FOR AUTO THEFT

For the first time, Swinney's name made its way to a front-page headline. His continued stealing of automobiles during the few months following his release from the Texas penitentiary made the "habitual" tag seem perfectly logical.

FBI agent Hallett walked out of the old courtroom feeling justice had been served, more or less. He felt Swinney had gotten off light but had been taken out of society's circulation, the objective.

Four days after the jury verdict, Judge Vance formally sentenced Swinney to life imprisonment in the state penitentiary.

The case ended so quietly that only a few in law enforcement on either side of the state line knew of it. It was legal, supposedly with the cooperation of Swinney himself, some of his family, and his attorneys. Officers and prosecutors believed he had been put away for the remainder of his years, and thus would never kill again, as they believed he had. If for some reason he managed to leave the penitentiary alive, the murder charges could be resurrected, possibly with stronger evidence.

It was the final act of the season of terror. Youell Lee Swinney had been taken off the streets in as effective and fast a way as could be designed.

The sentence came just less than a week after Swinney marked his thirtieth birthday.

Learning of the trial results, McVey wrote Cleo, saying that the Reverend Swinney had told him Cleo had made arrangements that Youell would get parole or a suspended sentence and would not be convicted under the habitual criminal act. McVey chastised Cleo for not confiding fully; if he had, Youell would not be under a life sentence. "This thing is not over yet. I intend to break this case . . . and that I am backed up by the 'Biggest Guy' in the world."

Slightly over a week later, Parson Swinney reacted with optimism. "They have done exactly the thing we hoped they would do," he wrote Cleo. "Convicted him without Counsel."

The manner in which the habitual criminal act was used to take Swinney out of society was strictly legal and, according to others, acceptable to Swinney as well as to his captors. Based on his previous record of early release on each of his falls, he probably expected to pull no more than ten or fifteen years. Hallett's memory was clear that Swinney attempted to plead guilty but was advised by the judge that he could not do so under the habitual criminal act.

Was the habitual criminal act a fair law? That was an issue the prosecutors in the 1940s had not created, nor Swinney's lawyers challenged. It existed. It was the law. It had been used with others. Whatever argument might be raised against its use, on the other side was Swinney's record of not only two previous convictions but of a multitude. Had the law required five prior jolts, they could have been documented. Additionally he could have been tried, and probably convicted, on a number of other crimes, in Texas, Arkansas, and Oklahoma. The two cases used for enhancement were representative of his criminal career at that stage. If he'd been convicted of the other crimes in which he was implicated and the sentences had been stacked, or served consecutively, he might have been assured of dying in prison.

In balancing the need for public safety against the prisoner's civil rights, the prosecutors appear to have served justice in the understanding of the law. Swinney's life was spared, as it might or might not have been with the filing of a murder charge, his major concern. And he was kept off the street, the guiding motivation of his prosecutors.

It was as effective a trade as could be achieved at the time. It did not "solve" the Phantom murders, but it resolved the salient concern.

Swinney remained in the county's custody for two months before he was transported to the state penitentiary at Huntsville. Following his conviction and sentence on February 15, he gave notice of appeal. On April 15, however, he withdrew it.

It is not difficult to reason why he appealed in the first place, once the significance of a sentence dawned upon him. It is less evident why he decided to withdraw his motion. It is possible that someone in authority, such as Sheriff Presley or District Attorney Welch, reminded him that should he succeed in overturning his conviction and sentence, he might face a charge in the Spring Lake Park murders, in which case the penalty likely would go beyond a life sentence.

Peggy's statement in Austin was like money in the bank for the prosecution. Once she divorced Swinney, she could be subpoenaed as a witness. With him now locked up for life, she might choose to do so anyway.

Three days after his request, Swinney arrived in Huntsville.

CHAPTER 21

BEHIND WALLS AGAIN

Youell Lee Swinney's mug shots as he reentered the Texas Prison System as Inmate # 108586 reflected the face of a man much aged from the one who had been processed less than three years earlier. He was still fairly good-looking with barbered and combed hair as he stared into the camera. But the boyish look was gone. The hard set of his mouth was grim. He was back in stir, beginning another chapter in his troubled life.

The data on his prison log, self-reported, provided a detailed accounting: five feet eleven inches tall, weight 154 pounds, with blue eyes, brown hair, and ruddy complexion. He wore size nine shoes.

The clerk recorded other features at check-in. A tattoo on his lower left arm included a heart with the word REVENGE spelled out. He used tobacco and considered himself "temperate" in his habits. He classified himself as a Baptist.

He told the processing clerk he'd attended school twelve years and had finished the twelfth grade. He could read and write, as he claimed, but he hadn't gone nearly so far in school. The sixth grade was closer to the truth. He probably hoped to get an inside office job by exaggerating his education.

There were other inaccuracies. He claimed he'd been born in Texas, although his birthplace was Arkadelphia, Arkansas. His mother and father, he said, were born in Texas; actually she was born in Georgia, the father in Arkansas.

As for occupation, he first gave *electrician* as his answer. That was marked out; *bookkeeper* replaced it. (While in Arkansas custody he no doubt had focused frequently on electrical operations.) He knew he ran a better chance of an inside job as a bookkeeper. As for his residence, he first gave San Angelo, Texas; it was marked over, substituting Texarkana, Texas. On the line for Ex-Service status, *Marines* was written but then marked through and left blank. Swinney was not a native of Texas, his mother and father were not born in Texas. He was not an electrician (nor a bookkeeper), his residence was not San Angelo, and he was never in the Marines or any other branch of the armed services. In a penal population where most inmates were not high school graduates, some of the false answers might be attributed to seeking better treatment as an electrician or bookkeeper with a high school education and as a World War II veteran. Other inaccuracies—if caused by him rather than the clerk—seemed to serve no purpose. His responses seemed to be aimed at avoiding hard labor on the prison farm. He knew how prisons operated.

Swinney'd never had to complete a sentence, for one reason or another. Why would this fall be any different? He hadn't been charged with murder, his greatest fear. Men with a murder rap sometimes got out in as little as ten or fifteen, even seven or eight, years. A life sentence for a stolen car? Unlikely! Swinney could convince himself that the more time passed, the farther he would be from having to stand trial for any killings, enabling him to gain release from a life sentence for a mere stolen car. He could do six or seven years, a good exchange.

Three entries reflected a bleaker future.

Offense: *Theft and prior conviction.*
Terms of Imprisonment: *Life*
Expiration of Sentence: *Death*

Outside, the world was in flux. A Cold War had emerged on the heels of the deadliest war in history. The Allies and the Soviet Union wrangled over arms control. Communists assumed power in Poland, with Hungary months behind. President Harry Truman dispatched aid to Turkey and Greece to thwart Soviet ambitions and contain Communism.

Great Britain endured turmoil. Her colonies in India, Pakistan, and Nigeria began breaking away. Beset by Middle Eastern strife, Britain signaled readiness to transfer her Palestinian woes to the fledgling United Nations, leading to the founding of Israel.

In the United States, President Truman faced a recalcitrant Congress. As if that was not enough, his aged mother broke her hip in a fall at home. In sports, Tony Zale held on to his middleweight boxing title, and Jackie Robinson broke the major league baseball color barrier with the Brooklyn Dodgers. As a hint of things to come, Edwin Land demonstrated his "instant camera," the Polaroid. Reports of unidentified flying objects (UFO) made the news from Washington state to Roswell, New Mexico. In mid-January, an unsolved brutal murder claimed the life of Elizabeth Short, known as the Black Dahlia, in Los Angeles. In early April, tornadoes swept viciously over Texas, Oklahoma, and Kansas, killing 181 and injuring 970.

Texarkana's crime and violence hardly slowed: six men indicted for attacking two policemen; Johnny Thompson, a local police character, in custody for automobile theft as part of a larger ring; a downtown fire ravaged Bryce's Cafeteria, Four States Business College, and the Mayflower Cafe; and a teenager, just out of reform school and in a stolen car, wounded by an officer's shotgun blast.

A new campaign to drive the "undesirable elements" out of town made headlines but no headway.

Swinney, untouched by the swirl of events outside, re-entered the prison population with a central idea in mind: to get out. His first assignment reinforced the intention. His keepers dispatched him to hard farm labor. After he thought it over, he decided someone from Bowie County was responsible. He settled on the sheriff, Bill Presley, as the culprit. But for the sheriff, Swinney concluded, he'd have an easier life. In early 1948, he wrote to Elmer Lincoln, the Texarkana criminal defense lawyer his father had written but never followed up on. In his letter, Swinney accused Sheriff Presley of giving him a negative report that consigned him to hard labor. He then brought up what he characterized as his unfair conviction. He hoped Lincoln would help him gain a better role in prison as well as find a way to liberate him.

Lincoln by return mail replied in a sympathetic tone, explaining why he couldn't help him. Lincoln by then was a member of the Texas Prison Board and thus unable to ask officials to do anything for a person he knew.

Lincoln recalled that the elder Swinney had made contact with him regarding Youell's case but that he'd heard nothing further from him. At the time, Lincoln wrote, he could have prevented Youell's conviction as a habitual criminal, but by the time he was writing the letter it was too late, as well as his being in no position to help.

Lincoln added: "If Mr. Presley gave you a bad report your record will probably disclose that. However, I am sure you understand that repeaters are almost invariably sent to Darrington or Retrieve Farm and it is not necessary for anybody to give a bad report on a man to get him sent there, if he has been in prison before."

As for the conviction, Lincoln continued, Swinney would need to have a lawyer explore the matter.

Whether Lincoln might have prevented Swinney's conviction as a habitual offender, as he wrote, is problematical. His claim was never tested. He evidently did not have access to the evidence that officers had compiled. Whether he might have, indeed, succeeded in freeing Swinney or reducing the sentence, it also would have tested whether a new series of murders would have followed.

On April 14, 1947, exactly one year to the day after Betty Jo Booker died, Gloria Donaldson, a sixteen-year-old Texas High School student, committed suicide with a shotgun in the bathroom of her home on West Eighteenth Street. She left a rambling note suggesting knowledge of the circumstances of Betty Jo's death. The girl's note was discounted as having any connection with the case, beyond her admiration of Betty Jo and unresolved guilt over her death. The suicide inspired rumors that swept the city, some of them persisting for decades. The girl could not have had knowledge of the facts of the murders, despite her contentions. It added another bizarre dimension to the tragedies of the previous spring.

Nor was Miss Donaldson's tragic act the only reminder of the murders. More than a year later, another young student's suicide revived the case after he left self-incriminating notes. In November, 1948, H. B. "Doodle" Tennison, the eighteen-year-old son of a prominent Texarkana family, swallowed rat poison at Fayetteville where he attended the University of Arkansas. His death made headlines over the nation, none outdoing the blazing front-page banner of the *New Orleans Item*. In his note, he apparently confessed to the murders, and so the papers said that:

'PHANTOM' KILLER TAKES LIFE

Despite their skepticism, Texarkana lawmen drove to Fayetteville to investigate, finding nothing to change their minds. His "confession" didn't fit the facts, to begin with. Young Tennison was buried in Hillcrest Cemetery, the resting place of Paul Martin and Virgil Starks. Family friend J. Q. Mahaffey was a pallbearer. His suicide-note confession was attributed to the mental illness and depression that caused him to justify the taking of his own young life.

Over the years similar groundless, but less tragic, confessions abounded. Max Tackett reported than nine men had personally told him they committed the crimes; none of their accounts meshed with facts that had not been made public.

Despite being behind bars for life as an habitual criminal, Swinney was not scot-free of a murder charge. This became evident in 1948 when he was returned to Bowie County on a bench warrant. The move coincided with a life change for Swinney's wife, whose statements had focused on him.

Peggy Swinney had sued for divorce, which was granted in Bowie County in August 1948. In one of those coincidences, her lawyer was Clyde Larey, who had obtained his son's divorce from Mary Jeanne Larey two years earlier. Days later, in September, Peggy married Buster Rymer in Texarkana, Arkansas, using her maiden name, Peggy Lois Stevens.

The bridegroom gave his age as twenty-two, born in 1926. She gave her age also as twenty-two, born in 1926 and two months younger than he. Actually, she had falsely stated her age as a year younger than she was; born in 1925, she was a year older than he and had already passed her twenty-third birthday. A prominent local Baptist minister, Dr. I. Keil Cross, performed the wedding ceremony.

This was the event lawmen had been waiting for. Once Peggy had severed her legal relationship with Swinney, she could be compelled to testify.

Sheriff Presley and a deputy, Zeke Henslee, fetched the prisoner from Huntsville with the judge's order. Swinney was held for about a month before returning to Huntsville on another bench warrant in October. The only extant records are the docket entries in the district clerk's office, which go no further than the enigmatic notations. Deputy Henslee years later testified that Swinney was ordered back to Bowie County for investigation of murder but remembered nothing more, not even the case involved. Supporting records for the docket notes could not be found in the district clerk's files, indicating they, like many other records of the Phantom period, had been lost or pilfered over the years. Such documents would have offered some detail as to the official reason for Swinney's month-long visit to the county.

With no documents to answer the question and those who would have personal knowledge dead, the most probable explanation is that, learning of Peggy Swinney's divorce, officers believed they could then use her testimony against him. If so, why then did they return him to prison? She may have continued to refuse to testify or her new husband may have pressured her to remain aloof. Under the circumstances, the prosecutor may have feared she would not be a reliable witness and decided to leave well enough alone. Swinney was already salted away for good. Why press their luck?

In addition to all the reasons a sheriff would have for solving a case, Bill Presley had a deeply personal motivation to see that the man he was certain had killed Betty Jo Booker and Paul Martin remained out of circulation forever. He had seen Betty Jo's corpse among the clump of trees north of Spring Lake Park, a fifteen-year-old girl who'd had her life before her until it was snuffed out senselessly. The image never left his mind. He had a daughter a few years younger than Betty Jo named Billie, and his empathy went out to Betty Jo's parents. He'd lost his first-born daughter, along with his wife, to a malicious drunken driver in 1936. He wanted a world safe for his Billie. He didn't want to see anyone else lose a daughter or son to a serial killer.

In 1949, nearly three years after her son Paul was murdered, Inez Martin wrote to Colonel Homer Garrison, Jr., director of the Texas DPS. She had lost faith in "the Rangers and the city police" doing anything about the case. Might Garrison help solve the murder?

Garrison replied that his men, especially Captain Gonzaullas and the Rangers, would continue to do all they could to bring the murderer to justice. He assured her that "we never quit the investigation of a case until it is finally solved."

She never knew that the man whom officers believed had killed her youngest son had been sent to prison for life for another, lesser crime. Her grief remained unmitigated, the mystery the greater. For some reason, Bessie Booker Brown, Betty Jo's mother, did know of Swinney's capture and that it was believed he had killed her daughter. She mentioned it in a taped interview, never published until this book, with journalist Georgia Daily years later. Bessie Brown mentioned Gonzaullas, as well as her neighbor FBI agent Hallett. Why Inez Martin was not also told is not clear. Arguably, her knowing the fact might have afforded her a measure of relief.

In 1954, Swinney earned thirty days of commutation time for donating blood.

In 1959, twelve years after his conviction, Swinney enlisted a sister in eastern Texas to plead his cause. She wrote her congressman, Wright Patman of Texarkana, one of the most powerful members in the Congress. Patman's kindly fatherly image inspired constituents to assign him a degree of omnipotence he surely would have denied, but he responded diligently to every letter the day it was received.

Her three handwritten pages highlighted her brother's poor health—a walking skeleton, with ulcers—and she didn't see how he could survive. He needed a transfer from the prison farm and, if paroled, help in finding a job. Her advocacy seems to have been filtered through her brother's eyes.

She soon focused on the 1946 murders, which must have come as a great surprise to Patman. Her brother didn't do that crime, she insisted, because he kept her child while she worked during the "Murder Rampage."

If she had been able to prove Swinney was baby-sitting during the crucial periods it would have been his first solid alibi. He had never before claimed a role in childcare.

Patman replied that he had no control over paroles but would make contact with the authorities. He wrote to the chairman of the Texas Board of Pardons and Paroles, enclosing her letter. He told her Swinney's case would be reviewed in February, after which the board would notify the inmate of its action.

The board denied parole.

Swinney's prison life was documented partially by his file at the Texas Department of Corrections office at Huntsville, examined in 1971. At that time inmate files were considered public records. On a later request the same records were no longer available and some were withheld from a Freedom of Information request. Over the years, his file bulged with correspondence and reports. A 2008 Freedom of Information request to the Texas Department of Criminal Justice revealed additional documents. Put together, the files reflected several patterns.

He wrote letters aimed at gaining better treatment, keyed to complaints. One memorable letter to the Warden spoke of young inmates coming into the prison and his fear of their forcing him to become an "oral queer." He also sought outside allies; letters to him demonstrated how he'd sought ministers to help in his attempts to make parole; one was from a Lutheran pastor in Texarkana whom he'd approached.

From time to time he also wrote short stories, some of which he submitted for publication. They demonstrated no particular literary talent; he strung words together but not in a coherent story.

He served time in solitary confinement—the Hole—for infractions of rules of behavior. One instance was for running a gambling operation with other inmates, but there were several other infractions. In 1954 he was placed in isolation and forfeited "good" time for operating a loan racket; in addition to the other evidence, he possessed a pocketknife, a forbidden weapon. Three years later he returned to isolation for illegal trading and trafficking. He admitted running a poker game but denied having a shakedown scheme. The warden commented: "This inmate's name has come up too many times on the wrong side of the ledger." In 1965 he was found guilty of fighting after starting the altercation with another inmate. It was back to solitary, with loss of good time. By then he had spent far more years behind walls than he had at any other time, nearing twenty years. He hadn't impressed his keepers.

A more serious violation came when he was caught in a sexual act with another inmate, with Swinney in the male position and his partner in the passive. This might have been related to the pattern among the Phantom's female victims—one apparent rape—and raises a question whether Swinney was bisexual or homosexual all along or whether the prison experience brought him to male-on-male sex because there was no other choice. The situation also might be viewed as an instance of domination over another person, relating to control more than a strictly sexual act, something which violent rape, like the sort that could have potentially happened to one or more of the female victims, would also have in common with this occurrence in prison. The document was viewed in 1971 but was not made available in 2008 and may have been scrubbed from his file by then.

If Bowie and Miller County officers felt Swinney would never again walk the streets of Texarkana, the prisoner had other intentions. Failing parole in 1967, he resorted to a new strategy. He wrote the Miller County Circuit Clerk, at the time Morris M. Haak. He requested a copy of the judgment and sentence of his February 11, 1941 trial. Swinney, Inmate No. 108586 at the Ellis Unit of the Texas prison system, by then had discussed his case with older convicts and eventually with an attorney representing prisoners for the state. Old cons usually have a wealth of experience with the legal system but hardly qualify as experts. Their incarceration itself, a certified venture into failure, branded them as losers. Despite their status, they often had been through enough contests in court to absorb considerably more knowledge of criminal law than the ordinary citizen or the novice defendant. Swinney's story was simple: He'd been in the pen since 1947 for car theft. Twenty years for stealing a car. The maximum penalty on that felony was acknowledged as ten years. The habitual criminal act for a mere stolen car?

If his had been an ordinary conviction for a single felony theft, his advisers agreed, he would have been out after no more than ten years—by 1957. But the habitual criminal act—some called it The Bitch—assumed other crimes. If he'd been tried and convicted of the other car thefts he'd been linked to, he could have netted up to ten years on each one, for a total forty to fifty years. If the terms had been stacked, or run consecutively, he wouldn't be cleared of one until he'd served out another. There was no telling how long he would have had to serve, perhaps even his natural life. But the key to freeing himself from the Bitch, his "experts" agreed, was to overturn any one of the previous convictions that had been used to enhance his sentence.

The weakest link in the convictions was likely to be the oldest one. The further back in time, the less likely witnesses, judges, prosecutors, and officers would remember details of the case. Some might not even still be alive. By this logic, the 1941 conviction in Arkansas for car theft, also being in another state, became a prime candidate for attack.

Having received a copy of the 1941 judgment and sentence, on July 4, 1967, Swinney wrote back to Circuit Clerk Haak, adding another request.

"Although the judgment seems to indicate that I was represented by an attorney at the above mentioned trial, I did not employ one and the court did not appoint one for me.

"If the indication mentioned above is correct please send me the name and mailing address of the attorney who claims to have represented me. May I have an early reply?"

Six days later Haak reported, through a deputy: "I'm sorry but we don't have any record of you being represented by an attorney. We have checked all records of your case."

Swinney had served, by then, twenty years of his life sentence. He was testing every means possible to gain his freedom. Time, it seemed, was on his side as more and more people involved with the case died off.

Meanwhile, he sought release through the standard parole process. Nothing worked. When he won a recommendation, the Board of Pardons and Parole sent a form to Bowie County. Uniformly, the judge of the court that had convicted him, the prosecuting attorney, and the sheriff—all different persons from those who had held the offices in 1947—protested his possible release, making it clear that they didn't want him back in Texarkana. The board wasn't bound by the protests but usually was influenced.

On July 7, 1970, Swinney, with assistance of a staff attorney, filed an application for writ of habeas corpus. Filed as petitioner *pro se*, that is, as his own attorney, Swinney cited his conviction in 1947 under the habitual criminal act which was based on two prior convictions used for enhancement. Alleging that he was "illegally confined and is illegally restrained," he attacked the 1941 Arkansas conviction, claiming he "was not represented by counsel at any stage of the proceedings, including trial," thereby making his conviction under the habitual criminal act invalid. He had served twenty-three years and should be released.

The application for writ went to Judge Stuart E. Nunn of the Fifth Judicial District, the court from which Swinney had been sent to prison.

Judge Nunn remembered a letter Swinney had written to him, which had nudged him into a more detailed investigation of the man, whom he had not known of previously. In it Swinney had stated that he was coming up for parole and "you dare not protest it." The veiled threat, or clear threat if interpreted on its face, immediately caught Nunn's attention. Why would an inmate, hoping to make parole, send such a letter to a judge who might influence the outcome of his application? Was he expecting the judge to be frightened into approving his release? What sort of man was he? What crime had he committed that had sent him to the pen? Nunn didn't know the name. His judicial career had come after that tense spring of 1946. Had Swinney not written the letter, and in that stern tone, he might have escaped the judge's notice and gained his liberty. His interest piqued, Nunn began looking into the prisoner's case. There was little in the county records to guide him. He called, among others, Bill Presley, who had been the sheriff in 1947. Presley briefed him on Swinney's record, including the Phantom case. Nunn reasoned that Swinney was incarcerated as a habitual criminal, and the threatening letter was proof enough that he hadn't been rehabilitated.

Although these thoughts remained in memory when Swinney took a new tack and sought a writ of habeas corpus as a vehicle for leaving the prison, the issue before Nunn now was a clear-cut one: Had Swinney had access to counsel in his 1941 Arkansas trial used to enhance his 1947 conviction? On the surface it seemed to be a simple matter of fact.

Judge Nunn had the record searched in the Miller County Circuit Clerk's office. In his assessment of Swinney's allegation, he found the judgment in Volume N, Page 174 of criminal cases as Case No. 5463, State vs. Youell Lee Swinney, with plea of guilty and sentence both dated February 11, 1941.

On October 3, 1970, Nunn delivered his decision on the motion, citing the exact language used in the 1941 record:

"On this Day the State, appeared by her Attorney, Dick Huie; and the Defendant Appeared in proper person and *by his Attorney*, whereupon the Court sentenced the Defendant to Three (3) years in the State Penitentiary."

Circuit Judge Dexter Bush had signed the document.

Judge Nunn concluded: "The Court finds from the record that the Petitioner Youell Lee Swinney had an Attorney when he entered a Plea of Guilty and was Sentenced in the Circuit Court of Miller County, Arkansas, on February 11, 1941. That his conviction in Bowie County, Texas, as an habitual criminal on February 11, 1947, is valid.

"Petition for Writ of Habeas Corpus is DENIED."

It closed, a little tighter, a door to the outside world for Swinney.

Several days later, Harry H. Walsh, a staff counsel for inmates at TDC, wrote the clerk of the Court of Criminal Appeals, forwarding copies of documents from the Miller County circuit clerk's office, asking for a review.

In a letter on January 21, 1971, Judge Nunn denied Swinney's appeal, ruling he *had* been represented by an attorney. He recommended denial.

Following protests from Bowie County officials, the board turned Swinney down for parole again.

In the spring of 1971, I freelanced an eight-part series of articles about the Phantom case. I had reviewed all of the records, including contemporary newspaper accounts, had interviewed numerous local officials associated with the case, and had made trips to the DPS offices in Austin, the Ranger office in Garland, and the main office of the Texas prison system in Huntsville. At the penitentiary I had studied Swinney's files, which were treated as public records. I had not used Swinney's name in any of the articles, on the advice of the newspaper's attorney. (The newspaper's attorney was Richard Arnold, who as a little boy had been pictured in *Life* magazine with his mother and his brother taking refuge in the Grim Hotel during the height of the Phantom scare, and who later became a federal appellate judge.)

The articles appeared in the *Texarkana Gazette* over an eight-day period. The first article, introducing and presenting the precursor event to the murders, appeared on a Sunday and triggered two events. That afternoon, I received a telephone call from a woman clearly distraught. My wife answered the phone and I never talked to the caller, but she forcibly told my wife that no more should be published of the case. I never knew for sure who the woman was, for she did not wait for me; she just left the message, without identifying herself.

The other event unfolded a few days later in my uncle Bill Presley's home. By then he had been out of the sheriff's office for years. That afternoon, a middle-aged man appeared at his door in a state of high anxiety. The former sheriff could see the man was practically vibrating with agitation.

He was concerned about the Phantom series being published. He was vague, but clearly nervous. The ex-sheriff, reading his emotional state, invited him to sit with him in the patio. It was a pleasant spring day, warm and comfortable.

As the visitor settled down, Presley learned the man was Peggy Swinney's younger brother. The articles stirred old fears, apparently in similar fashion as they had for the woman who had called my house, urging an end to the series. Specifically, the man expressed his fear of Swinney's getting out of the penitentiary, returning to Texarkana, and what he might do. He felt a personal fear of him and his actions. He was positive that Swinney was the Phantom killer and that there was cause for concern over his possible release.

He told the ex-sheriff of his own family's fears during the spring of 1946. He had been a teenaged boy at the time. His family had kept the house boarded up, windows covered securely, to discourage any intruder.

One day, he said, when his sister Peggy and Swinney came to their house, she told one of them, "If you knew what I know, you wouldn't be scared like this."

His family, he said, was convinced that Swinney was the man sought by the law, if not on that particular day, then later as events unreeled. Subsequently, when suspicions solidified despite lack of direct personal knowledge, the family had cooperated with officers to the extent they could.

If they had known what Peggy knew, it went without saying, they really would have been scared.

He was afraid Swinney would gain release from prison and return to Texarkana and wreak vengeance, perhaps even upon him and his family, although none of them had done anything to harm Swinney. Even Peggy's testimony, decades ago, played no role in sentencing Swinney. The prosecution had relied solely on the repeat-offender law. Just the knowledge of what Swinney was capable of doing, and that he might become a free man and return, was a terrible inciter to fear.

"Where is Peggy?" the former sheriff asked.

"I don't know," said her brother. "She left. I don't know where she went."

Twenty-five years after 1946, the images and memories continued to evoke emotional responses that hadn't been calmed by the passage of time. The nervous system, once conditioned, remembers, and reacts.

CHAPTER 22

BACK IN COURT

S winney had learned from fellow convicts that hammering away at the system might pay dividends. Time would erode memories of those who might testify against him. Whatever happened, he wouldn't be any worse off than he was; the right approach might, just might, liberate him.

In May 1972, he made another application for writ of habeas corpus. Judge Nunn had denied his previous application without holding a hearing. If he could get a hearing, he was advised, that could make a difference.

In the new application, he alleged that no attorney represented him in the 1947 trial. He further claimed he had signed no waiver and had no funds with which to hire a lawyer. The application, drafted by an attorney for inmates, covered virtually all bases

Although he had local assistance, Swinney hand-filed the application himself. It went to the Court of Criminal Appeals in the state capital. If the justices found a factual issue that, if true, would grant relief to the inmate, they would order a hearing.

Concepts of the law had changed. In the 1960s, the right to counsel clearly became a constitutional right. Before that, there were a lot of statutory rights in different states that afforded right to counsel, but the Bill of Rights applied solely to federal courts. By time Swinney applied, right to counsel was an acknowledged constitutional right. As he had before, he alleged that he had been denied access to counsel.

This time, Judge Nunn scheduled a hearing on the application and issued a bench warrant for Swinney to be conveyed, by the Bowie County sheriff, at that time C. C. Rachel, from Huntsville to the county jail at Boston, Texas. This came on August 18, 1972.

Three days later, Judge Nunn appointed a young lawyer to represent Swinney in the proceedings.

Jack Carter was sitting in his office that August day when his secretary said, "Judge Nunn is on the phone for you."

Carter picked up his phone.

"Jack," said the judge, "I'm going to appoint you to represent the Phantom killer, in order for us to have a hearing."

Then the judge laughed. Carter interpreted it as Nunn's way of joking. He really had no knowledge of his newest client and only a vague idea of who the Phantom killer might be. Carter had grown up in neighboring Red River County, had been out of law school at the University of Texas in Austin for five years, and was in the general practice of law. He mainly had tried civil cases and had done very little criminal law. When he received the appointment, he had to acquaint himself with the issues and the law.

After Swinney was transported back to Bowie County, Carter conferred with him in the jail at Boston. Swinney brought with him citations of cases and authorities that his legal counsel in Huntsville had provided. Clearly Swinney had been entitled to a lawyer, so that was not an issue. The question was, had he actually *had* counsel? Swinney maintained that he had appeared without counsel. The issue, a simple and narrow factual one, resisted ready resolution. The witnesses were decades older, did not always remember the trial clearly; others had died. The State's position was as uncertain as that of the prisoner's. The outcome would determine whether Swinney would go free or remain behind walls. If his conviction was proved to be suspect, he had to be released.

Reviewing the case, Carter soon gained a feeling that more was involved than appeared on the surface, an enhancement for felony theft. Each time Swinney came up for parole, local authorities recommended that the parole board turn him down. Although the legal issue was not complicated, whether or not he actually had a lawyer, Carter's job was to represent, to the extent of his ability, a client with a highly unsavory past that many believed included a series of murders. As a young lawyer, he wanted to do everything he could to represent his client, at the same time accepting its ethical difficulty.

It became one of the most challenging cases Carter had experienced. "It seemed like to me that it was hard to ignore the context of this, that *all* of these people were convinced, absolutely, that he *was* the Phantom killer. And for that reason, they had recommended against any parole. And I felt like that had to be in the record somewhere. That was kind of a touchy thing.

"I just felt like the Court of Appeals just needed another whole context of this. Not that I thought anybody had done anything improper. They didn't. I can certainly see why the people making the recommendations made the recommendations they did, 'cause they were convinced that he was the killer, of several people."

Carter lost no time in making preparations for the evidentiary hearing scheduled for September, a few weeks off. On August 31 he filed a motion to appoint an investigator for the case, in an effort "to locate any persons who may have some knowledge of the 1947 trial." On September 1, he went to the D.A.'s office and requested the file on Swinney. Gary Morgan, the D.A.'s investigator, handed Carter the file and provided a desk on which to review the documents.

That August, while Swinney was in the midst of his most serious attempt to gain release, his mother, Myrtle Chaffin, died in Texarkana. The obituary listed him among the survivors, his residence stated, simply, as Houston. By that time, the Texas Department of Corrections had a number of prisons beyond its central location at Huntsville.

One day while Swinney was housed in the county jail, the Reverend A. M. Adams, a young minister in his forties, dropped by to visit any of the prisoners who might be interested in discussing their spiritual, or any other, concerns with him. He had prayed and counseled with other prisoners before and made his jail visits a part of his ministry.

Before he could make his usual request, the jailer, Jesse Lynch, told him, "You can't go in today. We've closed the jail to outside visitors. I'm not supposed to tell you this, but we've got the Phantom killer in here now."

The label stirred old memories. As a boy in rural Bowie County, Adams's family, too, had lived in fear of the unknown marauder who killed by night.

The evidentiary hearing was held in two parts, the first beginning on September 11, 1972, and extending to the next day; the second, eleven days later. Carter had sought a delay for the hearing, in order to have more time to prepare his case, as well as to identify and summon witnesses. By this time a state's witness, former FBI agent Horace "Buzz" Hallett, had already traveled from his home in Durham, North Carolina. District Attorney Lynn Cooksey asked the court for permission to call Hallett out of turn so that he would be able to return home without unnecessary delay. The remainder of the evidentiary hearing was set for September 22. The lawyers agreed to hold the hearing in Texarkana, rather than in Boston, twenty-two miles away.

Three witnesses testified for the state: Winnie Stone, the district clerk; former FBI agent Hallett; and Gary Morgan, investigator for the District Attorney's office. Essentially, Hallett's testimony was the focal point, with the other two brief appearances framing his.

Hallett had retired in 1965 after thirty years as a special agent of the federal bureau and was head of security for a large telephone company. He had been stationed in Texarkana from September 1945 until January 1952 as the senior resident agent.

He testified that he had investigated Swinney's case and was physically present in court during Swinney's trial in February 1947.

"I was present during the entire trial."

Cooksey asked, "Was Mr. Swinney represented by an attorney?"

"Mr. Swinney represented himself," replied Hallett.

"And did you ever hear the Court admonish Mr. Swinney or tell Mr. Swinney that he was entitled to counsel?"

"Yes, I did."

Cooksey asked him to relate what the trial judge, Robert Vance, said.

Hallett said, "To the best of my recollection, Mr. Swinney asked the judge if he wasn't going to sentence him as a habitual criminal. And Judge Vance asked him if he was represented by counsel, and he said 'No, I'm going to represent myself.' And with that statement, Judge Vance told him that he was entitled to an attorney, that he would appoint him an attorney and would make one available for his defense, and he said, 'No—'"

"Who said, 'No—'?" Cooksey broke in.

"Mr. Swinney said, 'No, I'm going to defend myself.' And with that, Judge Vance said, 'Under the provisions of the Constitution of the United States, you are entitled to defend yourself and that will meet the requirements of the federal law.'"

"All right, sir. So Judge Vance, the trial judge at that time, did advise Mr. Swinney that he was entitled to counsel?"

"He did advise him of his rights to counsel and was willing to appoint him an attorney."

"And at that time, did Mr. Swinney appear to you to be rational?"

"Yes, he did."

"And he appeared to understand the Judge's warnings?"

"He appeared to understand the Judge's warnings and was given every opportunity to question any of the Judge's statements at the time."

Hallett testified subsequently, over Carter's objections, to his understanding that Swinney, in jail on the Arkansas side, had agreed through his attorney, William E. Haynie, to be transferred to the Texas-side jurisdiction, after which the Arkansas charges wouldn't be presented. In Texas he was tried under the habitual criminal act.

"And at the trial, Mr. Hallett, did Mr. Swinney enter a plea of guilty or not guilty?" Cooksey asked.

Hallett responded, "Mr. Swinney attempted to enter a plea of guilty and Judge Vance said he couldn't accept the plea of guilty to an habitual criminal act charge, that it would have to be a trial."

During the trial, Hallett said, he appeared as a witness on behalf of the State of Texas by reading Swinney's criminal record.

Cooksey asked, "And was Mr. Swinney given an opportunity to cross examine you?"

"Mr. Swinney was given an opportunity to cross examine me, and if my memory serves me correctly, he had me qualify myself as to my education and experience in identification matters."

On cross examination, Carter brought out that Hallett didn't think Swinney had questioned other witnesses during the trial, that he understood there was a deal made by Swinney's lawyer to transfer him from Arkansas into Texas but that he had no attorney for the trial itself when he tried to plead guilty. Carter displayed the docket record that reflected Swinney's plea of not guilty but not that he had tried to plead guilty. Hallett repeated his testimony of Swinney's attempted plea.

Carter asked, "Mr. Hallett, did Judge Vance ask Mr. Swinney if he had money to hire an attorney?"

"I have no recollection of his using the word 'money.' He said, 'Do you have means to hire an attorney?' And that's when he said he didn't want one again."

On cross-examination, Hallett testified that he had interrogated Swinney at least five or six times, an hour or two at a time. Carter then asked him of the 250 or more cases he had investigated during his FBI career, how many did he remember as vividly as he did this one.

The judge interjected, "Do you want him to tell you how he remembers it?"

"I'll be glad for him to," said Carter.

"All right," said Judge Nunn. "Tell him about the alleged murders, Mr. Hallett."

Under questioning by Carter, Hallett began. "Well, for your knowledge, on February the twenty-second, George Washington's birthday, there were two—a young couple assaulted here in Texarkana and they lived. A short time thereafter, a young couple were killed, the young girl raped. A short time thereafter, I'd say in a span of three or four weeks, without getting all of those old records out, another young couple, the boy was killed, the girl was raped, and the girl was killed. And a short time thereafter, and this date I can be as specific about as the first one because it was another holiday, May 30th, when a young farmer sitting on his porch over in Arkansas was shot, and his wife went to the phone and she was shot, but lived. They are the, what, five murders, eight people, four different offenses involved, and there was certain information developed during the investigation of these—let's say eight assaults, three assaults and five murders—that led to Mr. Swinney and his supposed wife."

Hallett's impressions were slightly distorted. There was no documented proof that the first murdered girl was raped, though that was the popular perception and seems to have been believed by many lawmen. His memory of the Starks shooting was seriously flawed on two points, that Starks was shot while on his porch (he was inside the house, by a window) and the date, which was May 3, not May 30. He was never contradicted on those points.

Carter drew out from the witness that Swinney had never been tried or convicted of murder and had never been charged with the Phantom killings.

Hallett explained the matter more fully. "You asked about why did he want to get from Arkansas to Texas where in Texas he could plead to an habitual criminal act. I don't know what was in his mind or his attorney's mind until, that kind of a deal—"

"Well, of course," broke in Carter, "he had no attorney when he tried the case, did he?"

"That's right."

After a brief exchange between the lawyers, Hallett continued: "It makes sense to this point that if he could go to Texas and be tried as a habitual criminal, he would not be faced with the possibility of the electric chair if he got convicted of murder in Arkansas."

"If he got convicted of murder," said Carter. "That's a big if, isn't it, Mr. Hallett?"

"I said *if*. That was his gamble at the time."

Hallett told the court that Sheriff Elvie Davis had informed him that Swinney was being moved from Arkansas to Texas. Hallett did not participate in conferences that led to the decision.

When Carter persisted in the point that Swinney had never been brought to trial for murder, Hallett replied, "He was never charged. You want to know the reason why?"

Judge Nunn said, "He asked you. Tell him."

"If you know the information," added Carter.

"I know the information," said Hallett, "is that we never could find the gun, but the same gun was used in all five murders."

Hallett's memory had failed him. The same gun was used in the first four murders, but a different caliber was used in the Starks shootings.

"Now, Mr. Hallett," said Carter, "isn't it a fact that the information that you have—I'd like to know where you're getting this information."

"From official reports of the FBI laboratory, from cartridge cases and bullets that were sent to them for examinations."

"So, what you're saying is that you think he's guilty of these murders."

"I didn't say that."

"Do you?"

"I didn't say that. You asked me why wasn't he tried for murder."

"That's right."

"Two reasons or maybe three good reasons."

"You didn't have the evidence is the reason, isn't it?"

Cooksey broke in, appealing to the Court. "Your Honor, let him answer the question. We're going to object to counsel—"

Hallett answered, "I say, the gun was never found—"

"All right, sir," said Carter.

Hallett continued. "—and a lot of testimony would have been presented by his alleged wife who cannot testify against her husband. With that, the prosecuting attorney did not present the case or cases to the grand jury for those two reasons."

Carter underscored the position that there had not been sufficient evidence to charge him with the murders. He then moved to Swinney's representing himself at the 1947 trial.

"Would you say that he conducted his trial, pretty good defense of himself?"

"He asked questions that most lawyers would ask, I mean particularly when he was qualifying me as an expert to be able to testify to his criminal record. Then he asked me one or two questions as to the entry on the criminal record which he knew as well as I did."

Carter returned to Hallett's memory of the trial.

"How does it happen, Mr. Hallett, that you remember the exact day that this took place, this trial?"

"I had an unfortunate incident following an operation," said Hallett, "and I was off on sick leave for some time, and that was the first day that I went back to work following that illness."

On re-direct examination, Cooksey established that the FBI had investigated Swinney for violation of the Dyer Act, interstate transportation of stolen motor vehicles, and that Hallett had interrogated Swinney in that connection.

"Now, at the time you counseled or interrogated Mr. Swinney, did you give him any type of warnings at that time?"

"At the beginning of each interrogation he was advised of his rights to an attorney; he did not have to make a statement if he didn't care to; that any statement he made could be used in any court against him."

"All right, sir. And was this done on the five or six occasions that you talked with Mr. Swinney?"

"On each occasion."

At the end of the day's session, the court recessed until September 22, enabling Hallett to return home to North Carolina while giving time for both sides to organize their witnesses.

A few days later, Carter filed, for Swinney, a new, revised application for writ of habeas corpus, alleging virtually the same as the one Swinney had filed from Huntsville, that he had been convicted in 1947 without counsel. In this instrument, however, Carter added that Swinney had been eligible for parole but had been rejected because of protests from Bowie County officials.

The evidentiary hearing resumed with give-and-take between Swinney's appointed lawyer and Judge Nunn. The issue was Carter's attempted subpoena of Charles Shandera, a member of the state Board of Pardons and Paroles, and all tangible records of the board relating to Swinney. The judge asserted that such documents were privileged communications and whether local officials protested was also a confidential matter, as ruled by higher courts.

The judge added: "But I don't mind telling you, all three of us did [protest] and the district attorney and the sheriff, everyone did connected with the case. I don't mind telling you. And the fact that we protested doesn't keep him from getting a pardon. The Board of Pardons and Paroles can still send him somewhere else, but he's not supposed to come back to Bowie County. That's up to them, but if he gets out and buggers up again, they can't say, 'Well, the judge and sheriff said it was all right to turn him out.' That's the only thing I care about.

"Let the record show that there is nothing in any of the correspondence from the three judges, the sheriff, and district attorney basing our refusal upon any alleged commission of any crime. It's just simply a protest which we have a right to lodge. There's nothing said about any crime; I'll put that in the record myself. . . . There's nothing in any of the correspondence with the board alleging that he has committed any crime or has been convicted of any crime other than the one that he's convicted on."

As the hearing progressed, it became evident that a quarter-century or more had made deep inroads into the witnesses' memories. Several jurors in the 1947 trial had no memory of the event, the defendant, or the case. Some had served on numerous juries; the youngest one was, in 1972, sixty-three years of age. Others had died. The judge, Robert Vance, had died. The district clerk at the time, Frank Cox, had only a vague memory of a case that mingled among a multitude during his three terms in office.

Carter called the prosecutor, Cooksey, acting as respondent for the State, to the stand. The purpose was to build a bill of exceptions keyed to the judge's ruling that actions taken by county officials, as well as by parole board members, were privileged communications.

Cooksey testified that he had merely checked the block on the letter from the parole board that noted "protest," without commenting why.

"But you did have a reason for checking that block?" asked Carter.

"I had subjective thinking, yes, sir," replied Cooksey.

"And what was that?"

"First of all, this man is an habitual criminal. He has been once again in the State of Texas convicted of a felony. He's a three-time loser and I believe in Article 63 of the penal code of the State of Texas and I believe that it should be a mandatory life sentence, and I do not believe in parole after the third felony violation and conviction."

Carter asked if the "alleged offenses" influenced him.

"Of course that would have to have some bearing on it, Mr. Carter," said Cooksey. "Certainly it does, and another thing, the manner in which he wrote the judge, Judge Nunn, the disrespect he showed for his high office of district judge, I can't personally see that this man is rehabilitated enough to come back out on the streets, and I personally don't want him on the streets."

Cooksey said he had "never, never" recommended parole for an habitual criminal. "I've only recommended parole, that I can recall, three times. They were all young and first offenders."

After several witnesses had stepped down, Carter said, "I guess I want to call Judge Nunn. "

Nunn testified he had recommended that Swinney not be paroled.

"I had never heard of Youell Swinney. I got a letter from him when he was in the penitentiary and he told me he was coming up for parole and to not dare protest it. I began to look into the thing, and I found out a whole lot about the man I didn't know, because if he's going to dare me to protest, why, he's going to have to get in line to find me. I'm not a bit afraid of him.

"As a matter of fact, he would have probably gone through unnoticed; it would have probably slipped through as a matter of routine if he hadn't written me that letter, but I got busy and seeing if I could find who this man was. I found out he was an habitual criminal, going back to reform school days, back in the thirties when he went to reform school. I don't feel that a man of that type should be turned loose on the public."

(Based on at least one other report, Nunn skimmed over more recent developments. According to Tillman Johnson, Swinney had been more vocal toward the judge, actually threatening him. Johnson said Swinney had told an informant that he was going to kill the judge as well as others involved in his case. The word reached authorities, including Judge Nunn, that Swinney intended to "get" all the officers involved in his arrest and conviction—a long list. Many were concerned about what might happen if he left prison. There is no official record of this, however, just Johnson's oral report; Johnson asserted that others knew of it as well.)

"Judge," said Carter, "are you familiar with the theory concerning Mr. Swinney's involvement—"

"I've heard of it, yes."

"And—"

"I don't know whether he's guilty or innocent, have no idea. That didn't influence me in any way. I guess subconsciously, in the back of your mind you know those things, but the reason was the fact that he was an habitual criminal and apparently he hasn't been rehabilitated."

He repeated that he had no objections to a state board to parole him "as long as he doesn't come back in this part of the world and commit some other crime," but he wasn't going to withdraw his protest. He said if he was unable to locate a file on a man up for parole, he inquired among people with knowledge of the case.

"In this case nearly everybody is dead, except Mr. [Frank] Cox and a few of those in there, and they can't remember much about it, and at that time Mr. Bill Presley was alive and that's where I got my information as to his prior criminal history."

Carter asked, "Did you get your information from Mr. Presley concerning this theory about these murders?"

"Yes, he told me quite a great deal about it which I didn't know about, but, as I said, that wasn't the dominating matter at all, but it was in Mr. Presley's mind, but it wasn't in mine at all."

"The dominating matter, you're saying, was the fact that he was an habitual criminal?"

"That was with me, yes. And, as I said, when the time comes, I can always consider again. I have no desire to keep a man in the penitentiary the rest of his life, but I want to make sure he'd rehabilitated and he's not going to get out and commit something else."

At that, Judge Nunn resumed the bench and declared a noon recess.

Following lunch, Carter called to the witness stand the key figure, who had initiated the action leading to the hearing.

CHAPTER 23

ON THE WITNESS STAND

The man on the stand could have been taken for any nondescript working man life had largely passed by: middle-aged, crewcut hair, sunburned from outside exposure—a day laborer, perhaps a truck driver. He was neither. He had just spent over a quarter-century in prison, this time around, and he was playing his last card in a continuing campaign to rejoin the free world. One more time he was seeking to overturn his conviction as a habitual criminal and a sentence of life imprisonment. He was fifty-five years old, an old con who had spent the bulk of his life behind bars, paying off a series of debts society had assessed him over the years since he was a boy. Most psychologists would have classified him as burned out, unlikely to commit the high-energy crimes of which he had been accused or suspected.

His words, hardly those of remorse, bristled with embittered denials.

Youell Lee Swinney, for the first time, was taking the stand.

Carter began. "Would you state your name, please?"

He responded in a low voice. "Youell Swinney."

"Speak up loud enough so everybody can hear, Mr. Swinney. You are the same Youell Lee Swinney that was convicted in Bowie County in 1947 for auto theft and as an habitual criminal?"

"Yes."

During the testimony, Swinney asserted that he remembered the 1947 trial well, including the names of the judge, Robert Vance, and the prosecutor, Maxwell Welch. His memory of the trial, he claimed, was vivid, a quite different response from the other witnesses. He said he had had no attorney but had spoken with the judge about representation.

Carter asked him to tell of the conversation.

"Well," said Swinney, "he asked me one time if I had an attorney present in court. I didn't hear him clearly and he asked me again the same question. I told him that I did not, and he saw that I was having difficulty hearing and he beckoned me to the bench. I approached the bench and he asked me if I had talked to an attorney about representing me. I told him, 'Yes, sir,' that I had talked to Mr. Bill Harkness and I hadn't been able to raise his fee. And about that time Mr. Maxwell Welch walked up and says, 'Your Honor,' says, 'we've got an open and shut case against this man and I can't see why we should delay the hearings any longer.' They began to talk and I sat down. The trial started."

(It is significant that Swinney claimed to have talked to the judge, by then dead, at the bench, a position from which no one else in the courtroom could hear and therefore remember hearing. In the correspondence between Swinney's relatives and several lawyers there is no mention, at any time, of Bill Harkness, a noted criminal defense lawyer in Texarkana who had also served as mayor on the Texas side. In addition to three lawyers involved in the case, Swinney's father had approached attorney Elmer Lincoln but had not followed through. Swinney's mentioning Harkness is almost certainly inaccurate, whether from a flawed memory or intent.)

Carter continued. "Were you ever advised by the judge or the D.A. or anyone that you should have an attorney?"

"No, sir, I wasn't advised—"

"Were you advised that you had a right to have an attorney?

"No, sir."

"Were you advised that if you couldn't pay for an attorney, that the State would furnish you one?"

"No, sir. I did not have an attorney and I did not sign a waiver of attorney."

He claimed he didn't tell the judge he wanted to represent himself. He didn't know he could have a lawyer, he said, or else he would have asked for one.

Swinney's memory of his conversation with Judge Vance conflicted with what former FBI agent Horace Hallett had recalled. Both witnesses, no doubt, were aware of the penalties of perjury, which would have been more of a serious risk to Hallett than to Swinney, who was already incarcerated, unlikely to fear a further penalty, and making his most serious bid for release.

Swinney claimed Hallett's testimony was the first he had heard of an agreement for him to go from Arkansas to Texas to be tried as an habitual criminal. He said he had fought extradition because he'd learned the Texans wanted to try him as a habitual criminal. The extradition hearing was in the governor's office in Little Rock, at which time the governor granted the extradition, he claimed.

"Did you want to come to Bowie County to be tried?"

"No, sir. I didn't want to come because, as I said, I'd heard that they were going to file an habitual criminal law in my case."

Carter segued into the February 11, 1941, proceedings when Swinney had been assessed three years in the Arkansas penitentiary. Swinney claimed he had no attorney, was not advised of his rights to have an attorney. Cooksey objected to bringing in the 1941 case. Judge Nunn referred to the previous writ application made by Swinney, based on that case, and noted that he, the judge, had searched the records and found Swinney *had* had an attorney.

Responding to Carter's questions, Swinney again said he had no attorney, did not waive his right to an attorney, never told the judge he didn't want an attorney.

The exchange then turned to Swinney's status in the prison. He said he was "a state approved trusty," which enabled him to earn credits for good time. He had been a trusty for ten years, had skills, and could make a living for himself if he were released.

"Do you know what the status of your parole possibilities are at this time?"

"Yes, sir."

"What?"

"Well, I have been recommended for parole. I'm recommended for parole now, but because of parole protests they won't parole protests."

On cross-examination by Cooksey, Swinney admitted he'd been represented by an attorney, William E. Haynie, in the 1944 jury trial for robbery by assault. He also admitted a federal conviction for transporting a stolen car across state lines, for which he had pleaded guilty, without an attorney. He testified to serving nineteen months of the three-year federal term, and of serving twenty months of his three-year Arkansas term. He also mentioned serving several months in reform school in the 1930s. He failed to remember a federal counterfeiting conviction during World War II.

"So, then, your testimony is your first conviction was in federal court?"

"Well, I'm not—it's been so long I don't remember. I mean, I'm not absolutely positive of the dates I was in federal penitentiary."

"Was that your first penitentiary to be in?"

"Yes, sir."

"Leavenworth?"

"Yes, sir."

Citing records from the Arkansas State Hospital crediting him with a high school education in 1947, Cooksey asked if that was correct. Swinney stated it was incorrect.

"I didn't finish the sixth grade. I went to Texarkana Junior High School. I didn't finish the sixth grade."

Cooksey also noted, referring to a 1946 record, "that the report shows in your personal history that you are on a charge of grand larceny in Texarkana and that your father's attorney in Montgomery City, Missouri, and attorneys Will McDonald and Ted Goldman, of Texarkana, are handling this case. Is that correct?"

"Yes, sir."

"Is that on a Miller County charge or a Bowie County charge?"

"Miller County charge."

"What were you charged with in Miller County in 1946?"

"I never was charged, as far as I know."

"You never were charged?"

"As far as I know."

"Well, what case were you telling the case worker about here when you told them that these attorneys were handling your case?"

"They was asking me about what the charge was and I told them that I didn't know what I was charged with."

"And until this day you still have no idea what the Miller County charge was?"

"Right."

"But yet you employed three attorneys—"

"I didn't employ them."

"Did your father employ them?"

"Yes, sir."

"You have a case here in Miller County in 1946, Miller County, Arkansas, that you don't know what the charge was—"

"No, sir. I was never informed."

"Never informed of it, yet your father employed three attorneys to represent you?"

"Yes, sir. He talked to the judge and then hired the attorneys."

"It also says here, Mr. Swinney, that you told whoever wrote this thing up that you were arrested and taken to jail. You came to Texarkana on a visit; you were arrested and taken to jail there on July 15th on a charge of grand larceny."

"Yes, sir."

"Is that correct?"

"I didn't say that."

"You didn't say that?"

"No, sir, I didn't tell that interviewer that. That information was brought down by the officer, I suppose."

Cooksey went on. "And then it says, 'states that he was not guilty when sent to the penitentiary to Texas and was not guilty of the present charge and knows nothing about it.'"

"Yes, sir."

"Now, then, what present charge did you tell the interviewer?"

"I didn't tell the interviewer any charge." Swinney persisted in denying he was guilty of any charges and that he didn't know what charge he faced in 1946, an amazing position in light of the series of daily interrogations he underwent in jail then. "Not guilty of any charge."

Cooksey next delved into the series of interrogations in 1946. "Did any of the FBI agents ever give you a warning and tell you that you had a right to an attorney?"

"No, sir, they did not."

"No one ever told you that you had a right to an attorney?"

"No, sir."

"Now, did Mr. Goldman [i.e., his attorney] ever consult with you about a charge in Miller County, Arkansas?"

"No, sir."

"And no other lawyer ever talked to you?"

"No, sir."

Swinney testified that he had fought extradition. He asserted the reason for extradition was for his having violated Texas parole. When Cooksey focused on the matter, however, he backpedaled.

"Mr. Swinney, you testified that you fought extradition and went to the Governor's office; is that correct?"

"I didn't actually—I didn't put up any opposition because I didn't know how. At the time the Governor asked me a few questions, if that's fighting extradition, well, then, I fought extradition that way. He asked me if I felt like ought to be returned to Texas and be put in the Texas penitentiary as a parole violation and I told him, No, that I didn't understand what the charge was against me."

"Well, Mr. Swinney, you see, you are confusing me, now, because I thought you told Mr. Carter a while ago that you understood that they were going to try you for an habitual criminal and that's why you fought extradition."

"Yes, sir, that's right. That's one of the reasons, yes, sir."

Swinney continued a pattern of evasion. Cooksey returned to the issue of extradition. Swinney insisted he'd been told parole violation was the only basis for his extradition. Cooksey asked for specifics. Was the Bowie

County D.A. in Little Rock for the hearing? He didn't remember. Were any lawyers representing Texas there? He didn't remember.

Swinney repeatedly contended that he didn't know the charge in Miller County, that he had been convicted previously at both state and federal levels without an attorney, that FBI agents had questioned him without telling him he could have an attorney, that he knew nothing about court procedure, and that Judge Vance had never asked him if he wanted an attorney appointed, the opposite of what FBI agent Hallett had testified. The court docket also recorded that Swinney was charged with felony theft in Miller County. He appeared in court and undoubtedly heard the charge.

Swinney seemed to have created his own interpretation of the extradition proceedings. (No record of a hearing before the governor in Little Rock has been found. Tillman Johnson, the last survivor of the lawmen, believed Swinney waived extradition. Other records indicate that Governor Laney did sign off on extradition. This was not pursued in the hearing.)

On re-cross examination, Cooksey returned to the theme. "Mr. Swinney, the truth of the matter is, when your father employed three attorneys for you, you knew that they were going to charge you with murder in Miller County?"

"No, sir, I didn't know that."

"And you knew that you had an attorney who made a deal with the Texas authorities that they would not pursue their murder case if you would go to Texas on the habitual criminal act?"

"No, sir, I didn't. I knew that they were going to file habitual criminal law, but I didn't know anything else."

The two local attorneys for Swinney who had filed the writ of habeas corpus in 1946 were Paul J. McDonald and Ted Goldman. By 1972 McDonald was dead. Swinney swore he had not conferred with either, nor with J. F. McVey from Missouri.

Carter called Goldman to the stand.

Goldman verified his signature on the petition for the writ but had no recollection of it. He could not remember if he had represented Swinney or not. That had been twenty-five years before.

The final witness for the State was Tillman Johnson, Miller County's chief deputy sheriff in the 1940s, now working as an insurance claims adjustor.

Johnson testified that he had investigated Swinney in 1946 and 1947.

Cooksey asked, "Now, are you aware of the agreement that was made between the officials of Miller County and Bowie County?"

"Yes, sir," said Johnson.

"What was the agreement, Mr. Johnson?"

"There was an agreement made between the courts of both counties through a attorney, W. E. Haynie, who represented Mr. Swinney, that he would be released from Miller County to Bowie County for prosecution over here, in Bowie County."

"All right, sir. And what was to become of the Arkansas charges?"

"Those charges were to be dismissed."

"All right, sir. And was this agreement carried out?"

"Yes, sir."

"Was Mr. Swinney delivered to Texas authorities?"

"He was."

On cross-examination, Johnson testified that the Arkansas charges were dropped, as agreed, but he did not know when. "It was agreement that was not reached in one day and immediately delivered to Texas. Everything worked over a period of time." Carter cited records that the charges hadn't been dismissed until June 21, 1951, four years after the trial.

The hearing had ended.

Several months later, on February 20, 1973, Judge Nunn recommended that the writ be denied.

Ten days later, Carter mailed an appeal to the Court of Criminal Appeals.

CHAPTER 24

"BEYOND BELIEF AND INCREDIBLE"

O n March 19, 1973, the Court of Criminal Appeals, the court of last resort in Texas for criminal matters, reviewed the case. Judge Carl E. F. Dally ordered the trial court to hold a supplemental evidentiary hearing, if needed, and certify the records to the Court of Criminal Appeals.

The appellate judge focused on the 1941 Arkansas conviction, for which Swinney earlier had contended he'd had no attorney. The judge's order noted the circuit court's form recitation that Swinney "appeared in proper person and by his attorney" but that the document was *silent as to named counsel.*" He further commented, in capital letters: "THE DOCKET SHEET IS SILENT AS TO COUNSEL BEING PRESENT." At the 1972 hearing, the judge observed, Swinney had claimed that at his 1941 trial he had no counsel, wasn't advised of his right, and had not waived counsel. This raised in Judge Dally's mind "a serious question to the validity of the 1941 Arkansas conviction for the purposes of enhancement." The prisoner, he said, "may be entitled to relief." To clarify these points, he ordered the trial court to hold a supplementary evidentiary hearing within forty-five days, to see if the State could produce additional evidence, and transmit all records back to Austin.

If the trial court failed to return the entire record within sixty days, the appellate court would presume that Swinney's allegations were true. In the summary sheet, the judge wrote: "Since there is no affirmative showing that P [i.e., Petitioner] was represented by counsel, I think P's evidence is sufficient to grant the writ."

In his summary, Judge Dally brought up a matter that suggested the issue of the Phantom murders had no bearing on the case or any decision. "For some reason, counsel appointed at the habeas corpus hearing subpoenaed all of the parole board records, Mr. Shandara, and went into tons and tons of evidence about all sorts of collateral matters, including that of the parole board's refusal to parole Petitioner due to some protests by the D.A. and the trial judge. This is the reason why this record is extremely voluminous, even though if Petitioner's counsel had stayed with contention #1, the hearing could have been about 5 minutes!"

(Carter, having no way to know which direction the higher court might take, sought additional points to cover unknown eventualities, a common tactic of lawyers.)

In a final note: "Petitioner has well in excess of 10 years credit, so granting of writ would allow immediate discharge without re-trial."

After more than twenty-five years, the tide had finally turned against efforts to hold Swinney.

Judge Nunn, previously diagnosed with cancer, filed an affidavit on April 6 that he would be absent from the bench for an indefinite period. He was going to M. D. Anderson Cancer Hospital in Houston for treatment. During his absence he requested that another judge be assigned.

Three days later, the presiding judge of the First Administrative Judicial District of Texas, in Dallas, named Morris Rolston of the 76th Judicial District to fill in for Nunn.

The supplemental evidentiary hearing, with Judge Morris Rolston sitting in the Fifth Judicial District, began April 17 in Boston.

Lynn Cooksey, as district attorney, represented the State. Jack Carter, of the firm of Newman and Carter, again represented Swinney.

Testimony from Tillman Johnson opened the session. Johnson recalled the 1941 case for car theft.

"All right, sir," said Cooksey. "Now in waiting on the court, did you ever see the circuit judge in Arkansas appoint attorneys for defendants?"

"Yes, sir, in nearly all felony cases, to the best of my knowledge, it was customary to. Where the defendant was unable to hire an attorney or was not represented by one."

"And what was the normal procedure for Judge [Dexter] Bush, if an indigent defendant charged with a felony desired to plead guilty?"

"He would always appoint one of the attorneys to confer with that defendant out of the courtroom, and to report back to him as to what they wanted to do."

Johnson had served as deputy sheriff from January 1939 until 1956. He acted as bailiff for the entire period, serving in Judge Bush's court.

"He died in office," said Cooksey. "Yes, sir. Now do you ever recall any defendant charged with a felony in Judge Bush's court not being represented by counsel?

"No, I don't."

"Mr. Johnson, on the conviction of Youell Swinney in 1941, to the best of your recollection did Youell Swinney have an attorney?"

"I can't say that the man was represented by an attorney. It was general procedure that the man would be represented by an attorney, but as far as remembering him as a individual having an attorney up there, I cannot."

Johnson, while certain that Swinney had representation, was unable to recall the lawyer's identity. Too many years had passed.

Swinney took the stand in his own behalf. On direct examination, Carter rapidly moved to the February 1941 Arkansas case.

"What transpired upon going down and pleading guilty, if you will just explain to the Judge?" asked the attorney.

"Well," said Swinney, "on the night of the tenth or the eleventh, Sheriff Elvie Davis came to the jail where I was at and asked me if I would plead guilty, and I told him that I would. And so he said, 'Well, I'll take you down to my office.' He said, 'Judge Dexter Bush and Prosecutor Dick Huie is down there, if you just want to enter your plea of guilty.' I told him that I would do that, that would be all right. And so about seven-thirty that night, he took me down at his office and I pled guilty there; and the only people who were there were Judge Dexter Bush, Mr. Dick Huie, the prosecutor, Sheriff Elvie Davis, and myself."

(By that time, the sheriff, prosecutor, and judge were all dead and in no position to refute any of the testimony.)

"All right, sir, and did you have an attorney at that time?"

"No, sir."

"Did the Judge ask you if you wanted an attorney at that time?"

"No, sir."

"Did you tell the Judge that you did not want an attorney?"

"I didn't tell him that I did not want one, no, sir."

"Did he ask you anything about an attorney?"

"No, sir, an attorney wasn't mentioned."

"Mr. Swinney, at that period in your life what was your financial condition?"

"Well, I had just been released from Leavenworth two or three months prior to that and I was living with my brother, C. C. Swinney."

"Did you have any job?"

"No, sir."

"Did you have any means or method of obtaining the funds to hire a lawyer?"

"No."

The lawyer introduced the letter Swinney had written to the Miller County circuit clerk asking if he'd had an attorney in that case and the reply.

Subsequently, Cooksey cross-examined Swinney, who said he was taken from the jail in the top of the courthouse, down to the sheriff's office on the first floor, at night. Cooksey asked if the judge was standing or sitting. After some hesitation, the prisoner said the judge was sitting behind Sheriff Davis's desk. Who had brought Swinney down to the office? The sheriff, himself; no deputies present. Was he taken down in handcuffs? No. Prosecutor Dick Huie, the witness continued, asked if he had talked to the sheriff about a three-year sentence; Swinney said he had. "I believe the judge asked me if I was willing to plead guilty for a three-year sentence, and I told him that I was."

"All right," said Cooksey, "then did the judge ask you to plead?"

"Well, as I said, he did. Said, 'You have talked to the—' I mean the prosecutor asked me if I had talked to the sheriff and agreed to a three-year sentence, and I told him that I had. I mean the judge was talking to me."

"All right, and then did the judge say, 'How do you plead?'"

"Yes, sir. He said, 'Well, you do plead guilty?' I said, 'Yes, sir.'"

"All right, did he take your plea and sentence you all at the same time?"

"Yes, sir, right there."

"Did he pronounce sentence on you?"

"Yes, sir."

"So you are telling Judge Rolston that the judge didn't know anything about the case other than just right there and—"

"Well, I know that Sheriff Elvie Davis told me that he was going to talk the case over with the judge and see if he could arrange a three-year sentence."

"Now, did this strike you as unusual, that they would take you down to the sheriff's office and hold court in the sheriff's office?"

"No, sir, I didn't know."

"Well, hadn't you just gotten out of Leavenworth?"

"Yes, sir."

"Were you sentenced to Leavenworth in a sheriff's office?"

"No, sir, I was sentenced in the courtroom, federal court."

"All right, but was your Leavenworth conviction your first conviction?"

"Yes, sir, it was; felony conviction, yes."

(Swinney had grossly understated his prison record, which went unquestioned. He'd spent time in three federal prisons—El Reno, Leavenworth, and Atlanta. Prosecutors apparently had not checked his FBI rap sheet, which would have painted a darker picture of his past than he had admitted.)

"First felony conviction?"

"Or—you know—"

"Now had you appeared in the courtrooms before?"

"No, sir."

"Before your Leavenworth conviction, you had not appeared in a courtroom?"

"No, sir, I hadn't actually gone through a trial, no."

"No, I didn't say go through a trial. I said appear in a courtroom."

"Well, I had probably been in some courtrooms, but I don't know anything—I didn't know anything at that time about court procedure."

"Okay, but now this didn't strike you as unusual, that the sheriff would take you down there to the sheriff's office at night—"

"No, sir."

"—and you plead guilty to the judge in the sheriff's office?"

"No, it didn't strike me."

"Well, when you were sentenced by the federal judge—I assume it was a federal judge, since you went to Leavenworth. Is that correct?"

"Yes, sir."

"That was done in a courtroom, was it not?"

"Yes, sir."

"Well, didn't you think that was the proper way to do it?"

"Well, I just didn't have any thoughts about it. I thought since the sheriff and the judge had me brought down there, it was all right. As I say, I don't know anything about court procedure."

"Well, you do now, though, don't you?"

"Yes, sir. Very little."

"Well, does that appear unusual to you now?"

"No, sir, it doesn't."

"All right, do you know that the sheriff is dead?"

"Yes, sir."

"Do you know that Judge Bush is dead?"

"Yes, sir."

"Do you know that the prosecutor is dead?"

"No, sir, I didn't know that."

"Didn't know that. And so nobody is here except you, who you say you were taken down to the sheriff's office, and that was not unusual."

"To me it wasn't, no."

"All right, was this on the night of the tenth, or the night of the eleventh?"

"I can't recall that, whether it was on the night of the tenth or the eleventh. The judgment says the eleventh. So I assume then that it was the night of the eleventh."

"All right, did they whisk you off to the penitentiary that night?"

"No, sir, a day or two later."

"All right, and no clerk was there?"

"No clerk; no, sir."

"Nobody was there but just the sheriff, the prosecutor, and the judge—in the sheriff's office?"

"And myself, yes."

"The four of you."

"Yes, sir, the four of us."

"So the court accepted your guilty plea, then, and sentenced you to three years without discussing anything with you except 'are you guilty?'"

"The judge, yes, sir."

"And the judge sentenced you at that time. Is that right?"

"Yes."

"Was he wearing a suit?"

"Yes, sir, he had on a suit."

"Had on a suit?"

"Yes."

"But nothing else in the circumstances there arouses your suspicion that that was kind of an unusual procedure?"

"No, sir."

His client's time in the witness chair ended, Carter then called as defense witness Swinney's older brother, Cleo C. Swinney, a solid working man with a clean record. On direct examination, Carter documented his client's testimony that in 1941 he was living with his brother and was unemployed.

"Did he have any means of employing a lawyer?" asked Carter.

"No, sir," said Cleo Swinney, "he couldn't get a job because he had been released from the federal institution, and at that time jobs were scarce and an ex-convict, it was impossible for him to get a job even on the farm."

Cooksey called, as a witness, a clerk in the Miller County circuit clerk's office, Brenda Roberts, who testified that defendants without an attorney were described in records as being in custody of the sheriff, whereas those with an attorney were designated as appearing "in proper person and by attorney." Thus Swinney's case indicated that he had been represented by an attorney, although unnamed. She displayed another case from the 1940s: "And comes the defendant hereto, in proper person and in custody of the sheriff," meaning, she said, the defendant did not have an attorney.

On cross-examination, Carter elicited from her that she had not been employed in the circuit clerk's office in 1941 and had no personal knowledge of how the records were kept at that time.

By mid-May, Judge Rolston, as Special District Judge Sitting for the Fifth District Court of Bowie County, Texas, had summed up the proceedings in his findings of fact and conclusions of law. He pointed out that the *typed* minutes from the circuit clerk's records were not a form recitation but "entirely original entries" and demonstrated that Swinney was represented by an attorney, citing the language, "Comes the Defendant hereto in proper person and by his attorney." The Arkansas practice of describing whether a defendant was represented by counsel or not, therefore, said the Judge, made clear Swinney had had counsel in 1941. Based on these records and the testimony of the clerk, the Judge wrote: "The Court further finds that the Petitioner was represented by an attorney in the 1941 conviction."

Judge Rolston went further, referring to Swinney's testimony about the circumstances of his guilty plea. "The Court finds that the Petitioner's testimony regarding his conviction . . . is in certain respects beyond belief and incredible. It is unbelievable that a Judge of a Court of Record would abandon his courtroom on the second floor of the courthouse at night in the dead of winter to go outside the courthouse and back into the Sheriff's Office to try an accused. The Circuit Clerk would then have had to conjure a proceeding in his head to enter into the Court record or would have had to record a falsehood at the direction of his Judge. The Circuit Court records introduced in this hearing specifically recite that the Court was convened at 9:00 A.M., February 11, 1941; that the Petitioner appeared in person and with his attorney on that Court day and upon being advised of his rights, entered a Plea of Guilty to the charge of Grand Larceny. There is nothing to support or give credence to the testimony of Petitioner that he was tried in the Sheriff's Office in Miller

County, Arkansas, by the Sheriff and the Circuit Judge the night before the entry made in the Court record."

Judge Rolston further found that Swinney was legally confined and was "not being held on any unproved crimes or illegal convictions but he is being held because he is an habitual criminal."

He concluded, on the basis of the records, that Swinney was represented by counsel, was tried before the Circuit Judge of Miller County, Arkansas, on February 11, 1941, and entered a plea of guilty after being properly admonished.

The judge further concluded that Swinney was "much more interested in being released from the penitentiary than in challenging the validity of his 1941 conviction and his 1947 conviction in light of the repeated applications for Writ of Habeas Corpus."

He found that the judgment in 1941 was valid, with all of Swinney's constitutional rights fully protected.

Another, out-of-district trial judge saw no reason to release the inmate. Swinney had hit another wall. The Court of Criminal Appeals, however, would have the final say.

Jim D. Vollers, an assistant attorney general serving as State's Prosecuting Attorney representing the State in all cases before the Court of Criminal Appeals, submitted a brief opposing the granting of the writ. He emphasized, and agreed with, Judge Rolston's characterizing Swinney's testimony as "beyond belief and incredible." He pointed out that the trial judge's finding was additionally supported by Swinney's criminal record, having been convicted of a federal offense before the 1941 case. "These prior convictions are certainly pertinent matters which the Court can and should consider in determining whether or not his present testimony is credible. The record also clearly reflects that the petitioner's first inquiry in regard to the status of the record in showing whether or not he had counsel in the 1941 conviction occurred in 1967, some 25 years after the conviction occurred."

Then he added another argument in support of Judge Rolston's finding, that Swinney's testimony was incredible: "the obvious reticence by the petitioner to answer the questions of the district attorney and his evasiveness in regard to such questions."

The brief concluded by emphasizing the importance of the psychological realities of the living courtroom as well as the immutable characteristics of the record.

"The trial judge obviously had the only opportunity to see and hear this testimony and was in the better position to determine credibility."

The appellate decision came in late September after judges of the Court of Criminal Appeals had sifted through what it described as "tons" of evidence and testimony. Stating that the appeals court was not bound by the trial court's findings in a habeas corpus proceeding, the justices turned immediately to the issues of the 1941 case. Both State and the petitioner had produced circumstantial, but not conclusive, evidence.

It noted that in some instances a delay in seeking relief via habeas corpus may prejudice the credibility of the claim. Swinney had waited until 1967 to seek information on the 1941 case, a delay of twenty years after his 1947 conviction. The court cited as the State's "strongest evidence" the statement made at the time: ". . . and comes the defendant hereto in proper person and by attorney. . . ." The contention was that if Swinney had not had an attorney, his statement would have read, "in proper person and in custody of the sheriff." In 1972, the summary continued, the Fifth District Court reviewed Swinney's contention and found that he *did* have counsel in 1941.

They then shifted over to the petitioner's argument, emphasizing that the record was "silent" as to the name of his counsel. On the other hand, Swinney had testified that he had no attorney, was not advised of his right to an attorney, and was indigent at the time.

In conclusion, the majority on the appellate court saw no reason to deny the writ. "This decision is not hastily reached—the question is obviously a close one. However, we feel that petitioner has sufficiently sustained his burden in attacking the 1941 conviction."

Once that step was taken, the way was clear for Swinney's release. The maximum punishment for the felony of which he was convicted in 1947 was ten years confinement. "He has clearly served in excess of this maximum. Therefore, his immediate release from the Texas Department of Corrections is in order."

The final line, signed by Judge Truman Ernest Roberts, one of the five judges on the court at the time:

"The writ is granted and petitioner's release ordered."

It would be October 16, 1973, before the inmate was processed and actually walked out from behind walls at Huntsville.

More than twenty-seven years after his arrest, Youell Swinney was free.

Soon after the news reached Texarkana, Jack Carter's telephone rang. It was Lynn Cooksey, his recent courtroom adversary.

"Jack," said Cooksey, "Texarkana's in trouble. Swinney's on the ground!"

Whether Cooksey's comment was just a good-natured lawyerly ribbing or a trifle more serious, Carter wasn't sure. By then, he had already experienced his most traumatic moment.

One day when he walked into his church, Central Christian, he saw a woman visiting with the pastor in his study. Carter didn't recognize her. As he walked by, she spoke to him and motioned him in.

As he entered, she said, "Mr. Carter, do you know you're representing the man who killed my daughter?"

He didn't know her. She was Bessie Booker Brown, Betty Jo's mother. Although a Baptist, she had been attending Central Christian with her husband.

Carter was stunned speechless. He struggled for the right word. There was none he could come up with. *What can I say?* He felt as if he had been knocked to his knees. It brought home to him how meaningful the case was to those who had gone through it, especially the families of the victims. He wanted to say, *I was appointed to defend him and had no choice—I didn't volunteer to represent him!*

CHAPTER 25

LIFE AFTER "LIFE"

On a Sunday afternoon after the decision in Austin, Jack Carter sat relaxing in his den, watching the Dallas Cowboys on television, when the doorbell rang.

He reluctantly rose from his easy chair, wondering who was there. He opened the door.

Youell Lee Swinney stood before him.

He was wearing a hat, the first thing Carter noticed. By then, late 1973, you hardly ever saw a man wearing a hat. It was striking evidence of how unaware of the outside world Swinney had become and of how it had changed during his long incarceration.

Swinney thanked him for representing him and credited him for winning his freedom. Carter asked about his plans. Swinney said he was going straight, for good, and never would be back in jail. He was getting a job and had promising years ahead. It was good to breathe the outside air for a change and he just wanted Carter to know how much he appreciated what Carter had done for him, and that's why he had come, to personally thank him.

They talked for fifteen or twenty minutes at the door. Carter wished him good luck. Swinney left.

Carter didn't invite him inside. He never saw him again.

When Youell Swinney asked an arresting officer in 1946, "Do you think I'll be lucky enough to get out in twenty-five years?" he had come, as it turned out, remarkably close to estimating the time he was to spend behind bars. It was his longest stretch, by far. Even that conviction, however, had one thing in common with his previous terms of servitude. He had gotten out before the intended release date, which, this time, would have been at death.

It is impossible to reconstruct the thought process involved in the decision of the five-judge panel of the Court of Criminal Appeals. Several factors leaned in Swinney's favor. Foremost was a life sentence for a nonviolent crime, that of stealing an automobile. His conviction immediately preceding that, however, had been for a violent act, robbery by assault.

His most obvious ally was time. The years had brought deaths of key witnesses who might have refuted his uncontested claims, while eroding the memories of those who did testify. In addition, during the interim the interpretation of the Constitution had confirmed individual rights that had not been spelled out in some states, which in turn had led to Swinney's claim that he hadn't had a lawyer in either 1947 or 1941.

Then there was another matter. The prisons were filling up with young lawbreakers, some extremely violent. An aging inmate, doing life for a stolen car, as an habitual criminal, was unlikely to be considered a risk to society. As he aged, he would be more of a liability to the state in terms of medical care. In 1973 Swinney turned fifty-six. It was an age by which sociopaths tend to burn out, or at least are not expected to perpetrate dramatic violent crimes that would require great spurts of energy. It is doubtful, however, that the appellate judges gave any thought to whether Swinney would commit such a crime, as they were not working with the knowledge of Peggy Swinney's testimony that named Swinney as a murderer, potentially the Phantom Killer.

Few in the Texarkana community entertained an inkling of Swinney's past or that he was the main suspect in the Phantom murders. The first public hint of his connection to the 1946 cases did not come until it was inserted into the evidentiary hearing. By then, nearly three decades had elapsed and though the crimes had become a part of Texarkana's history, even folklore, emotions had lost their edge. Memories, like those of witnesses, were blurred, faded, or evaporated.

At fifty-six, Swinney had the opportunity to start a new life.

Following release, Swinney relocated to Marshall, Texas, about eighty miles south of Texarkana. He lived there from October 1973 to July 1974. A sister lived in Marshall, which was one reason he took employment there. Another sister lived in Texarkana.

During this period, Swinney made a memorable appearance in Texarkana that drew more attention than he expected. On blistering cold Thursday, January 3, 1974, a day on which it was too cold to work, he drove up to visit the sister on the Arkansas side. Sheets of ice covered northeastern Texas and slowed traffic. Roads and bridges remained guardedly open. A tall, well-built middle-aged man with a crew cut wearing a hard hat, he parked an olive green 1973 Ford Maverick out front of the *Texarkana Gazette* office. A bumper sticker proclaimed: "Not Only Cars Recalled by its Maker."

Tugging a newspaper clipping from his pocket, he told the receptionist downstairs he wanted to talk to the woman featured as an author in the item that came from the *Gazette*. She glanced at it and directed him to Editorial.

Upstairs in the open newsroom, he showed the clipping to the first person he saw and repeated his request. The reporter pointed out the editor, Harry Wood, and returned to her work.

Swinney introduced himself to Wood and thrust out the clipping. Wood recognized his name and the lined, weatherbeaten face from a photograph the paper had run. The brief article was about a woman who had written a book. Swinney wanted to get in touch with her. He wanted her to help him write a book.

The editor scrutinized the clipping, of a syndicated book review. There was no local connection, but Wood was loath to dismiss the visitor. Maybe he had something newsworthy to say. What might it be? Swinney didn't seem eager to leave, either.

Busy reporters and copydesk personnel glanced at the stranger, then back to their work.

"Can we talk in some other place?" Swinney asked.

"We can go to the conference room," Wood said. Then he beckoned over an associate, Jim Reavis the news editor, sensing the need for a witness should a story develop.

As Wood closed the conference room door, the man in the hard hat introduced himself to the second editor.

"I'm Youell Swinney." Then he added, matter-of-factly but with a certain flair and a barely concealed tinge of pride, "I'm the man they say was the Phantom."

It was a startling, even shocking, way to introduce himself, and the two newsmen stood, expressionless, waiting for him to tell them more. He explained what he had in mind. He'd been framed for a crime he didn't commit. He wanted to write a book about how he'd spent twenty-seven years in the Texas penitentiary as an innocent man.

He spoke persuasively of the injustice done him.

Wood, aware of some details of the case, asked about his companion who had given statements implicating him. How did he explain that?

"The man they called the Phantom" shrugged it off.

"She just cooked up that story to collect the reward money. She made it up. I didn't have nothing to do with all that, and she knew it."

The editor told him that he knew a man who wrote books in collaboration. Would he like to talk to him? Sure, that'd be fine.

I hadn't been in my small office at the farm long that morning when Harry Wood called. It was still shivering cold inside from the prolonged hard freeze that had lingered for days, and I hadn't had time to heat the space and warm my hands sufficiently

Harry said, "Jim, Youell Swinney is here and would like to talk to you."

"Swinney?" I said. "You're kidding."

"No, he's here in the office. I wonder if you'd like to collaborate with him on a book."

The situation didn't ring true. Why would he show up at the *Gazette* and be brought into contact with, of all persons, me?

"Is this a joke?" I asked, a bit incredulous.

"No, it's not a joke," said Harry. "He's sitting right here in the office with me now. He's looking for someone to help him write a book about his experience."

Convinced he wasn't pulling my leg, I said, "Sure, I'll talk to him. But I doubt I can help him."

I was more than well acquainted with the case. Years before, I had explored it in a free-lanced eight-part series of articles.

I'd also studied Swinney's records at the state penitentiary's main office in Huntsville. I remembered, without referring to my files, a great deal of what I had read and noted there.

We talked.

"I want to write a book about how I was unfairly imprisoned and held for twenty-seven years," Swinney said. "The Court of Criminal Appeals finally released me last year. Back in 1946 they said I was connected to those killings. I didn't have anything to do with it.

"Steve McQueen and those other actors were at Huntsville making that movie, *The Fugitive*. I told 'em my story and they said it was a good one. They said, 'You oughta write a book and it'd be a best seller!' I can't write it by myself and I was looking for someone to help me with it."

He apparently referred to *The Getaway*, featuring McQueen with Ali MacGraw, filmed partly in the Texas prison system and released in 1972. *The Fugitive* was a television series; McQueen wasn't in it.

"Where were you when the Texarkana murders were committed?" I asked.

"I wasn't even here then."

I tried again. "Where were you at that time?"

"I was up in St. Louis," he said.

That was what he had claimed in his interview when he had entered the prison in 1947. In his version, he'd worked for the Green Tree Construction Company in St. Louis during a period that coincided exactly with when the murders were committed near Texarkana. I'd called Information for such a company and found there was none. I'd checked with the Chamber of Commerce there, to see if such a firm had operated in 1946. I was told none did. At the prison, the assistant warden told me they didn't check the inmate's claim. It was just part of his record. Swinney seemed to have forgotten that in 1946 he'd admitted he was in Texarkana but denied that he had killed. His own words disputed his claim to me.

"Do you live in Texarkana now?" I asked.

"No, I'm in Marshall right now. I'm foreman on a construction job there. It was too cold to work today, so I came up here to see relatives."

"What's your address there, in case I need to get back in touch with you?" I asked him.

He gave it in a low, cautious voice in control of himself.

"I live at 808 North Fulton in Marshall," he said.

"Well," I said, "I'm pretty busy now on another book"—very true, on a collaboration with an M.D. about preventive medicine—"but I'll get in touch if things change. Meanwhile, you might talk to a newspaper writer in Marshall, since you're there, about doing a book."

That ended our conversation. I called Information for a phone listing for him at the Fulton Street address in Marshall. There was none. That didn't disprove his statement, but only indicated that he had no listed telephone in his name.

In the *Gazette* office, as he hung up and turned to the editor, he said, "He's too busy now."

"The man they say was the Phantom" left the building. A reporter headed for the window to monitor his return to the car. On the street, a car with plainclothes detectives awaited him as he approached the Maverick. One of the reporters told the editor of the scene below. (Later the editor learned that one of his reporters had tipped off the District Attorney, who probably had spread the word to the police.)

Down the street, the policemen spoke sternly and earnestly with The Man They Say Was the Phantom, advising him, "We don't want you back here."

They then escorted him to the city limits and watched him drive south on U.S. Highway 59 toward Marshall.

I called Harry Wood afterward and asked his impressions.

"He just looked like an old con," he said. Harry had worked for the newspaper at Huntsville, the site of the state prison system headquarters, before going to Texarkana and was an old hand at sizing up old cons.

That night I called Tillman Johnson, who had been chief deputy sheriff during the murder spree. Johnson already knew of Swinney's appearance.

Policemen from both Texas and Arkansas sides had called him around noon. Swinney, they told him, had gone to an address in the College Hill neighborhood on the Arkansas side, the residence of a sister and brother-in-law. He never voluntarily returned to Texarkana after that.

FBI records document his short stay in Marshall. He worked for a construction company from November 1973 to July 1974. On the surface he seemed to be following the plan he'd told Carter—a job and staying out of trouble.

However, in an investigation made afterward a different picture emerged. One informant told an agent of a pattern contradicting the outward image.

"Swinney was believed to be a homosexual and spent most of his time around young people at the Dairy Queen in Marshall. He was also suspected of dealing in narcotics. Swinney had a young boy fourteen or fifteen years of age who was with him a lot and finally moved in with Swinney." When Swinney moved to Grand Prairie, Texas, the boy went with him. Grand Prairie is a northern suburb of Dallas. A nephew of Swinney said his uncle even took the teenaged boy to work with him, suggesting a level of control over the boy that Swinney had once exercised with Peggy.

(One family account has it that he grew angry with the boy one night and "almost beat the boy to death," as a relative put it. He escaped police scrutiny that time.)

Swinney's suspected homosexual behavior might offer counter-insight into why Mary Jeanne Larey and Polly Ann Moore had not been raped, though Betty Jo was, assuming Swinney was the culprit in all the cases. The Marshall informant's opinion meshed with Swinney's behavior in the Texas penitentiary when he was punished for sexual engagement with another inmate. On the other hand, he might have been bisexual or, despite the prison incident, possibly not homosexual either.

As for his possible involvement in the narcotics trade, that too added to a pattern in Swinney's 1946 actions in western Oklahoma when he'd sold bootleg whiskey. By the 1970s, drugs had replaced bootleg whiskey as the illicit stimulant of choice.

Swinney's relationships with relatives varied. When he lived in Arlington, Texas, he crafted a gold-plated necklace for his niece Joyce that proved to be durable and never tarnished. She didn't realize that he was also counterfeiting gold coins at the same time. (He also created bogus bills.) On the other hand he persuaded his nephew Clarence to sign a note with him. Clarence was stuck with paying off the loan.

There is no evidence that Youell visited violence upon family members, though he was vocal toward those he disliked, usually in-laws. He threatened to kill one brother-in-law, the husband of a sister. The sister remonstrated, "If you kill him, you might as well kill me." She was one of his favorites and often helped him. No actual violence occurred, beyond strong words.

Swinney did not make the best of his newly won freedom. He worked for a while, including the construction job in Marshall, followed by another construction job in the Dallas area, where he worked from August 1974 to March 1975 as a cement finisher.

In the spring of 1975 his criminal résumé took on renewed life. In March, U.S. marshals nabbed him for counterfeiting money, another old pattern. Police at Greenville, a short distance east of Dallas, levied an automobile theft charge, along with possession of bogus coins—counterfeited silver dollars and quarters he'd tried to pass as collectors' items. It was back to the marshals in Dallas, where he was convicted of counterfeiting. U.S. District Judge Sarah T. Hughes sentenced him to two years in prison. (Judge Hughes had sworn in Lyndon B. Johnson as President aboard Air Force One following President Kennedy's assassination in 1963.)

On April 18, Swinney was dispatched to the Federal Correctional Institution in Texarkana, Texas, a medium security prison. He was fifty-eight years old. As one psychiatrist put it, an aged, burnt-out psychopathic killer might kill again, if backed into a corner, but is not likely to commit a highly dramatic crime like those of the Phantom case.

In Swinney's case, the crime pattern of counterfeiting and felony thefts continued, but he was never held for murder again.

Ironically, his return to Texarkana was less heralded than his departure back in 1947. Only federal officers—marshals and prison authorities—knew Swinney had been placed in the Texarkana FCI. None was aware of Swinney's link to the terrifying days in 1946.

That relative anonymity lasted briefly. On May 8, less than a month after his arrival at the Texarkana FCI, Swinney escaped, a familiar pattern in his federal criminal record. That day, Swinney was assigned duty on an outside work detail at the institution's dairy farm. Shortly after noon, the guard realized a worker was missing. At that point Swinney— FCI prisoner 22232-149—by walking away, became an escaped federal prisoner. The warden notified local authorities and issued an all-points bulletin.

Unlike his previous escapes, this one garnered widespread attention, including front-page coverage in the *Texarkana Gazette*. An old con and counterfeiter who didn't know any better than to commit dumb crimes, he hadn't drawn any special attention from his keepers till then.

FBI records help reconstruct Swinney's itinerary for the next few days. At the dairy farm, he watched the guard out of the corner of his eye. As soon as the guard was out of sight, Swinney set down his tools and simply walked off. The Texarkana FCI is near Lake Drive, the local street that follows the route of U.S. Highway 59, which goes south to Marshall and on to Houston.

At the highway, he began hitchhiking. He had stored his clothes with his sister in Marshall. He needed to replace his prison khakis. He had no money.

It is not clear what happened on the road or where he spent that night. Along the way, he acquired a large knife about six inches long with a folding blade—and a red hat. Who would expect an escaped felon to wear a red hat? Where he acquired the knife and hat was never explained, whether they came from a motorist or a burglarized house.

At nine-thirty the next morning, he surprised his sister in Marshall by walking into her house through the open back door. He was wearing a tan khaki shirt and trousers, along with the red hat.

He wanted something to eat. She asked how he'd gotten out of prison.

"I tied up a guard," he said, "but I didn't hurt nobody."

She agreed to fry bacon and eggs but cautioned, "You can't stay here. You'll have to leave."

"Then take me out to the highway soon as I eat, so I can catch a ride to Shreveport."

First, she said, she had to go to Texarkana and pick up their sister.

"Okay," he agreed, "but I want to borrow some money."

As soon as he had finished eating breakfast, he sifted through a box of clothing he had shipped to her from the Texarkana FCI. He took out a brown dress suit and put it in a paper bag. He then changed into brown khaki trousers and shirt and set a brown corduroy hat on his head, leaving the distinctive red hat behind.

His sister took him to a point west of Hallsville, a town near Marshall. When she came to a sign, PASS WITH CARE, she let him out. He was to remain in the woods there until she returned. She drove on to Texarkana, where she picked up her sister. Her sister already knew of Swinney's escape. An FBI agent had visited her the day before, telling her that if Swinney made contact she should call immediately. He failed to tell her that she would be in trouble if she gave the escapee any assistance.

The two women returned to Hallsville, stopped at the sign where Swinney had gotten out of the car. Swinney spotted them and came out of the woods.

They tried to persuade him to turn himself in and save himself—and them—a lot of grief. He refused. They needn't worry about him. Just help him get away so he could go to Shreveport. They kept talking to him, pointing out that if he turned himself in, he would get better treatment, since authorities were bound to recapture him anyway. He resolutely refused.

Late that afternoon, his sister drove him out of Marshall on Interstate Highway 20. When he got out, one sister gave him twenty dollars; the other, thirty dollars. He said he was going to the Salvation Army in Shreveport for the night, and he would call in a week to ten days. He had no gun but was still carrying the large knife with the long blade.

At six o'clock, a special FBI agent arrived to interview the Marshall relative. She told him she had let Youell out on the highway about thirty minutes before.

This information set off a new alarm. The FBI agent sounded the alert that Swinney might be headed into Louisiana.

The FBI's all-points bulletin, sent out by Teletype immediately on learning of the escape, contained a full profile of Swinney, including his criminal record.

SWINNEY HAD BEEN CONFINED AT TEXAS DEPARTMENT OF COR-RECTIONS, HUNTSVILLE, TEXAS, FROM FEBRUARY 15, 1947 UNTIL OCTOBER 16, 1973. HE HAD BEEN CONFINED UNDER THE HABITUAL CRIMINAL ACT. SWINNEY IS BELIEVED RESPONSIBLE FOR SEVEN [sic] MURDERS AT TEXARKANA, TEXAS, IN 1945-46 [sic]; HOWEVER, HE WAS NEVER CONVICTED.

SWINNEY DESCRIBED AS WHITE MALE AMERICAN, DOB FEBRUARY 9, 1917, ARKANSAS, 6', 195 POUNDS, BROWN HAIR, BLUE EYES, WEARS EYEGLASSES. HE HAS TATTOO OF TWO INCH HEART WITH SKULL ON LEFT FOREARM AND WORD "MOM" ALSO ON LEFT FOREARM; SCAR ON RIGHT KNEE; SSAN 459-32-1164; BOTH PARENTS DECEASED; SWINNEY DIVORCED 1946 [sic] AND DID NOT HAVE ANY CHILDREN.

The description overlooked the tattoo, REVENGE. The oversight was corrected in subsequent FBI records.

The bulletin ended with a blunt warning:

CONSIDER ARMED AND DANGEROUS

Special instructions went to agents to interview individuals who knew him at Texarkana, Louisiana, Oklahoma, and Grand Prairie, Longview, Marshall, and Weatherford, Texas.

The manhunt took on greater urgency because of Swinney's history, now coming to light. He was not a run-of-the-mill escapee. Like many a time before, he had simply walked away. Nor had he tied up a guard, as he'd boasted to his sister.

Three days after Swinney walked off the FCI grounds, an FBI agent called the sister in Marshall. She was at her job in Jefferson, fifteen miles from Marshall. It was five-thirty in the afternoon. "He's here now," she said. "I'll try to talk with him, to keep him long enough for you to get here." The agent took off.

Fifteen minutes later, Swinney was gone, driving a dark brown compact car with the rear end square. She didn't know the license number.

The following morning—May 12, a Monday—Swinney's relative in Grand Prairie telephoned officers that Swinney, seeking money, had tried to contact him. Swinney, alone, was driving a bronze-colored American-made compact car, bearing Texas license plates, numbers unknown.

FBI agents swarmed into Grand Prairie. At nine o'clock a woman called from Swinney's former employer. Swinney was in her office in nearby Carrollton, trying to obtain money he claimed was due him. The FBI immediately notified Carrollton police. Minutes later a sergeant and patrolman reached the office. Swinney was on his way out of the building.

They stopped him, informed him he was under arrest. It was 9:10 A.M. Ten minutes later two FBI agents arrived, identified themselves, and took him into custody. One of the federal agents provided him a Rights and Waiver Form. Swinney read it, said he understood it, but declined to sign. He agreed to be interviewed orally.

Once in custody he verbally traced his itinerary over the past few days. He had hitchhiked to Dallas, not Shreveport, the first day. He left blank his visit to Marshall. Two days after his escape, he was in Lewisville, in the Dallas area. He took a used car from the Newt Miller Ford Agency for a test drive. He admitted he had no intention of buying it or returning it. He simply needed transportation. He slept in the car that Saturday and the following night. He remained vague as to where he went during that time.

He handed the car keys to the agents. It was a 1973 two-door Ford Maverick, bronze with 1975 Texas license number GTA 806.

The Carrollton police ascertained that the Maverick was, indeed, stolen from the Ford agency. The car's value was assessed at $2,900. Another felony.

Swinney spent the night at the Dallas County jail, with a hold for the U.S. Marshal Service.

His description remained basically as in his earlier arrests. His tattoos on the left forearm hadn't changed, including the heart and skull and crossbones and the word *Revenge*. The difference was his occupation: cement finisher, a trade he'd acquired in prison.

His level of education was stated as eighth grade, two steps above what he had testified to in 1973. His IQ was 95, considered low average.

A decision followed not to prosecute his family members for any aid they may have given him; they had cooperated with authorities in tracking him, had urged him to surrender. In late May he was dispatched to Leavenworth, a maximum-security prison where he had resided more than thirty years before.

In July he pleaded guilty in U.S. District Court in Topeka, Kansas, to one count of escape and received a sentence of two years, to be served after he completed his two-year term for counterfeiting.

His self-initiated freedom had been short-lived—four days.

The following year, a movie, *The Town That Dreaded Sundown*, was filmed in the Texarkana area and hit the theaters. Purporting to be a true account of the famous case, it was anything but that. The title, however, was an undisputed accurate reflection of the town's mood during the killing spree. Starring Ben Johnson, Andrew Prine, and Dawn Wells, it was directed by Charles B. Pierce, a regional moviemaker who had previously achieved a degree of success with another local incident, *The Legend of Boggy Creek*. The *Sundown* killer, left unnamed and his face never displayed, cavorted about with a pillowcase, with eyeholes, over his head, even in daylight. For anyone acquainted with the facts, the movie only vaguely paralleled what had happened in 1946. One of its most memorable scenes, in which the pillowcase–hooded killer tortures a female victim tied to a tree with knives on a trombone slide while he plays a mournful melody, evoked raucous laughter from those who knew the details of the case. There was never a knife used by the killer, never a trombone, never a girl tied to a tree.

"Poetic license has rarely been stretched so thin," wrote Dr. Robert Kerr, a Texarkana journalist who went on to teach at the University of Oklahoma. "Total fiction." Nonetheless, the "dreadful little horror" came to have a cult following, spreading, via translated subtitles, to Europe: *Kaupunki pelon valiassa* and *Verenpunainen auringonlasku* in Finland, *Staden som fruktade solnedgången* in Sweden, and *La citta che aveva paura* in Italy.

It became a new vehicle contributing to distortions of a hometown tragedy, on the heels of a vast array of published errors and word-of-mouth accounts that, aided by time's erosive nature, had seriously blurred, then kidnapped, the truth.

During the late 1970s, Swinney made another attempt at writing short stories, as he had done at Huntsville during his major stretch. His nephew Clarence said some of the stories were published in a "small Jewish publication," a newsletter from Temple Yaakov in Atlanta. Atlanta was one of his several federal "homes." The nine stories or sketches that are extant offer a range of topics from cotton picking to Independence Day to some superficial love stories. One gains the impression of a hard-luck loser striving for recognition but seemingly without a clue as to how to make it, beyond clichés of uplift philosophy.

Under a general heading of "Random Thoughts," he submitted a series of stories around 1979 containing titles like "King Cotton," "Fathers Are the Greatest," "A Lonely Vigil," "Angry Waters," "Love Is Forever," and "Each Dawn I Die."

"Angry Waters" tells of a typical summer's day in the long-forgotten year of 1927 when "Steve" was nine. (This is close to the time—1926— when Swinney's parents divorced and the age he would have been.) The piece bristles with words of violence—"lightning streaked the heavens like stabbing knives in quest of hidden victims," "maddened force," "fury," "angry waters," with "outings of fantasy," "envisioned himself as a pirate in search of loot or a captain of a luxury liner," "danger," "dangerous situations," "bone-chilling spasoms [*sic*] of wintery coldness," "the savagery of wild animals locked in battles to the death." This memory was of a boat in a millpond during a storm, employing a great many symbols that suggest violent inner turmoil and uncertainties.

In another, "Love Is Forever," he uses phrases like "devastation triggered by a hidden time bomb" and "fury of the fiery explosion." The lead in the story survives an explosion on an oil derrick but loses both legs, amputated at the knees. He had married his schoolhood girl friend, Beth, in a church, but because he is legless and can't support her, apparently he does not go back to her. It does not say she rejected him and doesn't explain how he could have gone away without her knowing it. He becomes a street singer. One day Beth and her new husband come by, hear him sing, but she doesn't recognize him. It is a jerky story in many respects, suggesting a pitiable man with low self-esteem amid a disturbed relationship.

His nephew, Clarence Swinney, called them "rather odd stories from a possibly disturbed mind." They were closer to a junior high effort that crammed in big words as if to impress. Most of all, they reflected an inner disturbance amid a violent background.

The seeds of his anger were planted early. His life story reveals numerous troubled relationships that may have become models for his acts of "revenge." The roots of his behavior can be traced to a childhood when he was ignored by his parents, left adrift, gaining attention by negative activities, and eventually acting out his emotional responses to the world around him.

It was small wonder that many, if not all, of the family believed that Youell had committed the murders.

His short stories, though poorly crafted, may have enabled him to express his frustrations and violent inner world in a nonviolent manner. If he had taken the literary route years earlier, instead of acting out his anger, the question arises whether he might have channeled his drive for revenge into a direction other than murder. Or if mental-health services had been available in his childhood, and used, would early intervention have prevented the multiple tragedies? It wouldn't have "cured" his psychopathy, which probably was set at birth or early in life, but it might have headed off the tragic violence.

Swinney's brushes with the law continued. He returned to Texas custody for felony theft in 1981 as Inmate # 326380 with a hold—yet again—for the U.S. Marshal in Houston. He was sixty-four years old. He subsequently returned to the Texas penitentiary as Inmate # 476635, much altered in appearance, old and seemingly embittered. Once paroled in January 1989, he had another hold on him by the U.S. Marshal in Houston. By then he was nearing his seventy-second birthday. He was a beaten, time-ravaged old man, a pathetic old con who had ruined a multitude of lives, including his own.

In his old age, Swinney was paroled from a federal institution in Fort Worth and moved to a nursing home in Dallas. He suffered a stroke but died of lung cancer in Southhaven Nursing Center in Dallas on September

15, 1994, technically and legally a free man, at the age of seventy-seven, a ripe age for a man with his record. He had spent the bulk of his life behind bars and at the end, as an indigent, was cared for infinitely better than he had treated any of his victims, including those on whom he had passed his counterfeit concoctions and whose cars he had stolen. He also had survived the three who had lived to tell of their attacks by the Phantom—James Hollis, Mary Jeanne Larey, and Katie Starks.

Because his body wasn't claimed by relatives, it was donated to The University of Texas Health Science Center in Dallas, which uses cadavers for teaching purposes. Medical students, unaware of the history of the body before them, dissected and studied the remains of The Man They Said Was the Phantom, who had once boasted of the label. The students, some of whom probably would practice medicine in the region terrorized by the serial killer, never knew what the body before them, when alive, had done. Once the body was no longer needed, it was cremated and the ashes disposed of. With the ashes unclaimed, it is not certain where the ashes went. His was a wasted life, whatever the outcome of a murder trial might have proved. He had besmirched the name of hardworking family members. He had cost society untold hundreds of thousands of dollars in law enforcement and incarceration expenses alone. Add the toll of Phantom victims—the dead and the survivors, along with their sorrowing families and friends—and the total loss is inestimable, stretching across decades.

In the end, he had literally burned, a fate many had sought for him back in 1946.

His official record belied any belief, by him or anyone else, that he was a "brilliant" criminal who had demonstrated that he was smarter than the men trying to catch him. "They"—the law—caught him over and over again. The only people he had ever managed to truly con were the parole board members, whom he somehow managed to convince each time that he would not commit any further crimes.

For the central crimes for which he had been blamed, but not charged, he had been no more brilliant than in the lesser theft, robbery, and counterfeit cases for which he had been convicted. In the crimes of murder for which circumstantial evidence and an eyewitness account existed, he had been uncommonly lucky. His only action even approaching brilliance was his marrying Peggy so that she couldn't be forced to testify against him. It didn't take a legal education to know that.

His wasted life was a cautionary tale so graphic as to defy explanation, forever beyond understanding.

In that sense, his victims—the dead and surviving loved ones—would never be avenged in full, though marginal justice had emerged in disguised form.

CHAPTER 26

CRACKING A COLD CASE

ad he gained political support for the idea, Glenn Owen, a Texarkanian born seven years after the murders occurred, intended to stamp SOLVED on the Phantom mystery. His mechanism followed a protocol effective in other jurisdictions.

Owen dedicated a significant portion of his time and energies to clearing the case through this overlooked process. Even with the culprit, witnesses, and officers all dead, his plan, proposed more than sixty years after the crimes, was reasonable, logical, faithful to the law, and practically guaranteed to succeed.

Owen was ten when he heard his older brothers and parents talking about the case. His family had a peripheral connection to the first double murders just off Highway 67. His grandfather, Hass Owen, operated Owen Brothers Livestock Sales, set back on the north side of the highway, a short walk to the death scene. In front of the livestock auction, a café sold beer. Swinney and Peggy, based on her statements, bought beer there several times. (They bought beer at a lot of other West Seventh Street cafés too.)

As an adult, Owen compiled an impressive résumé of investigative experience: ten years as an Army criminal investigator, twenty years of part-time work as a Texas police officer. As a part-time investigator for the Bowie County district attorney's office, he watched "experts" on TV talk about criminal cases. Doubting their authority, he began profiling cases as a hobby. His skill grew until he profiled, with great accuracy, a number of headline cases.

Eventually his intense interest brought him into contact with Tillman Johnson, who had pondered the case for decades. Owen decided the mystery could be reopened and settled with some satisfaction. The means would be the FBI-approved process set up for qualifying crimes, including murder as well as lesser transgressions.

The method was to clear the case *by exception*, following FBI guidelines. The FBI requires three steps.

1. Identifying the perpetrator
2. Sufficient information to justify an arrest, charge, and prosecution
3. The offender's location is known and he can be appre-hended, but there is an overriding reason why he can't be taken into custody and prosecuted.

If the culprit is alive and can be delivered, obviously he would be brought to trial.

If, however, he is in custody in another state and for some reason can't be extradited, proceedings could begin without him.

If the culprit is dead, so that he can't physically face the bar of justice, the case still may be resolved. Clearing a case by exception doesn't assign a penalty or sentence. It removes the mystery from its unsolved status.

The Phantom case, Glenn Owen reasoned, qualified on all counts. Sufficient evidence existed to meet the FBI standards, which would be administered by local authorities.

The approach had been utilized in a variety of jurisdictions over the nation. Owen followed a case so cleared in Indiana. Why not in Bowie and Miller Counties?

Before DNA became a trump card in criminal investigation, with the power to liberate as well as convict, the Phantom case had to depend on less dramatic findings. There were no reliable fingerprints. DNA studies *probably* would have helped at the time, but no such science existed. Other evidence, however, tied all of the cases together as the work of a single perpetrator.

Above all, one common feature characterized all four Texarkana attacks. They were "stranger" crimes. Neither attacker nor victims knew the other. This alone doesn't prove the same stranger committed all the acts, but is a starting point.

The killer was a very angry man, obvious in the February beatings before the murders began. The assault victims suffered the man's vicious acts; he came close to killing them. Hollis and Larey had witnessed his rage up close. Hollis, describing the man as "desperate," warned officers that he would kill next time. The warning went unheeded. Hollis was right; it cost Richard Griffin and Polly Ann Moore their lives the following month.

Bearing in mind that all of the incidents were committed by a stranger driven by deep anger, the victims then become innocent surrogates for the persons whom the criminal blamed for his own distress. Emotionally he was getting even with those who, he perceived, had done him wrong. Such twisted logic fit snugly within the framework of his behavior.

Hollis was lucky to survive. The assailant had intended to kill him, had left him for dead. The brutal February beatings, as precursor event, set the stage for the murders to come.

The Griffin-Moore murders presented the same MO as the beatings. The thug attacked a couple parked in a lovers' lane late at night. He wielded a pistol and, in February, a very strong flashlight. A pistol was the centerpiece of the subsequent attacks. A flashlight was used—and left—at the Starks house in May.

Another part of the MO linked the Hollis-Larey beatings to the Griffin-Moore murders. In February, in which we have a clear, up-close eyewitness account from Hollis, the gunman forced Hollis to drop his trousers. The gunman obviously knew this would limit his male victim's movements.

A month later, Richard Griffin's body was found with his trousers around his ankles. This was a similar attempt to control the male victim, hobbling Griffin so that he would be unable to move freely. Thus the killer controlled the scene more effectively than in February. He'd corrected his errors. He'd improved his technique, as serial killers usually do. The first attack is a learning experience. Afterward he goes over the event in his mind, devising ways to improve the next one. In effect, he perfects his methods in his fantasies. At the next opportunity he puts into practice what he has learned.

The February beatings can be read as the seminal event from which the murders grew. The lawmen to a man misinterpreted the case, believing the victims knew their attacker, despite having no such proof, despite the couple's consistent, forceful certainty that they had never seen him before—and that the man was a potential killer. Four bodies later, lawmen tardily acknowledged the connection. At fault was lawmen's refusal to believe what Hollis and Larey kept telling them, that a stranger had beaten them.

Usually the first incident in a string of attacks or murders will reveal much about the killer. The February attacks tie in with subsequent MOs. He failed to control the crime scene then and, most of all from his viewpoint, he had left witnesses. He apparently hadn't intended to leave either one alive. His lapses in the February attacks probably generated a degree of anxiety. Might they identify him if he was arrested? As the weeks passed and the story faded from the newspapers, supplanted by other violence, he could relax and meditate on his next venture, a month later.

Glenn Owen, like others, saw money as a motivation but believed humiliating the victims was part of the plan, sexual humiliation in the female and possibly in the male. "Having the male drop his trousers helped control the scene, to keep him from running off, but maybe there was a little sexual perversion there. The criminal may have wanted to humiliate the man in front of his girlfriend. Maybe he wanted to look at him, you know. Maybe he got off by doing that, by humiliating somebody in that form or fashion."

The connection between the February beatings and the March murders was obvious. Richard Griffin was forced to drop his trousers, as had happened to Hollis, and was killed before Polly Ann Moore. The February attacker had assaulted the male first. The sequence of deaths was a pattern throughout: disabling or killing the male first, then dealing with the female at a more leisurely pace. This thread runs through all of the four incidents, except that he enjoyed no leisure at the Starks home when his plans were short-circuited, causing him to panic and leave his flashlight.

(The pattern of disposing of the male first, then focusing upon the female, especially for an extended period of time, as in the Betty Jo Booker incident, outwardly suggests an Oedipal model, despite the ages of the victims. Risky though such speculation is, one is reminded of Dr. Luther White's 1971 analysis along these lines, that a sexual relationship with a respectable woman would seem incestuous, leading to the killing of the female. The tattoo MOTHER may add to the theory.)

While the February crime scene was chaotic, the March murders reflected a more organized offender. He'd had a month to fantasize and improve on his crimes. Instead of slugging his victims, he shot each victim execution-style, in the back of the head: two shots each from a .32 automatic pistol, a Colt with a left-handed twist. No witnesses.

He also posed the bodies inside the car, so that they might be supposed at a glance to be sleeping. Postponing their discovery gave the killer time to distance himself.

The killer learned from his flawed February experience. He had once more exacted revenge—on surrogates—in what was to become his near-perfect crime. He was helped by rain later that night and clumsy police practices that permitted curious crowds to trample the scene and destroy possible evidence.

Still, officers failed to suspect a stranger or see a link with the beatings, despite fervent attempts by Hollis and Larey to point out the similarities and their certainty that their attacker had now killed others, as they'd warned.

The Martin-Booker and the Griffin-Moore murders are tied together without any doubts whatsoever. Irrefutable ballistics evidence proved that the same gun, a .32 Colt automatic pistol with a distinctive left-handed twist, killed all four victims. The same death weapon; therefore, the same killer. There were other similarities, but no other physical evidence was needed. One killer had taken four lives.

The MO also was the same—defenseless couples parked in lovers' lanes. The same gun shot each one. There was the same pattern of two shots each, as in the Griffin-Moore case, to kill Paul Martin and Betty Jo Booker, with a slight exception. Martin was shot four times but in two-shot bursts, with an interval between. Although wielding an automatic weapon, the killer seemed addicted to shooting each target twice only.

Unlike the previous case, Paul Martin's and Betty Jo Booker's bodies were left some distance apart. No effort was made to conceal Martin's body—the mark of a disorganized offender—while Betty Jo Booker was killed in a clump of woods and her body not discovered for hours after Martin's was found. These facts pointed toward a mixed offender as an overall pattern.

Again, the perpetrator had left no witnesses, in the Spring Lake Park crimes selecting a much later time in an even more isolated atmosphere. In effect, the killer had *hours* in which to execute his plans at a more leisurely pace. Every bit paralleled the earlier case.

On top of all else, the ballistics evidence makes the connection airtight.

Tabloid-like headlines to the contrary, modern forensic psychology leads us now to believe that sex was not a primary motive in any of the crimes. The gunman could have done as he wished with any of the females. He had a gun. His bizarre behavior in February was not rape or attempted rape, but a novel way to inflict pain. Possibly there was an intention to rape Polly Ann Moore, but if so, it did not occur. As for rape of Betty Jo Booker, he had been in no hurry to do so, all the while with his female companion, Peggy, near, presumably making it more difficult. He had total control over Betty Jo before he killed her. There is no evidence of rape in any of the other cases.

One difference in Betty Jo Booker's death is that it came "up close and personal." She was not shot in the back of the head as the first two victims were. The killer faced her and shot her in the face and heart, after considerable time with her, taking her with him as he moved the cars. This suggests an attempt at a "relationship" with her. She was a respectable girl and probably was so in his eyes, but she resisted him. Recalling psychiatrist Luther White's insight, this would constitute rejection in his eyes. Even more important, she was an eyewitness to Paul Martin's murder. Feeling rejection and fear of discovery, he shot her, facing her, up close. This was the most personal shooting of all of the murders.

If any doubt remained of a stranger's role in the Starks case, it's dispelled by the fact that the killer had to be unaware that Starks had one of the few rural telephones in the community. Anyone who knew the Starkses would have known of their telephone. He didn't know them; assuredly they didn't know him. That is almost always the way serial killers operate, targeting victims they do not know, which makes them much more difficult to track.

Katie Starks had not seen the killer that night nor had any consistently definite ideas about him. After all, she had no way of knowing, which exacerbated her anxieties. She, like nearly everyone else, felt the killer had to be someone who knew her husband and her—that there had to be a recognized motive. It was a common, understandable concept. Killers almost always know their victims, and they have reasons, in their minds, to kill. It made no sense to her that a stranger would kill her husband and try to kill her. But with serial killers that's exactly what happens. A stranger had beaten Jim Hollis and Mary Jeanne Larey, had killed Polly Ann Moore, Richard Griffin, Betty Jo Booker, and Paul Martin. It's what serial killers do. They kill strangers, over and over.

When Katie entered the room, the killer made no attempt to do anything until she turned and went to the wall phone and started to use it. This caught him by surprise, indicating he was not aware of the phone; else he would have cut the line or would have shot her as she stood in horror before her husband's body, a much closer target than when she was at the phone. Seeing he hadn't killed her, he panicked, forgot the flashlight he'd set down while he braced his weapon, and dashed to the back of the house to force his way in. At that point he exhibited a touch of disorganization. When he got into the house and realized his quarry was no longer inside, he panicked again, and raced to his car to escape.

He shot Katie two times. The pattern in all the shootings, almost like a signature, was the firing in two-shot bursts in every instance beginning with the first double murders. It was as if the killer believed that two shots were all that were needed to ensure death. Every murder victim in the series was shot twice except Paul Martin. The same pattern continued at the Starks home.

If, as some believed, Virgil Starks was the target of someone he had angered, his killer would hardly have stopped at two shots. Nor would he have lingered outside till Katie entered the room. And if he knew Starks well enough to want to kill him, he would have known of the phone lines and cut them.

It has been tempting for many to discredit the single-villain argument simply because a different weapon was used in the Starks case and the locale had changed from a lovers' lane. These objections deserve consideration and shouldn't be dismissed out of hand. But a careful analysis tilts the argument in favor of the same gunman in all four incidents.

The MO at the Starks home—intruding at a home instead of a parked car, using a .22 automatic instead of a .32 automatic—does constitute a shift from the previous pattern in the Texas-side crimes, but the differences are superficial. The killer already knew lawmen were looking for his .32 automatic; any half-savvy criminal would know a change of weapons was necessary. By then, as officers patrolled nightly and set traps, the killer knew better than to scout out parked cars. He would have encountered officers on a stakeout or armed lovers just waiting to shoot anyone who showed up. Vulnerable couples were hard to find. As a further indication that the killer was an experienced criminal, he had broken into the Starks home with a speed and skill no novice was likely to match. Swinney had experience as a burglar. A lot of experience, dating back to childhood.

A belief in a copycat perpetrator enters into serial murders because many can't believe one person could kill so many. In the Starks case, this belief was supported by the slightly different MO. Instead of killing couples in lovers' lanes, the killer struck at a home using a different caliber gun, but still an automatic. There should be no surprise. Serial killers intentionally change their MO after a time to confound police and hope someone else will be blamed. But in the Starks case, other features remained consistent—the shooting pattern, an automatic weapon, and the hunting of vulnerable couples under cover of darkness.

The Starks killer arrived armed, prepared to kill, equipped with a flashlight as had the February attacker. A flashlight was part of his planning for those two crimes, if not for all of them.

Furthermore, the Starks case fits snugly within the three-week intervals of the Texas-side murders.

If the same hand committed all the crimes, whose hand was it?

Evidence in the Phantom case fulfills the FBI requirements for clearing the cases. There was a suspect—Swinney—and a variety of evidence in all the cases, but an arrest couldn't be made and the suspect prosecuted because he was dead and witnesses were dead. But statements implicating Swinney are extant, as well as physical and circumstantial evidence. The rules are not as strict as in a formal trial. The process is more like an inquest with a presentation of evidence zeroing in on the perpetrator.

"We have the evidence to prove this person, Youell Swinney, committed these crimes," Owen said. "When you close a case by exception, you're going to be able to lay it out and show that this guy was the killer."

Owen had worked out a profile of the killer based on evidence he knew, his crime-scene studies, and his personal experience.

Classifying the killer as a mixed offender—displaying mostly organized but some disorganized features—Owen linked all of the Texas-side crimes to the same MO: the same .32 Colt automatic, attacking couples in lovers' lanes. He connected Swinney through Peggy Swinney's signed statement given at DPS offices in Austin. He concluded that her minute details of the Spring Lake Park crime scene could not have been imagined. Nor were they known to the public or released to the press. She had to have been there to know exactly where the bodies were left, where the saxophone was thrown. Additionally, Bill Presley's finding Paul Martin's date book, and Peggy's description of where Swinney tossed it, definitely proved she was there.

A psychological profile of the Phantom killer fits Swinney.

An FBI report contained the medical assessment of his psychopathic personality, which coincides with observations of others.

"The Phantom killer was a sociopath," agreed Glenn Owen, "which means he didn't care about anybody but himself. He was just a cold-blooded killer, and he probably also suffered from other mental disorders.

"The organized offender usually comes from a family that is not broken. The father is usually a dominant figure, and the organized offender is usually skilled labor, or he may be educated. But the disorganized offender, in this day and time, usually comes from a broken family. May live with an aunt or an uncle or a grandmother. Was physically abused, whereas the organized offender who had a dominant father figure may have been mentally abused but not physically. He's average or below average in intelligence.

"With our suspect we're seeing that mix, a combination of both. You had a broken family. You had a dominant father figure. And then you get to the disorganized killer; they usually work low-paying jobs. They're not skilled laborers. They usually live with relatives. They usually do not have transportation. I think the reason the suspect in the Phantom killings was an organized offender, he showed that he had been *schooled* in prison, to know police tactics and to know what they were looking for, and that's why he was organized; but he was disorganized too."

Swinney telegraphed his anger with body art that was concealed most of the time by his shirts. He wore his feelings not on his sleeves but literally on his arm with tattoos: REVENGE, a heart, and MOTHER. It was symptomatic, if not intimately revealing, of Swinney's inner turmoil. The beatings and the murders all pointed toward acting out of vengeful emotions. (Told of the tattoos, Glenn Owen said, "That tells me that he may have had a real shady relationship with his mother and disliked her, and in his mind, that may have played a part in his revenge.")

Criminal profiling narrows a search to a type or pool of suspects. Though it may lead to the villain, it is used to identify, not convict. In Swinney's case it makes the argument that he was capable of the acts, which may become strongly suggestive.

While the highly complex process leading to the making of a serial killer may never be fully understood, Swinney fit the general profile of a serial killer. He was a career criminal. He came from a broken family at a critical age. Early trouble and contact with other problem youths engendered more law-breaking. "Trained" in prison by other felons, he learned his "trade." He was classified as a sociopath, suggesting his moral development was short-circuited early in life. But most sociopaths are not murderers. To kill and to kill repeatedly is a step beyond common killing. Swinney's record documented steps in that direction, beginning with burglary and robbery by assault. By 1946, Swinney's background contained the ingredients that would produce violence ahead.

There is a possibility—even probability—that Swinney was involved in some of the robberies in Texarkana from December 22, 1945, forward. He'd served time for robbery by assault. Some early 1946 robberies were by assault, some with a gun. According to Peggy, Swinney would leave her at the movies, be gone for a half-hour or hours. He would return with money. Where did he get it? Assuredly not from the Salvation Army, nor on the sidewalk where a negligent citizen had dropped it. More likely he robbed someone. Repeatedly he raised funds without working.

In the February beatings, Owen cited Swinney's conviction for robbery by assault and the same MO that would appear in the murders later on. The February assailant left witnesses, hadn't controlled the crime scene, the sign of a disorganized offender. But he had displayed organized behavior, arriving prepared with flashlight and gun. He subsequently improved his technique, as serial killers do, leaving only bodies.

"He was organized enough to keep himself out of the electric chair," said Owen.

Moving to the Starks case, Owen cited the boot or shoe impression as "roughly" the same as Swinney's and the shirt with the laundry mark STARK with slag metal in its pocket matching that found in Virgil Starks's shop. He explained the different MO as the killer's adjusting to a changed situation—finding victims in a house and using a different caliber gun at a time lovers' lanes were well populated—one might say clogged—with lawmen.

Swinney, released from prison in December 1945, returned to Texarkana shortly before the crimes began. The homicides ended following Swinney's arrest.

Owen compiled a strong case. Yet additional evidence, much of which he hadn't seen, dovetails with his to build the case even tighter. Owen had not seen material gained by Freedom of Information requests for this book nor interviews from many of the officers already dead.

The reader of this book already knows more of the evidence than, probably, any single investigator knew in 1946. The Arkansas State Police files, as one example, have produced statements not seen by Texas lawmen or by many Arkansans. Building upon Owen's case, a prosecutor or sheriff would be able to present convincing evidence—much of it circumstantial but damning—that Swinney committed all of the crimes.

Taken together, the preponderance of evidence weaves a web of guilt around Swinney that cannot be discounted. What stands out is that Swinney had no proven alibi for any of the incidents, the beatings or the three murder nights. Peggy never provided him cover for sensitive time periods and, in fact, could not document her own alibis. She went out of her way to ensure that Swinney had no solid alibi for the Starks incident, even telling officers he'd gone to Texarkana that night, thereby practically shouting that he had the opportunity to commit the crime.

An important matter generally overlooked in the February case locks Youell Swinney in. There is proof that Youell Swinney possessed a .32 automatic pistol at the time, according to witnesses, including Peggy Swinney. This is the same caliber that took the lives of four victims. It is not known to a certainty the caliber of the pistol brandished by the February bandit, but there is other evidence that Swinney attacked Hollis and Larey.

There apparently was a triggering event in February, involving Swinney, and it suggests revenge, not simple robbery, was a motive. Swinney's tattoo, REVENGE, would prove to be significant.

One statement reveals that Peggy, Swinney, and another man had an argument in a beer joint. The upshot was that the other man took Peggy away from Swinney, leaving Swinney humiliated and angry. Swinney had no transportation of his own but rarely went without a car. He could steal one in a matter of minutes and usually did when he needed a vehicle.

Dr. Shervert Frazier said the way the couples were killed indicated the killer was reacting criminally to a disturbed relationship. The beer-joint dispute could have been the event that set Swinney off on the series of attacks. Afraid to confront the competitor, he took out his anger on surrogates, although the REVENGE tattoo, already on Swinney's arm, suggests there were precursors to that triggering experience which reminded him of them.

The statements do not clearly establish that the dispute occurred *before* the beatings, but it can be argued that it did. This would account for the violence toward Hollis, who was left almost dead, and a special type of violence toward Hollis's teenaged companion.

In his statement, Swinney gives a different date—February 23—when the argument happened, and probably did so to deceive or confuse his captors. His interrogators seemed to believe February 23, not February 22, was the crucial date of the Hollis-Larey attack. His version went uncontested. But the incendiary spat left Swinney bested by the other man and lusting for revenge. Swinney did not risk confrontations unless he clearly had the upper hand. A man in the dark with a lethal weapon almost always has the upper hand.

That triggering event, it seems likely, led to the attack on Hollis and Larey and their close brush with death. Though the man—Swinney— sought money, his actions spell out a deadlier motive—revenge.

The beating of a man who made advances toward Peggy in Waynoka, Oklahoma, later in the year also ties in with the February attack. The burden of proof leans toward Peggy holding the gun on the man, at Swinney's order, while a jealous Swinney beat the man with a chain. An angry Swinney derived pleasure in the beating, just as did the enraged intruder back in February north of Texarkana. In both cases, the victims were at a distinct disadvantage, held defenseless by a person wielding a gun. In Waynoka, no surrogate was sought, but the technique was similar, and Swinney had the means at hand to enforce the punishment.

The Swinney couple bought beer at the café in the vicinity of the Griffin-Moore murders. If they'd done so that night, it would have been but a short drive or stroll to where the couple was parked. There is a possibility—no more than that—Peggy was with Swinney. By then she accompanied him almost everywhere, though not necessarily that night. Her alibi was unsupported for that time period, when she claimed to be in a motel. At best they were each other's alibi, likely to raise, rather than satisfy, suspicions. Officers did not probe beyond the surface when she gave her account of the weekend.

There is also the statement by a brother-in-law that Swinney appeared that morning in a highly nervous state and went to bed and pulled the sheets over his head and slept all day. This would fit the time and emotional state of the late-night killer in the March murders.

Three weeks later, the Spring Lake Park murders gave a clearer pattern of the series of crimes. The bullets matched those taken from Richard Griffin's body, thereby linking the two double murders. Again, the killer shot the male first. Once Swinney was apprehended that summer and Peggy gave her first statements, Swinney's guilt was established, from her eyewitness account. His .32 automatic had killed four persons.

Her statements are crucial to identifying Swinney as the culprit. She may have modified her position from one statement to the next, causing officers to believe she might be an unreliable witness, but her presence at the Spring Lake Park crime scene is undeniable. The overall picture didn't change. Two points firmly establish her presence.

As Owen said, her descriptions of the crime scenes coincided with the facts. She had to have been there. He also pointed out how she had described where Swinney had thrown Betty Jo Booker's saxophone, at a time when the precise facts were not known by the public.

Another fact, never released to the public, proved that she was there and strengthened her statement. Sheriff Presley asked her during a Spring Lake Park visit, Did Swinney take anything from Paul Martin and if so what did he do with it? Without hesitation she replied that Swinney took a small item—she wasn't sure what it was—which he tossed toward some bushes. Presley had found Martin's datebook exactly where she said Swinney threw it. The existence of the datebook was known only to Presley and a very few others on the Texas side. He'd presented the datebook for the first time—after she'd described where Swinney had thrown it. This linked her to the scene, as an eyewitness, more than anything else, strongly supporting her other memories.

The exact role, if any, she played in the teenagers' deaths may never be known. What is certain is that Swinney shot both of them with a .32 automatic pistol—the same one that killed the couple three weeks earlier—and that Peggy saw him shoot Paul Martin on two occasions in two-shot bursts, fatally wounding him the second time. Her accounts of Paul Martin's shooting remain consistent in all tellings, further supporting her version. Although she denied seeing Betty Jo Booker die, she reported hearing Swinney's gunshots.

The bullets that snuffed out the lives of Richard Griffin and Polly Ann Moore matched those in the Spring Lake Park murders, thus connecting all four murders. Peggy documented Swinney's actions at Spring Lake Park.

Other statements coincided as to time and place in support of her account. Tom Moores heard the gunshots that killed Betty Jo Booker at about the time Peggy reported. Ernest Browning saw the car that had to have been driven by Swinney in the early dawn but was unable to see the license number. Thus unrelated, objective witnesses backed her up on the time and place. Coupled with her description of the crime scene, she had to be believed. Additionally, Mark McClish's analysis of her statements supports her version.

Peggy told of Swinney's washing blood off of his clothes at the spring at the park. This indicated how he dealt with possibly incriminating evidence, which resurfaced in the Starks case. According to her, Swinney took care to leave no fingerprints, wearing a glove; he also instructed her not to touch surfaces where she might leave her prints. He fit the organized offender category in this respect. Yet he left Martin's body in plain view, though on a little-traveled dirt road or path. As an ex-convict, Swinney, as Owen pointed out, had learned police tactics from other criminals and knew what to do to avoid detection. The results showed a mixture of offender traits.

Even the discarding of the saxophone, which at first he'd considered pawning, showed his organized side dominating his impulse to profit from the crime. A pawned saxophone would have tied him to the murders. It didn't take him long to realize that and to dispose of the evidence. At that point his sense of self-survival had burst forth.

Peggy's statements fail to reveal an immediate triggering event for the two double murders in March and April. There need not have been one close to the crimes. His tattoo, REVENGE, documented an emotion long festering. If he was intent on killing surrogates to satisfy his deep-seated anger, he would not have required an unsettling experience on that particular night. Seeing couples apparently happy would have been enough to set him off. He would ensure that they suffered. It was as if they were flaunting their relationship, and it was all he needed to get even. It was a strange, but effective, means of revenge, with his innocent victims unarmed in the dark with his gun upon them.

Some of Swinney's short stories written in prison also touch upon shattered relationships and further support what Dr. Frazier concluded about the motivation of the gunman.

A mountain of evidence, everything but eyewitness testimony, points to Swinney's guilt in the Starks case.

The triggering event in the Starks case was Swinney's blowup with Peggy's sister on the afternoon of May 3, a few hours before Virgil Starks died. The Swinney couple, not yet married, left after a volatile argument over Swinney not paying for their board. (He also didn't pay his rent to Jim Mays, which led to his downfall.) Swinney was in a foul mood. Peggy stated that he left for Texarkana. He would have passed the Starks home.

She claimed to have been in the hotel at Delight while Swinney drove to Texarkana. She wasn't, nor was he. The couple operating the hotel remembered the two had arrived after midnight, several hours after the murder.

This indicated that they were together that night, but not where they claimed to be. She stated that Swinney had gone to Texarkana. She must have gone with him. From other evidence, they must have been at the Starks home, she waiting for him in the parked car. Cigarette butts near the parking space indicated that more than one person was there.

Though ownership of the flashlight left behind at the Starks home could not be traced, two pieces of evidence linked Swinney to the scene: the shirt with the laundry mark STARK and shoes found among Swinney's possessions.

The shirt would have fit Starks but not Swinney. Swinney was known to steal clothing. Contents of the shirt pocket matched materials found in Virgil Starks's shop. The laundry mark was close enough to STARKS to leave little doubt whose shirt it had been. Katie Starks's initial identification of the shirt as being Virgil's lent further credence to his having owned it, even though she subsequently said she wasn't sure. It was understandable that she decided she could not be absolutely certain that the shirt belonged to Virgil. A man's life hung upon her testimony. Upon reflection she cited the mending, which she at first had identified, was that which any wife would have done. Most of all, she realized her testimony could send a man to the electric chair. It was an awesome responsibility.

The shoes found among Swinney's possessions had been washed and put away wet, which distorted their size and shape. A reasonable explanation is that the shoes had made the tracks crossing the plowed field, sinking into the soft, wet soil. Going into the house, the shoes may also have picked up blood from the floor, either Virgil's or Katie's blood, or both. In either instance, a skilled criminal—which Swinney was—would recognize the need to remove any trace of evidence linking him to the scene. The obvious solution would be to wash any suspicious taint from the shoes. This could have been done in a stream between the death house and Delight, an area with a number of creeks, or at any other source of water.

Peggy's statements indicated how Swinney disposed of incriminating evidence. He washed blood off his clothing and shoes. His once-wet shoes, which might have been worn the night of the Starks case or on another attack night, fit into her observations. At the Starks farm it was virtually impossible to match a specific shoe or boot with the muddy impressions left. The killer's shoes, as a certainty, were muddy, possibly bloody, and needed to be washed off—as Swinney did his shoes.

A .22 caliber weapon killed Virgil Starks and critically wounded Katie. Many officers assumed it was a rifle because of the accuracy. The bullets were so battered that no conclusion could be drawn as to whether they had come from a pistol or a rifle. Today, improved ballistics science might establish which type of weapon fired the bullets.

A document not included in Owen's studies suggested that some officers considered the Starks murder weapon to be a .22 caliber automatic *pistol*, rather than rifle. In January 1949, Captain Gonzaullas wrote, referring to the Starks case, that the shootings were "committed with a .22 caliber Colt's Woodmaster Automatic pistol, or some foreign type of automatic of the same dimensions and characteristics." Max Tackett in a 1971 interview also believed the murder weapon was an automatic pistol. Testimony from Waynoka, Oklahoma, proved that Swinney had owned, and sold, a .22 pistol.

Witnesses, aside from Peggy, confirmed Swinney had owned a .22 automatic pistol, as well as a .32 automatic pistol. He had sold them in western Oklahoma following the murders. These fit the calibers of all the shootings.

Thus, he'd owned pistols like those in the murders, with the strong probability that they were the ones that took five lives.

In addition, at the Starks home the killer broke into the house like an experienced burglar, which Swinney was, having served reformatory time for burglary as a youth. In one of Peggy's statements about the Martin-Booker slayings she told of Swinney's taking a gate off its hinges, another sign of a skilled intruder. A novice would have taken more time to get into the Starks house, might have botched it.

Though the Starks case may have begun as an opportunity to steal from the shop, it also showed the work of an organized offender—most of the time. He went prepared, with gun and flashlight. The work shirt in Starks's shop would have caught his eye. When he saw the light through the window and Virgil Starks's head a few feet away, he'd found a tempting way to exact revenge—through a surrogate. He was armed, ready to kill, or he would not have taken a gun. It may be interpreted as a way to strike back at Peggy's sister and her husband, who had kicked Youell and Peggy out of the house. He took revenge at another house, belonging to strangers. Starks was shot twice in the back of the head, just as Richard Griffin had been. The killer knew the surest way to deliver death.

The Starks case was linked, then, by physical evidence to Swinney—the once-wet, dried-out shoes, the stolen shirt—and circumstances: witnesses that Swinney went to Texarkana that night, passing the crime scene, that he owned a pistol matching the death weapon, the two-shot bursts, and that he had no alibi to account for his presence anywhere else. The couple at the Delight hotel shredded his claimed alibi, and Peggy's along with his.

Most telling was his heated argument with Peggy's sister over money owed her for their board. Many serial killings are preceded by a triggering event. Swinney's encounter that Friday afternoon was a trigger that stirred his anger and led to Virgil Starks's murder—a twisted form of revenge that led to the shooting of surrogates.

The flashlight abandoned at the Starks home also is a reminder that the February attacker carried a flashlight, possibly the same one. It is not known if Swinney used a flashlight in the Texas double murders.

Of particular interest, outside the evidence of the beatings and the murders themselves, is the incident in the Texas prison in which Swinney was caught in a sexual act with another male inmate. Though one female murder victim was raped, sex was not the main motive. The prison encounter may have been strictly a homosexual act, which might explain the relative absence of rape in the killings, or more likely it may have been an expression of violent dominance with sex a secondary meaning. Swinney's relatives believed, based on his post-release behavior with a young boy in Marshall and Dallas, Texas, that he was homosexual or at least bisexual. Whether they believed it earlier in his life is uncertain. He cohabited with a woman in Texarkana in the 1930s or 1940s—before Peggy—and was said to be "married" to her. A search of Miller County marriage licenses failed to turn up one with his name on it; apparently the earlier liaison had no legal basis. His later marriage to Peggy in Shreveport, of course, is solidly documented.

Added to this is the belief held by some in Marshall during Swinney's brief sojourn in the free world—and noted in a FBI report—that he was homosexual and kept a young boy. Even so, he may not have been an actual homosexual but was merely exerting dominance over another, weaker individual as he once did with Peggy, and this time the person he felt he could manipulate and control at the right level was a boy. Chances are, sexuality wasn't a factor. He got his kicks through violence, especially killing, and control.

My own encounter with Swinney, briefly by telephone, revealed a pattern of evasion, not uncommon for an ex-convict. He never said he hadn't killed anyone. Instead, he said he "wadn't even here then," something that was not true at all. He concentrated, with officers as well, on unsubstantiated alibis rather than proving he didn't kill. He also didn't claim he was illegally convicted for the charge of automobile theft. Instead he sought to profit from writing a book about being unjustly imprisoned as the Phantom. The case was crucial to his story. He hadn't been charged with those crimes. Jurors in 1947 hadn't known of any connection. By thrusting himself forward as a victim, with the Phantom highlighted, he would link his name forever to the notorious deeds without suffering the consequences. He was indulging in fantasy, with a grandiose view of himself. Swinney seemed to yearn for recognition by associating his name with the crime wave, perhaps even reaching the status of Jesse James, glamorized by Hollywood and a hero to Swinney.

If Swinney believed he'd been falsely imprisoned, more logically he would have filed a lawsuit against the State of Texas and Bowie County. He never took that approach. It seems not to have entered his mind. He would have had great difficulty sustaining his contention, or finding a lawyer to handle it. He no doubt recognized its futility.

Swinney came close to identifying himself as the Phantom years before he dubbed himself as The Man They Said Was the Phantom. Jones Floyd, a U.S. marshal who later served as sheriff, then county judge, of Howard County, Arkansas, told newspaperman Louis Graves that Swinney sent word back to Texarkana that he was ready to admit he'd done the murders, then changed his mind. Like other lawmen, Floyd was convinced that the convict Swinney was the serial killer.

Graves's report of Jones's comments is hearsay, of course, but meshes with other, stronger evidence. At Swinney's arrest, he came close to admitting his guilt when he blurted out, "Do you think they'll give me the chair for this?" As a psychiatrist had noted, sociopaths exhibit no sign of anxiety except when apprehended, and then they become very anxious. This described Swinney to a T. Once he realized his captors didn't know what he knew, he regained his composure and refused to cooperate or further incriminate himself.

Mark Bledsoe, a Texarkana probation officer who maintained a keen interest in the case in the 1990s, acquired material revealing that Swinney had boasted of his exploits to others. Bledsoe talked with men who had interviewed Swinney's cellmates over the years.

"He gave the cellmates vivid tales of what had gone on," Bledsoe told the *Texarkana Gazette* in 1996. "But when the Rangers went to interview him, he would not [confess]. There were those that had been his cellmates that had the same stories and details that were not in the newspapers. I think he felt like he was bulletproof, he was omnipotent. No one was going to get him."

Bledsoe also interviewed Swinney in 1992 in a Dallas nursing home, videotaping the session in hopes of gaining a confession. Results were disappointing. By then, Swinney had suffered a stroke and he revealed little. Swinney grew angry when Bledsoe asked about the murders, claiming, "I got off for that and I was cleared." Yet he had not been tried or found not guilty of murder and was never "cleared."

Why would Swinney even consider admitting to such high-profile murders? A probability is that he was proud of his "accomplishments" and wanted recognition for his "brilliance." An impulsive gesture would have soon paled upon realizing the consequences. No judge or jury would have been impressed by his dubious claim to fame. At an earlier time, resigned to his life sentence, he may have reasoned that so long as he could negotiate himself out of the electric chair, he wouldn't be any worse off, while gaining recognition as the Phantom. The moniker, Phantom, was an appealing label. It gave him status.

Despite the passage of decades, key physical evidence may still exist. The .32 automatic that killed four persons and the .22 automatic that killed Virgil Starks could be in the possession of innocent individuals who have no inkling of their importance, especially if the guns were handed down from an older person—who also would have no knowledge of the events. Unless either gun was tossed into a lake or river, it probably was sold or traded or given to someone unaware of its history. A surviving relative or friend of the man who bought or traded for one of the guns might still own it.

The pistols that Swinney sold at Waynoka, Oklahoma, would be of crucial importance. A person turning one in to authorities would render a major public service. Do the guns exist? Possibly. So far away from 1946, the most likely vehicle for attracting the present owners' attention would be through detailed exposure on television. It's a long shot, but might be productive. (It could also result in thousands of candidate guns being proposed.)

If the victims were innocent surrogates, who were the original targets they represented? There are several possibilities, which may merge or supplant each other at different times. Swinney complained of a stepfather's mistreatment of him. From other sources we learn his real father, the minister, also treated him shabbily, at least on occasion. At best their behavior toward each other may be described as uneasy. He probably was also dissatisfied with his mother's role in selecting another husband who was unkind to him. His anger grew as he stewed over perceived slights.

We know at least two events that precipitated his anger—the hot dispute in February over Peggy, a deeply personal relationship issue, and the argument with Peggy's sister on May 3. Max Tackett reasoned that Swinney, in search of Peggy and his rival in February, had headed to the vicinity of Peggy's parents' residence, relatively near the attack site, believing they had gone there. En route—continued Tackett's scenario—Swinney discovered the parked car, believing he'd caught up with the couple. When he learned he'd made a mistake, instead of backing off he intensified his punishment of the substitute man and woman. If he did wear a mask, as his female victim insisted, it would make sense, to conceal his identity from those whom he at first thought he was attacking.

Flawed relationships frequently shaped his life. Yet a normal person would not have chosen such a bizarre and deadly way to strike back. One may take out spite on the proverbial innocent bystander, but not in such a violent manner. Even though violent language may occur, murder does not become a key to the solution. But for whatever reason, Swinney was not normal. He probably at birth, or early in life, suffered "an accident of genetics," as Professor Paul Bloom put it. He seems not to have developed a normal conscience. He was classified as a sociopath. He had behind him decades of criminal pursuits and incarcerations, and seemingly never learned from his mistakes, repeatedly offending for more than fifty years. He was a troubled youth, breaking the law at twelve, in a broken family. He reacted differently than did his siblings to these events. Over the years a great rage had built up. Prison time only added to his resentments, especially after his state terms, beginning in a harsh Arkansas system. Sometime in that period he had ordered his tattoos, indicating he'd reached a boiling point, that his deep anger was a pre-existing condition just waiting to explode. Especially the tattoo REVENGE, as documented in prison records, established his frame of mind long before the attacks, suggesting the idea had festered in his psyche over time. He had failed repeatedly. As he entered his late twenties, he must have envisioned his situation as desperate, the state Jim Hollis had ascribed to his assailant. The behavior of 1946 was a way to lash out, to get even.

Although it is not evidence, it is interesting that, according to several reports, both Swinney relatives and Peggy's family believed that he had committed the murders. Their beliefs were based on a variety of observations and behavior. Some of them had offered testimony that backed up their opinions.

Swinney himself may not have been fully aware of his motivation, even as he regularly reviewed his perceived hurts and grudges in the security of his mind. Many "normal" people do the same in their minds. But acting on those thoughts, as he did, constitutes the crime—and disturbs society and endangers its citizens.

The totality of evidence—physical, eyewitness, circumstantial, and psychological—linking Swinney as the perpetrator in all of the crimes is voluminous. Taken as a whole, it zeroes in on him and no one else as the offender. Although Peggy Swinney, Max Tackett, Bill Presley, Lone Wolf Gonzaullas, Elvie Davis, Tillman Johnson, and Katie Starks were all dead by the time this analysis was conducted, the compelling web of evidence left behind fills out a wealth of incrimination: Peggy's signed statement while connected to a polygraph; .32 caliber bullets from the first two double murders; .22 caliber bullets from the Starks case; statements from a number of persons regarding Swinney's itinerary and behavior in Arkansas and Oklahoma; and FBI reports, one of which assessed him as a sociopathic personality, plus his prison behavior and lengthy records of felonies.

In essence, the story of Youell Swinney is one of an abnormal break at birth or in the first few years thereafter and his responses to the world around him, eventually touching the lives, negatively, of almost all those with whom he came into contact. He probably didn't think of it in the way normal persons would have, ensuring tragedy for everyone, himself included.

One of the most intriguing ideas is that of his emotional environment during his childhood and youth. Assuming he somehow suffered a "genetic accident" that contributed to an abnormal mind, would he have turned to violence even if he had had a stable, supportive family experience as he grew up? If the answer is No, untold tragedies might have been prevented and lives saved. While too late for this American tragedy, it is a question worth considering in future mental-health studies, arguing for intervention. Yet even if his was a case of "bad seed" entirely, that is, being sociopathic, that abnormality alone doesn't lead to repeated murders. Sociopaths are vastly more numerous than sociopathic killers, indicating much more is at work in serial killers' minds, probably tracing back to life experiences making a difference.

Glenn Owen's plan to clear the case by exception, following FBI guidelines, would accomplish what hadn't happened in 1946 and has been elusive since then. It would provide a public service rare enough in so many serial killings: stamp CLOSED on the case, laying out for the first time all of the evidence attesting to Swinney's guilt, and offering some modicum of closure to the victims' extended families.

The approach could be used in both Texas and Arkansas, as well as in Oklahoma for the lesser felonies committed there.

EPILOGUE

Time transformed Texarkana, sending all the major players of 1946 to their graves.

Youell Lee Swinney died in a Dallas nursing home in 1994 at age seventy-seven. His wife Peggy, as noted, divorced him and remarried. She died, also in Dallas, in 1998 at seventy-two.

Ultimately Swinney received the notoriety he craved, in this book. He wanted credit without the consequences. His guilt is nailed down, with him beyond the reach of the law—but the small comfort is that he is unable to enjoy the "credit" that comes with being revealed as the Phantom. Conversely, relatives and friends of his victims are more likely to benefit from the enlightenment.

All of the lawmen and prosecutors died over the years, long before Tillman Johnson finally passed away in 2008, at age ninety-seven. Max Tackett left the state police in 1948 to become Texarkana, Arkansas, police chief; in 1951 he became president of the Arkansas Peace Officers Association. Tillman Johnson left the sheriff's office where he had served as chief deputy and accepted a job as an insurance claims adjuster until he retired. As he was leaving the sheriff's office in October 1957, he conveyed to Max Tackett, by then police chief, a pasteboard box containing a cast of the shoeprint he'd found in the field next to the Starks home, along with a piece of linoleum from the house with a shoeprint on it, and the flashlight. He thought having the box in Tackett's hands was the best way to safeguard it. They'd also found .22 cartridge hulls at the murder site.

Tackett retired as police chief in 1968 and died in 1972, only fifty-nine years old, remembered in his obituary as "a colorful, outspoken, and sometimes controversial figure." Johnson never found out what happened to the evidence, now long vanished.

Johnson wrestled with the Phantom mystery for the rest of his long life. Deep into his nineties, still agile of mind, he reflected on clues, records, interrogations, and memories, always searching for new insights and fresh ideas.

Even in sleep the case haunted him, invading that most intimate zone of dreams, rendering detailed, vivid, unambiguous scenes. It was as if his unconscious mind was determined to highlight signals overlooked in his waking hours.

For years he'd believed the Starks case was unrelated to the Texas crimes. As he examined material he'd not seen before, much of it from official files acquired through Freedom of Information requests for this book, he revised his opinions. He concluded, as his friend Max Tackett had years before, that Swinney had killed all five victims and had shot Katie Starks, and that Peggy had accompanied him.

Both sheriffs—Elvie Davis and Bill Presley—were gone by the end of the 1970s. Davis was defeated for reelection as Miller County sheriff in the 1950s. Presley did not seek reelection in Bowie County when his second term ended in 1948. He characterized his four years as sheriff as the worst time of his life, which included Army service in France during World War I. "I haven't averaged six hours sleep per day—or night—since I became sheriff, and financially I figure I'm about where I was four years ago." Out of office, he sold cars for the local Ford agency until the political bug bit him again and he served three four-year terms as Bowie County treasurer. He died in 1972 at seventy-seven.

Captain M. T. "Lone Wolf" Gonzaullas retired from the Texas Rangers in 1951 after thirty years' service, consulted for a Hollywood studio filming movies about the West, later helped dedicate the Texas Rangers Hall of Fame and Museum in Waco. He died in Dallas of cancer in 1977 at eighty-four. He never wrote the memoirs he had in mind. Eighteen days before he died, he gave his last interview, for an oral history project for the Texas Rangers museum. Several of his comments seemed in conflict with previous statements and the facts. He said the killer knew the murdered couples and they knew him—clearly not true. Just as surprising, he claimed the Rangers got no credit for their work, that newspapers "never said anything in any paper from all over the United States." On the contrary, the Rangers—and Gonzaullas—were front and center in almost every article. The most likely explanation is that the cancer and its treatment led to his confusion and impaired memory.

Newsmen who covered the story locally joined the parade of death. Editor J. Q. Mahaffey retired from the *Gazette* in the 1960s, worked in public relations for the Model Cities program before retiring again. He lived to ninety-two. Calvin Sutton, the *Gazette* city editor who labeled the Phantom, subsequently joined the staff of the Fort Worth *Star Telegram*, where he retired as executive editor, after which he ran a smaller newspaper in Arkansas, where he died of a massive stroke. Louis "Swampy" Graves, who'd served as sports editor and the *Gazette*'s greeter for out-of-town news people, a few years later went into the printing business, then bought a country newspaper in Nashville, Arkansas, which he and his family ran till his death. Others who'd covered the big story—Bob Mundella, Ernest Valachovic, Lucille Holland, Sally Reese—died over the years. Charles B. Pierce, who had focused attention anew on the case with his movie, *The Town That Dreaded Sundown*, died in 2010. He was seventy-one. (Occasionally the film showed, late at night, on Turner Classic Movies, as it did twice in 2012. A MGM-funded remake of the movie was completed in 2013.)

The judges and prosecutors in both counties were gone. Stuart Nunn, who'd presided over Swinney's evidentiary hearing, died of cancer. Lynn Cooksey, who as D.A. had opposed Swinney's release, died in 2008. His adversary in the hearing, Jack Carter, the sole survivor, became a district judge, later gaining a seat on the appellate bench; he retired in 2013.

Bessie Booker Brown mourned her young daughter till her own death in 1977. She lived among her memories, hoping justice would be served in the murder of Betty Jo, who would always be, in her mind, fifteen years old with a promising life before her. Paul Martin's mother and brothers died not knowing who had wantonly taken his life at sixteen, on the cusp of adulthood.

Mary Jeanne Larey remarried and led a rewarding life cut short by cancer in Montana at age thirty-eight in 1965. James Hollis, her date that night, remarried after his own divorce, siring a set of twins before his second marriage ended, and finally settling down in a subsequent marriage with a family of four. As a Civil Service employee, he traveled far and wide and served a stint with NASA in its early days. He died in 1975 in Oklahoma, where he'd travelled for his older brother's funeral. He was fifty-four.

Lizzie Moore, Polly Ann's mother, died in 1958. Polly's brother, Mark Moore, survived them both and in retirement lived in northeastern Texas. Of Richard Griffin's brothers and sisters, only David Griffin in his nineties remained at this writing.

Richard Griffin's niece, Andrea Anderson, who never knew him, probably spoke for other victims' families, though they never knew her, when she said, "It has always been like there was a hole in the family where Uncle Richard should have been." The same large hole existed in other families as well.

Katie Strickland Starks, like other surviving victims and relatives, never fully recovered emotionally from her night of terror and near-death. As soon as she was physically able, she attended business school and lived with a sister and brother-in-law for ten years, working as a secretary. In 1955 she remarried, to Forrest Miller Sutton, who worked for a milk company. She carried on a normal life, except for those fearful moments that haunted her for the rest of her life. A noise at night would wake her; she would ask her husband to investigate. He would go outside, usually find nothing, and temporarily soothe her imagination.

Katie Sutton died on July 3, 1994, at age eighty-four—a few months before Youell Swinney died—and was buried in the family plot at Hillcrest Memorial Park beside Virgil. A gravesite on her other side was reserved for her second husband, Forrest, who died in 2009 and was buried there.

Hillcrest Cemetery, on the Texas side, became the final resting place for several of the Phantom victims, including Paul Martin, Virgil and Katie Starks, as well as any number of prominent figures of the time such as

William Rhoads Grim, Judge Stuart Nunn, Congressman Wright Patman, publisher Clyde E. Palmer, editor J. Q. Mahaffey, their graves all situated a short stroll from each other.

As if to replace notables who had faded into yesteryear, the city continued to export noteworthy natives to achieve fame elsewhere. H. Ross Perot, billionaire founder of Electronic Data Systems and a 1992 third party candidate for President, made Dallas his headquarters. Arthur Temple, Jr., with Temple-Inland, became a major business influence. Golfers following Byron Nelson included Miller Barber and Rick Rogers, joining football sensation Billy Sims (from Hooks) and other athletes to lead a crowded parade of those starring in different sports. Others gained recognition belatedly: Scott Joplin for his ragtime compositions (his opera *Treemonisha*, which won a posthumous Pulitzer Prize, was set near Texarkana) and player piano composer Conlon Nancarrow, who did most of his work in Mexico City.

As Texarkana changed over time, quirks of its bi-state status lingered.

Today a water tower on Interstate 30, which slices through the north side, emphasizes both oneness and twinness: Texarkana—Twice as Nice. The slogan didn't exist in 1946. Neither did the Interstate. The city limits, which didn't reach nearly so far, expanded to include Spring Lake Park. A bank sits near where Betty Jo Booker's saxophone was recovered. Popular Bryce's Cafeteria, like other businesses, relocated alongside the Interstate.

Downtown, the massive federal courthouse and post office, astride the only bi-state road in the U.S., remained a dominant fixture. It reportedly is the second most photographed courthouse in the nation after the U.S. Supreme Court. In 1960, Democratic nominee John F. Kennedy drew an estimated 100,000 for his speech there. A plaque now commemorates the event. The iconic Confederate soldier still stares south.

Old landmarks underwent a variety of fates. A decrepit, empty Grim Hotel, a shell of its former glory, lies like a scar, awaiting restoration or other final disposition. Once-bustling Union Station became another shell. The Amtrak station nearby operated from a small office. The old Paramount Theater, refurbished, became the Perot Theater. It no longer screens movies but is the venue for musical and dramatic performances.

For years, the twin cities shared Texas ZIP codes—75501 and 75502. Arkansas-side Mayor Londell Williams, the first—and, so far, only—African-American mayor of either city, lobbied his city to its own, Arkansas ZIP code—71854. State Line Avenue also divides the area codes—903 for Texas; 870, Arkansas. For years Jim and Linda Larey operated a printing shop on the Arkansas side of State Line. Its telephone area code was 870; its fax code, in the same room, 903 as if in Texas. Explanation: they had once been across the street; when they moved, the phone company let them keep the fax area code. In the town where Willie Vinson was brutally lynched, interracial couples occasionally could be seen, setting off no incidents, raising no eyebrows.

The tricky boundary continued to bewilder unwary visitors. The Texas Liquor Store sported a billboard in 2010 advertising Lone Star beer, brewed in San Antonio.

ONE MORE

REASON TO NEVER

LEAVE TEXAS

To read the sign, you had to drive north, meaning you'd already left Texas. Both the Texas Liquor Store and its billboard were in Arkansas.

Decades after the murders, incidents continued to open old wounds and raise questions. In 1999 an anonymous woman called the home of Paul Martin's brother, R. S. Martin, Jr., and talked to his wife Margaret. The caller wanted to apologize for her father. "I never understood why my daddy shot Paul." Efforts to trace the call failed. In light of facts of the case, it hardly seemed credible even as a "confession by proxy," adding stress rather than closure to survivors.

The case, resisting oblivion, attracted international attention. Inquiries came from as far off as Sweden and the United Kingdom and all over the U.S. One day a couple from North Carolina appeared on Tillman Johnson's porch, the man eager to have his picture taken with the old lawman. In 2003 a camera crew from Italy showed up, unheralded, to film Johnson's version of the crimes.

Everyone wanted to solve the case. In 1977, students from Drury College in Springfield, Missouri arrived in Texarkana, accompanied by their sponsor, Dr. Jay Bynum, intent on cracking the, by then, thirty-year-old mystery. As the *Texarkana Gazette* reported, the students "were bathed directly in the pool of icy fear immersing the case." Dr. Bynum explained: "We found out the motel we were staying in was just a hundred yards or so from where Paul Martin's body was found. The girls were fairly frightened by it, and they even put a chair under the doorknob." They spent a week in Texarkana researching the case.

On the Internet, Wikipedia expanded its entry. Websites such as crimelibrary.com, angelfire.com, TruTV.com/library/crime/serial, and thedarwinexception conveyed their reports. A few foreign entities joined in—Thai, Russian, Greek, and Italian. A rapper, Nas, mentioned "stabbin' bitches like the Phantom," although the Phantom stabbed nobody and no victim was a "bitch."

In 2010 a play, "Phantom Killer" by Jan Buttram, opened off Broadway in New York's Abington Theatre. The same year Jane Roberts Wood's novel, *Out the Summerhill Road*, turned a fragment into fiction. Casey Roberts and his students at Texas A&M University at Texarkana worked on a projected film about the case. A musician in northeast Arkansas performed under the name Youell Swinney, as if to assume a cloak of dark fame, transforming multiple tragedies of innocent persons, mostly teenagers, into a celebration of a multi-fall convict.

Sometime over the years, decades afterward, far from Texarkana, someone labeled the crimes the "Moonlight Murders," alliterative and slick but inaccurate, pure imagination. Certainly the Hollis-Larey and Griffin-Moore attacks occurred in the dark. There was some waning moonlight in the Martin-Booker case, and the moon was setting during the Starks shootings. The killer operated in the dark. Any moonlight was purely coincidental and slight, never a factor in the killer's motivation.

The murders put the town on the map, in a negative way. In 2007 a national tour featured it among sixteen locales that had sustained senseless violence, such as Chicago's St. Valentine Day massacre. At Texarkana, a musician played John Lennon's peace anthem, "Imagine," on the piano on which the Beatle composed it. Afterward the film crew pushed on to Dallas, where President Kennedy was assassinated.

As its signature crime the case seemed woven indelibly into Texarkana's cultural fabric. *The Town That Dreaded Sundown* came to be shown annually in Spring Lake Park, sponsored by the City of Texarkana, Texas. A country club held a Phantom Ball. The chamber of commerce once included the Phantom legacy in its brochure. More recently it gave out DVDs of the movie. In 2013 a Hollywood remake of the movie, backed by MGM, headed to theaters.

Criminologist Jack Levin has observed that residents of a small town in which a high-profile murder occurred often feel stigmatized. This seems not to have happened in Texarkana, except at the time of the murders. The city has almost wallowed in the notoriety, as well as expressing a certain local pride in the fictionalized movie filmed on location there.

The murders represent a case history of domestic terrorism as threatening as any other. Domestic terrorists have abounded over the 20th century, creating a long line of serial killers—the Green River killer, Zodiac, the D.C. sniper, Son of Sam, B.T.K., the Boston Strangler, all named by the media—and mass murderers like Timothy McVeigh, with his Oklahoma City federal building bombing. The Long Island Serial killer has started the 21st century, and still remains at large, as do the tragic legacies left behind by other mass murders, including the Columbine shooters, Eric Harris and Dylan Klebold, Jared Loughner of Arizona, and Adam Lanza of Sandy Hook. Arguably, domestic terrorists like these have, collectively, inflicted more carnage upon the U.S. than did the foreign terrorism of September 11, 2001, in New York City and Washington. The incidents, because they stretch over decades, lack the dramatic impact of killing thousands on a single day, but the overall toll rapidly mounts in any full accounting. For the victims, their families and friends, the emotional shock and the rampant fear are as great as that of any other tragedy.

Psychiatrist Helen Morrison wrote that the victims of serial killers, whose deaths all too often go unsolved, are numerous enough to populate a small town. Somewhere, she suggested, they deserve a memorial in recognition of what they and their families have suffered. Texarkana would be as good a site as any.

END

SOURCE NOTES

Details of weather, moon and sun data, and temperatures came from U.S. Geological Survey data, newspaper weather reports, and Farmers Almanac for 1946 in online archives. When data were not available for Texarkana, the author used that for nearby Shreveport, Louisiana. The Texarkana City Directories and 1946 telephone book provided other information. In addition to interviews and archival material, the *Texarkana Gazette* and *Daily News* were among the major sources for the events and, especially, headlines. MeasuringWorth.com was consulted when translating 1946 dollars into present-day values. Comparisons, of course, are approximate.

THE TOWN

Early Texarkana history: "that lively railroad village," Leet, *Texarkana, A Pictorial History*, p. 33. "Texarkana is the gateway." quoted in Leet, p. 38. Paragon Saloon tragedy, pp. 33-34.; "great majority . . . gamblers, gunmen," *Images of Texarkana*, p. 6. The city's 88 saloons: *Texarkana Gazette*, Sept. 26, 1948. The crimes described were reported in the *Texarkana Gazette* of relevant dates. Tillman Johnson's files and memory covered the O'Dwyer and Hasselberg murders. "As a puzzle": Kent Biffle to Mark Moore, July 7, 2008; "most notorious and intriguing": Deborah Bauman (Segment Producer for The Ultimate 10) to Jerry Atkins, Aug. 14, 2000.

CHAPTER 1
STRANGER IN THE DARK

Events of late 1945, including the Fulton shootout, and early 1946 came from articles in the *Texarkana Gazette*. The author personally viewed the movie, *Three Strangers*, on Turner Classic Movies. The night of the attack is based primarily on an unpublished manuscript, "The Texarkana Phantom Killer" by James M. Hollis, an eyewitness first-hand account in which he recalled his exact thoughts from the beginning of the ordeal, a copy of which is in the possession of the author. His memoir was supplemented by contemporary *Gazette* and *Daily News* accounts, including an interview of Mrs. Larey published in May 1946 in the *Gazette*. James Hollis's background came from a variety of family sources: an ex-sister-in-law from his second marriage Mary Ann Williamson, a niece Diana Burris, his widow of his last marriage Peggy Francisco, as well as marriage and divorce records in Union County, Ark., along with census records. Mary Jeanne Larey's background came from census records, marriage and divorce records, and relative interviews.

CHAPTER 2
CONFLICTING PERCEPTIONS

Billie Presley Edgington provided many details about her father, Bill Presley. His brother, J. A. "Alex" Presley, recalled the Red Springs community in which they grew up. Other material came from a *Gazette* feature as the sheriff was leaving office in 1948. Hollis recalled his hospital experiences in his unpublished memoir. That article and newspaper reports of the *Texarkana Daily News* and *Gazette* combined to fill out his post-hospital period. The *Gazette* reported the Hooks house fire, as well as the two-car crash on Highway 67 around that time. Mary Ann Williamson told of the gunshots startling Hollis. The *Gazette* reported on the returning servicemen, crimes, and social events, as well as the arrival of baby chicks at the post office.

CHAPTER 3
DOUBLE DEATH IN A CAR

Richard Griffin's background is based on interviews with his brothers, Welborn Griffin and David Griffin. Polly Ann Moore's information is based on interviews with her brother, Mark Moore.

CHAPTER 4
A BAFFLING CASE

Mark Moore and Patti Bishop provided details of the tragic day Polly's body was found. *Texarkana Gazette* stories contained some details of the couple's activities. The *Gazette* reported accidents at the Canary Cottage. Most of the accounts of individuals mentioned came through interviews with those persons; for instance, Byron Brower, Jr., Mark Moore, Patti Richardson Bishop, Ray Rounsavall, Sandy Burnett (then Sandy King), David Griffin, and Welborn Griffin. A physician's report that she was not "criminally assaulted" appeared in the *Texarkana Gazette*, supported by Max Tackett's interview that there was no rape. Verdicts were written in death certificates of each victim. In addition to accounts at the time, Texas DPS records provided details of the murder weapon, to which Max Tackett and Bill Presley also contributed. The filing label for the bullets is specified in numerous DPS letters then and subsequently, as in Fred R. Rymer, firearms examiner, to W. H. Presley, Aug. 12, 1948. The finding of the Spanish-made revolver three years later was reported in the *Texarkana Gazette*, Oct. 17, 18, 19, 1949, confirmed by telephone interview with Marie Barlow Tammen. Mrs. Larey's trip to Texarkana was told in a May 1946 *Gazette* interview.

CHAPTER 5
A BOY, A GIRL—AND A GUNMAN

Sue McCrossen told of Girl Scout hikes; Bill Horner, of park water beliefs. The *Gazette* reported the stolen car of April 11. Tillman Johnson explained how to hot-wire a car. Jerry Atkins and Bill Manning described the band and the atmosphere at the time. Mrs. Grace Guier contributed details of Betty Jo Booker's life. Tillman Johnson supplied insight on the background and death of Betty Jo's father. Bessie Booker Brown's taped interview with Georgia Daily provided additional details, as did Bob

Mundella's interview with Mrs. Brown. Paul Martin's background came from his sister-in-law, Margaret Martin, Herbert Wren, Thomas Torrans, Bob Matthews, and Tom Albritton, as well as newspaper accounts. His correct age, repeatedly reported as seventeen, was established as sixteen on his death certificate, information given by his mother. Sophie Anne White Redditt told of the afternoon swim and the evening's band performance; Jerry Atkins also contributed. Bessie Brown's taped interview described Paul Martin's visit. Jim Morriss explained the little-known cancelled date. Both Tom Albritton and Ramona Putman Ruggles gave versions of the Saturday night that went awry. Charlsie Schoeppey Boyd remembered her fellow students dancing in Spring Lake Park.

CHAPTER 6
PALM SUNDAY HORRORS

The ordeal at the Brown home came from Bessie Brown's interview by Georgia Daily. Janann Gleason verified that the slumber party, which Betty Jo failed to attend, was at her home. What Tom Moores heard was reported in the *Gazette* and confirmed by his son, Richard Moores. Ernest Browning's and the Weavers' reports were in the *Gazette*. The *Gazette* provided details of the death scene for Paul Martin. Bill Presley told the author of the unpublished report of the evidence he recovered nearby, of Martin's date book, which no one else knew of. Jerry Atkins's memories were shared in an interview with him and his own unpublished account of that weekend. The site where Martin's car was found was toured with Bill Horner, who visited it the day of the murders. Tom Albritton and Herbert Wren told of the Sunday morning receipt of the bad news. Charlsie Schoeppey Boyd told of the discovery of Betty Jo Booker's body by the search party. There also was an account in the *Gazette* in 1996. Jim Morriss recalled the morning and his reactions.

CHAPTER 7
RISING TERROR

The death certificates provided the coroner's comments. The author examined the DPS report regarding the condition of Betty Jo Booker's body. The FBI memo of April 20, 1946, reported findings of semen, noting it was not known if Polly Ann Moore was raped. A copy of the Ernest Browning report by the Texas Rangers came from Tillman Johnson's papers. Other details came from newspaper articles and from the Texarkana City Directory and 1946 telephone book. Grace Guier told of her husband Nathan Guier's plans to photograph Betty Jo upon his return from New York. Sue Phillips MaGouirk told of the woman holding up the child at Betty Jo's funeral. J. Q. Mahaffey explained how the brand, Phantom, came about. Texarkana newspaper ads documented the familiar use of the term Phantom at the time, in the movies, the comics, and wrestling.

CHAPTER 8
A LEGENDARY RANGER

Captain Gonzaullas's biographers published background and a variety of details, as did a number of newspapers and magazines. A major source was Brownson Malsch, *Captain M. T. Gonzaullas: Lone Wolf, The Only Texas Ranger Captain of Spanish Descent* (Austin, Texas: Shoal Creek Publishers, 1980), especially pp. xiii-xvi, 1-2 ff., 159-168, 206-209. Chapter XV (159-168) deals with the Texarkana murders. Mike Cox's *Texas Ranger Tales* features the Texarkana case in a chapter, "Lone Wolf Versus the Phantom," pp. 246-265. Several oral histories from the Texas Rangers Hall of Fame E-Book Project added details, especially those of Gonzaullas himself and Lewis Rigler. The author also spoke with Gonzaullas by telephone in 1976 during research for another book but in no detail about the murders. Louis Graves offered his memory of Gonzaullas's first news conference in Texarkana. A copy of the all-points bulletin was in the Tillman Johnson papers. Weldon Glass and J. Q. Mahaffey provided details of the investigation and the type of suspects picked up. Mahaffey recalled the incoming newsmen and Wick Fowler's anecdote. Billie Edgington told of her father Bill Presley's feelings about the outside lawmen. Sue Wilson McCrossen told of Gonzaullas's approaching her father to acquire a secret meeting room.

CHAPTER 9
FEAR STALKS BY NIGHT

Travis Elliott recounted the case of "Sammy" and his examination under hypnosis. Newspaper accounts were sources for numerous incidents. Max

Tackett's comments were made in an interview. Byron Brower, Jr., told of his mother's reaction to the visitor. A feature in the *Texarkana Gazette* described the French war bride's arrival in Texarkana. J. Q. Mahaffey's interview by Georgia Daily provided his reaction to the fatal plunge of the woman from the hotel. The event was confirmed by examining a *Gazette* article. John Norman Henshaw recalled how his classmate Betty Jo Booker's chemistry lab book remained in place. Max Tackett in 1971 told of stopping the motorist.

CHAPTER 10
MURDER STRIKES HOME

Background on the Starks couple and their farm was compiled from a variety of sources, census reports, marriage license, city directory and telephone book, oral history, correspondence, and newspaper reports. Max Tackett told of his and Charley Boyd's itinerary and observations. Parts of Katie Starks's version of the shootings were in the *Gazette* the next morning; Max Tackett and Tillman Johnson also provided details. Bill Presley recalled the night. Tillman Johnson's papers include photos at the Starks house. Johnson, in numerous conversations, reviewed the night and the community. J. Q. Mahaffey remembered the experience in an interview with Georgia Daily. Arkansas State Police Lt. Carl Miller's reports are in the ASP files. Calvin Sutton's letter to the author explained how he sent the news onto the Associated Press wire.

CHAPTER 11
NOBODY IS SAFE!

Tillman Johnson described his investigation and the tracks. Forrest Sutton, for one, told of the cigarette butts found near the car's parking spot. Howard Giles explained the fingerprinting setup in Texarkana, Ark. Max Tackett told of the forensics lab report on the .22 caliber weapon. Death certificate for Virgil Starks cited facts of his death. Calvin Sutton and J. Q. Mahaffey described the flashlight photo and its distribution. The *Gazette* interview with Dr. Anthony Lapalla was a major article three days after the Starks shootings. Paul Burns described flying Lucille Holland to Oklahoma to interview Mary Jeanne

Larey. Holland's story of the interview ran on page one the following morning.

CHAPTER 12
A MEDIA INVASION

J. Q. Mahaffey and Louis Graves cited Kenneth Dixon's arrival and his much-quoted lead. Dixon background came from Wikipedia entry and other sources. Mahaffey read his speech to the American Society of Newspaper Editors into his taped interview with Georgia Daily. *Time* and *Life*: Sheet of instructions for producer in Wayne Beck collection. Morris Arnold's memory of the times was printed in the *Texarkana Gazette*'s series in 1996, marking the 50th anniversary of the murders. "UNIVERSAL NEWSREEL" Garrison to Gonzaullas, telegram, May 15, 1946, Wayne Beck collection. A *Newsweek* article ran May 20, 1946. Bob Carpenter: Mahaffey told of the MBS broadcast from Texarkana. Gonzaullas to visiting press: "Ranger Asks 'One Little Break'" under byline of Dick Allen, newspaper clipping, May 9, 1946, publication unknown. Photocopy of AP newspaper story, undated but apparently in mid-May 1946, quoted an unnamed officer as claiming the killer smeared his hands in the blood on the floor, which didn't happen, according to reliable sources. Mahaffey's interview with the author described the attempt by an unknown man to enter his house one night. Jo Hurst, Bettye Matthews, and Leslie Greer described aspects of Phantomania. Mahaffey recalled the Gonzaullas anecdote at KCMC in an interview with the author. Mahaffey and his son John Mahaffey told of the reactions from afar.

CHAPTER 13
LAW AND DISORDER

Tillman Johnson told of the unshuttered house on County Avenue. Louis Graves recalled the "bodies" in a yard. A number of far-off crimes were investigated for possible Phantom connections. News reports provided most of the incidents, while others came from official files, such as Texas DPS correspondence. For instance, data on Fort Lauderdale, Florida, murders came from correspondence: Glen H. McLaughlin to Walter E. Clark, Oct. 11, 1946, and Glen H. McLaughlin to M. T. Gonzaullas, Oct.

23, 1946, and a clipping, *Dallas Morning News*, Oct. 12, 1946. The Black Dahlia case in Los Angeles received front-page attention over the nation, one example of which was *Dallas Times Herald*, Feb. 10, 1947; the elimination of a Fort Dix, New Jersey, soldier as a suspect in the Phantom case, having been overseas at the relevant times, is in Gonzaullas to Glen H. McLaughlin, Feb. 24, 1947. Regarding a couple assaulted in a suburb of Los Angeles, United Press report, April 21, 1950; Glen H. McLaughlin to W. A. Worton, April 27, 1950; W. A. Worton to Homer Garrison, Jr. Across McLaughlin's April 27 letter copy he had printed boldly, ELIMINATED; a double murder in Amsterdam, New York. United Press report, Oct. 3, 1950 (in typescript); Glen H. McLaughlin to W. E. Kirwan, Oct. 4, 1950.

Re letters to Gonzaullas, *Texarkana Gazette* feature by Sally Reese, May 19, 1946. The Tresnick divorce was in the Miller County Circuit Clerk's records; the marriages cited, from the Miller County Clerk's books. Georgia Daily remembered the comment: "If the Phantom ever walks into John's Place." "Ten thousand dollars worth": Mahaffey interview. "I'm not going to leave" Tillman Johnson recalled his conversation with Gonzaullas while riding with the other officers. Incidents with Gonzaullas told the author by the women involved. Lights in Starks house and Tackett-Gonzaullas conflict came from Mahaffey interview. Louis Graves supplied information on Texarkana Bears. Tillman Johnson recalled how touchy it was to approach law-abiding citizens at night in the line of duty. Bill Presley told of stakeout in interview, *Texarkana Gazette*, May 31, 1970. He told the author of falling asleep on his feet.

CHAPTER 14
BEHIND A SERIAL KILLER'S FAÇADE

Accounts of the Alexander Pichushkin case: *Texarkana Gazette*, October 2007; Associated Press, August 14, 2007. Definition of serial killings and material from the FBI Symposium: Morton, Robert J., and Mark A. Hilts, eds., *Serial Murders—Multi-Disciplinary Perspectives for Investigators*. Symposium, Aug. 29-Sept. 2, 2005, San Antonio. FBI National Center for the Analysis of Violent Crime; types of multiple killers, with quote by John Douglas, from Douglas and Olshaker, *The Anatomy of Motive*, pp. 190-191. Re organized and disorganized offenders, Ressler,

130; "He thinks he will never be caught," Ressler, 139-141. The author interviewed the Texarkana psychiatrists in 1971. Another insight is by psychologist James Grigson in Carlton Stower's excellent article, "The Phantom Menace," *Dallas Observer*, Feb. 1-7, 2001. Thought preceded the act: Robert K. Ressler, Ann W. Burgess, John E. Douglas et al., *Sexual Homicide: Patterns and Motives* (New York: The Free Press, 1988), pp. ix-33; "the way they think," Ressler et al., 40, 43; re accomplices, teams, Levin, *ibid.* 31-34; James Alan Fox and Jack Levin, 80, 101; on driving at night, Douglas and Olshaker, *Mindhunter*, 57; "It is not that serial killers want to get caught," Dr. Jack Levin, *Serial Killers and Sadistic Murderers: Up Close and Personal* (Amherst, N.Y.: Prometheus Books, 2008), 56. Experts: "a complex process" FBI symposium. See also Morrison, *My Life Among*, cf. psychopath, 67, 71-72, 128-9, 194. "Serial killers may be compensating," Levin, 34. "Taunting law enforcement," Levin, 31. Levin quote, target strangers, Levin, *op. cit.*, 157; re changing MO, re copycat: beliefs: Morrison, 137, Levin, 38-39; "branch out," Fox and Levin, 101; re sociopaths: Fox and Levin, 65-66; quote on p. 69. Paul Bloom quote in Leanne Italie, Associated Press article keyed to Bloom's book, *Just Babies: The Origins of Good and Evil*, in *Texarkana Gazette*, Nov. 17, 2013, contained a quotation not in the book. Telephone interview with Dr. Shervert H. Frazier. See Shervert H. Frazier, "Violence and Social Impact," in Joseph C. Schoolar and Charles M. Gaitz, eds., *Research and the Psychiatric Patient* (New York: Brunner/Mazel, 1975, pp. 183-194. Rehab of serial killers, Fox and Levin, 71; Levin quote, 186.

CHAPTER 15
AN ACCIDENTAL BREAK

These events have been reconstructed primarily around interviews with Max Tackett and Tillman Johnson. Peggy Swinney's background data—birth, previous marital status, her recent marriage—all came from official documents, including 1930 census, two marriage licenses, divorce records. A great deal of information exists on marriage licenses. Similar information for Swinney was also required for their marriage license. Sources for the Atlanta, Texas, portion of the chase included Ollie Jaynes, Nancy Partain, Paul Boone, Ralph Allen. Ray B. Fultz's Oct. 2, 1977 article in

The Atlanta Times provided additional information. Tackett and Johnson corroborated each other's version of the chase and arrest.

In the photograph, Hibbett Lee previously has been identified as "Mr. Partain," but Partain remained at the car lot in Atlanta. Those acquainted with the incident agreed Hibbett Lee is the one photographed.

A tour of the old Miller County jail, in the company of Johnson, then in his nineties, with County Judge Roy John McNatt, clarified the layout of the jail, by then no longer in use for its original purpose.

CHAPTER 16
INCRIMINATING REVELATIONS

Swinney's statements to FBI agent Calhoun came from ASP files. Swinney's note to Peggy is in the ASP files pertaining to Swinney and the Starks case. Copies of Peggy Swinney's statements are in Johnson's papers. Details of the movies showing at the Nashville theaters were found in ads in the *Nashville News*, courtesy of Cecil Harris. The plot and critic's comment on *Jesse James* are in the online Wikipedia entry about the movie. The author viewed the film on Turner Classic Movies.

Copies of her statements are in the Johnson papers. The trip to Dallas with Peggy is documented in the ASP files, with report by Dallas detective Will Fritz. Bill Presley related the scene in Spring Lake Park where Peggy Swinney confirmed that Martin's datebook had been taken from his pocket and thrown into the brush, a fact not reported in the newspapers and not known to anyone else, a critical bit of evidence assigning definite credibility to her on that specific matter. Bessie Brown's statement about Swinney returning to the room after the Griffin-Moore murders and laughing is from Georgia Daily's interview with her.

CHAPTER 17
THE PRIMARY SUSPECT

The 1920 census contained the data about Swinney's family and himself as a child. The Swinney parents' divorce records are in the Miller County Circuit Clerk's office. Myrtle Swinney's marriage records are in the Miller County Clerk's office and divorce from Travis in Miller County Circuit

Clerk's records. Additional material came from Clarence Swinney and Joyce Swinney Ward.

Because he was a juvenile, at twelve years of age, there is no regular record of young Youell Swinney's 1929 brush with the law. However, it was reconstructed by comparing his name on the Bowie County District Court's docket, which does list him by name, and the front-page news story in the *Texarkana Evening News*, September 25, 1929. There can be little doubt but that this is the same boy, for both match in age and all other aspects.

His FBI rap sheet documents the subsequent arrests and dispositions. Swinney's 1941 Arkansas conviction: Miller County Circuit Court, Case # 5463, State of Arkansas vs. Youell Swinney, page 174, Criminal Court record, Volume N. The Texas prison system roll of inmates, in the Texas State Archives, contains detailed data about each prisoner as he's processed in, including such matters as Swinney's tattoos and scars. Data about the other inmates from Bowie County at that time also came from the prison rolls. Tackett's reports to his supervisors, in the ASP files, provided details of the once-damp shoes and other information. Swinney's statement to the Arkansas State Police is in ASP files. The Texarkana City Directory of that year contains addresses and residents of the Rose Hill community where Youell and Peggy lived briefly.

CHAPTER 18
TIGHTENING THE NOOSE

The several witness statements are in Arkansas State Police files, in regard to the Starks case. Tillman Johnson and Max Tackett each independently related how they collected samples from the welding shop to compare with slag found in the shirt pockets. A copy of J. Edgar Hoover's message is in Johnson papers. Johnson described his search with the laundry mark and his visit with the brothel madam. Tackett's log of Swinney's day-to-day activities is in Tillman Johnson Papers. Sandie Olson, director of the Waynoka Historical Society, supplied the Waynoka, Okla., background.

Tackett's reports also are in the state police files. Tackett's attempt to find out what happened to a painter picked up by Swinney is in Tackett to Scroggins, Sept. 27, 1946, ASP files. Other reports from ASP files include O. D. Morris to W. B. Jones, Oct. 1, 1946; W. L. MacGregory to W. B. Jones, Oct. 5, 1946; Albert O. Calloway, Oct. 4, 1946; MacGregory to Jones, Oct. 5, 1946, W. B. Jones to Sgt. O. D. Morris, Oct. 11, 1946; Morris to Scroggins, Oct. 13, 1946.

Regarding tracing of the pistols Swinney had disposed of and the Waynoka scene: Arkansas State Police files—Morris to Homer Garrison, Nov. 25, 1946; Morris to Scroggins, Nov. 26, 1946; Carl Miller report, Oct. 27, 1946; Tillman Johnson report, in Miller report, Oct. 27, 1946. Tackett notes in Tillman Johnson papers.

CHAPTER 19
MOUNTING PRESSURES

Memo drawing down Ranger force in Texarkana: Gonzaullas to Rangers, Aug. 15, 1946 (Johnson papers). Subsequent letters: Presley to Gonzaullas, Oct. 10, 1946, and Gonzaullas to Garrison, Oct. 12, 1946. Material in this section regarding the Reverend Stanley Swinney and family is based on Swinney family correspondence in Clarence Swinney papers, with each item of information coming from a letter, most of which the Rev. Mr. Swinney wrote. One of Youell's sisters, Mildred Whetstone to her mother, Myrtle Chaffin, Sept. 15, 1946. "If something is not done." Stanley C. Swinney, Sr., (SCS) to Cleo Swinney (CS), Sept. 20, 1946. "Perhaps we may." Claude E. Love to SCS, Sept. 22, 1946. "something must be done . . ." SCS to CS, Sept. 23, 1946. re Supreme Court on appeal, SCS to Maxine Whetstone, Sept. 26, 1946; *ibid.*, Sept. 27, 1946. re reward money, SCS to CS, Oct. 4, 1946; re the minister's case involving missing funds, SCS to Maxine Whetstone, Oct. 4, 1946. Substitute suspect, SCS to CS, Oct. 5, 11, 19, 1946.

Discovery of saxophone: *Texarkana Gazette*, Oct. 25, 1946: Gonzaullas to McLaughlin, Oct. 26, 1946; Glen McLaughlin to W. H. Presley, Oct. 29, 1946. re insanity plea, McVey to CS, Nov. 4, 1946. SCS affidavit, same date. SCS's "substitute Phantom" and insanity plea are in SCS to CS, Nov. 4, 1946. McVey's tirade, McVey to Goldman and McDonald, Nov. 9, 1946. His letter to John Frederick, Nov. 9, 1946. Judge's order is in Book O, p. 120, Docket 5968, Miller County Circuit Court. Swinney's records at the Arkansas State Hospital are also in Swinney's files from Texas State

Archives. Tackett and Johnson told of their own memories of the trip to Little Rock and impressions at the time.

McLaughlin, re "strawberry blonde," Mike Cox, *Texas Ranger Tales*, 261. Presley's letter to Gonzaullas, Nov. 19, 1946 (Johnson Papers). Copies of Peggy Swinney's statements at Austin are in Johnson Papers, as well as in other hands. McLaughlin's assessment of Peggy's polygraph questioning is in Cox, 261-262. The author applied Mark McClish's techniques, as detailed in his book, *I Know You Are Lying!*, to analyze the statement. McClish supplemented the analysis with his own comments, e-mailed to the author. Cleo visits Youell Swinney in jail, McVey remarks, McVey to CS, Nov. 25, 1946. McVey's theory of crimes and instructions, McVey to CS, Dec. 3, 1946; McVey on his substitute villain and analysis, McVey to Love, Dec. 3. McVey's contact with Gov. Laney and his bill, McVey to CS, Dec. 2, 1946.

CHAPTER 20
A QUIET "SOLUTION"

Bill Presley told the author about taking condemned prisoners to Huntsville. Sources for material on the Swinney family reactions and strategy in Youell's case came from the Clarence Swinney papers, consisting, as in a previous chapter, of correspondence among the various members, as well as the attorney McVey. The extradition request by Texas Gov. Coke Stevenson to move Swinney from Arkansas to Texas is in: Record of requisitions and extraditions, 1939-1965, Texas Secretary of State fugitive records, Archives and Information Services Division, Texas State Library and Archives Commission. Extradition, call to Gov. Laney, Frederick's reactions and conversation with Maxwell Welch reported in McVey to CS, Dec. 10, 1946. Youell Swinney's postcard of Dec. 9 is in Clarence Swinney papers. Details of the Titus County jail and the sheriff came from Robert Russell. "Phantom Lead . . . Dud," *Gazette*, Dec. 11, 1946; two suspicious characters, McVey to CCS, Dec. 12, 1946; SCS to CS. undated (circa Dec. 12). McVey suspicious, etc., McVey to CS, Dec. 18, 1946. Tackett and Johnson escape death, *Texarkana Gazette*, Dec. 23, 1946. SCS and Seconal, SCS to SC, Nov. 17, 1946; Nella Swinney to CS, Nov. 24, 29, 1946; Rev. Swinney's loss of pastorate, SCS to CS, Jan. 11, 1947. Rev. Swinney advice to Youell Swinney, enclosing letter from

Elmer Lincoln, Jan. 13, 1947; Rev. Swinney belief in light sentence, asks for Seconal. SCS to CS, Jan. 17, 18, 1947; Rev. Swinney advice to plead not guilty by reason of insanity, SCS to CS, Jan. 22, 1947. Buzz Hallett related what he saw and heard in the courtroom during his testimony years later at Swinney's evidentiary hearing on a writ of habeas corpus. Hallett's address is in the Texarkana City Directory of that time. The judge's charge to the jury is a part of the evidentiary hearing documents. "This thing is not over," McVey to CS, Feb. 17, 1947. "They have done exactly," SCS to CS, Feb. 26, 1947.

CHAPTER 21
BEHIND WALLS AGAIN

The Texas prison roll, a part of the Texas State Archives, contains the inmate's information as noted. Inmate photos are in Texas Department of Corrections files. The elder Swinney remained, CSC to CS, May 6, 1947. "I am wondering," McVey to CS, Dec. 17, 1947. In midsummer 1948, SCS to CS, July 31, 1948. "Would you get me . . ." SCS to CS, Aug. 13, 1948. Elmer L. Lincoln to Youell Lee Swinney, #108586, March 10, 1948 (Clarence Swinney papers). Donaldson suicide, death certificate; Ted Asimos, Jerry Atkins interviews. Peggy Swinney's divorce, remarriage: divorce records, Bowie County District Clerk's office; marriage license, Miller County Clerk's office. Bench warrant, Bowie County District Court docket, which provides no details; other documents providing more details could not be produced; Henslee testified to the trip to Huntsville during Swinney's evidentiary hearing. Inez Martin to Garrison, March 14, 1949; Garrison to Martin, March 18, 1949, Johnson papers. The correspondence of Swinney's sister with Patman is in the Youell Swinney folder, Wright Patman Papers, LBJ Library, Austin, Texas: Maxine Childs to Wright Patman, Jan. 12, 1959; Patman to Childs, Jan. 16, 1959; Patman to Jack Ross, chairman, Board of Pardons and Paroles, Jan. 16, 1959; Childs to Patman, Jan. 19, 1959; Ross to Patman, Jan. 22, 1959; Patman to Childs, Jan. 27, 1959.

The author reviewed Swinney's records at Texas Department of Corrections in 1971 and obtained extant records permitted under Freedom of Information requests subsequently. Items not released in the FOI request but seen in 1971 included a letter to the warden of his fear of becoming an "oral queer," his short story, and records related to the sexual act, from which notes were taken. Documents related to Swinney's application for writ are in the complete file of the evidentiary hearing, Texas State Archives. Visitor to Bill Presley in 1971, told by him to author.

CHAPTER 22
BACK IN COURT

The documents and transcripts of the evidentiary hearing and related motions and papers provide the details of this chapter, supplemented by interviews with Jack Carter, A. M. Adams, Tillman Johnson, and others.

CHAPTER 23
ON THE WITNESS STAND

The transcript of the evidentiary hearing provided the chapter's material.

CHAPTER 24
"BEYOND BELIEF AND INCREDIBLE"

The proceedings in this chapter come from the transcript of the hearing and related documents, Texas State Archives. The five members of the Texas Court of Criminal Appeals at the time included Carl E. F. Dally, Leon Burr Douglas, Wendell Albert Odom, John Frank "Jack" Onion, Jr., and Truman Ernest Roberts. The court later was expanded to nine. Jack Carter told of the call from Lynn Cooksey and his meeting Bessie Booker Brown.

CHAPTER 25
LIFE AFTER "LIFE"

Judge Jack Carter recalled Swinney's visit to his home. Swinney's record after release from prison in 1973 has been documented from FBI files obtained through a Freedom of Information request. The files contained Swinney's rap sheet, or record of criminal arrests, and statements from witnesses and federal agents related to his various activities. Robert Kerr's review of the movie appeared in the magazine *Arkansas Times*, November 1986. He also published an excellent report on the case after forty years, along with a review of the movie, in the *Texarkana Gazette*, March 23, 1986. An online search yielded the foreign title versions. Other background came from Clarence Swinney and the short stories are in the Clarence Swinney collection.

CHAPTER 26
CRACKING A COLD CASE

Interviews with Glenn Owen presented his argument for closing the case by exception. Facts regarding closing cases by exception were found online. Among others, the FBI website details conditions for the process. Go to *http://www.fbi.gov/about-us/cjis/ucr/frequently-asked questions/ nibrs_faqs_inspec* and then scroll to Exceptional Clearances, which lists the conditions to be met. Other searches offer information on how such a clearance is accomplished in various locales, as well as discussion about whether specific clearances were proper or abused. See, for example, the Goldwater Institute in Arizona and its brief, "Justice Denied: The Improper Clearance of Unsolved Crimes by the Maricopa County Sheriff's Office." Similar searches may yield information about the process in Portland, Oregon, and Miami, Fla., the latter of which may be read in the article by Wanda J. DeMargo and Jay Weaver, "How reform turned into curse for sheriff," *The Miami Herald*, posted March 13, 2005. For a breakdown of Clay County, Florida, 2005 crimes solved by arrest and by exception, see *www.claysheriff.com/documents/AnnualUCR2005_ool.pdf*

Louis Graves told of his conversation with Jones Floyd in an interview with the author in Nashville, Ark. Mark Bledsoe recounted his experience to the *Texarkana Gazette* in 1996.

EPILOGUE

Tillman Johnson reported his dreams during several conversations. The transcript of Gonzaullas's final interview, conducted by Bob Mitchell and Alva Steen on January 26, 1977, at his home in Dallas, is a part of the E-Book Project of the Texas Ranger Hall of Fame and Museum, Waco, Texas. It was at this interview that he made the statement on the epigraph of this book, regarding the panic that he found in Texarkana. Andrea Anderson, Richard Griffin's niece, made her remark at a Griffin family reunion in 2010 which the author attended as a guest and spoke about the case. Helen Morrison's idea of a dignified memorial for serial-killer victims is in her book, *My Life Among the Serial Killers*, 213.

SELECTED BIBLIOGRAPHY

MANUSCRIPTS, RECORDS

James M. Hollis, "The Texarkana Phantom Murders." Unpublished manuscript.

Jerry Atkins, Unpublished memoir of the spring of 1946 and aftermath.

Records in Bowie County, Cass County, and Cameron County, Texas, and Texas State Archives; Miller County and Union County, Arkansas.

Records in Texas State Library archives, Texas Department of Public Safety, and Texas Department of Corrections, and Arkansas State Police files.

FBI records for Youell Lee Swinney and Phantom case.

U.S. Census records for 1920, 1930, 1940.

Social Security Death Index (online).

City Directory, Texarkana, 1940s, 1950s.

Texarkana Telephone Directory, 1946.

Tillman Johnson Papers.

BOOKS, ARTICLES

Bowman, Bob and Doris. *More Historic Murders of East Texas*. Lufkin, Texas: Best of East Texas Publishers, 1994.

Clemmer, Donald. *The Prison Community*. New York: Holt, Rinehart and Winston, 1958.

Cox, Mike. *Texas Ranger Tales: Stories That Need Telling*. Republic of Texas Press, 1996.

Douglas, John, and Mark Olshaker. *Mind Hunter: Inside the FBI's Elite Serial Crime Unit*. New York: Pocket Star Books, 1996.

Douglas, John, and Mark Olshaker. *The Anatomy of Motive: The FBI's Legendary Mindhunter Explores the Key to Understanding and Catching Violent Criminals.* New York: Scribner, 1999.

Fox, James Alan, and Jack Levin. *Extreme Killing: Understanding Serial and Mass Murder.* Thousand Oaks, Calif.: Sage Publications, 2005.

Frazier, Shervert H. "Violence and Social Impact," *in* Joseph C. Schoolar and Charles M. Gaitz, eds. *Research and the Psychiatric Patient.* New York: Brunner/Mazel, 1975, pp. 183-194.

Greer, Leslie B. *Pages of Time.* Texarkana, Ark.

Keirsey, Tex. "Riding With the Rangers on a Phantom's Trail." *Amarillo Globe-Times,* Feb. 7, 1956.

Kerr, Robert. "Unmasking the Phantom at 40." *Texarkana Gazette,* March 23, 1986.

Kerr, Robert. "Texarkana's Phantom Killer." *Arkansas Times,* November 1986, 24, 26.

Leet, William D. *Texarkana, A Pictorial History.* Norfolk/Virginia Beach, Va.: Donning Company, 1982.

Levin, Jack. *Serial Killers and Sadistic Murderers: Up Close and Personal.* Amherst, N.Y.: Prometheus Books, 2008.

Malsch, Brownson. *Lone Wolf: Captain M. T. Gonzaullas. The Only Texas Ranger Captain of Spanish Descent.* Austin, Texas: Shoal Creek Publishers, 1980.

McClish, Mark. *I Know You Are Lying: Detecting Deception Through Statement Analysis.* Winterville, N.C.: Police Employment, 2000.

Minor, Les, Ruth Evans, and Ethel Channon, ed. and compiled for *Texarkana Gazette.* *Texarkana II: The Two County Collection.* Marceline, Mo.: D-Books Publishing Co., 1994.

Minor, Les, and Ethel Channon, eds. *Images of Texarkana: A Visual History.* Marceline, Mo.: Heritage House Publishing Co., 1991.

Morrison, Helen, and Harold Goldberg. *My Life Among the Serial Killers: Inside the Minds of the World's Most Notorious Murderers.* New York: William Morrow, 2004.

Morton, Robert J., and Mark A. Hilts, eds. *Serial Murders—Multi-Disciplinary Perspectives for Investigators.* Symposium, Aug. 29-Sept. 2, 2005, San Antonio. FBI National Center for the Analysis of Violent Crime.

Newton, Michael. *The Texarkana Moonlight Murders: The Unsolved Case of the 1946 Phantom Killer.* Jefferson, N.C.: McFarland & Co., 2013.

Presley, James. "The Phantom Murders," 8-part series. *Texarkana Gazette,* May 1971.

Rasmussen, William T. *Corroborating Evidence II: The Cleveland Torso Murders, The Black Dahlia Murder, The Phantom Killer of Texarkana, The Zodiac Killer.* Santa Fe: Sunstone Press, 2005.

Ressler, Robert K., Ann W. Burgess, John E. Douglas, et al. *Sexual Homicide: Patterns and Motives.* New York: The Free Press, 1988.

Stowers, Carlton. "The Phantom Menace." *Dallas Observer,* 40-51. Feb. 1-7, 2001.

Texarkana Gazette. "The Phantom at 50," May 1996.

The Tiger 1946. Texarkana, Texas: Students of Texas High School, 1946.

NEWSPAPERS

Amarillo Globe-Times
Arkansas Democrat
Arkansas Gazette
Atlanta (Tex.) Times, The
Billings (Montana) Gazette
Dallas Morning News, The
Dallas Times Herald
Nashville (Ark.) News
New Orleans Item, The
New Orleans Times-Picayune
Shreveport Times, The
Texarkana Daily News
Texarkana Evening News
Texarkana Gazette
Two States Press

ORAL HISTORY

Interviews were conducted with most of the individuals quoted, either in person or by telephone in 1971 and in the 1990s and up to 2013. These included, but are not limited to, Max Tackett, Tillman Johnson, Bill Presley, Dr. Shervert Frazier, and hundreds more.

MAGAZINES

Active Years (Little Rock, Ark.)
Arkansas Times
Life
Newsweek
Time

FILMS

Getaway, The
Jesse James
Three Strangers
Town That Dreaded Sundown, The

ACKNOWLEDGMENTS

Without the contributions of hundreds of individuals, this book, long in the making, would have been incomplete. I appreciate each one.

I'm going to reverse the usual order of acknowledgments and first name my agent, Mickey Novak of Writers House, for his enthusiasm, support, friendship, and skills. I also want to shine the spotlight on my editor, Pegasus Books associate publisher Jessica Case, and Pegasus publisher Claiborne Hancock for their enthusiasm (that word again!) and good deeds. Michael Fusco produced a splendid jacket design.

Of the major contributors, Tillman Johnson deserves to be singled out. We often talked till two or three in the morning as we pondered both major and minor evidence and documents. He was mentally alert until his death at age ninety-seven. Jerry Atkins repeatedly answered questions as I reconstructed the times, especially the tragic night when Betty Jo Booker last played in his band. Georgia Daily generously shared audio taped recordings of interviews she'd conducted with J. Q. Mahaffey and Bessie Booker Brown, as well as clippings from a variety of newspapers.

I thank Les Minor, editor of the *Texarkana Gazette*, for his goodwill in use of microfilmed copies of the *Gazette* and *Daily News*. Bill Maddox, a previous editor of the *Gazette*, had opened the newspaper's old copies to me earlier. Grace Guier shared photographs and other material related to Betty Jo Booker and her family.

Billie Presley Edgington provided memories and photographs of her father, Bill Presley, and other events, as did her late husband, Don Edgington. I interviewed Max Tackett at some length and later talked with his son John Haynie Tackett and daughter Sandra Tackett Zaleski and nephew Boyd Tackett, Jr.

Peggy Gastineau Francisco shared James Hollis's manuscript account of his night of terror. Paul Burns told of the Frederick, Oklahoma, flight for Lucille Holland's interview with Mary Jeanne Larey.

My cousin Billie Hargis House and Heather McEntee, then with the Shreve Memorial Library in Shreveport, guided me in genealogy. Wayne Beck shared genealogical data and postings on his website.

Mark McClish, in his book *I Know You Are Lying*, helped me understand Statement Analysis®, adding his to my interpretation. Dr. Shervert H. Frazier gave insights from his work with killers, as did Dr. Jack Levin and Sheila Kendall. Robert Stevens was helpful with photographs.

I am grateful to Clarence Swinney for providing correspondence about the case. His sister, Joyce Ward, was similarly helpful. Judge Jack Carter recalled his representation of Youell Swinney during the evidentiary hearing. Reconstructing the events in Cass County, I thank Paul W. Boone, Ralph Allen, Ollie Jaynes, and Nancy Partain. Nancy particularly helped correct an old error related to the arrest photo.

Juanita Bloodworth helped bring order to my office, while Auzie White maintained my work environment in good repair. Jane and Pat Davitt and their staff, particularly Robbie Bowers, were helpful when I needed copies and reproductions.

Librarians and archivists played major roles: Alice Coleman and her staff at Texarkana Public Library, especially Roann Moore and Lesley Sandlin. Texarkana College's Palmer Memorial Library produced newspaper files on microfilm. The Moss Library at Texas A&M University at Texarkana also was helpful, as were the Frederick, Oklahoma, High

School staff, Dallas Public Library (Rachel Garrett Howell, history and archives division), Fort Worth, Texas, Public Library, Frederick, Okla., Carnegie Library, Shreve Memorial Library, Sheryl Spencer at Sam Houston University Library Archives in Huntsville, and Gayle Brown at Amarillo (Texas) Public Library.

County clerks and their staffs over a broad reach of Texas, Arkansas, Louisiana, and Oklahoma spent considerable time responding to my many requests. I must single out Velma Moore and her capable staff in Bowie County, Texas, Ann Nicholas and staff in Miller County, Arkansas, and Texarkana, Texas, city secretary's staff. Bowie County District Clerk Billy Fox and her staff, especially Dean Maddox and Martha Roberts, dredged up old criminal files, as did Carolyn Williams in the civil section. On the Arkansas side, Circuit Clerk Mary Pankey and staff helped me find old records. The county clerk's and circuit clerk's offices in Union County, Arkansas, supplied records, Linda Hinson shouldering the major burden. In Louisiana I benefited from clerks and clerks of court in Caddo and Bossier Parishes; in Texas, in Cameron, Cass, and Dallas Counties; and in Oklahoma, McCurtain, Oklahoma, Cleveland, Johnston, and Tillman Counties. Oklahoma State Health Department and Arkansas State Health Department provided death certificates, as did Texarkana, Texas.

Other organizations include Pioneer Heritage Town Site, Frederick, Oklahoma; Tillman County Historical Museum (Jimmy Espinosa, director); Waynoka (Oklahoma) Historical Society (Sandie Olson, director); Pioneer Telephone Company; Texas Prison Museum (Jim Willett, director). There is no way I can enumerate the cold calls, made virtually all over the country, from California to Virginia, from Texas to Montana, in tracing individuals of interest.

The Texas State Library and Archives, the keeper of old state records, including prisoners' rolls, provided transcripts of Youell Swinney's evidentiary hearings and related papers. Tony Black and Laura Saegert especially made the search easier, as did Robert Tissing at the Lyndon B. Johnson Library at The University of Texas at Austin.

The Arkansas State Police responded ably to my FOI requests. I thank Ron Stovall, Miller County sheriff and former Arkansas State Police supervisor, for advice on finding the documents and Tina Witt in the file room for locating and copying them.

The Texas Department of Criminal Justice at Huntsville, in the persons of Jason Clark, Michelle Lyons, Patricia Fleming, and Rachel Williams, responded to my Freedom of Information requests. The Federal Bureau of Investigation responded fully to my FOI requests as I sought rap sheets and other documents related to the murders.

Men I interviewed earlier but who were dead when I began the book provided information I otherwise might never have learned. These include Max Tackett, Bill Presley, J. Q. Mahaffey, and Calvin Sutton. I interviewed Louis F. Graves, Sr., after undertaking this book; he, like others, did not live to see its publication. Prudence Macintosh and John Mahaffey helped add to their father J. Q. Mahaffey's story.

Thanks to Andrew Lusk for his map of the Spring Lake Park crime scene.

Finally, I thank the families of the victims, who have been victims themselves, deprived of the lives and company of their murdered relatives. Almost everyone I talked to was helpful in telling family stories, enabling me to recreate the historical and emotional environment. These include Richard Griffin's brothers Welborn and David Griffin, and other members of the Griffin family, especially nieces Ruth Proctor Mahoney and Andrea Anderson; Polly Ann Moore's brother, Mark Melton Moore; Paul Martin's sister-in-law, Margaret Martin; and Katie Starks's second husband, Forrest Sutton. Of the victims who survived but died before my research, I found their survivors helpful: James Hollis's widow Peggy, his niece Diana Burris, his son by his second marriage David Hollis and daughter Rebecca Wivagg, and former sister-in-law, Mary Ann Williamson, and children by last marriage (with Peggy) son James Hollis, Jr. and daughter Cherie Lydick.

Others who contributed in various ways include: The Rev. A. M. Adams, Milam Albright, Tom and Pat Albritton, Sybil Alexander, Ralph Allen, Ted Asimos, Sonny Atchley, Charles Raymond Barlow, Gene Barlow, Tom Binger, Patti Bishop, Barry and Lyn Blackmon, Charlsie Boyd, Edward Brettel, Jr., Byron Brower, Jr., Doris Brower, Sandie Burnett, Diana Burris, Dale Buster, Oran Caudle, Don Coleman, Wanda Evaige, P. H. Fairchild,

Joe Forgy, Herbert G. Freeman, Sidney Fricks, Javier Garcia, Howard K. Giles, Frances Goodknight, J. C. and Ruth Gray, Earl F. Greene, Neoma Guyton, Cecil Harris, William Carson Harris, Mark Hazel, Noah H. Hilliard, Ernest Holcomb, Bill Horner, Dorothy Humphrey, Henry Jackson, Wynnell Jackson, Laverne Jester, Robert Kerr, Betty King, Jackie Larey, James Larey, Tony Leal, Mara Leveritt, B. C. Lyon, Frances Machette, Wanda Mapp, Ray and Bettye Matthews, Robert E. Matthews, Sue McCrossen, Ruth McCutcheon, Stuart McDonald, Roy John McNatt, Evelyn Anne Minor, Richard Moores, Robert Morris, James A. Morriss, Archie Munn, Wayne Murdock, Sally McClure Patton, Norman Powell, W. Dewey Presley, Don Preston, Sophia Anne White Redditt, Casey Roberts, Willie Marie Robinson, Traci Russell, Bill Sharp, D. Henry Slaton, Ellen Stewart, Ken Stewart, Marie Tammen, Alfred A. Tennison, Jr., Bill Thomas, Brad Thomas, Gwen Tice, Thomas Torrans, Richard Tuck, Darlene Vanderpol, Haskell Walker, Tammie Watson, Evelyn Miroir West, Laverne Wilson, Ann Winger, and Herbert Wren.

Tillman Johnson read the first third of an early version before a health crisis led to his death. Billie Hargis House also read the early first half. James Williams, a retired newspaper editor with a special interest in true crime, read the entire manuscript. He was particularly helpful in suggesting shorter chapters. Katie Grimm read the manuscript and offered helpful comments. My son, Dr. John F. Presley, read the manuscript in its entirety twice, resulting in changes in organization and emphasis. John was a mainstay in many ways, throughout encouraging and providing feedback. My daughter Ann and wife Fran, though not devotees of the true crime genre, were supportive and read portions of the book, to my benefit.

Any errors, oversights, or misinterpretations are mine.

JAMES PRESLEY
Texarkana